Physical Education
for the Handicapped

SECOND EDITION

Physical Education for the Handicapped

RUTH HOOK WHEELER, M.A., P.T.

Associate Professor, Physical Education, The Ohio State University
Columbus, Ohio

AGNES M. HOOLEY, Ph.D.

Professor of Physical Education, Bowling Green State University
Bowling Green, Ohio

LEA & FEBIGER · 1976 · PHILADELPHIA

Health Education, Physical Education,
and Recreation Series

RUTH ABERNATHY, Ph.D.
Editorial Adviser
Professor Emeritus, School of Physical and Health Education
University of Washington, Seattle 98105

Library of Congress Cataloging in Publication Data

Wheeler, Ruth Hook.
  Physical education for the handicapped.

  Bibliography: p.
  Includes index.
  1. Physical education for the handicapped persons.
I. Hooley, Agnes M., joint author. II. Title.
GV445.W49 1976   371.9'1   75-22477
ISBN 0-8121-0538-9

Published in Great Britain by Henry Kimpton Publishers, London

PRINTED IN THE UNITED STATES OF AMERICA

Preface

"The purpose of this book is to aid those who seek satisfaction in educating the atypical child, and better preparation for this chosen task." This is one of the few statements from the preface of the first edition which can be repeated in the second. Or to phrase it another way: happily, it *IS* necessary to write a new preface. This is so because there have been many changes in the world for which, and about which, the book is written. The printed material reflects these changes.

Probably the biggest change concerns the attitudes of people toward the handicapped. The fear, anxiety, curiosity, rejection, and over-solicitousness which had been common reactions for so long have given way to other attitudes; the common ones range from tolerance to acceptance, paralleled by a belief that all persons (including the handi-capped) must receive fair treatment in educational, vocational, and social realms (26, pp. 4–7). Because this is true, one chapter of the first edition (Chapter 8) has been omitted from the present edition. That chapter explored solutions to the basic adjustment problems which society's maturing attitudes toward the handicapped have now all but eliminated.

Many of the predictions and hopes expressed in Chapter 11 of the first edition, Future Directions in Adapted Physical Education, have come about; for example, government funds have been spent to "spark" research and see it through, and handicapped youngsters who were just beginning to come to schools for typical youngsters are now there in large numbers, and as full participants. That chapter has also been eliminated.

There are two completely new chapters, one devoted to mental retardation and learning disabilities (Chapter 4), and another to camping for the handicapped (Chapter 10). A reading of the new Chapter 4 will disclose the careful researching, collating, and synthesizing which has been achieved to present the vast amount of recent information about learning. Specifically, such information concerns ways in which people learn, why some learn and some do not, and how the root causes of non-learning can be recognized, and maximum learning achieved under whatever circumstances exist.

Because the handicapped have been provided with many opportunities denied to them earlier, they have become more confident, more willing to "try" new experiences, and more socially competent. There have been many results of this "new" image; one is that many handicapped persons now go camping. Some camp with their families, others attend organized camps during the summer, and a few go to school camps during the regular academic year. Camping is an experience which returns immense dividends to the handicapped person; yet, there is a dearth of information on camping for the handicapped. Hence, the new Chapter 10, which is devoted to a complete analysis of the needs of such campers, and the ways in which those needs can be met through proper personnel, programs, equipment, and facilities.

Certain portions of the book which are still very relevant have been retained, but references suggested in those portions have been up-dated. Case studies have been inserted in some chapters to explain and exemplify better various theories, directives, and recommendations. The bibliography has been culled of irrelevant listings, and new references have been added.

It is the hope of the authors, one a physical therapist and physical educator, and one a physical educator and former camp program director, that we have presented a book which will be useful to beginners in the field, and to those with considerable experience. But even beyond that hope is the ultimate one: that we shall have done something which will motivate all who work with the handicapped to help them to learn, achieve, and prove themselves TO themselves, and to a doubting world which is more ready to believe in them than at the time of the first edition.

Ruth Hook Wheeler
Agnes M. Hooley

Columbus, Ohio
Bowling Green Ohio

Contents

Historical Review and Developing Trends in Adapted Physical Education and Therapeutic Exercise

"The wise, for cure, on exercise depend."—John Dryden

Introduction

Many systems of exercise, some developed in past centuries, are available to the physical educator as he works to improve both the normal and the atypical child. Much of the exercise performed in the United States and throughout the world today, as well as in ancient times, is in the form of sports. In this decade, however, the employment of therapeutic exercise has increased significantly. Formal gymnastics are used now more than in previous years, and corrective exercises for therapeutic purposes have developed to a high degree. The trend is toward national and local sports activities and the introduction of specific gymnastics in the school systems. Our thirty-fifth president, John F. Kennedy, did much to promote youth and adult fitness during this decade.° Also, the escalation of rehabilitation has presented a challenge to the physical educator who is a member of the educational team for the atypical child.

The physician may be asked to prescribe exercises for normal, healthy adults, particularly for persons of middle age and older or for adults with particular problems. For example, he may prescribe care-

° *Sports Illustrated*, Dec. 26, 1960. President's Council on Youth Fitness.

fully graded exercises for patients with heart disease to increase the heart's tolerance to exertion. These exercises will affect the strength of the skeletal muscles, although this is not the primary purpose. More and more physicians are aware of the potential of exercise therapy for the functional or physiological body conditions of the so-called normal individual, as well as for the individual with pathological body conditions. *Therapeutic exercise* may be defined as the scientific application of bodily movement designed specifically to maintain or to restore normal function to diseased or injured tissues (105). *Adapted physical education* is the appropriate term which implies that a program or skill has been altered in accordance with the individual's capacities, limitations, and physical or social needs. The handicapped individual should be able to adapt to his environment.°

The Influence of Exercise as a Curative Agent

Despite its current popularity in aiding the atypical individual, therapeutic exercise has been practiced for centuries. From archeological findings and the writings of historians, we can trace the study of therapeutic exercise from ancient China and other old civilizations. The Cong Fou (105, p. 426) was a series of ritualistic movement patterns consisting primarily of body positioning and breathing routines prescribed by the Taoist priests about 2700 B.C. (105). A Jesuit priest, Father Amiot, returned to France from China in the eighteenth century with a full description of the Cong Fou. Thus, Juvenal's well-known saying *Mens sana in corpore sano* (a sound mind in a sound body)† had significance in ancient China. Father Amiot also recorded that the ancient Chinese emperor, Yin-Kang-Chi, commanded his people to perform military exercises to prevent diseases caused by the frequent rains. Emperor Yin-Kang-Chi developed a "turning" dance to aid the relief of the miasma (relapsing fever). Subsequently, about 1000 A.D., the Chinese established T'ai Chi Chuan (pronounced Tye Gee Chwan), an exercise method to develop composure and mental equilibrium. This system can lead to the art of self-defense as well as to tranquility. Since the interpreted T'ai Chi Chuan system demands inner control of the mind and body, alertness and concentration have explicit exercise structures. There are 108 structured positions and variations which apply two intrinsic principles of softness and circular movement. The five essential qualities are categorized as slowness, lightness,

°Hubbord, K. T.: Who Shall Be in the Adapted Physical Education Program. AAHPER National Convention, Chicago, 1966.

†A concept of the eighteenth century (age of enlightenment) was advised for educational context by Locke, Rousseau, Basedow, Guts Muths, and Ling.

clarity, balance, and calmness, with the cause and effect syndrome a total crystallized entity (31).°

The present oriental culture includes exercises for strength and agility of the body, the fundamental principle for basic progress being perfection of self.

Ancient Greece

Despite this ancient oriental heritage, therapeutic (Gr. *therapeutikos:* art of healing, curative) exercise in the modern context had its philosophical birth in ancient Greece. The medical practitioners of ancient Greece were priests, physicians, philosophers, and gymnasts who studied the bodily effects of exercise and diet. The Greek term for exercise is *ascesis,* so an Ascete was an individual who exercised his mind and body. The individual who exercised for a prize (*Athlon*) was called an *athlete.* The word *exercise* is derived from *ex,* which means *out* and the *erc* component which means to *lock;* so, exercise means *to free a part* or *unlock.*

Legend tells us that the first Olympic game was a religious and athletic festival taking place near the temple of Zeus at Olympia in 776 B.C. (58). Archeologists testify that the temple of Hera and other temples had games and religious ceremonies before 776 B.C. (123), but the Greeks began to reckon time by the Olympiads (192).† The games were opened by the priests, who sacrificed a pig to Zeus and a black ram to Pelops. The games lasted only five days, but the temples and altars were open all year. These Olympic games continued until 394 A.D. when Theodosius, a Roman emperor, discontinued all Greek festivals.

Hippocrates (460 B.C.), the famous Greek physician and Father of Medicine, recognized the importance of exercise for strengthening flesh (muscles), hastening convalescence, and improving mental attitude. He was a student of Herodicus (480 B.C.), who claims to have cured himself of an incurable illness through exercise. His complicated system of exercise was accepted in part by Hippocrates and other physicians. Hippocrates' book, *On Regimen,* is largely concerned with illness and exercise for physiological and pathological diseases, including mental disease and medical rehabilitation. This keenest of all ancient observers

---

° The movements have specific names such as "Single Whip." The wide appeal of this system was shown from the results of a television program which Sophia Delza presented in 1960. More than 1,000 responses from people in 40 states asked for more information on how to perform T'ai Chi Chuan.

† The blind bard, Homer, preserved the primitive civilization through the *Iliad* and *Odyssey.*

of the human body had practical mechanical views on anatomy and physiology.

Such Greek philosophers as Socrates, Aristotle, and Plato recommended medical gymnastics for their citizens.° Plato advised training for women to produce a perfect physique. Aristotle's treatise, "De Motu Animalism," investigated muscle action in an elementary way as compared with present scientific methods.

The Athenian culture enveloped gymnastics and self-testing sports (games) as individual achievements for citizens of Athens. Many festivals were held for this type of participation. Originally, giving thanks to the gods was among the basic reasons for these festivals. The Spartan culture identified its citizens with state goals, shunning the personal goals of the Athenians.† In Sparta, the boys were drilled as soldiers; women were conditioned to bear sturdy children. The exercise training centers (*Gymnasia*) were focused to develop physical efficiency, perfect physique, and military stamina. Claudius Galen (130–200 A.D.) ‡ recorded that physicians such as Herodicus recommended medical gymnastics; Diocles, walking exercises; Erasistratus, walking for dropsy; Themison, passive and active exercises. Also, Praxagoras, Philotinus, and Theon advised specific movement patterns for illnesses. Galen was a forerunner of the twentieth century physiologist, Charles Scott Sherrington, in that he interpreted gross muscular effort and relaxation, coming close to the later law of Sherrington (Reciprocal Innervation), which states that tension is never increased simultaneously and in the same degree in both agonist and antagonistic muscles. Thus, as with much of medical science, the mechanics of locomotion had its philosophical birth in ancient Greece.

After the Persian Wars, the Greek empire's victory nurtured unlicensed freedom and eventual downfall of the empire. Professional men were hired for the military, and physical training for the young lost its religious significance. The individual's physical efficiency was analyzed in the medical gymnasia, with success in athletics seemingly the primary goal. Competitive brutality developed, resulting in the discontinuation of these festivals.

° Around 450 B.C. the Athenian city-states had populations comprised of 20 per cent citizens, 5 per cent foreigners, 75 per cent slaves. "Citizenship came with birth and proper education." Citizens served the state, owned land, and were educated (105, p. 41).

† Like the Homeric Greeks, they cultivated the body rather than the mind for their military government. Under the harsh laws of Lycurgus, eugenic procreation was compulsory. Crippled and deformed infants were exposed to the weather or thrown into the Eurotas.

‡ A Greek physician and prolific writer, assumed to have written 500 treatises, of which 80 are found in print. He kept many scribes busy.

Ancient Rome

Prior to the fall of Greece to Rome in 146 B.C., the Greek philosophers, Aristotle, Socrates, and Plato,° had deplored the whimsical character of the children to which permissive parents and teachers had contributed by disregarding the old Greek training ideals for the perfect physique.† The Greeks were profound, versatile thinkers, while the Romans exhibited more natural, energetic, and practical views.

The Roman home was well organized, although the father, as head of the household, determined if an infant should live or die. Marcus Tullius Cicero (106–43 B.C.), Roman orator and philosopher, tells how the weak were isolated on an island (22). This patriarchal power continued even after the marriage of the child. Father and son attended daily religious ceremonies, the forum, business discussions, and exercise programs with a thoroughness to duty that adult life needed. The Roman Republic and Empire (27 B.C. under Augustus) assimilated the Greek culture and carried enlightenment from Africa to northern Europe. Exercise had a specific purpose: to make men strong and skillful warriors. In the declining years of the Roman Empire, exercise was "to prevent systemic weaknesses, for recovery from illness, or to avoid the unpleasantness of overindulgence (180)."

Greek physicians were imported by the Romans for practical health purposes, and many were glad to come to the flourishing society. The value of Greek gymnastics was recognized by some Roman philosophers and orators as a help in the training for poised gestures in public speaking, but Cicero felt exercises had a proper place, not an end in themselves. The entertainment at the Roman festivals was provided by slaves and was not a demonstration of personal physical prowess.

Despite these attitudes, great treatises on scientific physical exercise were recorded. Claudius Galen of Pergamus, Asia Minor (130 A.D.), lived in the Roman Empire and served as physician to Marcus Aurelius Antoninius. Galen's knowledge of traumatic surgery and the musculoskeletal system, gained while caring for gladiators in Pergamus, gave him a sound basis for exercise postulates. He is credited with using pulse count to determine physical condition of gladiators for the emperor of Pergamus. He recommended moderate exercise for health training of the body and mind. In his book, *On Hygiene*, he classified exercises according to their vigor, duration, frequency and use of apparatus, and the body part involved. Galen had (1) specific exercises for muscle tonus, (2) quick exercises, and (3) violent exercises with re-

° Plato. *Republic*, dialogue 563.
† Socrates. Plato's *Apology*

sistance and uninterrupted drill. Galen° was sensitive to contraindications of vigorous movement patterns and felt that the quasi-medical
anointers of the bath and the gymnasts prevalent in Rome harmed the
profession of gymnastic exercise.

Other Romans, mostly priest-physicians, who supported moderate
exercise were Asclepiades;† A. Cornelius Celsus; Aretaeus, who felt
exercises in the erect position for the chest and shoulders helped a
headache; Antyllus; Philostralies; Callius Aurelianus, who in the fifth
century, and Paulus Aegineta, who in the seventh century recorded
catalogs of exercises selected from their predecessors. These men followed Galen's writings, but Aegineta defined exercise as violent motion
which renders the body organs fit for their functional action (105).

In Rome, the public bath, with light exercises and competitive
games as part of the participation, was popular. Emperor Nero tried
to revive Grecian contests, but the evils of professionalism were too
strongly associated with the decline of Greece. Julius Caesar set up
festivals for athletic displays, chariot races, gladiator contests, dramatic
and musical performances; but Greek type athletics in Roman games
did not hold the interest of the Romans, and the bath remained their
preference for exercise participation. Private contests were held in
Rome, but in time they became barbaric with heavy gambling and ex-
hibitions of a base character. Present day physical education has developed principally from that of Greek philosophers and Roman orators.

Middle Ages

After the fall of Rome in 476 A.D. and throughout the early Middle
Ages, Christianity renounced material things, including strength of body
and preservation of beauty. The Christian church nurtured the souls
of men but had little concern for their bodies. Until the ninth century,
only the higher class, such as the lords and knights, exercised. The
severity of these times and the effect on physical contests were significantly apparent around the end of the tenth century.

The Arabians, through Syrian and Hebrew translations, stored and
kept alive ancient oriental, Greek, and Roman writings throughout the
Byzantine period (476–730 A.D.) (50, p. 121). During the tenth and

---

° His *Exercises with the Small Ball* was especially recommended because the ball
could be used for light or strenuous activity. The exercises resembled our handball
game.

† One of the first Greek physicians practicing in Rome—born 174 B.C. and regarded
by Pagel as the Father of Physical Medicine, since he used physical agents for helping
the sick.

eleven centuries, the value of exercise was again revived by Rhazes, an Arab physician. Avicenna wrote that "if men exercised their bodies by motion and work at the appropriate times, they need neither physician nor remedies (105, p. 434)." Isaac Judaeus, in the tenth century, "felt idleness was harmful for health (105, p. 435)." Johannes Actuarius, of the thirteenth century, prescribed exercises and diet for disease, especially mental diseases. Catalan, in the fourteenth century, wrote of the "need for medicines, exercise and gladness (105)." Francesco Petrarch, also in the late fourteenth century, expressed need for natural remedies, including exercise, in place of drugs, and he satirized the doctors on their gorgeous clothes and pompous airs (58). During this time, St. Thomas Aquinas gave limited praise for the value of body exercise, while other scholastics usually ignored physical development for the intellectual and religious training of logical analysis, reasoning, and debate on educational curricula.

During the time of the Eastern Roman Empire (390–1450), compassion for human suffering arose as a result of the teachings of Christ. Hospitals were formed and nursing care was organized (50, p. 176). Licht (105, p. 434) relates that during this period a large hospital in Cairo erected a pavillion in the garden so that patients could take walking exercises in the shade.

The Renaissance

The Renaissance in Europe introduced new thinking in both academic and physical matters. The school of Salerno, Italy, developed in a mysterious way, with evident access to Greek and Roman writings for teaching purposes. Despite the many wars following the downfall of Rome, other schools and universities arose, including the University of Paris (1110), Bologna (1113), Oxford (1167), Padua (1222), and Naples (1224). This period was characterized not only by intellectual, religious, commercial, and industrial upheavals, but also by destructive influences. The Plague, or black death, in 1348, killed one fourth of all the population. The secular authorities became concerned about men's bodies, and in the thirteenth century some hospitals were administered by municipalities instead of by the churches. The invention of the printing press contributed to social progress during this period. Michelangelo, Columbus, da Vinci, Raphael, Montaigne, Magellan, Cellini, Galileo, Copernicus, Luther, Gutenberg, Juan Luis Vives, Rabelais, and others challenged the intellectual decadence of the previous centuries.

Humanism manifested itself during the Renaissance, followed and/or paralleled by moralism and realism. Petrarch, the Italian scholar, was a forerunner of the humanistic movement, which advocated a broad, liberal training for students. The influence of therapeutic exercise within the educational program was furthered by Pietro Vergerio (1349–1428). He wrote a letter about physical education which Vittorino de Feltra, a physician, used when he founded the Mantua School, in 1423, to educate young noblemen mentally and physically. (105, p. 435)°

Greek classics appeared in print, and books stressing the values of health and exercise were available. Leonard Fuch's book, *Institutiones Medicae,* had a chapter on motion and rest which contained a resumé on the art of exercise: "There are two kinds of exercise; the first is simple exercise; the second is both exercise and work (105)." *Libro del Exercicio* by Christobal Mendez of Jaen was printed in the sixteenth century. The book, *De Arte Gymnastics,* by Hieronymus Mercurialis, a professor at Padua, was reprinted five times. Mercurialis set definite principles for medical gymnastics which included (1) exercises to maintain an existing healthy state, (2) regularity in exercise, (3) exercise for sick people with conditions that might exacerbate, (4) special individual exercises for convalescents, and (5) exercises for persons with sedentary occupations. He particularly advocated mountain climbing for those with weak lower limbs, and discus throwing for people afflicted with arthritis of the wrists, but no jumping exercises for pregnant women.

The writings of Mercurialis were followed by those of other scholars advising exercise for the preservation of health. Timothy Bright, Joseph Duchesne, Sanctorius, and Martin Luther stressed the value of exercise. Luther preached, "Music chases chagrin and melancholy; gymnastics produces a strong and robust body and keeps it in a state of health. It can keep young people from idleness, debauchery and drink (105, p. 438)." Pope Pius II expressed his approval of humanistic education: "A boy must be won to learning by persuasive earnestness and not be driven to it like a slave . . . (50, p. 156)." Tuccaro, a famous Neopolitan physical educator, also wrote and put into print dialogues on hygienic exercises.

European Cultures

Despite the difficulties of the sixteenth and seventeenth centuries, the education philosophies and practices of humanism, moralism, and realism continued to be of great importance to modern physical education. The Frenchman, Francois Rabelais (1483–1553), wrote the *Life of Gargantua.* This monk felt that training of the intellect and nurturing of the body was the aim of education. Michel de Montaigne (1533–

° The pioneering work at Mantua School influenced John Locke to write an essay on education, "Thoughts Concerning Education," in 1693. In 1572, Michel de Montaigne also advised a balanced education.

1592), the well-known essayist, preceded John Locke in his idea on the value of exercise as a hardening process for the body, which contributed toward developing a healthy, thinking, acting person. As an aristocrat, Montaigne felt tutors were better educators than parents or schools. Francis Bacon (1561–1626), the masterful English author and statesman, stirred many educators to interest concerning physical education. Garrison (50) calls the seventeenth century the age of individual scientific endeavor. Some call it the age of Shakespeare. During this era new universities developed, scientific societies were formed, and much periodic literature was printed. René Descartes (1596–1650) of Tours, France, propounded work on neurophysiology. Giovanni Borelli ° (1608–1679), an Italian mathematician, recognized muscle tone and muscle contractions and developed the center of gravity point for the body. William Croone (1633–1684) in his *London Lectures* discussed muscle structure and muscle contractions. Thomas Willis (1621–1675) developed microscopic data on muscular motion. Leonardo da Vinci also was known for his work in biomechanics of the body and illustrations of the muscular system. Toward the end of the seventeenth century, Thomas Sydenham, the English physician, prescribed horseback riding for patients with tuberculosis. His influence was significant for many years. John Locke (1632–1704), the English philosopher and disciplinarian, had a strong influence on education and physical education. One of his writings, *Some Thoughts Concerning Education,* stressed the natural development of the child. Physical education was the hardening process counterbalanced by recreation. To Locke, the health of the body in maintaining business and happiness was too obvious to need proof. Robert Hooke (1635–1703), an English physicist, is credited with many original experiments. He built a microscope to observe the cellular structure of living things. His law (1676) states that the deformation bears a constant ratio to the stress (172, p. 11). Thus, the principle that all tissues are elastic within certain limits is assumed. When subjected to stress, body tissues change their form but return to the original shape when the stress is removed, with a constant arithmetical relationship between force and elongation.

In the eighteenth century, the writings of the many Renaissance philosophers influenced the scholars of this age of enlightenment, also known as the age of theories and systems (50). The theory of "natural laws" evolved with rebellion by many brilliant scientists and philosophers against inequality, oppression, and enslavement of the individual. Jean Jacques Rousseau (1713–1778) attacked French society and the poor practices of French education. He rebelled against the practices

° Borelli was a student of Galileo and a contemporary of Isaac Newton. Barthez went into analysis of walking, running, and posture (105, p. 439).

of the child being a miniature adult and mandated a "return to nature" philosophy for education. This philosophy followed that of Comenius and Locke, whose natural environment theories for child development were familiar. Comenius felt the will of the Bible should be the authority for education, and Locke focused on the demands of society (172). Rousseau's contributing ideas to education were set forth in *Emile* (1762). As a theorist, he did not test his ideas in practical school situations, but his zealous attacks for reform in education had a great appeal for many followers and influenced other educators. The French Revolution saw the naturalistic education doctrine outlawed in France, but other countries began experimentation in naturalism.

Johan Bernhard Baselon (1723–1790) of Germany followed Rousseau's theories at his school, the Philanthropinum. His writings outlined his methods of educational reform. Vieth (1763–1836), also influenced by naturalism in education, contributed an *Encyclopedia of Bodily Exercises* or system of exercises. C. G. Salzmann (1744–1811) established an Educational Institute with Johann Friedrich Guts Muths (1749–1839) as one of his teachers. Guts Muths contributed volumes on physical education. He categorized games into natural classifications by specific skill development. His *Gymnastic for the Young* was translated into many languages.* He was a prolific writer in physical education and geography. Many regard him as the "grandfather of modern physical education." His work at the Salzmann Schnepfenthal Institute was preceded by that of Christian Andre, who included movement patterns to improve the posture of the students. Thus, so-called "free exercises" began (180, p. 207). Guts Muths continued Andre's program of exercises and/or physical education and delved into the ancient classics for further information on body development.

Friedrich Ludwig Jahn (1778–1852), father of German gymnastics and the Turnverein system, aimed educationally at developing the body, mind, and character of youth through heavy apparatus gymnastics, mass drills, and games of skill (23, p. 3).

This age of formalism and methodistic "systems" in exercise also had parallel scientific and medical achievements related to physical education. Francis Fuller believed he cured hypochondria by horseback riding. His book, *Medicina Gymnastica*, (1705) had nine editions printed plus a German translation. Friedrich Hoffmann (1660–1742) established the importance of exercise in hygiene and medical treatment. His book, *Dessertationes*, published in 1708, has a chapter on movement advo-

---

* The chapter headings are 1. Leaping, 2. Running, 3. Jaculation, 4. Wrestling, 5. Climbing, 6. Balancing, 7. Lifting and Carrying, 8. Dancing, Walking and Military Exercises.

cated as the best medicine for the body. He felt patients at medicinal spas gained more through body movement than from the famous drinking water. He is well-known for his observation that "Exercise improves the action of many medications to such an extent that without it the desired effect cannot be obtained." He quoted Galen's premise, "Exercise prevents gout (105, p. 440)." Hoffmann's prominent name contributed to the reestablishment of physical exercises in daily life. Nicolas Andry ° (1658–1742) was the first to relate exercise to the musculoskeletal system. At a Medical Faculty meeting in Paris, he read a paper titled "Is Exercise the Best Means of Preserving Health?" He advised corrective exercise, specific exercise and sports for reducing weight, increasing mobility, strengthening the spine and correcting postural deformities. He coined the term *orthopaedics,* and published his book, *L'Orthopedic,* in 1741. Orthopaedics is that branch of surgery which is especially concerned with the preservation and restoration of the function of the skeletal system, its articulations, and associated structures.

Luigi Galvani (1737–1798) of Bologna developed experiments on muscle-nerve preparations. He discovered the electric properties of excised muscle. Alessandro Volta (1745–1827) continued the animal electricity studies of Galvani. Albrecht Von Haller (1708–1777), a Swiss physiologist, experimented with irritability and excitability of muscle tissue and the physiology of locomotion (171). The study of the operation of the body was followed by many physicians and the physical education context employed by the well-known ones. Theodore Tronchin of Geneva, President of the College at Leyden, persuaded his patients to take long walks in the fresh air, as well as other exercises. Exercise machines were invented. Even Voltaire was pleased with a vibrating chair.

The latter days of the eighteenth century witnessed changes in human thought and action. The parallel of present-day therapeutic exercise appeared in a book by Joseph-Clement Tissot (1750–1826) in 1785. This book, *Medical and Surgical Gymnastics,* contained an essay on the use of motion and exercises in the cure of disease. The significance of Tissot's written work was not recognized for some years, and exercises continued to be prescribed for their overall effect rather than for the strengthening of weak muscles and the mobilization of stiff joints. Tissot analyzed craft and manual motions, insisting that one should have knowledge of anatomy for prescribing orthopaedic exercises. He also prescribed recreation therapy and adapted sports for the disabled. He preceded Ling in prescribing fencing as a curative exercise

---

° Nicolas Andry was born in Lyons. He was an ordained priest but studied medicine at Reims and Paris. He was Dean of Paris Medical School, 1724.

and stated that fencing is an active gymnastic exercise which strengthens the limbs, increases the range of the joints as well as the circulation of the viscera. Tissot's medical management for many illnesses was advanced, but evidently because of the provocative times his recommendations were ignored.

John Hunter, the English anatomist and surgeon, preceded Tissot although they were contemporaries for a while. He was a strong believer in early mobilization after illness or injury through active exercise. He endorsed John Pugh's system of exercise. In 1794, Pugh's book, *A Physiological, Theoretic and Practical Treatise on the Utility of the Science of Muscular Action for Restoring the Power of the Limbs,* was published. This book presented the kinesiology of each muscle and was well illustrated with specific exercises. Other physicians to prescribe this treatment of exercise were John Abernethy, Dally, Jean David, and Watson.

During this age of enlightenment and naturalistic educational systems, America was involved with many conflicts. Therefore, physical education was not a specific part of education in America until the nineteenth century, but many medical men were attracted to it for its health values. John Morgan (1735–1789), a surgeon in the French War and a native of Philadelphia, along with William Shippen, helped found the Medical Department of the University of Pennsylvania in 1765. Morgan was appointed Director General and Physician in Chief of the American Army in 1775. For political reasons, he was replaced as the Surgeon General to the Army by his contemporary, Shippen, in 1779. Benjamin Rush (1745–1813), an English Quaker from Philadelphia, also contributed much to early medicine in the United States. Therapeutic exercise and/or part of the reconstruction aid work used by the above men contributed to physical activity of patients with neuromuscular injuries.

Modern Cultures

The nineteenth century saw the start of universal education. The civic virtues and cultural heritage of each nation gave nationalistic identification. In this age organized scientific advancements had their beginning (50). Along with advances in medicine and education came the rapid growth of the gymnastic movement, often credited to Pehr Henrick Ling, (1776–1839) whose thesis was "physical and moral perfection (105)." Ling's physical education experience started with fencing in Copenhagen, where he taught poetry, mythology, and history (180). The improvement of his afflicted arm through fencing exercises inspired him to study the effect of exercise on the body. With much vigor, he developed a system of gymnastics as the fencing master at the University of Lund. In 1813, the Central Institute of Gymnastics of Stockholm was created to train teachers. Here, Ling developed a system of medical gymnastics which attracted physicians. His system introduced dosage, counting, and detailed directions with classified starting positions and degrees of activity. Ling classified muscle contraction into two types: concentric, or shortening of a muscle by the origin and insertion moving toward each other, and eccentric, or increasing the length of the muscle while contracting. Concentric and eccentric muscle movement also has a third category called "isometric contraction" where the muscle tenses with no joint movement. Isometric muscle contractions are also called "muscle setting" or "dynamic tension." Ling's physical education theory was to achieve military, medical, pedagogical, and aesthetic results (172, p. 247). The educational values of exercise as set forth by Ling are those found in the encyclopedic *Gargantua* by the sixteenth century physician, Rabelais (105). Ling authored many books on fencing and gymnastics, including *Manual for Gymnastics*, 1836; *Manual for Bayonet-Fencing*, 1836; *Soldiers' Manual of Bayonet-Fencing*, 1838. After his death, his pupils published a book, *General Principles of Gymnastics* in 1839, which Ling started in 1831. Reaction to his work was virtual worship by most of his students and followers and mixed emotions and abhorrence by a few. Du Bois-Reymond, a physiologist, felt that Ling was dogmatic and that his underlying facts were not true physiologically. Pickery of France opposed gymnastics and felt that Ling's statement, "Every movement is a thought expressed by the body (105)," was just obscure words. Despite these reactions, the Swedish exercise movement spread throughout Europe and the United States.

The Ling system was introduced into the United States before the Civil War by George H. Taylor, Medical Director of the Remedial Hygienic Institute of New York City. The latter part of the nineteenth century saw the Ling (Swedish) and Guts Muths (German) gymnastic systems put into educational practice. Physicians maintained an interest in therapeutic exercise and prescribed it. In 1821, the French physician, Charles Londe, published the book, *Medical Gymnastics*. In 1822, an essay on exercise for scoliosis won Dr. Bampfield the Hunter prize. John Shaw believed scoliosis was caused by weak spinal muscles and prescribed graduated exercise, massage, and intermittent rest for patients. The French physician, Jacques M. Delpech (1777–1832), established a school for girls with scoliosis. He wrote a book on posture correction, which advocated apparatus for exercises—particularly suspension movements of the body by the hands—and an espousal on the value of swimming for the vertebral column.

Dr. Gustav Zander, a follower of Pehr Ling, felt that the one-to-one ratio of patient and gymnast was unwise economically. He set up wheels, levers, and weights for exercise assistance and resistance, so that the gymnast could continue the patient's program with occasional supervision. He demonstrated his twenty-seven machines for mechanotherapy before Swedish doctors in 1864 and shortly thereafter opened his Medico-Mechanical Institute in Stockholm. Zander Institutes have been opened in the United States, on the Continent, and in South America.° By 1893, seven countries had fully equipped Zander Institutes. At first, the patient's muscles powered the Zander machines; then steam engines were used; and, later, electric motors. When Zander equipment, which was manufactured in Wiesbaden, Germany, was unavailable during World War I, exercise with no apparatus was emphasized.

In 1854, William Stokes of Dublin prescribed regulated exercises and planned walks for heart cases. Oertel of Munich set up planned walking for heart conditions, and other physicians followed. In 1874, S. Weir Mitchell included graduated exercise and massage in his patients' prescriptions.

Albert Frenkel, in the late nineteenth century, developed a system of coordination exercises for ataxic conditions. At this time, tertiary syphilis with spinal cord deterioration was common, presenting ataxia, an associated syndrome. Now ataxia is a rarity among civilized people.

Many other individuals furthered the advancement of education and science during the nineteenth century. The Webers† studied biokinetics or the dynamic action of muscles and the mechanics of locomotion. The structure of bones was Herman Von Meyers' great interest. Julius Wolff and William Roux (1850–1924) researched in developmental mechanics of the body. Wolff's law of bone growth states that the external stress affects the internal architecture. Fischer and Braune (1891–1905) investigated locomotion by kinematograph. Rudolph Fick and Strasser set up a guide on modern kinetics and human locomotion. Helmholtz investigated the velocity of nerve currents. C. B. Duchenne de Boulogne (1806–1875) studied the electrotherapeutics in diseases of nerves (171). Charles Scott Sherrington (1857–1952), one of the greatest physiologists of all times, set up his law of reciprocal innervation and reciprocal inhibition of reflex stimulus which states: excitation of one

---

° Ernesto Aberg, who had a Zander background, settled in Argentina and published *Mechanotherapy of Zander* in 1884. A woman physician continued Aberg's work and finally, in 1937, a School of Kinesiology was founded in Buenos Aires. Twenty-five monographs in five volumes on therapeutic exercise were completed in 1958 by Claudia Ceci and Juan Nagera of this school (105).

† Edward Weber, 1806–1861; Heinrich Weber, 1795–1878; Wilhelm Weber, 1804–1891.

center is simultaneous with inhibition of another reflex center. His "all or none law" stipulates that the individual muscle fibers can only be in a state of absolute relaxation or in maximum contraction (171), p. 90).°
Thus, muscle tension is a quantitative procedure rather than a qualitative one. Henry Pickering Bowditch (1814–1911) of Boston investigated the indefatigability of nerves and the so-called staircase phenomenon of fatigue. He used curare for blocking nerves and, subsequently, curare came to be used by anesthetists. Bowditch proved that nerves cannot be tired (171, p. 90).†

The term, *rehabilitation*, was first used in a book on medical exercises published in Spain in 1864. The special exercises were called orthopaedic gymnastics to rehabilitate the weak muscle groups (105, p. 453).

Thus, the physiology and the physical therapy taken for granted by many today are based on specific fragments of knowledge contributed by many persons from various professions and homelands.

American Cultures

Physical education as a specific discipline of education in America was strongly affected by the investigations and achievements of the physicians, scientists, and educators of the nineteenth century. Many physicians became physical education leaders during the genesis of teacher training in this field. Some prominent pioneers of physical education are Edward Hitchcock, Amherst College; Dio Lewis, Boston; Dudley Sargent, Harvard University; W. G. Anderson, Yale University; Fred E. Leonard, Oberlin College; Luther Gulick, Springfield College; James McCurdy, Springfield College; R. Tait McKenzie, University of Pennsylvania; Kate C. Hurd, Bryn Mawr College; Alice J. Hall, Goucher College; Margaret Bell, University of Michigan; William Skarstrom, Boston Normal School of Gymnastics; Thomas Storey, Stanford University; Thomas Wood, Columbia University; Clark Hetherington, Stanford University; Charles Leroy Lowman, University of Southern California; Delphine Hanna, Oberlin College; Carolyn Ladd, Bryn Mawr College; Helen Putnam, Vassar College; and Margaret Lightring, Michigan State University.

Among the early proponents of physical education in the United

---

°In 1932, Charles Sherrington shared with Edward Douglas Adrian the Nobel Prize for advancement of physiology.

†Sadi Carnot in 1824 demonstrated the principle of dissipation of energy which Mayer, Helmholtz, and Joule in 1842 formulated as the law of conservation of energy. Energy consumption during work is based on the laws of muscle thermodynamics investigated by Haldane (1860), Hill, Myerhof, Harttru, and others.

States were such well-known men as Benjamin Franklin,° Thomas Jefferson, Noah Webster, and Benjamin Rush. The first gymnasia to appear were at Round Hill School, Northhampton, Massachusetts, in 1825, and at Harvard University, Cambridge, Massachusetts, in 1826. The Normal Institute for Physical Education, established in Boston in 1861 by Dio Lewis, graduated around 250 students during its six or seven years of existence. The co-educational curriculum consisted of participation in gymnastics six to twelve hours a day for nine weeks.

The Jahn system† was introduced by the Germans, Charles Beck and Charles Follen. Teacher training for physical education was started in 1861 by the North American Turnerbund at Rochester, New York. German Turnverein Clubs served the new German residents in the United States. The National Turnerbund, established in 1850, eventually had about 150 societies. The annual Turnfests included mass participation in exercises and games for all members. However, the Civil War saw the decline of most physical education activities.

Physicians were partial to the Swedish medical gymnastics during the last half of the nineteenth century. The gymnastic fad of the 1820's exacerbated in the 1850's. The culture of the American population was absorbing many changes, so vacillating interests were normal and to be expected.

The physical education focus in America started in Boston in the 1820's. The Swedish system‡ and the German system of gymnastics came with immigration of the Swedes and Germans to America. Their basic aim was the development of the physical organism. In 1879, Dudley Sargent, M.D. of Harvard University listed four aims of physical training:

1. Hygiene: the consideration of the normal proportions of the individual, the anatomy and physiological functions of various organs and a study of the ordinary agents of health such as exercise, diet, sleep, air, bathing, and clothing.
2. Educative: the cultivation of special powers of mind and body used in acquisition of some skillful trade or physical accomplishment, such as swimming, golf, or skating.
3. Recreative: the renovation of vital energies to enable the individual to return to his daily work with vigor and accomplish his tasks with ease.

° Credited as one of the first to propose that physical training be made a part of the educational institute curriculum.

† Friedrich Ludwig Jahn; 1778–1852, father of German gymnastics and the Turner societies.

‡ Hartvig Nisson and Baron Nils Posse came to Boston from Sweden in the 1880's and are credited with selling Swedish gymnastics to the school.

4. Remedial: the restoration of disturbed functions and the correction of physical defects and deformities (180, p. 389).

The modern aim and philosophy of physical training can be credited to Thomas D. Wood, M.D. of Stanford University and Columbia University. In 1893, he stated before the National Education Association: "The great thought in physical education is not the education of the physical nature, but the relation of physical training to complete education, and then the effort to make the physical contribute its full share to the life of the individual in environment, training, and culture (180, p. 391)."

The twentieth century marks the beginning of internationalism in education and the appearance of specialization in medical practice, and both enhanced the development of the physical education program. Garrison calls this the era of organized preventive medicine. Physical educators* developed anthropometric measurements and strength tests adopted by schools and colleges. Formal corrective physical education programs were incorporated in the school curriculum. Teacher training courses included "correctives" to correct postural defects, to ease pathological conditions, and to develop weak muscles. The physicians identified physical education as a contribution to the individual's mental, emotional, social, and physical effectiveness. The orthopaedists, neurologists, and spa physicians specialized in therapeutic exercise and electrotherapy. Dr. Rudolf Klapp in 1904 and 1928 experimented with creeping exercise for spinal deformities or scoliosis. His principles for strengthening muscles of the spine are still widely used.

Poliomyelitis, which is rare now, was a serious problem in the early twentieth century.† Robert W. Lovett, M.D., a Boston orthopaedist, set up "muscle training" for polio patients and, with his senior assistant, Wilhelmina G. Wright, developed ambulation techniques for paraplegics. When a polio victim was trained to ambulate on crutches, it was a great achievement (105). In Sweden, J. Arvedson recognized the value of exercises for musculoskeletal diseases, particularly poliomyelitis, in preventing contractures of the limbs. The gymnastic and supportive treatment of polio is still used with the addition of Charles Leroy Lowman's idea of utilizing the Hubbard tank for hydrogymnastics in 1924.

World War I found many young people physically unfit for military service. This spurred the expansion of physical education, and by 1932, thirty-six states required it in their school curriculum. Expansion in education brought vacation schools, playgrounds, social centers, and

---

*Dr. Hitchcock of Amherst took measurements for students to see their development. Dr. Sargent of Harvard was interested in perfect body proportions for the harmoniously developed man (180, p. 416).

†Salk vaccine and Sabin oral vaccine were developed in the 1950's. Polio epidemics took their toll of American youngsters before that time.

special classes for the crippled, tubercular, and retarded. The Parent-Teacher Association, Rhodes Scholarship, and Carnegie Endowments for International World Peace were started at this time. Military hospitals used "restorative exercises" to aid in the recovery of disabled patients. Occupational therapy, as a part of medical gymnastics, was practiced in many military hospitals and convalescent centers.° Reconstruction and re-education of the disabled were planned in Germany ten years before World War I. Vocational rehabilitation adumbrated by Juan Luis Vives (1531) became a national administration matter (50, p. 792). In 1918, E. G. Brackett and Joel Goldthwait, M.D., organized the Reconstruction Department of the United States Army. Aides were trained in the Physiotherapy Division of this Department. Their contribution to therapeutic exercise had great value.

Following the First World War, the attitude toward exercise expanded. Scientific techniques were developed for measurement of posture as well as athletic achievement tests or motor performance tests and cardiovascular tests. "Reconstruction" exercises recognized the value of relaxation techniques. Jacobson, of the University of Chicago, developed an encyclopedic system of movement for relaxation.† Todd and Josephine Rathbone of Teachers College, Columbia University, and Maja Shade of Wisconsin also formulated relaxation techniques.

The great number of neuroses caused by the War and its aftermath resulted in relaxation being identified with "remedial" exercise. August Bier, M.D. of Germany believed sports and games more relaxing than conventional exercises. Special "correctives" classes were inaugurated in the schools. Teacher-training courses included study of examination and testing programs to determine individual needs. Joel E. Goldthwait, M.D.‡ and co-authors in 1934 wrote a book entitled *Essentials of Body Mechanics in Health and Disease*. Celia Mosher, M.D.§ in 1900 suggested that poor posture caused many human ailments, but later some research did not substantiate this hypothesis. Arthur Steindler, Professor of Orthopedic Surgery at the State University of Iowa, wrote *Mechanics of Normal and Pathological Locomotion in Man*, in which the thesis of myokinetic coordination was studied intensely.

Physical educators, such as David Brace, began applying statistical methods to physical education. In 1924, Brace's tests for women's bas-

° Bergonie of France is credited with starting occupational therapy.

† Jacobson, Edmund: *You Must Relax*, New York, Whittlesey House, McGraw-Hill Book Co., 1962; *You Can Sleep Well*, New York, Whittlesey House, McGraw-Hill Book Co., 1934.

‡ Goldthwait, J. E.; Brown, L. T.; Swaim, L. T.; Kuhns, J. G. and Kerr, W. S.; *Essentials of Body Mechanics in Health and Disease*. Philadelphia, J. B. Lippincott Co., 1934.

§ Exercises for dysmenorrhea.

ketball were set up, and in 1927, he organized motor ability tests of twenty stunts. Elizabeth Beall, in 1925, set up tennis tests. Dudley A. Sargent, M.D. in 1921, used the "jump" test for power and efficiency in performance. Frederick Rand Rogers devised a Strength and Physical Fitness Index. Charles H. McCoy in the late 1920's developed a classification index using age, height, and weight to estimate homogeneous grouping as a criterion for activities. Behavior types, as determined by moral and social qualities, were studied to determine character outcome.

Knowledge expansion, specialization, and the complexities of twentieth century society had a significant influence on educational objectives. In the 1930's, Jesse F. Williams of Columbia University and Jay B. Nash of New York University reinforced the concepts of Thomas D. Wood and Clark Hetherington.

Nash believed in four levels of life:

1. Organic powers (basic to other three levels).
2. Neuromuscular (Hetherington's psychomotor).
3. Interpretive-cortical, or meaning through activity (Hetherington's intellectual education).
4. Emotional-impulsive (Hetherington's character education).

Coordination of all four, he believed, developed the integrated individual.

Preparation for leisure time activity became necessary due to economic changes in society. Establishment of desirable health habits was stressed, such as improvement of posture and prevention, detection, and correction of physical defects; development of normal growth and organic development; and coordination of effective mental and motor activity. Social psychology advances promoted (1) the compensation theory of imagination and vicarious satisfaction in play, and (2) the self-expression theory allowing direct achievement and satisfaction in play, through habits as well as instinct, to enrich living and fully develop the personality (180). Deaver of New York University and George Stafford of Illinois proposed physical opportunities adapted to the abilities of the handicapped, and, in 1935, the Social Security Act authorized the Federal government to match state money for the care of crippled children.

Between the two World Wars, physical education expanded greatly, and leadership shifted from physicians to men and women with Doctor of Philosophy or doctoral degrees in the philosophy of education and Doctor of Education degrees. Formal calisthenics used in foreign countries were replaced by natural activities of play, sports, games, and dance. Individual needs of the student were identified and considered by many educators. Programs to alleviate and improve neuromuscular deficiencies of students' personal needs were continued. Many texts on "corrective" physical education and body mechanics illustrate and document this philosophy. The contributions of well-known physical educators promoted the personal and individual needs of students. Among them were George T. Stafford, Josephine L. Rathbone, Ellen D. Kelly, Arthur S. Daniels, Mabel Lee, Eleanor Metheny. The associated field of kinesiology had writers such as Gladys Scott, Katherine Wells, Gertrude Hawley, Philip Rasch, and Roger Burke. Books on physiology of exercise were prepared by Peter Karpovich, Arthur Steinhaus, Laurence Morehouse, Don Mathews and Benjamin Ricci.

Therapeutic exercises were developed by both physical educators and physicians. Leo Buerger, physician, developed a system of exercises, the Buerger System, for peripheral vascular disease. So-called segmental breathing exercises were used by physicians, and in 1936, T. Holmes Sellers established a program of breathing exercises for his patients with pathologic conditions of the chest and lung. Physical therapy and occupational therapy were two new specialties using therapeutic exercises. Frank Krusen, Charles Leroy Lowman, and Claire Colestock were among the pioneers in these new allied medical services.

Great emphasis was placed on physical fitness during World War II. Selective service statistics showed that of 4 million men rejected, 700,000 had remedial defects. Many held physical education responsible for this condition, but Delbert Oberteuffer* refuted this unwarranted criticism. A 1943–44 survey of the United States Office of Education pointed out that physical education was, indeed, inadequate in many schools. A 1948–49 survey conducted by the National Education Association recorded progress for physical education in the schools, but by this time non-school agencies had been developed to promote fitness and recreational programs.

In 1943, Dorothy LaSalle† reported 232,000 American women in uniform. Although official information was unavailable on their physical condition, evidence points to some of the same problems as the men presented. In the autumn of 1944, the Surgeon General's Office reported one-third of the volunteers for the Women's Army Corps (WAC's) were rejected—primarily because of obesity (101, p. 9).‡

During World War II, a great motivator to therapeutic exercise and specific training techniques was a method called the Progressive Resistive Exercise Program (PREP) for developing muscle strength. A

---

* Professor at The Ohio State University. Nationally known leader in health and physical education. 1966 Professor Emeritus.

† Dorothy LaSalle: *Dance and Fitness of Women.* Health and Physical Education. 14: 309, 1943.

‡ Mabel Lee and Miriam M. Wagner: *Fundamentals of Body Mechanics and Conditioning,* Philadelphia, W. B. Saunders Co., 1944, p. 9.

young Alabama physician and amateur weight lifter, Thomas DeLorme, experimented with the application of increasing resistance to weak quadriceps following knee surgery. This idea was not new, but DeLorme's method was different. He applied a boot, frequently called the DeLorme boot, strapped to the foot, to which weights could be added. The weight, the repetitions, and the tempo of the exercise were constant for one week. The maximum weight that could be carried through ten normal ranges of motion was determined each week—Ten Repetitions Maximum (10 R.M.). In 1948, DeLorme revised his method so that after the maximum resistance was determined, the Load Resisting Exercise was

(*a*) first set of 10 repetitions = one-half of 10 R.M.
(*b*) second set of 10 repetitions = three-fourths of 10 R.M.
(*c*) third set of 10 repetitions = full 10 R.M.

The Load Assisting Exercise was

(*a*) first set = use twice the 10 R. Minimum
(*b*) second set = use one and one-half 10 R. Minimum
(*c*) third set = use 10 R. Minimum

Variations of this method are prescribed by physiatrists, some similar to the "Oxford Technique" which advocates that the first set of 10 R.M.'s and each successive load—progressively 1 pound—and the 10 R.M. be increased each day by the same amount of weight.

During the 1940's, Harvey E. Billig, M.D. introduced postural exercises for dysmenorrhea. Industrial absenteeism, partially due to menorrhagia, was a problem of women employees. Billig held that postural defects contract ligaments which compress the nerves (iliohypogastric), thus causing cramps, low back pain, and nausea (see Chapters 7 and 8).

The development of new drugs in this decade was a milestone in therapy. "Drug potentiated gymnastics" (105, p. 467) was the term given for the use of drugs to improve muscle metabolism and produce a more rapid response to strengthening exercises. Muscle relaxant drugs are sometimes prescribed for acute strains and sprains. Hoffmann in the seventeenth century stated that exercise improved the action of drugs, but in the latter half of the twentieth century the idea could be changed to "Drugs improve exercise."

While many of the curricular aspects of physical education were developed in the 1940's, a standardized college physical education curriculum was developed by a committee of the National Education Association in the Department of School Health and Physical Education in 1931 under the chairmanship of N. P. Neilson. In February, 1942, President Franklin D. Roosevelt established a Division of Physical Fitness for all age groups in the Office of Defense, Health and Welfare Services. By 1949, forty-one states reported a physical education law, and many states employed directors or supervisors. Teacher-education requirements improved, and by 1950 more than 400 colleges and universities offered a major in physical education.

The discipline of physical education at women's colleges and universities in the latter part of the nineteenth and early twentieth centuries sometimes used the title, Department of Physical Culture and/or Physical Training. The staff members were usually trained at Boston Normal School; the private schools of Dudley A. Sargent, William G. Anderson, Baron Nils Posse; or by a skilled performer. Women usually shared men's facilities or used a basement area on campus. Delphine Hanna of Oberlin College introduced a sports program for women, and Blanche Trilling at the University of Wisconsin organized the Women's Athletic Association (WAA) about 1913, with guidelines for intramural and extramural sport days for women. The earlier women's programs had gymnastics, corrective exercises, and dance; later, sports such as archery, golf, cycling, riding, tennis, hockey, basketball, baseball, swimming, diving, and track and field athletics were added.

The enthusiasm for sports participation by women was high, and publicity was given the women contestants when they performed in local and national events. During this period a special costume for women's sports was designed by Amelia Jenks Bloomer (Fig. 1-1).

The rise of American physical education societies reflects the development of interest in fitness. College physical education meetings for men started in 1897, but in 1933 the name of College Physical Education Association (CPEA) was adopted. Professional requirements were set up and coordinated in 1947 when Delbert Oberteuffer was president of the CPEA.

William G. Anderson of Yale University in 1885 organized a group of men to set up a national association to represent professional workers in physical education. Edward Hitchcock was the first president. In 1937 the name became the American Association for Health, Physical Education and Recreation. The journal (JOHPER) *Journal of Health, Physical Education and Recreation* is the AAHPER's publication, as is the *Research Quarterly*. Special interest groups were organized early in the twentieth century: the therapeutic section dates from 1905.

The National Association of Physical Education for College Women (NAPECW) was organized in 1924 in Kansas City. Amy Morris Homans of Wellesley College started the Association of Directors of Physical Education for Women in 1909 with eastern college teachers. Subsequently similar organizations in the Midwest and West were organized.

FIG. 1-1. Bloomer girls of 1923 on a physical education class hike.

At Kansas City sixteen members with twelve guests met and organized the national association. The purpose has been to study problems relating to physical education in colleges and universities to increase the usefulness of physical education. The NAPECW meets biennially and conducts workshops for college physical educators. *Quest* is its official publication. In the 1930's, the southern district affiliated with the national association. Long-range planning committees were established in research, finance, public relations, and publications, and a placement service was created for women physical educators. Scholarships are available to aid the women in physical education from Central and South America (133–134).°

Delta Psi Kappa, a professional fraternity for women in health, recreation, and physical education, which was organized in 1916, is affiliated with the Professional Panhellenic Association. Its goals are promoting high professional standards and extending professional opportunities for women. Delta Psi Kappa provides (1) educational loan funds, (2) research fellowship funds to give professional women grants for investigations of merit, and (3) *Foil*—its official semiannual publication.

Modern programs, principles, and standards were established for the preparation of teachers in health, physical education, and recreation at a national conference held in May of 1948, at Jackson Mills, West Vir-

° AAHPER: JOHPER: *17:* 525, 1946. NAPECW Report: 1964, p. 138.

ginia. Graduate program conferences were held for suggested standardization, and Seward Staley of the University of Illinois promoted a national conference in Illinois (Pere Marquette State Park) in January, 1950. The Athletic Institute, a nonprofit organization of sporting goods manufacturers, financed this and other conferences. The Committee on Curriculum Research chaired by William Ralph LaPorte, sponsored by the CPEA, contributed to this field and to the development of modern trends. Some CPEA contributions include:

1. Sponsorship and publication of "The Physical Education Curriculum—A National Program," a suggested program for all grade levels;
2. Publication of the proceedings of the annual meetings.°

Professional organizations reflected the development of Physical Education. In 1950 the AAHPER reached a membership of 18,000 (180, p. 483). The primary purposes of this organization are "(a.) to promote and awaken a wide and intelligent interest in physical education, (b.) to acquire and disseminate accurate information and (c.) to provide such means of promotion as will secure an adequate program of physical education." "In 1958 the AAHPER inaugurated a positive plan for action called Operation Fitness—U.S.A. This operation distributed fitness kits for testing elementary and secondary youths to educational authorities in the United States (59, p. 500)." "In 1962 the AAHPER established the Peace Corps Project. This Project distributes information on Peace Corps needs to key personnel in colleges and universities, contacts uncommitted physical education graduates, and assists in the selection of institutions suitable for training programs (59, p. 505)." The purpose of the Peace Corps set up by Congress in 1961 is to promote world peace and friendship by providing interested foreign countries with the services of Americans to help them meet their needs for trained manpower. Physical education is helping meet the Peace Corps' purpose through the AAHPER Project.

In 1921 the American Physical Therapy Association was established. This association publishes a monthly journal which has articles on specific physical aberrations and the medical uses of therapeutic exercise relative to these deviations. *The Archives of Physical Medicine and Rehabilitation* is the official journal of the American Congress of Physical Medicine and Rehabilitation. These publications have scientific articles of interest in this field, including electromyography. Electromyography reveals what a muscle actually does at any moment during various movements and postures. It records muscle fiber movements on a graph.

° Since 1959, books (8 Volumes) *Completed Research in Health, Physical Education and Recreation* including International Sources have been published by the AAHPER.

This specialized technique used in the Allied Medical Services is also being explored by some research personnel in physical education.

In the 1950's Hans Kraus, M.D. and Sonya Weber tested 4,000 students from ages six to sixteen in a minimal fitness test. Their conclusions showed that 56.6 per cent failed this test. They continued this test of very minimal fitness with 2,000 children in Austria, Italy, and Switzerland to see if the performance was generic to all children. European children had a failure incidence of only 8.2 per cent. Kraus published the results of his research, and this comparative test of the American and European children had general news value. In 1956, the President's Council on Youth Fitness was established by President Eisenhower after Vice President Nixon had chaired a committee to develop a national fitness program. Shane McCarthy was appointed executive director of the council, and his office became a clearing house for information on youth fitness.

Following the establishment of the President's Council on Youth Fitness, Paul A. Hunsicker of the University of Michigan was appointed director of the Youth Fitness Project of the AAHPER. A battery of six tests (a seventh was added later) was set up for a pilot study of the fitness of the nation's school children. The AAHPER youth fitness battery of tests included pullups, situps, shuttle run, standing broad jump, 50-yard dash, softball throw, and 600-yard walk-run. By June, 1958, this test had been administered to 8,500 boys and girls in grades five through twelve. The statistical compilations showed low scores on the pullups, thus substantiating the Armed Services' observation that Americans were deficient in arm and shoulder girdle strength.

President John F. Kennedy continued this stress on the improvement of physical fitness, with subsequent development of many types of modified fitness programs being used by the entire country (schools, clubs, and commercial spas). During the late 1950's and 1960's a great impetus was given to developing new concepts in therapeutic exercise and physical education, which Arthur Steinhaus called the "New Image (173)."

Since 1954, the trend in most institutions has been toward individual sports, aquatic activities, dance, and body mechanics. Adapted physical education is designated for the atypical student. By 1958, the average enrollment for adapted physical education was 33 students (59, p. 509). In 1965, the University of Illinois had over 300 handicapped students enrolled. Seventy-five were at the "wheel chair olympics" in Queens, New York, in June, 1965. In 1975, when 51 per cent of young adults are anticipated as college and university students, the number of handicapped students will be greatly increased.

A brief overview of learning problems is included. The development of terms used to classify people's mentalities has been a continuous concern. According to Leland and Smith (102) "feebleminded" is derived from the Latin word *flebelis,* meaning tearful. This word is similar to foible, implying a weakness of character similar to tearfulness with the implication that the individual is at fault. Mental deficiency, a common term, comes from the Latin word *deficere,* meaning to fail. It implies a lack of success or a lack of brain, which is scientifically inaccurate. Now the term mental retardation is used to mean a "state of being slow." A redundancy of terms seems to refer to essentially the same condition. The word moron may derive from the Greek word *moros,* meaning dull, or from Dr. Benjamin Rush's term moral idiot, which was made into the contraction "moron" by Dr. Goddard at the Vineland Training School in New Jersey. Another familiar term is imbecile, from the Latin *imbecillus,* meaning weak. It has been used, generally, to identify a person in contact with the world but of weak mind. The word idiot or Greek *idiote* means "private person" or one separated from other people. This indicates that the person's mind is out of contact with the rest of the world.

Still other terms familiar to educators, psychologists, and others are dull-normal, mental impairment, and borderline retardation. In 1969 the National Act for Children with Learning Disabilities identified children in terms of learning problems, not mental retardation, and in 1973 The American Association of Mental Deficiency deleted the borderline retardate from its classification. Thus, it is evident that terms are arbitrarily used to classify mentalities. Labeling a child may have serious complications for his future (see Chapter 4).

The following chart, which is adapted from Robinson and Robinson (144), illustrates very well the suggested classification systems according to the Stanford Binet IQ (1965).

Professional Preparation

Many meetings since the Jackson Mills Conference have established the need of accreditation for physical education training institutions. The American Association of Colleges for Teacher Education (AACTE) Coordinating Committee, with the Committee for Improvement of Professional Education in Health, Physical Education, and Recreation of the AAHPER, evaluated professional teacher training in Minnesota under Carl Nordly's leadership. Evaluation was done in a number of other states.

The AACTE accrediting function was transferred to the National Council of Accreditation of Teacher Education in 1944. In 1960, at the National Convention of the AAHPER in Miami Beach, the NCATE was accepted as the accrediting committee for professional preparation

A.A.M.D. Current Educational Practice, Cruickshank's Suggested Modification.

IQ			
100	No Retardation	No Retardation	No Retardation
90	Borderline Retardation	Dull–Normal	Slow
80	Mild Retardation	Educable M.R. Moron High-Grade	Learning
70		Slow Learner	Mentally Handicapped Educable M.R.
60	Moderate Retardation	Trainable M.R.	Mentally Deficient
50	Severe	Imbecile Mid-Grade	
40	Profound Retardation		Trainable M.R.
30		Severely Retarded	Custodial
20		Custodial	
10		Idiot	
0		Low-Grade	

institutions of health, physical education, and recreation. Thus, the various state departments of education grant certification to graduates of institutions accredited by the NCATE. In 1962, the Professional Preparation Conference met in Washington and developed criteria for student personnel, faculty, professional courses, laboratory experiences, facilities, instructional materials, and the first phase of graduate education. Definite commitments on acceptable criteria of professional preparation were established (59, p. 514).

In 1947, H. Harrison Clarke reported a survey from 192 institutions stating that 53 per cent required a course in corrective physical education, 49 per cent required tests and measurement, and 34 per cent required physiology of exercise.

In 1974, Agnes M. Hooley surveyed the fifty states of the United States concerning state requirement or recommendation with regard to training in adapted physical education for their teachers of physical education. Thirteen states required a course in adapted physical education for certification in physical education; 16 states recommended it.

The modern trend in teacher preparation institutions seems to be a thorough review of courses with the primary concern to present the best academic education to future teachers of physical education. Research in human movement and performance is progressing rapidly with the focus on physiology of exercise, kinesiology, and perceptual motor studies through physical education.

The teacher of adapted physical education should (1) have understanding and knowledge of therapeutic exercise, sport, and diversional recreation activities; (2) have knowledge of physical conditioning and body functioning; (3) be skilled in the use of body mechanics and understand the principles of its operation; and (4) help all individuals fulfill their need for movement.

Summary

The historical background of therapeutic exercise and physical education is highlighted by specific principles and practices.

1. Physical education was used to improve body condition and health in old civilizations. Military preparedness was important, and men trained through military exercises.

2. The early Grecian and Roman cultures associated physical activities with the values of mental effectiveness, aesthetics, entertainment, and state purposes. European philosophers expressed and practiced formal physical education for the total development of the individual during the sixteenth and seventeenth centuries.

3. Therapeutic exercises originated in ancient China. They were practiced and taught by the priests and scribes there and in the Grecian and Roman cultures.

4. The humanistic movement stressed the total individual with physical education a part of the academic curriculum for the student. Various systems of gymnastics were developed at this time. The Germans and the Swedes developed well-formulated gymnastic programs. Early physical education in the United States was patterned after the German and Swedish gymnastic programs.

5. Leadership in physical education preceding World War I came from men and women doctors of medicine interested in fitness, who prescribed therapeutic exercise for the development of the complete individual.

6. Professional organizations of local, sectional, and national scope were formed by the leaders in physical education and therapeutic exercise during the first half of the twentieth century. The role of these organizations is professionally multifaceted to serve all areas of physical education and therapeutic exercise. Some publications which serve personnel in these disciplines are:

   a. *Quest* published by the National Association of Physical Education for College Women (NAPECW).

   b. *Journal of Health, Physical Education and Recreation* (JOHPER) published by the American Association for Health, Physical Education and Recreation.

c. *Research Quarterly* published by the American Association for Health, Physical Education and Recreation.

d. *Physical Therapy Journal* of the American Physical Therapy Association.

e. *Archives of Physical Medicine and Rehabilitation* published by the American Congress of Physical Medicine and Rehabilitation.

Many other valuable services and guidelines are provided by the professional organizations.

7. Now, the leadership role in physical education lies with persons trained in the fields of education, education psychology, philosophy, and physical education; the doctor of philosophy (Ph.D.) trained person. Specialization with diversified training has arrived in both fields of physical education and therapeutic exercise.

8. Several other milestones of the twentieth century which have added and identified new dimensions to therapeutic exercise and physical education are the ambulation techniques for paraplegic patients set up by Wilhelmine G. Wright of Boston when she was working with R. W. Lovett, orthopaedic surgeon; Thomas DeLorme's progressive resistive exercise program has influenced the dimension of the isometric programs for the development of neuromuscular strength.

9. Clinical therapeutic exercise prescribed by the physiatrist and orthopaedic surgeon follows the pressure of the current epidemiology. If a focus can be stated, the upper motor lesion conditions, as cerebral palsy and brain damage, overshadow the lower motor neuron and peripheral nerve injury lesions. The incidence of paralytic poliomyelitis encountered before the Salk and Sabin vaccines of the early 1950's is almost gone.

10. The stress on youth fitness by Presidents Dwight D. Eisenhower and John F. Kennedy developed dimensions in physical fitness. The Youth Fitness Project of the AAHPER directed by Paul A. Hunsicker of the University of Michigan set up an activities test for school children used on a nationwide basis.

11. The increased use of electromyography (EMG) for clinical diagnosis of neuromuscular conditions by the doctors of medicine presents a future direction for exercise and kinesiological research. Basic scientific electromyography should improve the investigations of fatigue, muscle conditions, muscle mechanics and posture.[*]

12. The current terms used in the mental retardation dichotomy compared with earlier words chosen to designate subnormal intellects.

[*]Basmajian, J. V.: *Muscles Alive: Their Function Revealed by Electromyography.* Baltimore, The Williams & Wilkins Co., 1962, p. 228.

Broer, Marion R. and Houtz, Sara Jane: *Patterns of Muscular Activity in Selected Sport Skills: An Electromyographic Study.* Springfield, Charles C Thomas, 1967.

Thus, the disciplines of physical education and therapeutic exercise have expanded beyond the therapeutic values of ancient times. Although adapted physical education has its own stated goals and sponsors studies which are not bound by the barriers of other academic areas, it has not expanded as much as some physical education programs. It is estimated that by 1975, when approximately 50 per cent of our young men and women will be enrolled in higher education, improved program facilities should be available for the atypical student. There is currently great national interest in physical activity for all students, and national support and aid is being made available through the Department of Health, Education and Welfare. Title V of the Higher Education Act should result in more teachers being educated to work in adapted physical education.

Nonprofit organizations also are providing assistance for motor skill learning; such a one is the nationally known Joseph P. Kennedy, Jr. Foundation. Since 1966, this fund has sponsored many "grants-in-aid" to professional persons who are interested in working with the mentally retarded for the improvement of motor learning.

Dr. Julian Stein, as Consultant of Programs for the Handicapped with the AAHPER, and his staff communicate information about adapted physical education nationwide through articles, films, and IRUC.° So the 1960's and 1970's show a forward movement in adapted physical education; and they also disseminate information on job placement.

Chronology of Therapeutic Exercise: Physical Education

B.C.

Hieroglyphics, bows and arrows
    3000
Aesculapius   circa 2500
Cong Fou   2700
Yin-Kang-Chi   circa 2000
Homer   circa 1000
Lycergas   circa 900
Ayur-Veda (India)   800
Olympiads   776
Persian Empire   558–331
Confucius   551–480
Roman Republic   500–476 A.D.

88th Olympiad Herodicus   480
Socrates, Plato, Aristotle   469–332
Hippocrates   460–357
Alexander the Great   323
Philip of Macedonia   382–226
Cicero   106–43 A.D.
Caesar   100–44 A.D.
Augustus   63–14 A.D.

A.D.

Nero   37–68
Galen   120–200

° Information and Research Utilization Center in Physical Education and Recreation for the Handicapped. AAHPER, a Project of the U.S. Department of Health, Education, and Welfare.

Roman Empire 390–1450
Theodosius 394
Byzantine Period 470–730
Callius Aurelianus 700
Paulus Aegineta 650
Avicenna 980–1037
T'ai Chi Chuan 1000
Alexander III 1000
Isaac Judaes 10th century
Rhazes 1050
University of Paris 1110
University of Bologna 1113
University of Oxford 1167
University of Padua 1222
University of Naples 1224
School of Salerno 11th century
St. Thomas Aquinas 1225–1275
Petrarch 1304–1374
Hospitals with exercise pavilions
Virgerio 1349–1428
Vittorino de Faltre 1378–1446
Fuch's *Institutiones Medicae* 16th century
Mendez's *Libro de Exercicio* 16th century
Mercurialis *De Arte Gymnastica* 16th century
Tuccaro, Neapolitan dialogues: 3rd on exercise 16th century
Leonardo Da Vinci 1452–1519
Rabelais, *Life of Gargantua* 1534
Descartes neurophysiology 1596–1650
Giovanni Borelli 1608–1679
John Locke 1632–1704
Robert Hooke 1635–1703
Harvard University 1636
William & Mary 1693
Nicholas Andry 1658–1742
Francis Fuller 1705
Friedrich Hoffmann 1660–1742
Albrecht Von Haller 1708–1777
Jean Jacques Rousseau 1713–1778
Benjamin Franklin 1706–1790
Johann Friedrich Guts Muths 1759–1839
Luigi Galvani 1737–1798

Alessandro Volta 1745–1827
Friedrich Ludwig Jahn 1778–1852
John Hunter ?-1720
John Morgan 1753–1789
John Pugh 1794
Pehr Henrik Ling 1776–1839
Jacques M. Delpech 1777–1832
University of Pennsylvania 1740
Transylvania University 1780
Round Hill School Gym 1825
Dio Lewis 1823–1886
Julius Wolff 1850–1924
Turnerbunds 1861
Normal Institute P. E. 1861
Rudolf Klapp 1873–1949
S. Weir Mitchell 1874
Niels Bukh 1880–1950
Baron Nils Posse 1885
Chautauqua Summer Schools 1886
Dudley A. Sargent 1849–1924
de Coubertin 1863–1937
Charles Scott Sherrington 1857–1952
Delphine Hanna 1885–1941
CPEA 1897:1933
Joel E. Goldthwait 1918
NAPECW 1909:1924
AAHPER 1885:1937
Therapeutic Section 1905
Charles Leroy Lowman
Arthur Steindler
Arthur Daniels
Jesse F. Williams
Lillian Drew
Frank Krusen
Ernest W. Johnson
Earl C. Elkins
Richard D. Burk
Mabel Lee
Delbert Oberteuffer
Bruce Bennett
Dorothy Ainsworth
Catherine Ley
Eleanor Metheny
Ann Jewitt
Ruth Abernathy
Ellen Kelly

Edward, Heinrich, and Wilhelm
    Weber　1795–1891
Henry Pickering Bowditch　1814–
    1911
Edward Hitchcock　1828–1911
University of Michigan　1817

Esther Gilman
Celeste Ulrich
Newell C. Kephart　1960
Carl H. Delacato　1965
Evelyn A. Davies　1965
Bryant J. Cratty　1971
Julian Stein

Rehabilitation and Habilitation: Physical Medicine, Allied Medical Services, and Physical Education

The team of specialists for assisting handicapped people to achieve efficient, effective living should include a doctor of medicine, therapists, physical educators, teachers, and parents. Rapport and understanding among the members of this team will develop a successful activity program for the handicapped person, providing goals of rehabilitation, habilitation, development, prevention, restriction, and adaptation.

1. *Adaptation* involves modifying the working activity program for the student. Depending upon the condition of the student, this adaptation may be short-lived or long-lived.

2. *Restriction* pertains to activities that are dangerous for the student and should be avoided permanently or temporarily.

3. *Prevention* activity may be set up from a physician's referral order so that a student with a potential physical weakness will not increase this condition.

4. *Development* involves activities for the student who may be subpar in motor skills and in stamina and endurance as well as in coordination.

5. *Habilitation* pertains to learning to live with specific disorders and relating to environment. The habilitation, or maintenance, concept involves teaching to the handicapped, as well as to those subjected to particular restraints, the facts that they must learn to live with certain disorders. This involves specific conditions with organic malfunctions of

a hereditary nature or an environmental nature. The person must understand what he can and cannot do with safety and learn how to maintain a state of fitness in spite of his condition (109, p. 185).

6. *Rehabilitation* is defined as "the restoration, through personal health services, of handicapped individuals to the fullest physical, mental, social, and economic usefulness of which they are capable, including ordinary treatment and treatment in special rehabilitation centers (96, p. 1)." This involves treatment, training, and re-education of the individual so he can attain his maximum potential for normal living and adequate functioning in his or her individual situation. A dictionary definition states that *habilitate* is derived from the Latin *habilis*, which means "suitable"; how much more important it is to remember that rehabilitation is derived from the same word and may be defined "to make suitable." It calls for programs for those who need help to live successfully in the society in which they were born. Rehabilitation centers provide allied medical service work with the individual for the development of the needed activities of daily living (ADL) including vocational training. Rehabilitation requires special attention for the activities of the student with close interrelationships of the team of specialists.

These six concepts have reciprocal values for the student. Procedural tools in addition to the medical examination to obtain these goals include (1) tests or measures of the physical abilities of each student, (2) assessment of the test to see where he is deficient, (3) prescription or selection of activities to improve the deficiency, and (4) evaluation of his abilities by retesting to see if the activities achieve improvement. (TAPE) (67, p. 9).

Physical Medicine

Physical medicine is the diagnosis and treatment of disease, employing the physical modalities of light, heat, sound, cold, water, electricity and mechanical agents such as massage, exercise, and mechanical apparatus, excluding those employed in radiology. Although physical medicine is an ancient branch of the medical sciences, the term is relatively recent. It started with the Reconstruction Department of the United States Army in 1918. Then medical and lay workers labored successfully to restore thousands of maimed soldiers to habilitation. Their work helped document the value of therapeutic exercise and physical medicine early in the twentieth century.

A physiatrist is a doctor of medicine who specializes in physical medicine during his residency training. He examines the patient to diagnose the condition which causes the disability. Then, using the physical modalities, he prescribes the treatment to be given by the allied medical service technicians such as the physical therapist, occupational therapist, and corrective therapist. In rehabilitation centers he is in charge of the patients and decides upon the admissions and discharges. The physiatrist is usually the director of the medically-oriented clinics of the rehabilitation center. Many physicians refer patients to the allied medical services to be treated, rehabilitated, or habilitated.

Rehabilitation for the disabled person requires the skilled treatment of the therapists if the individual is to adjust to group living. The treatments are prescribed daily and sometimes twice a day to restore the person's physical function as quickly as possible.

Habilitation for the handicapped usually employs a longer time, as the focus is on successful self-maintenance in daily living activities.

Allied Medical Services

Physical Therapy

The physical therapist applies technical skills in keeping with the physiatrist's prescription. The therapist's curriculum has three areas: (1) the broad cultural and basic science prerequisites, (2) specialized physical therapy courses in the junior and senior years, and (3) clinical training which requires a curriculum quarter of full-time clinical affiliation following the academic program. A Bachelor of Science degree is conferred.° Thirty-five schools award the baccalaureate degree.† Students who already have a degree may enroll as special students for twelve months for a certification course. A state license is obtained after successful completion of the curriculum. In the United States there are 45 approved schools of physical therapy.

The therapist, through the physiatrist's or orthopaedic surgeon's prescription, treats patients with the physical modalities for the restoration of body function. This treatment includes application of the modalities and (1) measurement of the joint range of motion, (2) muscle tests to assess muscle strength, (3) tests of the individual's potential in activities of daily living which require ambulation (walking and climbing), and of his ability to use prosthetic and orthotic devices, (4) specialized treatments for shaping, wrapping, and conditioning stumps of amputee patients, and (5) muscle re-education of the peripheral nerve injuries and upper motor neuron injuries. Earl C. Elkins, M.D., Director of the Mayo Clinic Physical Medicine Clinic, states: a good neurosurgeon and

° The Ohio State University School of Allied Medical Services, College of Medicine, Columbus, Ohio.

† Worthingham, Catherine A.: Curriculum Patterns for Basic Physical Therapy Education. J. Amer. Phys. Ther. Ass., 48:9, 1968.

a therapist well-trained in muscle re-education are invaluable for the neuromuscular refunctioning of nerve injury repairs and muscle transplants.*

The physical therapist is a specialist in the various types of exercise:

1. *Passive exercise.* When this type of exercise is prescribed, the patient remains passive and relaxed, while the therapist gives the desired movement. Great care should be used, since the occurrence of muscle spasm is a danger signal. When muscle spasm occurs, the movement should be stopped, since muscle tightening precedes pain and to secure the best results all movements should be under the pain limit. One movement through its fullest range is better than a series of partial range movements. The aim of passive exercise is to prevent contractures and the formation of adhesions. It is employed for early mobilization of the joints, when the patient cannot perform exercises himself or has pain on active movement. Motion is taken to the point of pain.

2. *Active Assistive exercise.* When this form of exercise is given, assistance is needed at the beginning and end of the normal range; sometimes a mechanical agent (pulley) assists. Active assistive exercise is used to mobilize a joint with muscle weakness. When fibrillation occurs, the muscles have been given too great a task. The aim is to develop normal range active movement.

3. *Active exercise.* This is voluntary contraction and relaxation of the muscles responsible for that particular motion. No assistance is needed for normal range. Postural exercises are in this category as are exercises for such conditions as scoliosis, lordosis, and kyphosis. Active exercise is employed for muscular and circulatory disturbances restoring function to the part.

4. *Progressive Resistive exercise.* From active motion, resistance is added to increase muscle strength. The maximum load a person can lift 10 times is first determined; this is divided into thirds. If an increase in strength is desired, the program is modified and high resistance with low repetitions is used. When an increase in endurance is desired, low resistance and high repetitions are prescribed. PRE's are modified by the physiatrist for the patient's need: for example, 10 repetitions of full weight against gravity; 10 seconds rest; 10 repetitions with $\frac{3}{4}$'s of the load through normal range; 10 seconds rest; 10 repetitions with $\frac{1}{2}$

* Alumni Symposium of Physical Therapists: The Mayo Clinic, Rochester, Minn., August, 1965.

load through normal range. Each week a new weight load is determined to increase progressively the muscle strength. Contraindications for PRE include sensory disassociation, osteoporosis, and conditions in which a pathological fracture is a danger.

5. *Other exercises.* (*a.*) Corrective—specifically graded routines for physiological and pathological abnormalities. (*b.*) Postural—used in chronic back conditions, muscle weaknesses and imbalances. (*c.*) Scoliosis, kyphosis, and lordosis exercises. (*d.*) Breathing exercises for asthma and emphysema. (*e.*) Buerger-Allen for circulatory conditions. (*f.*) Frenkel exercises for incoordination. (*g.*) Codman exercises for shoulder joint conditions. (*h.*) Williams exercises for back conditions. (*i.*) Cervical traction for whiplash injuries, migraine, headaches, and cervical disc injuries.

A recent survey indicates that of the approximately 7,000 hospitals in the United States 80 per cent employ physical therapists. The anticipated need is 4,000 new therapists each year.

The physical therapist administers, on prescription by a physician, heat treatments, dry or moist; light treatments, ultraviolet, infrared or radiant; electrotherapy and diathermy, microwave, ultrasound, sinusoidal, faradic, and galvanic currents; massage and exercise, with, or without mechanical devices; paraffin treatments; cold therapy; traction; and hydrotherapy. New techniques are being explored and used by these allied medical services.

Occupational Therapy (O.T.)

The occupational therapist is another member of the allied medical team. His role is to carry out the treatment plan prescribed by the physician to attain previously established psychological or supportive physical or functional and vocational or prevocational objectives.

The occupational therapist has four years of college in the basic sciences and specific professional classes. Before he becomes licensed, he spends ten months in clinical affiliations: three months at a rehabilitation center, three months in a psychiatric hospital, and four months in a general or other type hospital. The degree of Bachelor of Science is conferred upon students who have successfully completed the curriculum.[*]

Training for maximum use of the hands to perform necessary daily living activities is a prime goal of the occupational therapist. Stressed for rehabilitation are (1) preparatory activities of reaching, grasping,

[*] The Ohio State University School of Allied Medical Services, College of Medicine, Columbus, Ohio.

FIG. 2-1.   Clinical Training. Ohio State University Physical Therapy Department, Ernest Johnson, M.D., Director (Bulletin on Physical Therapy: The Ohio Rehabilitation Center, Columbus, Ohio.) A. Students acquire proficiency in teaching techniques. B. Advances in patient care necessitate a constant adjustment of the physical therapy curriculum.

releasing objects; (2) manipulation skills of holding objects and turning objects; (3) feeding activities such as drinking and using spoon, fork and knife; and (4) writing activities with pencils and typewriters.

The occupational therapy program is coordinated with the physical therapy prescription to help the patient to improve motion of the joints,

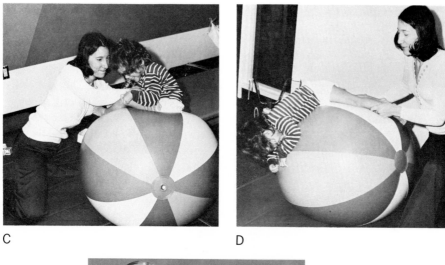

C   D

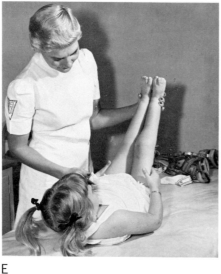

E

FIG. 2-1. C & D, Student working with a child with a learning disability on a 36-inch diameter mushroom ball to improve perceptual motor skills (Nassau County Medical Center, Garden City, New York.) E, Physical therapist applying muscle re-education on a child with a physical handicap (Easter Seal Society, Miami, Florida.)

muscle strength and coordination, motor skills, and work tolerance. The occupational therapist uses constructive, specific procedures such as woodworking. These procedures help the disabled person to see the degree of function he is gaining in manual skill. The occupational therapist follows the principles of therapeutic exercise, uses the muscle test grades as a guide, starts with active-assistive exercises, and works toward active and active-resistive movements (146).

As the patient improves, the physiatrist may discontinue physical therapy but continue occupational therapy to develop the individual's muscle strength, work tolerance, and manual skill to aid his habilitation. The activities in therapeutic exercise are flexible. The first characteristic of such activities is that they provide action rather than position. If the patient has joint movement limitations, alternate contraction and relaxation of the muscles is needed, not static contractions. Sawing wood, for instance, gives active exercise to the shoulder girdle, elbow, and wrist. Hand exercises require grasp and release and opposition of the thumb with the fingers to achieve manual skill. A second characteristic is that the activities provide repetition of the motion. This type of activity should be self-sustaining, with the objective being to control the number of muscle contractions and relaxations in a given period. The endurance of the individual is developed when machines (foot-driven as stapling or punch press) give active and repetitive motion. Finally, activities for occupational therapy provide gradation in the activity, range of joint motion, progressive increase in resistance, and coordination of muscular action. Hammering metal to gain range of motion in the wrist requires arm stabilization so that joint action is limited to wrist action. The increased resistance necessary to strengthen muscles is achieved by increasing the weight of the hammer gradually from three-fourths of a pound to two pounds. Coordination comes by grading the activity from gross to fine movements.

Corrective Therapy (C.T.)*

Corrective therapy is the application of the principles, tools, techniques, and psychology of medically oriented "physical education" to assist the physician in the accomplishment of prescribed objectives. Corrective therapy is prescribed by a physician who supervises and determines the goals and limits of the therapist. The physician is preferably a physiatrist or orthopaedic surgeon. Corrective therapy, formally organized as a specialty in 1946, grew out of the expansion of corrective physical rehabilitation in the Veterans Administration and the highly successful reconditioning units of the armed forces. In 1953, the American Board for Certification of Corrective Therapists was set up to establish a National Certification Registry. To be employed as a corrective therapist the man or woman with a Bachelor of Science degree must

* C.T.'s are employed in veterans hospitals, domiciliaries, and in some private hospitals.

successfully pass the registry examination given by the American Board for Certification of Corrective Therapists.

Treatment by the corrective therapist involves:

1. Conditioning and reconditioning exercises to develop or maintain strength, endurance, neuromuscular coordination, and agility; to aid in both physiological and psychological improvement.

2. Exercises and resocialization activities for the psychiatric patient specifically oriented toward the accomplishment of psychiatric objectives.

3. Teaching of functional ambulation techniques, including all types of prosthetic and orthotic devices. Programs are carefully geared to the individual's level of behavior providing progressions in physical and social complexities that the patient is able and/or willing to accept with responsibility.

4. Teaching self-care activities, including personal hygiene.

5. Therapeutic swimming (hydrogymnastic) program.

6. Corrective exercises prescribed and administered for specific conditions.

7. Conditioning, reconditioning, self-care, and motivational activities for the aged and infirm person.

8. Special activities for re-orientation of the blind person.

9. Prescribed training in the operation of adaptedly controlled motor vehicles.

10. Adapted physical education and recreational programs for the atypical children's groups in schools, camps, and hospitals. This phase of the treatment is often used by others—not just the corrective therapy technicians (3).

The allied medical service technicians are concerned with the management of all disabling conditions for efficient adjustment in daily living. Men and women are accepted for preparation in these allied services. As new advances in medical science develop, the dimensions of the allied medical service grow. One new phase in the science of medicine that will affect the ancillary medical area is explained below.

James E. Appleby, past president of the American Medical Association, explains a new phase of medicine called "Predictive Medicine" (currently in its infancy). It includes computerizing medical histories of individuals on a longitudinal scale, starting at birth. The individual medical history is stored by the computer so that when the physician desires or needs this complete record, it can be fed back quickly for his examination. Potential susceptibilities are pointed out in this stored record.

"The idea is likened to a 'medical DEW Line'—an early warning system. During the course of a disease there is a stage in which it develops but goes unrecognized, without symptoms. . . . Through multiphase screening tests, physicians who interpret the results can gather information about the whole patient more quickly, freeing them or attending physicians to do actual treatment more effectively."°

To evaluate and assess the individual's predictable tendencies toward diseases, this new medical phase should subsequently include the services of the various therapies.

Therapeutic Recreation

One of the faster growing professions of our day is therapeutic recreation (or recreation therapy, as it is sometimes called). Recreational therapists, a group of dedicated professionals, use recreation as a vehicle which can bring joy, social communication, skill improvement, and many kinds of adjustment to ill, disabled, and handicapped persons. Patients are often involved in the program on a pre-discharge basis in order to be helped in adjustment to home and community when they leave the institution.

Recreation therapists work in a variety of settings with persons of all ages, and with persons with most handicapping conditions. Their association is known as The National Therapeutic Society, one of several branches of the National Recreation and Park Association. The group publishes a quarterly entitled *Therapeutic Recreation Journal.*

Physical Education

In company with many other areas within the whole concept of education, physical education provides opportunities for the development of the individual within a social environment. Stated in more usual fashion, physical education is one of the many fields in which the student may gain knowledge and understandings, build wholesome attitudes, develop good health, and increase in skill-ability. Generally, physical education is defined as a discipline with a program of vigorous physical activities through which some education of the person is achieved.

° Irwin, Theodore: Forecasting Your Future Health, *Today's Health*, 45:25–29, 1967. The American Medical Association, Chicago, Illinois.

What can be accomplished through physical education? Hopefully this method of operating "through the physical" involves such goals as upgrading the development of:

1. Organic vitality—as in exercises for increasing circulation, respiration, muscle strength, body flexibility, and body efficiency.

2. Neuromuscular skills—through activities such as those for eye-hand coordination, opposition, follow-through, energy conservation, and total body movement assembly during movement.

3. Social capabilities—as confidence, satisfaction, fair play, courtesy, respect for others, and problem-solving techniques.

4. Safety habits and practices.

5. Better adjustment to life—as in release of tensions through vigorous activity or in development of leadership through directing games and scoring them.

6. Fundamental motor skills of work and play commensurate with ability and body mechanics.

A basic program should provide an appreciation of the role that recreational sports play in our modern world.

More and more states provide for physical education through legislation which spells out the minimal amount of time which the student is to spend in the program during his school life. The program operates through the following overall areas: dance and other rhythmic activities; individual, dual, and team activities; aquatic activities; body mechanics; and movement exploration.

Range of Offerings in the Activity Areas

1. Dance and Other Rhythmic Activities

    a. Ballroom dance.
    b. Folk dance.
    c. Modern dance.
    d. Square dance.
    e. Tap dance.

2. Individual, Dual, and Team Activities

    a. Archery.
    b. Badminton.
    c. Bait casting.
    d. Baseball.

e. Basketball.
f. Billiards.
g. Boxing.
h. Bowling.
i. Deck tennis.
j. Fencing.
k. Field hockey.
l. Football (flag, touch, tackle).
m. Golf
n. Gymnastics.
o. Handball
p. Horseshoes.
q. Ice skating.
r. Lacrosse.
s. Paddle ball.
t. Paddle tennis and platform tennis
u. Rebound tumbling (trampoline).
v. Riflery.
w. Roller skating.
x. Skiing.
y. Soccer.
z. Softball.
aa. Speedball.
bb. Stunts and self-testing activities.
cc. Table tennis.
dd. Tennis.
ee. Track and field.
ff. Tumbling.
gg. Volleyball.
hh. Wrestling.
ii. Weight lifting.

3.   Aquatic Activities

a. Swimming.
b. Diving.
c. Lifesaving.
d. Scuba and skin diving.
e. Synchronized swimming.
f. Boating.
g. Canoeing.
h. Sailing.
i. Water skiing.

4.   Body Mechanics

    a. Applications of principles of movement in such tasks as lifting, carrying, pushing, pulling, stair-climbing.

    b. Posture work as needed by the individual.

    c. Relaxation techniques.

    d. Remedial exercises as needed by the individual.

5.   Movement Exploration (first few grades)

    a. Problem-solving with reference to body movement potential.

    b. Problem-solving with reference to time and space.

    c. Problem-solving with reference to sharing ideas with others (62, pp. 52, 53, 171–217).

Criteria for Sound Programs

1. The program is led by qualified personnel.

2. The program is designed for all students, with modifications as indicated.

3. Needs and interests of students are considered and are provided for through such media as a wide range of offerings and varying degrees of competition.

4. The program increases in variety and complexity as students progress through the years of school life.

5. Record-keeping begins with the first medical examination upon entrance into school and includes such data as that obtained from skill-tests, intramural participation, and earned placement in such groups as leadership clubs and varsity teams.

6. Safety is considered important and is reflected in safe practices, equipment, facilities, and adequate insurance coverage of all who are involved in the program.

7. The required program is established first; as conditions warrant, the intramural program may be added, to be followed in time by the extramural and/or varsity program where circumstances make this an appropriate move.

    Unfortunately programs in many school systems cannot meet these criteria. Often state laws are neglected or waived; sometimes extramural and varsity programs supersede regular instruction and intramural programs. Other ills exist. The poor programs are of doubtful benefit to the typical student and usually overlook or eliminate the atypical student who needs the advantages of a good program much more. Hopefully, the increased emphasis on physical education by industry, unions, and the government will lead to improved programs.

The Physical Education Program for the Handicapped

Of all advice that might be given when introducing the program for the handicapped, one directive takes precedence over all others: *Start it early.*

Childhood is the time for the program to begin. The average child, typical or atypical, is interested in his growth and development and is eager to succeed among his peers and win the praise of his parents. Children do not expect success to come easily; a child will try many times for the attainment of success. He will accept help more enthusiastically than an adult, succeed more often, and will profit far more in every way—physically, socially, mentally, and emotionally.

The atypical child differs in some ways from his age-mates, but he has the same needs and can soon develop the same interests as they. Ambition and will to succeed are present in him as in most humans. And in addition to the goals set forth for all children in physical education, a special one must be included when considering the atypical child—*conservation of human resources.* As the handicapped child moves toward self-realization in the educational climate of the school, he moves toward the total development and the attainment of a high level of efficiency which are characteristic of the typically successful person (103, p. 67). His success wins him a place among his companions where he can express himself, develop loyalties, and enjoy new experiences. Achievement takes time and effort, but, when the atypical child has achieved success, he is on a par with children whom he once feared and whose critical or pitying looks and gestures were the overt source of many anxious moments. Such a child is ready to move forward into the many phases of life, secure, accepted, recognized, loved, and capable of creative and adaptive behavior in many situations (152, pp. 50–55).

Physical education is not solely responsible for such attainment, but without the experiences which come through physical education at a time when motor expression and success are of paramount importance, a child tends to have maturational difficulties. Particularly is this true of the often frustrated atypical child, who may have experienced no other paths to satisfactory achievement.

Teachers must remember the importance of genuine instruction in the physical education program. The normal child may find other ways to learn skills if he is unfortunate enough to take part in a program which is little more than "free play." But the atypical child must have instruction in order to build both muscles and confidence and to become as fine a performer as it is possible for him to be. Kraus reminds us that "since we tend to enjoy most that which we do well, it is essential that the school experience involves a real learning experience. . . ." (94, p. 86).

The seriousness of learning to the atypical can be seen wherever good programs are in effect. Recently a concert was to be given by students of The Lighthouse.° One of the children, hearing a visitor say that the printed program looked nice, asked to know "how far down the list" her Mozart selection appeared. Here was a child who could not see, yet had mastered a difficult classical composition. Only the good instruction at the music school could have helped this child, whose kinesthetic and auditory senses must substitute for the visual sense.

Arthur Danger of the Professional Staff of Just One Break (JOB) alluded to another kind of learning when he said, "most of those (handicapped) who are turned down for jobs fail to make it because of personality difficulties."†

Danger feels that the handicapped adult needs to join others in constructive and meaningful recreation in order to develop the ability to react positively to other people, to adapt quickly to unusual situations, and to act with confidence and decision. The handicapped can learn these skills through social contacts both on and off the job. Danger noted that many of the handicapped who are employed admit that their after-work activity is primarily sedentary, with television the main pursuit. Some may not know of the instructional programs available in many locations throughout New York City; others may choose not to participate in such programs. They mirror the attitudes of typical adults who do not perform well those skills which are learned best in childhood. Such learning involves instruction. If handicapped children are taught well, they will carry over to adulthood skills which can bring satisfaction into their lives as they associate easily with others.

Skill-learning is a serious matter for these people, even the children. The skeptic need only watch the film, *Adaptation of Children to Prosthetic Limbs.* It is one of several such films undertaken by the Michigan Crippled Children's Commission.‡ After viewing such a film one is aware of the intensity of interest of the learner and of the remarkable progress which can be made through good instruction.

And now to a question which is of great importance to both teachers and learners in the situation: How are the interest, need, and willingness of the handicapped being provided for in the physical education program? Generally this question is answered in one of five ways:

° The Lighthouse is the name given to the building of The New York Association for the Blind, 111 E. 59th St., New York, N.Y.

† Statement made at a personal interview with Agnes M. Hooley. Arthur B. Danger is Director of Information for JOB (Just One Break), a nonprofit placement agency for disabled men and women. JOB is located at 717 First Ave., New York, N.Y.

‡ State of Michigan, Crippled Children's Commission, 252 Hollister Building, Lansing, Michigan.

1. The handicapped are "excused."

2. They are assigned to some kind of "leadership" position, often on a par with custodial work, requiring little of them, producing few benefits, and advancing their physical abilities very little, if at all. The chores assigned to such students may include collecting used towels, taking roll call, or umpiring and scoring contests. They remain spectators.

3. They are assigned to a remedial and generally individualized program of exercises and apparatus work. This is corrective physical education, although it is occasionally labeled *Adapted Physical Education*.

4. A remedial program is provided; it includes the therapeutic approach through individualized work, but with absorption into the regular physical education classes, perhaps on a modified basis, as soon as possible. This is genuine Adapted Physical Education.

5. An integrated program is offered, wherein the handicapped person is assigned immediately to a regular physical education class and takes part as much as possible. This also is genuine Adapted Physical Education.

Such a list of possibilities points up sharply the differences in opinion about physical education for the handicapped. Many school administrators believe in it and provide for it; for a whole host of reasons others provide little or no worthwhile physical education experience for this group. It is encouraging to note that physical education programs are on the increase. Hopefully, as attitudes toward physical education and toward the handicapped improve, the handicapped will not only hope for, but begin to insist upon, participation in the physical education program.

Choice for each handicapped student will have to be made among the three types of programs listed as 3, 4, 5; this assumes that professional workers will eliminate 1 and 2. At one time the therapeutic approach evident in 3 and 4 was the only approach. Physicians and physical therapists gave leadership and carried out their work with such equipment as dumbbells, plinth tables, iron boots, and shoulder wheels in laboratory-like facilities. The work was known generally as Correctives or Corrective Physical Education.

Later physical educators argued that the activities of the regular program should be modified or changed for the individuals who would use them in part as remedial work and in part for the same reasons which motivate the average nonhandicapped participant. Thus the term *Adapted Physical Education* came to be used.

There was considerable rancor over this difference of opinion, and separate sections operated for years within the American Association for Health, Physical Education, and Recreation—The Therapeutic Section and the Adapted Physical Education Section (141, pp. 3–5).

At present the programs for the handicapped might be described in the phrases which have earned them the title of the Second Three R's— Remedial, Rehabilitative, and Recreation-Educational. Successful programs meet the needs and interests of the student and by so doing involve the natural corollary: *motivation.* Such programs stress the potential capacities and respect the established limitations of the students.

The teacher may provide the answer to the type of program which will be used. Sometimes a teacher with a bias toward one of the various methods is sought; sometimes a teacher is called in to choose and administer the type which he considers best. Given such choice, the teacher will tend to make a selection on the following bases:

1. His point of view on degree, amount, and kind of participation by the handicapped in physical education.

2. His goals for the program in physical education, and a knowledge of the goals of the handicapped in such a program. (Research on the differences between student and teacher goals has been very revealing) (73).

3. His knowledge of the possible content of a physical education program. (A lapse here may be serious; for example, many teachers seem to know little about movement exploration, currently the "backbone" of physical education in the lower grades.)

4. His knowledge of research and of evaluation techniques. (The efficacy of flotation devices has been studied, for example; the positive results might point up their possible value in aquatic programs for the handicapped who lack buoyancy.) (105, pp. 6, 277–281.)

5. His willingness and ability to profit and progress from the results of the applied evaluation techniques.

6. His willingness and capacity to lead a mature life as a self-accepting person who respects others and is able to operate with them in the psychosocial world of the school and the community. Conversely, he does not operate through behaviors which bring "vicious, destructive, or neurotic kinds of satisfactions (135, pp. 3, 20)."

It is sad but safe to assume that some teachers will be forced to choose in the future, as others have in the past, on the basis of expediency. Administrators, unimaginative or anxious parents and children, and inadequate facilities and equipment may determine that the handicapped will be directed in useless or rigid programs. But other teachers will be able to take advantage of the developing climate of education which seeks the best for each child. There are over 4 million exceptional children in the United States. Regular schools see the attendance of 89 per cent of this 4 million. These are extraordinary people with extraordinary needs.°

Funds for facilities and personnel and the approval of ongoing administrators have begun to take effect. In such an atmosphere it is highly probable that the integrated program (No. 5 in the list of types) will become the accepted method of programming for the handicapped. A good physical education program includes the appropriate activities for each child and group of children. This is exactly what the handicapped child needs, if genuine modification of and occasional withdrawal from activity is considered acceptable behavior. In the integrated program such is the case. Built on understanding and motivation among all concerned, this program is ideal for the handicapped student. It is truly Adapted Physical Education.

The importance of the teacher in this situation cannot be minimized. He should be:

1. Well educated in all phases of physical education, especially in such areas as anatomy and kinesiology in order to know the normal from the atypical in such items as growth and development.

2. Well versed in possible methods and materials within the field so that he can set up worthwhile programs for the handicapped.

3. Capable of interpreting medical terminology so that he can discuss cases with the physicians, nurses, and therapists and carry out agreed-upon procedures.

4. Adroit in the area of public relations so that he can become the catalyst among physician, parents, and school authorities to the better adjustment and all-round improvement of the child.

In physical education activities, the principles of specificity, adaptation, and progressive overload are basic to help determine what the individual may achieve.

1. *Specificity* means neurophysiological adjustments of the body to specific demands in terms of movement patterns, load, rate, repetitions, and duration (123). Special exercises are valuable to improve endurance and strengthen the neuromuscular system, but performance is the best way to get specific improvements in an activity.

° Hubbard, K. T.: Who Shall Be in the Adapted P. E. Program? AAHPER National Convention, Chicago, March 20, 1966. P. E. Adapted Section, from handout sheets of Dr. Hubbard's speech.

2. *Adaptation* means that the body—heart, lungs, muscles, mind, and emotions—adapts to the level of activity it is accustomed to maintaining each day. Repeated efforts and vigorous exercise aid the adaptation of the neurophysiological body system (123).

3. *Progressive overload* involves intensity of effort more than quantity of work. This means that fast or maximal work of short duration can improve endurance and strength, both cardiorespiratory and neuromuscular. In World War II, Thomas DeLorme applied progressive resistance exercise (PRE) to the quadriceps following knee surgery to restore full muscle strength rapidly (105, p. 464). This PRE method, or overload principle, was widely adopted by physicians and physical educators to increase muscle strength and stability of performance.

   Other principles that were investigated by Hettinger and Muller pertained to Brief Repetitive Maximal Exercises (BRIME). This method of six-second maximal muscle contraction has developed rapidly, and its significance on the performance and strength of a muscle needs more investigation (105, p. 316).

   Another theory for improving muscle strength is the cross transfer theory. This theory of cross education means exercise of one limb may produce an improved performance in the opposite limb by restoring strength and endurance (123).

Biological laws affect the interrelation of the structure and function of our bodies. The basic biomechanical principles of movement are well-known to the physical educator.

Biomechanical Principles of Movement

1. Body joints allow certain types of motion.

2. The movement of the body comes from the muscles (116, p. 58).

3. The muscle fibers have nerve strands that fire up to 75 nerve impulses each second (174, p. 4). The higher the number of impulses, the stronger the muscle contraction.

4. The lever system gives movement and equilibrium through the muscles and joints working together. (*a*). First-class levers analogous with a teeter-totter and a pair of scissors are found at the lumbo-sacral joint and at the elbow with the triceps action. (*b*). The second-class lever, comparable to a wheelbarrow and a nutcracker, is used to open the mouth against resistance or to stand on tiptoe. (*c*). The third class lever compares with the spring which closes a door. An example is found when holding a weight in the hand, the biceps becoming the force.

5. Newton's Laws of Motion—the Law of Inertia, the Law of Momentum or Acceleration, and the Law of Reaction.

6. Two forces create movement: the internal force of muscular contraction and the external force of gravity.

7. Equilibrium or balanced movement requires the center of gravity over the base. The base must be enlarged in the direction of the moving force; the external weight affects the center of gravity in the direction of the external weight; a large base and a low base increase stability and kinetic chain, which means a situation exists where muscle action is used to establish stabilization and equilibrium rather than free motion (172, p. 8).

8. Movement has a pattern of timing or rhythmic organization; it may be linear (up and down, forward and backward, side to side) or rotary (clockwise and counterclockwise and/or forward and backward).

9. Friction, air resistance, gravity, and water resistance modify motion.

10. Activity skills are concerned with the production of force, the application of force, and the receiving of force.

The physiologists and chemists have explored thoroughly muscle chemistry and fatigue and the formation of lactic acid. Energy requirements of work and sports are found in many books. Work is hard to measure, since a part of energy becomes mechanical work while a great part is changed to heat.

Guidelines for Working with Physicians

1. For patients and students with circulatory irregularities, the physical educator generally must stress progressed activities.

2. For those with heart disease, congenital and acquired, the sports prescription should be therapeutically understood. Distress symptoms, as dyspnea and cyanosis or shadows and circles under the eyes are contraindications for continued activity. Joyful play for these students is important with guarded controls to insure safety.

3. For the patient with organic coronary insufficiency, overload is injurious, but complete rest is also contraindicated.

4. For individuals with vascular disturbances (HBP) relaxation or massage may be prescribed.

5. For persons with lung disease, light athletics—hiking, rowing, and swimming—may improve the mucosal health. Relaxation is good exercise therapy as is practicing breath control while walking (inhale

PHYSICAL EDUCATION DEPARTMENT

_____School

Date_____Month_____Year

Dr. _____ M.D.'s Signature _____

We desire 100 per cent participation in our Physical Education Program. This check

list is for your prescription of_____for

Name of Student

integrated adapted sports and specific therapeutic exercises.

Team Sports	Individual Sports	Therapeutic Exercise
(List)		
	Archery	Mimetic of sports
	Bowling	Rest
	Billiards	Relaxation
	Badminton	Isotonic exercise
		Isometric exercise
		Sitting games
		Officiating
		Posture control exercise
Low organization games	Dancing	Flexibility exercise
(List)		Cardiorespiratory exercise
	Modern	Endurance exercise
	Folk	Strength exercises
	Country	Progressive resistive
	Ballroom	or overload exercise
		General conditioning
	Basic Movement	exercises

Indications and Contraindications_____

_____

Physician's Remarks: _____

Individual progress notes will
be sent every 3 months or on
_____ your request.

_____Teacher's name

FIG. 2-2. A suggested chart for the physician's prescription of activity.

during two steps, exhale during four steps). Correct breathing during
work can be practiced through the motions of sports. Adequate rest
periods are important. Swimming with exhaling against water pressure
is prophylactic as well as beneficial psychologically.

6. Persons with diseases of metabolism usually should not participate in team sports because of tempo variations. The anthropometric deviations of overweight need progressive swinging type endurance exercises for approximately twenty minutes followed by table tennis, walking, rowing, or other endurance activities with a slow tempo. Profuse sweating is recommended (105, p. 372). With any joint involvements, however, endurance sports are contraindicated. Persons with diabetes may benefit from systematic exercises or from rest.

7. For those with constitutional weaknesses, as general asthenia with quick fatigue, rest should precede and follow any activity. Sidney Licht, M.D., recommends relaxation and good pelvic (posture control) exercises and breathing for anterior neck musculature (105).

8. For those with mental disturbances, sports are prescribed to develop relaxation and contentment and to help overcome undisciplined, unnatural behavior.

9. Endurance activities are kinder to older persons, who usually have aging changes of joints and blood vessels, than speed and power physical activities.

Criteria for an adapted physical education program should include the needs of the individual as determined from the medical examination, the screening physical fitness test (Chapter Five), the functional physical skill test, the interest of the student, and support from the parents in developing his motor abilities and physical capacity. The program design should include considerations for the student with physical conditions that are permanent, those with slight body deviations and the student with temporary body deviations so that the adjustment in physical activity will allow him to participate in sports and recreational activity now and later. Medical clearance for the participation of the student is necessary (Fig. 2-2). The physical educator is a specialist in movement: (1) the analysis and assessment of basic movement patterns are his discipline; (2) the refined evaluation for improved skill in body dynamics, kinetic and static, for work and play uses therapeutic exercise, general exercise, or sport. The teacher becomes one who sees, refers, confers, follows directions, and helps the child and the parents.

Essentials of the Nervous System

This chapter was written to meet a definite need in the area of motor education for teachers. The teachers of normal students, those with slight faults in the mechanics of human movement, and those with atypical physical divergencies need basic factual knowledge of the central nervous system for the assessment of movement from the neuroanatomical and neurophysiological point of reference. This should serve the physical education area, the special education area, and the allied medical services of physical medicine and rehabilitation for the analysis of the body mechanics, static and dynamic. It also provides some of the etiology for the abnormal functioning of the musculoskeletal system from the neuroanatomy and the neurophysiology aspect.

General causes of the body deviations are usually classified as (1) genetic, (2) organic, (3) cultural, and (4) idiopathic. The genetic, organic, and idiopathic causes have a neurological basis that all persons who relate to the individual with a disability should understand.

Neuroanatomy and neurophysiology are relatively new fields. Research and exploratory studies are developing constantly and are adding newer dimensions to the present knowledge.

All movement has a neurological basis, since the nervous system is intimately integrated with the musculoskeletal system, as well as with all other body systems. Exercise produces vascular changes in working muscles and compensatory circulation changes in the organs. The common injuries of this system point out the development of the motor unit and postural motor activity.

The Central Nervous System

The brain and the spinal cord make up the central nervous system (CNS). Three membranes give support and protection to the brain and the spinal cord: the dura mater (outer), the arachnoid (middle), and the pia mater (inner).

The brain consists of the cerebellum, the cerebrum, and the brain stem. The brain stem refers to the midbrain (mesencephalon), the pons, the medulla oblongata, and the interbrain (diencephalon). The cerebellum is connected to the brain stem, and the hemispheres of the cerebrum are divided into lobes.

The pons serves as a bridge between the cerebellar and cerebral areas. It contains nerve tracts and the nuclei of cranial nerves V, VI, VII, and VIII.

The Neuron

The neuron, or nerve cell, is the genetic, trophic, and anatomical unit of the nervous system. The functional unit is the reflex arc or the two neuron chains. Each neuron has a cell body and one to several dozen processes of different lengths called "nerve fibers" (Figs. 3-1 and 3-2). Dendrites are short fibers which receive impulses at their periphery and conduct them to the cell body, and the axon is a single long fiber conducting impulses from the cell body. The axon may be bi-directional under certain conditions. Nerve cell bodies are located in groups. Outside the central nervous system such groups are called "ganglia." In the central nervous system the cell bodies comprise the gray matter. The white matter is primarily the nerve fibers.

Most nerve fibers (peripheral) are encased in a sheath called the "myelin sheath" and a neurolemma (sheath of Schwann). Peripheral autonomic fibers have just a neurolemma, and fibers of the white matter have a myelin sheath with no neurolemma.

Nerve fibers which have a common origin and destination constitute a tract. The fibers or tracts are named from their origin and termination; *i.e.*, the corticospinal is an efferent motor tract from the cerebral cortex to the spinal cord.

The transmission of impulses from neuron to neuron occurs at a synapse. Neurons (nerve cells) usually send impulses in one direction, away from the area which receives stimulation. In the peripheral nervous system, the afferent fibers carry impulses from the receptor to a specialized area in the spinal cord through the dorsal roots of the spinal nerves. The efferent fibers conduct impulses away from the spinal cord through the anterior or motor root of the spinal cord known as the

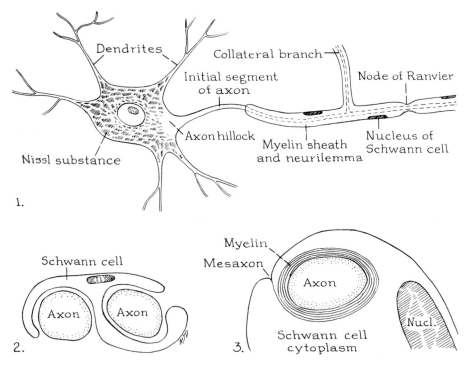

FIG. 3-1. (1) Diagram of typical neuron, (2) diagram showing relation of Schwann cell to axons, (3) diagram illustrating relation of Schwann cell to myelin sheath and axon. (Everett, *Functional Neuroanatomy*, 5th ed., 1965, Lea & Febiger.)

motor fibers to the area from which the stimulus arose. From the dorsal horn of the gray matter the impulse travels through the anterior horn cell to the peripheral muscle effector (49, pp. 85, 86).

The Spinal Cord

The spinal cord (Fig. 3-3) is a slender cylindric mass of nerve tissue sheathed by three meningeal coverings. The subarachnoid space contains cerebrospinal fluid. The cord is enlarged in the cervical region and in the lumbar region because of the greater neuronal density supplying the upper and lower limbs. The spinal cord is continuous with the medulla oblongata and ends at the level of the border of the second lumber vertebra with the meninges continuing to the coccyx. The spinal cord is encased in the vertebral column, which maintains the body in the upright position. The cord functions as a system of reflex centers controlling activities of the numerous glands, the visceral organs, and

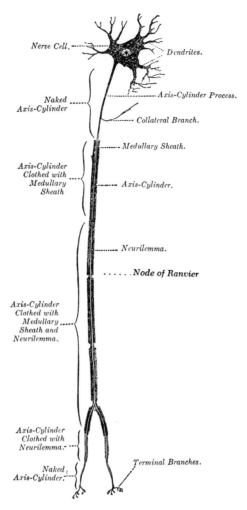

Nerve Cell.

Dendrites.

Naked
Axis-Cylinder

Axis-Cylinder Process.

Collateral Branch.

Medullary Sheath.

Axis-Cylinder
Clothed with
Medullary
Sheath

Axis-Cylinder.

Neurilemma.

· · · · · ·*Node of Ranvier*

Axis-Cylinder
Clothed with
Medullary
Sheath and
Neurilemma.

Axis-Cylinder
Clothed with
Neurilemma.

Naked
Axis-Cylinder.

Terminal Branches.

FIG. 3-2.   A motor neuron. (After Stohr, from Rasch and Burke, *Kinesiology and Applied Anatomy*, 3rd ed., Lea & Febiger.)

the voluntary muscles and is a path of conduction to and from the brain. These functions are subject to modifications by the higher centers.

Transversely, the spinal cord has an H-shaped or butterfly-shaped area of gray cells with surrounding white substance composed of longitudinal nerve fibers of the ascending and descending nerve tracts (Fig. 3-4).

The gray matter is located in the center of the cord with the white matter surrounding the gray matter. The gray matter has two com-

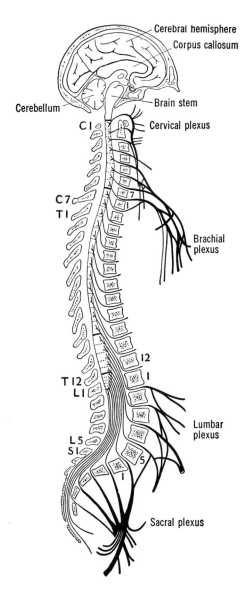

FIG. 3-3.   Drawing of the brain and cord *in situ.* Although not illustrated, the first cervical vertebra articulates with the base of the skull. The letters along the vertebral column indicate cervical,
thoracic, lumbar, and sacral. Note that the cord ends at the upper border of the second lumbar
vertebra. (Gardner, *Fundamentals of Neurology,* 6th ed., 1975, Courtesy of W. B. Saunders Co.)

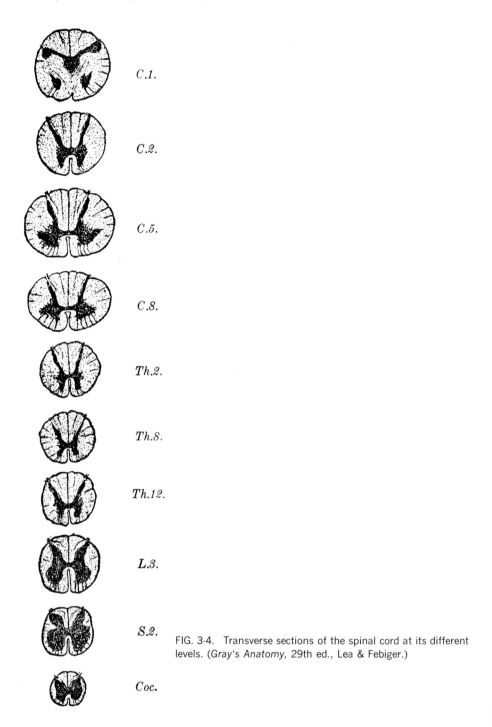

C.1.

C.2.

C.5.

C.8.

Th.2.

Th.8.

Th.12.

L.3.

S.2.

Coc.

FIG. 3-4.   Transverse sections of the spinal cord at its different levels. (*Gray's Anatomy*, 29th ed., Lea & Febiger.)

ponents: the motor and the receptor. The anterior (ventral) horn cells supply the voluntary muscles. The receptor component of the spinal cord consists of the posterior (dorsal) horn cells. Nerve tissue can be traced from the ventral (anterior) horn cells to the periphery. These are the ventral roots of the spinal nerves.

The white matter of the spinal cord has distinct regions termed "columns." These nerve fibers serve to link different segments of the spinal cord and to connect the cord with the brain. The columns immediately surrounding the gray matter contain short ascending and descending fibers which end within the spinal cord.

The important tracts of the spinal cord are (21, p. 69):

	ANTERIOR COLUMN	LATERAL COLUMN	POSTERIOR COLUMN
Ascending Tracts	Spinothalamic (light touch) Spino-olivary (reflex) proprioception	Spinocerebellar (reflex proprioception) Spinothalamic (pain and temperature) Spinotectal (reflex)	Tract of Goll Areas of vibration, passive motion, joint and two-point discrimination, equilibrium reflexes, muscle tone regulators
Descending Tracts	Corticospinal direct pyramidal (voluntary motion) Vestibulospinal (balance reflex) Tectospinal (audiovisual reflex) Reticulospinal (muscle tone)	Corticospinal (voluntary motion) Rubrospinal (muscle tone and synergy) Olivospinal (reflex)	Tract of Schultze Association and integration areas

These tracts do not function autonomously. Specific and general movement patterns require coordination of the spinal cord reflexes with the cerebral centers for the normal function of the body.

The lower motor neurons have large cell bodies in the anterior horn cells of the spinal cord and in the motor nuclei of some of the cranial nerves. With the dorsal root fibers they form the spinal nerves and are distributed through the trunks and branches of the peripheral nerves to the voluntary or skeletal muscles. Since one axon may branch several times, one neuron may supply 100 to 300 separate muscle fibers. Voluntary or reflex action is dependent on the motor nerve for activation of the skeletal muscle. Sherrington called the lower motor neuron the "final common pathway," since it shows an interplay of impulses from other descending association fibers (efferent), usually the extrapyramidal and reflex circuits. The character of movement displayed comes from this interplay of impulses.

Disorders

Some lower motor neuron injuries are shown in Figure 3-5, and these illustrate the area of the lesion. Figure 3-6 points out disorders of the lower motor neuron pathway.

Autonomic functions, as the visceral activities, are lost or depressed. The upper limit of the area of sweating identifies the level of the cord lesion.

Severance of the spinal cord above the fourth cervical segment causes death because respiration is prevented (49, p. 226).

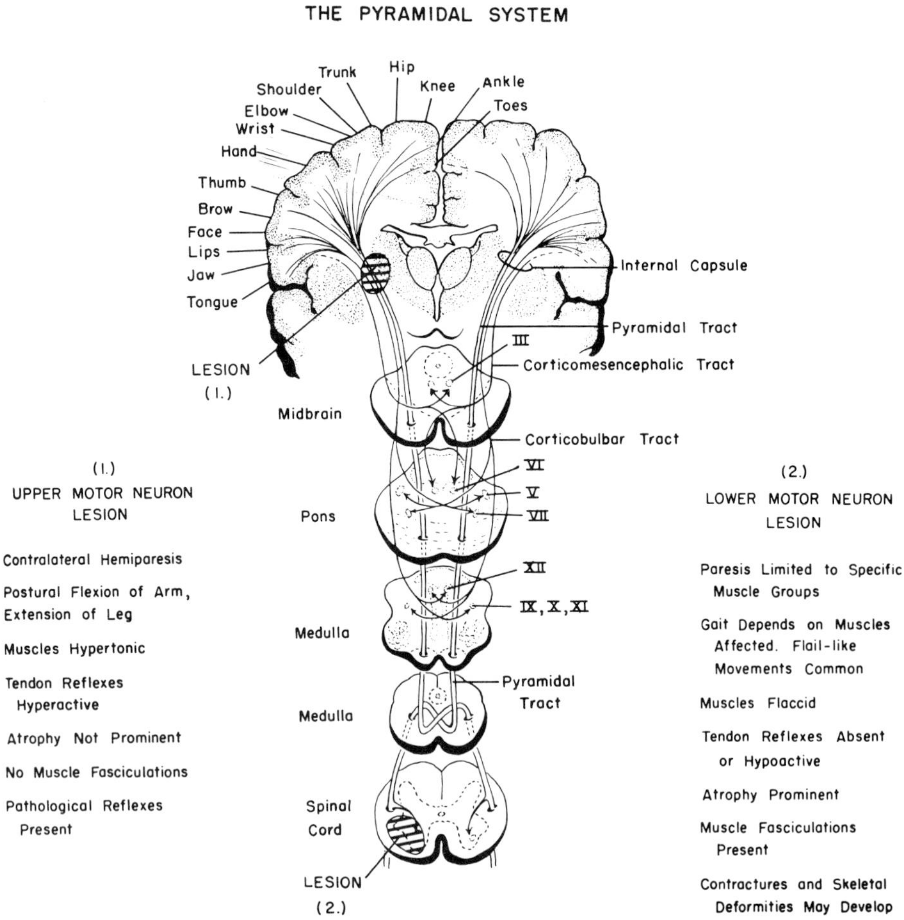

THE PYRAMIDAL SYSTEM

FIG. 3-5.   Pyramidal System. (Manter and Gatz, *Essentials of Clinical Neuroanatomy and Neurophysiology,* 2nd ed., Courtesy of F. A. Davis Co.)

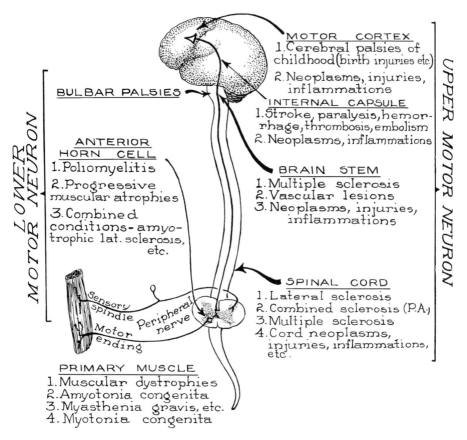

FIG. 3-6.　Motor Pathways. (Chor: Some Problems in Muscle Disorders. Physiotherapy Rev. 16:2, 1936.)

The Reticular Activating System

The reticular activating system is formed by nerve cells scattered throughout the brain stem. Impulses from the labyrinth, midbrain, and cerebrum modify the reticular mechanisms. This reticular circuit (1) receives impulses from the (*a*) spinal cord, (*b*) cerebellum, and (*c*) cerebral areas, and (2) sends impulses to these areas. The formation extends from the sacral part of the spinal cord to the thalamus (49).

The reticular system relays sensory impulses to the cerebral cortex through the subcortical centers. Functionally this formation is significant, since it effects (1) wakefulness; (2) conscious states; (3) attention; (4) learning; (5) excitation and inhibition of motor neurons through the reticulospinal tract (Fig. 3-7); (6) visceral functions as blood pressure,

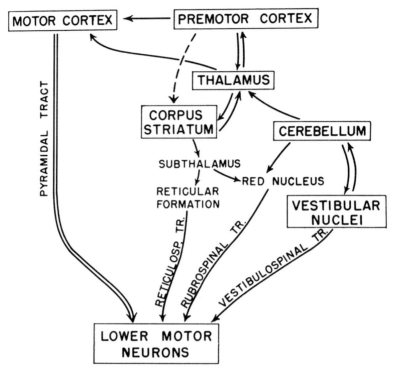

FIG. 3-7. Schematic diagram of the pyramidal and extrapyramidal systems. (Manter and Gatz, *Essentials of Clinical Neuroanatomy and Neurophysiology*, 2nd ed., Courtesy of F. A. Davis.)

heart, respiration, and alimentary canal movements; and (7) auditory and visual reflexes.

Disorders in this diffuse system present aberrations of the above characteristics (114, p. 99).

Peripheral Nervous System

The peripheral nervous system is made up of cranial, spinal, and autonomic nerves with their associated ganglia. Like the muscular system, spinal nerves are symmetrically arranged in pairs with two roots— a sensory (dorsal) root and a motor (anterior or ventral) root. The sensory fibers of nerves receive stimuli from the receptor end organs called "proprioceptors."[*]

[*] Dorland's *Medical Dictionary. Proprioceptive* (automatic motor control) means "receiving stimulations within the tissues of the body"; *Facilitation* means "hastening of a natural process"; thus the term *neuromuscular proprioceptive facilitation* is applied to motor learning in the allied medical services, as a specific mode of treatment in physical medicine.

Thirty-one pairs of spinal nerves arise in the spinal cord. Each nerve has a posterior (dorsal) and anterior (ventral) root. The spinal ganglion or root contains 6 to 8 bundles of nerve fibers and is a swelling in the posterior or dorsal area of each nerve. There are 8 cervical nerves, 12 thoracic, 5 lumbar, 5 sacral, and 1 coccygeal nerve. They leave the cord obliquely and at the lumbosacral region descend vertically. This region is called *cauda equina* because of its appearance (Fig. 3-8). The anterior nerve roots are the motor efferent fibers which terminate in the skeletal muscle, and the posterior nerve roots are the sensory or afferent fibers from the nerve cells in the spinal ganglion and the proprioceptors of the muscle. The spinal nerves and cranial nerves with their associated ganglia make up the peripheral nervous system.

Disorders

When the nerve is injured, paralysis and loss of sensation occur in those muscles and skin areas supplied by the nerve distal to the lesion. The muscles are flaccid, and gradually atrophy is accompanied with loss of sensations. In neuritis there may be partial destruction of several peripheral nerves, usually on both sides, marked by muscle weakness and poor skin sensations.

Lesions of the spinal and peripheral nerves vary because (1) a spinal nerve provides impulses for several different peripheral nerves and composes only part of each, and (2) a peripheral nerve may contain parts of several spinal nerves.

A peripheral nerve lesion has some capacity to repair itself. When cut, the nerve may divide and sprout axons which enter the neurolemmal tubes leading to the motor end-plates or sensory terminal and thus restore function. If chance determines this regeneration, the growth rate is normally 1 to 2 mm per day (114). Fibers of the spinal cord and brain do not normally regenerate.

Nerves to and from the Muscles

The nerves to the muscles are 40 per cent sensory and come mainly from the muscle spindle, Golgi tendon organs, and pacinian corpuscles which conduct impulses to the spinal cord and the brain (Fig. 3-9). The Golgi tendon organs are found in the tendon fibrils, and the pacinian corpuscles are located in the muscle fascia, particularly beneath the area where the tendon inserts at the joint. There are many spindles and organs in each muscle. Boyd reports the soleus muscle of a cat has 55 spindles and 45 tendon organs (13). The spindles and tendon organs are classified into groups, with some conducting impulses at velocities of 60 to 120 miles per second with the average being 10 to 15 impulses

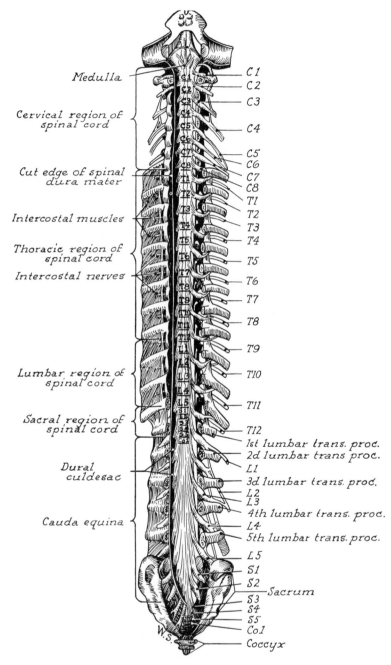

Fig. 3-8.   Dorsal view of the spinal cord *in situ* (vertebral laminae removed) to show the relation of the spinal cord segments to the vertebral column (after Tilney and Riley). (From Everett, *Functional Neuroanatomy*, 6th ed., 1971, Lea & Febiger.)

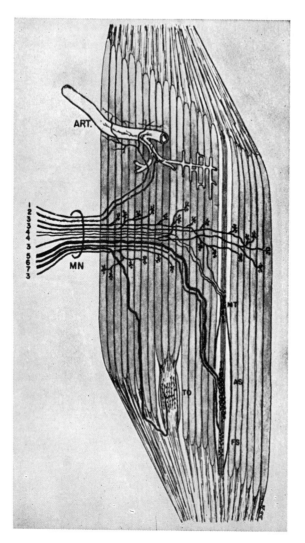

FIG. 3-9. Distribution of nerve fibers to a striated muscle. The muscular nerve (MN) contains approximately 50 per cent of fibers derived from the anterior roots. Of these the medium-sized fibers (3,3,3) are distributed to motor end-plates, and the small fibers (4,4) to the end-plates of muscle spindles. Of fibers derived from the sensory nerve roots the largest (5,6,7) are distributed to muscle spindles (to the annulo-spiral ending, AS, and the flower-spray ending, FS) and to tendon organs (TO). Small sensory fibers (1), often non-medullated in their peripheral part, are distributed in the connective tissue surrounding blood vessels. Fibers derived from the sympathetic nervous system (2) are distributed to the muscular coats of arterioles and the smaller arteries. (Adams, Denny-Brown, and Pearson, *Diseases of Muscle,* 3rd ed., 1975. Courtesy of Hoeber Medical Division, Harper & Row).

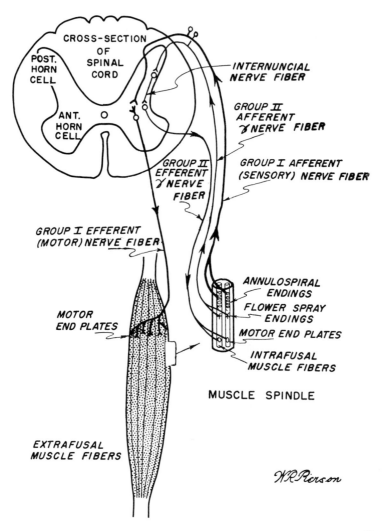

FIG. 3-10. Schema of alpha (α) and gamma (γ) neural systems. (Rasch and Burke, *Kinesiology and Applied Anatomy*, Lea & Febiger.)

per second. The muscle spindle is formed by a bundle of 4 to 10 muscle fibers. It has sensory connections with the spinal cord (dorsal) and the brain. It receives efferent impulses from the central nervous system changing the proprioceptor muscle sensitivity; increasing the sensory input fed to the cord. The muscle spindle is the sensing element of the reflex system. Steady voluntary or postural contraction may be considered a result of tonic innervation and alpha motor neuron innervations via the gamma loop. The role of the supraspinal (alpha route) controls the gamma system as follows:

The large alpha motor neurons from the anterior horn cells innervate the main muscle mass directly from supraspinal centers (Figs. 3-10 and 3-11). The small gamma motor neurons activate the motor units via the stretch reflex arc. Supraspinal motor centers are thought to send impulses to the skeletal muscles through the large alpha motor fibers from the anterior horn cells to the main muscle mass and the small gamma motor neurons. The gamma loop through a stretch reflex may serve as a "starter" for nerve firing of the alpha motor neuron which activates the main muscle mass. Graded strength of muscle contraction varies with the number of active motor units (114, p. 13).

The remaining 60 per cent of the muscular nerves are the motor fibers (efferent). The large size group axons (fibers) supply the striated skeletal muscles through the anterior horn cells of the spinal cord (13).

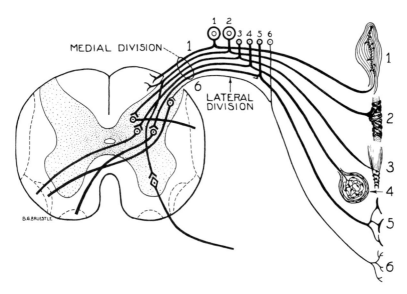

FIG. 3-11. Diagrammatic cross section of spinal cord showing principal sites of termination of dorsal root fibers. 1 and 2 represent large medullated fibers having large dorsal root ganglion cells and passing to the dorsal columns; they arise from pacinian (1) and muscle spindle (2) endings. 3 and 4 terminate on dorsal horn cells that cross and give rise to spinothalamic and spinocerebellar tracts. 5, a similar cell terminating on a neuron that gives rise to anterior spinothalamic tract. 6, a small fibered neuron (pain) giving rise to fiber of ascending the spinothalamic tract of opposite side. (Fulton, *Physiology of the Nervous System*, 3rd ed. Courtesy of Oxford University Press.)

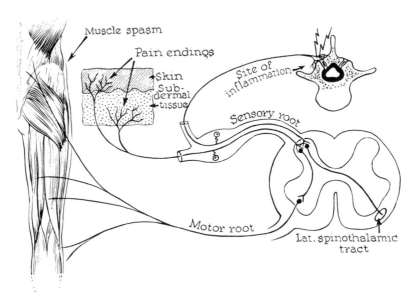

FIG. 3-12.   Reflex arc showing that the stimulation of an inflamed joint will cause muscle contraction and sensory changes. (Hauser, *Curvatures of the Spine,* 1962, Courtesy of Charles C Thomas.)

Reflexes

The term *reflex* (Fig. 3-12) originally applied to an involuntary action, an inborn stimulus—response mechanism, but now includes learned acts which may be voluntarily initiated, then completed without voluntary action. Learned, semiautomatic conditional responses are important for skilled and smooth movements of complicated activities (42).

The reflex is described as involuntary reaction to a sensory stimuli conducted to an effector by a motor nerve. The reflex arc may be one synapse or complex with multiple synapses. Reflex motor action shows that some muscles are inhibited, while others are stimulated. This reciprocal inhibition prevents antagonist muscles from acting when an agonist contracts. The lower brain stem centers are thought to modify the primitive reflexes, and the reflexes of the brain stem are modified by the motor cortex.

The Stretch Reflex and Muscle Tone

The normal muscle which appears to be relaxed possesses some tension. It is not flabby but has a quality of resilience called "muscle tone." Tonus is defined as attention expressed in neuromuscular terms. The stretch reflex or myotatic is the neural mechanism for maintaining tone in the muscles. The stretch reflex differs from the normal reflex arc, since its two fibers make a direct synapse without the intermediary neuron. Stretching of a muscle evokes a firing of impulses in its neuromuscular spindles so that the afferent nerve fibers enter the spinal cord through a dorsal root and turn anteriorly across the gray matter to the anterior horn for a synapse with the motor nerve. The axon conducts the impulse from the spinal cord to the motor end-plate in the muscle fibers which produces increased tension in the muscle. The motor response takes place in the same muscle that is stimulated so that the stretch reflex is primarily a monomuscular reflex. The anterior horn cell is the motor neuron in the stretch reflex.

Posture comes from the reflex impulses of the antigravity muscles. They have tone, or postural contraction, and exhibit static stretch reflexes. The extensor reflexes concerned with the action of gravity on body posture are myotatic reflexes. With increased stretch, more motor units are brought into action so that prolonged muscle tension continues without alteration or fatigue through neuromuscular adjustments. The flexion reflex stimulates the smaller nerve branches of the periphery. Many motor units are affected, as several segments are involved. This is a withdrawal mechanism from a pain or harmful stimulus.

Several types of static postural reflexes are recognized:

1. Local static reflexes which affect single limbs with positive and negative supporting reactions.

    a. The positive supporting reaction of touching the foot causes the toes to separate and the limb to extend.

    b. Negative supporting reaction applies to inhibition of the weight-supporting posture by flexion of the distal parts of the limb.

2. Segmental static reflexes are those which with stimulation of one limb affect the opposite limb.

3. General static reflexes originate in one segment and affect the motor responses in other segments, as muscles stretched due to corrected shoulder and pelvis position bring about reflexly the needed tonus in the legs for the correct upright position.

Some primitive reflexes are:

1. Tonic neck reflexes—when the labyrinth is destroyed at the midbrain level.

    a. Rotation of the head causes extension of the limbs on the jaw side and flexion of the opposite limbs.

    b. Deviation of the head without rotation may cause extension on the jaw side of the limbs and flexion of the limb on the opposite side.

  c. Extension of the head produces extension of the upper limbs and relaxation of the lower.

  d. Flexion of the head produces flexion of the upper limbs and extension of the lower (49, p. 285).

 2. Righting reflex (maintain topside up)—positional reflexes which arise from stimulation of the labyrinth and

  a. Maintain the head's orientation in space if the midbrain is intact.

  b. Act upon the head and keep the head oriented with respect to the body.

  c. Act on the body, coming from skin receptors to keep the body oriented.

  d. Arise in the neck to keep the body oriented with the head. These arise in the medulla.

  e. Keep the head in proper orientation and depend on an intact occipital cortex (Area 17).

Vagal System Reflexes

The *carotid body reflex* produces inspiration through the medulla where the rate of respiration is influenced. The stretch receptors in the walls of the bronchioles send impulses to the medulla by the vagus nerve and, by inhibition, stop inspiration. The hypothalamus seems to maintain the rhythm.

The *cough reflex* (Fig. 3-13) is usually a response to an irritation of the larynx, trachea or bronchial tree. The afferent impulses reach the solitary tract by the vagus nerve through efferent impulses of the larynx and pharynx muscles. The respiratory center forces expiration.

Inhibition

Inhibition is a phenomenon which diminishes reflex muscle contraction. Increased frequency of impulses at the synapses gives increased discharge frequency. If the impulses increase beyond certain limits, the motor cell discharge may diminish in its velocity. If the internuncial neurons carry impulses at a higher frequency than the impulse can enter the anterior horn cells, inhibition sets up. This plays a role in reciprocal innervation. Another hypothesis states that a type of inhibitory knob decreases the excitation state of the synapse blocking the activated anterior horn cell. The anterior horn cells in one segment have afferent impulses, internuncial impulses, and short spinal cord paths with afferent impulses from a different level of the spinal cord. The reticulospinal tracts descending in the lateral columns present inhibition of the motor neurons, particularly the stretch reflexes.

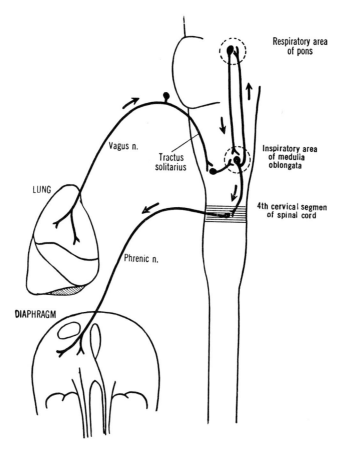

FIG. 3-13. A schematic diagram of the pathway in a respiratory reflex. (Gardner, *Fundamentals of Neurology*, 6th ed., 1975, Courtesy of W. B. Saunders Co.)

Changes in reflex activity sometimes occur by degeneration of the anterior horn cells at a slow and progressive rate during normal aging. This may explain why the ability to learn new motor skills may decrease with age (42, p. 743).

Proprioception

The large fibers are proprioceptors coming from the neuromuscular and neurotendinous spindles. The proprioceptors carry sensory reports from the muscles, tendons, ligaments, and joints regarding awareness of limb position and movements called *"kinesthetic sense."* All proprioceptor impulses going to the central nervous system are not sent to the sensory perception areas of the brain; some are concerned with the automatic motor control. When the muscle tension is caused by muscle activity, the sensory impulses from the muscle spindles decrease and those from the Golgi tendon increase in the proprioceptor pattern. Where the muscle tension is caused by passive stretch, the impulses from both types of proprioceptors increase. Patterns vary for joint position and the velocity of joint movement. Three proprioceptor paths are:

1. Direct fibers to lower motor neurons. This is the stretch reflex where the fibers synapse within one or two spinal segments of the level at which they entered the spinal cord.

2. Fibers to the nucleus dorsalis (a group of cells in the medial posterior horn) which send a second set of proprioceptive fibers and serve as a relay station to the cerebellum through the spinocerebellar tract. This tract reports movements and muscle activity, and the cerebellum modifies muscle group action for accuracy and smoothness.

3. Fibers which turn directly upward to the cortex, ascending the posterior portion of the cord to relay nuclei in the medulla. They cross and continue ascending to the thalamus, then to the cortex or somatesthetic area. Conscious recognition of body and limb posture takes place at the cortical level.

Disorders

Disorders of proprioceptor paths may show abnormal sway in standing, inability to recognize limb position, loss of vibration sense, two-point discrimination, and astereognosis or the inability to recognize an object by touch with the eyes closed.

Medulla Oblongata (Bulb)

The medulla oblongata (Fig. 3-14) is continuous with the spinal cord at the foramen magnum and has the pyramid-shaped part of the brain stem; it also borders the pons. The medulla oblongata contains (1) various nerve tracts, and (2) important nerve cells concerned with such vital functions as respiration, circulation, and special senses. The lower half contains the central canal of the spinal cord; the dorsal upper part forms the floor of the fourth ventricle, which is a cavity filled with cerebrospinal fluid. The pyramids, which contain the pyramidal tracts, show crossing, or decussation. The arrangement of the fibers and gray substance of the medulla is comparable to the spinal cord but more complex. Some long fibers of the spinal cord pass directly through the medulla with no position changes. The nuclei of the hypoglossal, acces-

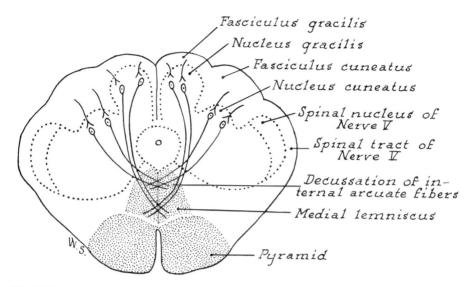

FIG. 3-14. Cross section of medulla at the level of the decussation of the internal arcuate fibers. (Everett, *Functional Neuroanatomy*, 6th ed., 1971, Lea & Febiger.)

sory, vagus, glossopharyngeal portions of the cranial nerves, the trigeminal sensory nuclei, and some afferent fibers of the acoustic and vagus nerves are found in the medulla.

The medulla has afferent fibers of the vagus system which supply the pharynx, larynx, or voice and influence the rate of respiration through the carotid body reflex (respiratory center). The prominent oval swelling on the ventrolateral medulla is the *oliva,* where olivocerebellar fibers arise and decussate to the opposite cerebellar area.

Disorders

Disorders of the brain stem produce symptoms in the motor and sensory pathways going through it, particular to the involvement of the nuclei of the cranial nerves which lie within the brain stem. The medulla is functionally concerned with these cranial nerves: the eighth, or hearing and balance nerve; ninth, or mucous membrane and throat muscle nerve; tenth, the nerve of the mucous membrane, pharynx, and larynx; eleventh, the nerve of the pharynx, larynx, trapezius, and sternocleidomastoid; and the twelfth, the nerve which supplies the tongue muscles. Some basic postural reactions are associated with an intact medulla. Many visceral centers lie in the medulla and may be affected by any pathologic condition involving this structure.

The Cerebellum

The cerebellum (Fig. 3-15) is located in the posterior cranial fossa and is attached anteriorly to the pons, posteriorly to the medulla by cerebellar peduncles, and inferiorly to the occipital lobe. A transverse fold of dura mater is over it and separates the occipital lobes from the cerebellum. The cerebellar cortex is a layer of gray matter which covers the surface and encloses the core of white substance. Nuclei are buried within this white substance. The dentate nucleus is the largest and most important, since it receives most of the afferent fibers sending impulses to the motor cortex.

Some neurologists believe that the cerebellum has no direct motor function, but that it controls muscular activity and is the main integrative center for sensory proprioceptor data, facilitating smooth, graceful motion. Sensory afferent fibers are much more numerous in the cerebellum than are the efferent fibers. Efferent, or motor fibers, come from the vestibular nerve, olivocerebellar, spinocerebellar, and accessory nucleus of the medulla. The efferent (motor) fibers arise in the dentate nucleus, go to the red nucleus, then proceed directly to the lower motor neuron of the spinal cord by the rubrospinal path. The path crosses twice, so that the origin and terminus are on the same side of the body (Fig. 3-15). The second efferent route is by the dentate and thalamus to the cortex; crossed fibers bypass the red nucleus to the thalamus and then the impulse travels to the motor area and influences the pyramidal system.

Muscle synergy comes through the cerebellum. Voluntary movements without cerebellar assistance are clumsy and unskilled, resulting in cerebellar ataxia, which is swaying and staggering with the eyes open.

The general scheme of operation of the cerebellum allows nerve impulses to be returned, or fed back, to the same region from which they originated. In this respect cerebellar circuits are analogous to modern automatic control devices, or servomechanisms. The guided missile, for example, transmits radar signals which are picked up and fed to a mechanical computer. The computer, which may be thought of as analogous to the cortex of the cerebellum, detects any error in the missile's tract and returns the proper radio messages to adjust its controls and put it back on course (114, p. 73).

Disorders

1. The individual with ataxia resulting from cerebellar aberrations may show:

    a. Disturbances of posture and gait. Antigravity muscle impulses make it difficult for the person to maintain an upright stance. Lack of

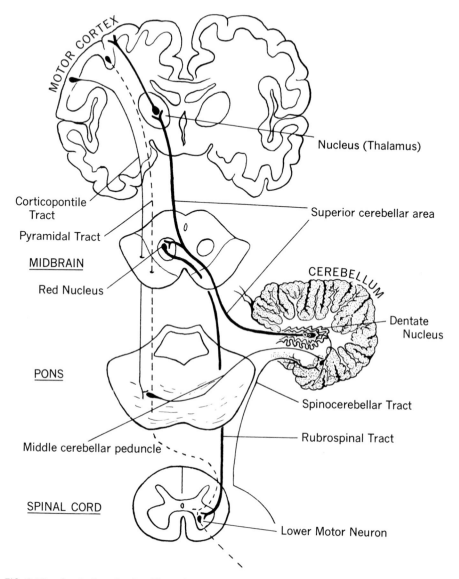

FIG. 3-15. Cerebellar circuits. The spinocerebellar and corticopontocerebellar pathways to the cerebellum are represented by thin fibers. Thicker fibers show efferent paths from the dentate nucleus to the red nucleus and to the precentral gyrus. The pyramidal tract is shown as a dotted line. (Manter and Gatz, *Essentials of Clinical Neuroanatomy and Neurophysiology*, Courtesy of F. A. Davis Co.)

muscle synergy presents a loss of equilibrium. A stumbling gait on the side of the lesion occurs and a loss of position sense develops.

b. Decomposition of movement when the movement of several joints is needed for coordination. Synchronized movement is difficult.

c. Dysmetria, or the inability to control the range of movement as a result of overshooting the goal, stopping too soon, finger to nose check, or loss of timing at the end of a movement.

d. Inability to stop a movement and change to an opposite action— for example, pronation and supination of the hands.

e. Scanning, or spacing sounds irregularly or using wrong pauses because of asynergy of speech muscles.

2. Hypotonia, or a decrease of the tendon reflexes—for example, knee jerk.

3. Asthenia, or weak muscles that tire easily.

4. Tremor or jerkiness—as in the intention tremor—which is diminished following rest.

Cerebellar defects usually are slow, progressive, less severe, and more difficult to localize regionally than defects of the cerebral cortex. The same side is affected in cerebellar symptoms, but cerebral lesions have opposite body effects. The defects are manifested as disorders in timing and coordination.

Midbrain (Mesencephalon)

The midbrain, a part of the brain stem or central core of the brain, is the short portion between the pons and the cerebral hemispheres. The functions of the midbrain and medulla relative to the integration of muscular action are at present incompletely known. The ventral (anterior) aspect has ropelike bundles of fibers which are the fibers of the pyramidal tract and is skirted by the optic tract system with the oculomotor nerves exiting from this surface. The dorsal aspect shows the nucleus of the trochlear nerve and its exit from this surface. The red nucleus (Fig. 3-15), an oval mass of gray substance in the rostral half of the midbrain, has nerve fiber terminations with the rubrospinal and tectospinal tracts arising in this part of the midbrain with decussating near their origin. The auditory and visual reflex sensory centers appear as protuberances on the dorsal aspect of the midbrain.

Disorders

Lesions to the midbrain may involve the upper motor neurons and may be caused by birth injuries, trauma, inflammation, and degenerative processes. Disorders may be manifested as spastic paralysis, hyperactive deep reflexes, and eye abnormalities. Red nucleus lesions may show involuntary movements, rigidity, and tremor. Benedikt's syndrome is characterized by eye aberrations on the same side and movement abnormalities on the opposite side (21, p. 106).

The Cerebral Cortex

The modified Brodmann chart (Fig. 3-16) illustrates the cortical areas. Their functions are described under Frontal Lobe, Parietal Lobe, Temporal Lobe, and Occipital Lobe.

Frontal Lobe

Voluntary movements are started by nerve impulses from *Area 4,* the motor cortex. The *pyramidal system,* or corticospinal tract, sends impulses to the muscle effectors. Most of these fibers decussate (cross) in the medulla and have two components—(1) upper motor neurons (pyramidal fibers) and (2) lower motor neurons (peripheral nerve fibers) (Figs. 3-5 and 3-7). When the motor cortex is destroyed, conscious effort is ineffective and paralysis results.

Three subdivisions of the pyramidal system are (1) corticospinal tract whose fibers descend from the cortex to the spinal cord; (2) corticobulbar tract whose fibers descend from the cortex to the brain stem with the cranial nerves V, VII, IX, X and XI, XII; and (3) corticomesencephalic tract whose fibers descend to the cranial nerves III, IV, and VI and furnish the motor supply to the extrinsic muscles of the eye. *Area 8* has the corticomesencephalic tract, but it is associated with the corticobulbar of the medulla. This area is concerned with eye movements and pupillary changes.

Area 6 is a part of the extrapyramidal tract. This premotor area, which lies in front of the motor area, has many short association fibers and is concerned with the development of motor skills of a more complex character. It has subcortical connections with the thalamus and corpus striatum (basal ganglia) and the cerebellum. The functions of the extrapyramidal system are concerned with associated movements, *postural adjustments,* and autonomic integration. It is considered a functional unit of the CNS, since it is difficult to separate it from the pyramidal system. This area has a *suppressor strip,* a phenomenon giving inhibition to the skeletal muscles, and is thought to influence the stretch reflexes of the spinal cord. Injury to the area shows a spastic paralysis.

Areas 9 and 10 are frontal association areas, and 8, 9, and 10 form the prefrontal region. This region is associated with all other lobes and may be essential for thinking, foresight, mature judgment, tactfulness,

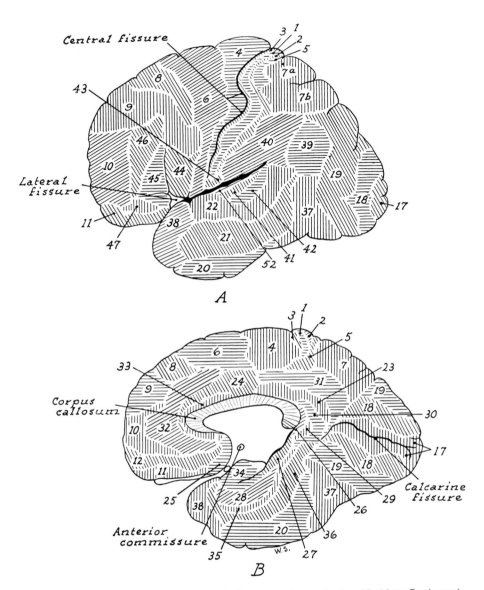

FIG. 3-16.   Structurally distinctive areas of the human cerebral cortex (modified from Brodmann). A, Dorsolateral surface. B, Medial surface. (Everett, *Functional Neuroanatomy*, 6th ed., 1971, Lea & Febiger.)

and forbearance. Tested intelligence is not relevant to this area, but injury presents personal irresponsibility, slovenliness, clownish behavior, impulsive anxiety, obsessions, and pain. When surgery is required, epilepsy may develop from the cortical scar.

Parietal Lobe

The principal sensory areas are 3, 2, and 1, while 5 and 7 are the sensory association areas. The somatesthetic area—3, 2, and 1,—receives thalamic impulses giving skin, muscle, joint, and tendon sense from the opposite side of the body. Pain is also perceived here. Injury will produce numbness to the specific area or alter pain sensibility. Unilateral lesions seem to show no effect on hearing, as association fibers to the temporal lobe do not affect the ears. The areas formulate sensory stimuli into object images and comprehend their meaning. For example, the visual association areas must be called upon when a friend is recognized in a crowd. *Areas 5 and 7* are necessary for correlating the cutaneous sense so that a person can recognize objects with his hands (eyes closed), a function called *"stereognosis."* Astereognosis is the absence of this ability.

Temporal Lobe

Area 41 is the primary auditory cortex which conveys impulses, particularly the low and high tones, from the ears. Buzzing and roaring sensations are also received in this area. *Area 42* is the associative auditory cortex, and *Areas 38, 40, 20, 21, and 22* are association areas. The auditory and visual association areas have a "silent area" in the temporal lobe in which visual and auditory sensory experiences are thought to be stored as if they had been permanently recorded on sound film. The mechanisms of memory, hallucinations, and dreams appear to be located here. Lesions in the associated area may present word blindness, the inability to understand written words although vision is normal. A temporal lobe seizure presents temporary memory suspension or amnesia. Removal of the temporal lobes permanently abolishes memory of past experiences. Amnesic aphasia is the inability to recall specific names and is associated with injury to the posterior section of the temporal lobe. Motor aphasia, or loss of vocal expression, comes with injury to the left auditory area in right-handed persons (114, p. 112).

Occipital Lobe

Area 17 is the principal visual cortex. *Areas 18 and 19* are the visual association areas. Peripheral vision comes from the anterior part of this lobe; spotted or macular vision and central vision arise in the posterior lobe. *Area 19* may receive stimuli from the entire cerebral cortex, while *Area 18* gets stimuli primarily from *Area 17*. Lesions which block the optic pathways in the occipital and temporal lobes cause visual field defects. Visual hallucinations resulting from lesions in the temporal lobe area are of objects, people, and buildings. The action of the eye muscles is important in determining the posture of a body in space.

The Interbrain (Diencephalon)

The posterior portion of the brain stem is the diencephalon, or interbrain. Three of its subdivisions are the thalamus, subthalamus, and hypothalamus.

Thalamus proper

The thalami (Fig. 3-17), large, ovoid gray masses located either side of the cerebral hemisphere, are continuous with the hypothalamus and are bounded by the caudate nucleus and laterally by the internal capsule. It is agreed that the axons of the nuclei pass through the internal capsule to connect with the cerebral cortex with a return set of fibers. It serves as a relay station with subcortical connections. Since brain wave records of the cortex and thalamus show that each has a degree of independence and a degree of cooperation, it is felt that they exert an influence on one another through "nonspecific" fibers. The thalamus may be the crucial structure for perception of some sensations such as the focusing of attention and the processes of correlation and integration. When affected, pains are persistent and aggravated by emotional stress and fatigue. The thalamus (a) receives sensory impulses from the spinal cord and brain stem, (b) receives integrative information of a motor nature from the cerebellum and the corpus striatum (basal ganglia), (c) sends and receives a variety of impulses from the cerebral cortex, (d) sends and receives visceral information from the hypothalamus, and (e) sends information caudally back down the brain stem.

Subthalamus

The subthalamus which lies anterior or ventral to the thalamus is closely related to the internal capsule and the basal ganglia. It contains the subthalamic nucleus. It forms a part of the afferent, descending path from the basal ganglia.

Hypothalamus

The hypothalamus (Fig. 3-17) lies ventral to the thalamus and is concerned with visceral functions. This region of gray matter contains diffuse cells and nonmyelinated nerve fibers. Sixteen nuclei have been

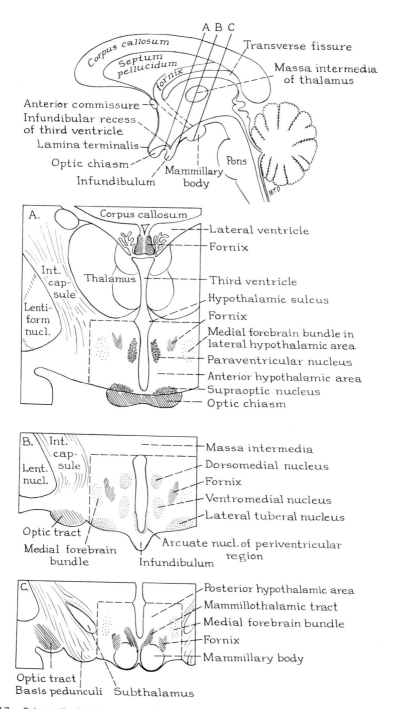

FIG. 3-17. Schematic drawing of a sagittal section of the brain stem to show the relations of the hypothalamus to surrounding brain structures. A. Supraoptic area. B. Tuberal area. C. Mammillary area. (From Everett, *Functional Neuroanatomy*, Lea & Febiger.)

identified. Fibers of the hypothalamus are passed into the reticular (network) formation of the midbrain through many synapses, and they have sympathetic and parasympathetic system connections in the brain stem and spinal cord with counterbalancing mechanisms. The efferent hypothalamic path descends through the medulla, with fibers going to the respiratory center and vasomotor center giving stimuli that influence the respiration rate, heart rate, and blood pressure. The hypothalamus is believed to (a) alert the cerebral cortex and produce alert awakening from sleep, (b) produce physical expressions of emotion, (c) regulate body temperature, (d) affect the appetite, (e) influence the pituitary hormones as well as the gonadal hormones developed at puberty, (f) circuitously affect the limbic system of the brain, and (g) regulate water balance. It is suggested that the hypothalamus through the limbic system, a midbrain circuit, has association fibers which produce emotional coloring of thought through psychic activity, thus reinforcing or intensifying an emotional experience. The thalamus and hypothalamus are sometimes included in the brain stem.

Disorders

Lesions of the hypothalamus may result in problems of obesity, somnolence, loss of sexual appetite, sexual dystrophy, visual defects, and neurogenic fever or a rise in blood temperature or may prevent sweating (21).

Limbic Lobe or System

The limbic system is defined as the visceral brain and is concerned with various aspects of emotion and behavior. It may circulate impulses continually and, by reinforcement, intensify an emotional experience. The limbic lobe is formed by the gray matter areas of the temporal and frontal cortex, thalamic and hypothalamic nuclei, parts of the basal ganglia, and other associated areas. Electrode stimulation of this area may result in a person becoming more alert, sharp, and talkative and generally reporting a pleasant feeling.

A temporal lobe lesion causes emotional disturbances with symptoms of hallucinations, disorder of memory, dream states, clouding of consciousness, unpleasant smell or taste syndrome, and psychomotor epilepsy. Lesions of this system are important in psychiatric disorders.

Surgery of the temporal lobe may correct some of the above symptoms. Removal of the lobe produces an attitude of indifference and a total loss of emotional responses (114).

Basal Ganglia

The basal ganglia are nuclei of the gray matter deep within the cerebrum. The basal ganglia regulate and control motor integration and posture. Associated with the basal ganglia are the pyramidal and extrapyramidal systems. Separating them anatomically is difficult. The pyramidal is the more direct corticospinal voluntary motion system. To carry out motor acts correctly, the pyramidal system needs the cooperation of the (1) vestibular system (Fig. 3-18), (2) the cerebellar and (3) corpus striatum, which includes some of the basal ganglia.

The vestibular system (C VIII) has peripheral endings on the hair cells in the three semicircular canals. The nerve furnishes afferent fibers for coordinated reflexes of the eyes, neck, and body for maintaining equilibrium in accordance with the posture and movement of the head. Vertigo and motion sickness develop with prolonged stimulation of the vestibular system (Fig. 3-18).

The extrapyramidal system reaches segmental levels after many detours, with interruptions in basal ganglia and midbrain. The midbrain contains the red nucleus (Figs. 3-15 and 3-19), which forms a part of the efferent descending path from the basal ganglia. The basal ganglia are presumed to (1) "tone down" or inhibit activity, (2) give two-direction motor facilitation through the premotor and motor cortex and the lower neurons of the spinal cord through the midbrain components, (3) show that the left basal ganglia influences the right side of the body,

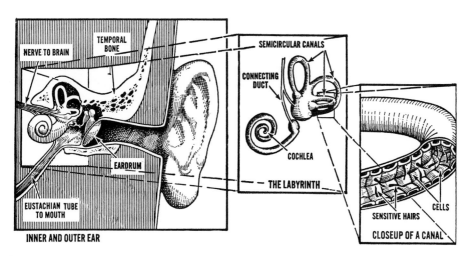

FIG. 3-18. Schematic drawing of vestibular (labyrinthine) system. (Courtesy of World Book Encyclopedia Science Service, Copyright 1965.)

and (4) serve as the connection for the skeletal muscle extrapyramidal system.

The extrapyramidal system functions are concerned with postural adjustments, association movements, and autonomic integration (Fig. 3-19). This system includes all descending pathways, exclusive of the

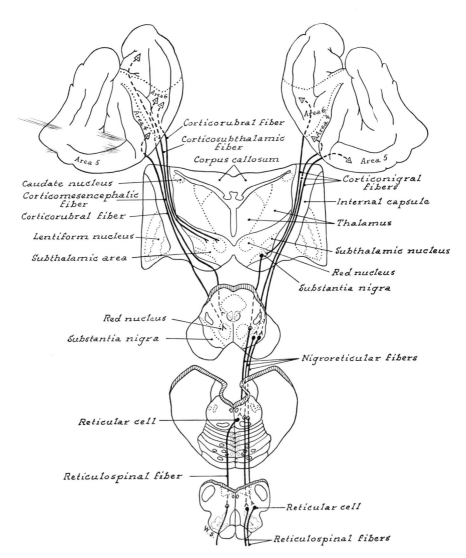

FIG. 3-19. Diagram to show the origin and distribution of some of the cortically originating extrapyramidal projection fibers. (From Everett, *Functional Neuroanatomy*, 6th ed., 1971, Lea & Febiger.)

pyramidal tract, which act directly on the motor neurons. Injury at any level may abolish voluntary movement which is replaced by involuntary movements.

Disorders

Motor disorders of basal ganglia present:

1. Parkinsonism or shaking palsy associated with degeneration. The person has normal deep reflexes, but Parkinson's disease is characterized by increased muscle tonus or rigidity, resting tremors, and short, shuffling, walking steps. Surgery sometimes stops tremors on the opposite side of the body.

2. Athetosis, chorea, and torsion spasms. Athetosis is associated with spastic paralysis with worm-like movements and lead pipe limbs often caused by brain damage at birth. The person with chorea shows jerky, purposeless movements. Two types are (a) Huntington's, an inherited form which appears in adult life and includes cerebral cortex damage, and (b) Sydenham's or St. Vitus' dance which may be part of rheumatic fever with subsequent complete recovery.

3. Internal capsule lesion with spastic movements of the opposite side of the body. They may result from a cardiovascular accident.

4. Post-traumatic epilepsy—a result of scar formation in the motor or sensory cortex.

The extrapyramidal system is a complex and interrelated system, since injury or disease may give hypertonic, or rigid, and hyperkinetic syndromes including choreic, athetoid, and myotonic syndromes.

Coordinated Muscle Movement

The functional organization of coordinated muscle movement is developed in the central nervous system through the reflex system and voluntary control cortical centers. Complicated skilled movements have participation of:

1. Full proprioceptor and sensory information to the cerebrum and subcortical centers.

2. Primitive reflexes.

3. Receptor conduction tracts to motor effector and the final common pathway.

4. The cerebral cortex.

5. The semiautomatic reflex patterns which are learned.

6. The integrative reticular activating system of the brain stem.

Daily experience shows that learning a new motor skill by a normal person is possible due to general neurophysiology. The use or disuse of a synapse repeatedly used by neurophysiological conditions of temporary facilitation or inhibition leads finally to a permanent facilitation or permanent inhibition for later passage of the motor unit impulses through the synapse in question (42).

Summary

The scientific basis for motor learning and/or the sensorimotor functions of learning is neurological.

1. The central nervous system involves the brain and the spinal cord.

2. The neuron with its cell body and nerve fibers is the functional and anatomical unit of the nervous system. Nerve tracts are named by their direction.

3. The spinal cord starts below the medulla oblongata at the level of C-1 and goes to the border of the second lumbar vertebra. This is the final common pathway, as impulses descend to the motor units of the muscles, joints, and tendons through the peripheral nerves and reflex circuits. Movement comes from these circuit interplays. Injuries to the cord are called lower motor lesions.

4. The peripheral nerves have dorsal roots for sensory impulses and anterior roots for motor impulses. These nerves are arranged in pairs as in the muscular system.

5. The medulla oblongata is at the superior end of the spinal cord. Here the pyramidal tract crosses to the other side of the cord to affect that body area's motor activity. Other tracts also cross here.

6. The midbrain, a part of the brain stem, contains the red nucleus and the rubrospinal tract that help complex voluntary movement.

7. The pons serves as a bridge for many nerve tracts.

8. The cerebellum, posterior to the pons and the medulla, has a cortex and nuclei which receive sensory impulses and send them to the cerebral cortex. The cerebellum coordinates skilled motor activities and has feedback capacities.

9. The interbrain (diencephalon) of the thalamus and hypothalamus lies between the cerebrum and the midbrain. The thalamus (a) receives sensory impulses from the spinal cord and brain stem, (b) receives integrative information on the motor side from the cerebellum and corpus striatum, basal ganglia, (c) sends and receives a variety of impulses from the cerebral cortex and visceral information from the hypothalamus, and, (d) with the hypothalamus, integrates all pathways.

It is the site of the limbic system with its aspects of emotion and behavior.

10. The frontal lobe of the cerebrum or brain has the motor cortex and the pyramidal, corticospinal, nerve tract, the premotor or suppressor cortex, and the extrapyramidal nerve system.

11. The parietal lobe has the principal sensory area of the brain. The skin, muscle, joint, and tendon sense is discriminated in this lobe.

12. The temporal lobe is the main auditory cortex.

13. The occipital lobe has the visual cortex.

Injuries to the cortical areas are called "upper motor neuron lesions" presenting aberrations in voluntary motor functions. The upper motor neuron injuries in the brain cause a spastic paralysis; the lower motor neuron injuries present a flaccid paralysis with atrophy of the skeletal muscles. Hypertonic muscular action is associated with brain injuries, and lack of movement comes with the spinal cord or lower motor neuron injuries.

Movement can be organized into three levels:

1. The lowest level of motor organization is in the gray matter of the spinal cord.

2. The next level of motor control comes from the reticular formation in the brain stem. The basal ganglia and cerebellum give coordination to motor skills.

3. The highest level of motor control comes from the cerebral cortex. Most cortical reflexes are conditioned reflexes developed through the repetition of a given stimulus. Voluntary motor activity depends upon sensory perception from the sensory impulses.

Mental Retardation and
Learning Disabilities

Approximately six million children in the United States require special education but only 38 per cent of them are receiving such assistance. Special education may be defined as all those instructional services specially planned for children of elementary and secondary school age who are physically handicapped, seriously retarded in learning ability, or emotionally maladjusted. The term the exceptional child includes both the gifted and the handicapped. He is one who requires a modification of school practices or an addition of some special educational service to develop his maximal capacity because of some definite deviations in mental, neuromuscular, or physical, emotional, or social, sensory communication or multiple handicaps. In other words, the child's ability to learn is reduced in the conventional classroom. The 1970 Annual Report of the U.S. Department of Health, Education and Welfare stated that 52 per cent of the one and one-half million retarded children are receiving special educational services. This should be higher due to local and state mill levies and more federally funded grants for such children. Even so, of the 46 million children of school age, 12 per cent need some form of special education.

Children with learning disabilities or learning disorders have highly visible behavior, not because of early developmental impairment but usually because of a lack of ability to respond adequately to conventional classroom teaching. These children show disorders in listening, thinking, talking, reading, writing, arithmetic, and sometimes in motor patterns. The maladaptation generally occurs in school. Often when the child's home adjustment is chaotic, parents assume that school will help, but there the full problem emerges and the child does not respond to demands for specific learning. Learning disorders have been called

91

perceptual handicaps, perceptual-motor conditions, brain injury or Strauss Syndrome, minimal brain dysfunction, dyslexia, developmental aphasia, or neurological handicaps. The various labels of learning disabilities depend not only on the child's difficulty but also on the professional person who makes the diagnosis. A physician may diagnose a child as dyslexic, while an educator might label him as one with a reading disability. A neurologist might call him brain damaged; a psychiatrist may label him as emotionally disturbed; and a psychologist may say his trouble stems from poor visual perception (McCarthy and McCarthy) (118). This case illustrates the various labels applied to some school children.

John, after four months in the first grade, was recommended for an evaluation by the school psychologist due to reading disabilities and behavior problems. The results of his Stanford-Binet were CA, 6.3, MA, 5.5, and IQ 95. The Peabody test showed MA, 6.4, and IQ, 104. John passed all items at the four and one-half year level and failed all items at the seven year level. His Bender-Gestalt test showed poor eye-hand coordination. The psychologist recommended that he return to kindergarten on a half day schedule with a half day in first grade. The parents preferred the first grade. John became defiant and impudent and the school principal suggested professional counseling for John to the parents. In the third grade John was evaluated again by the school psychologist. His Stanford-Binet results were CA, 8.11, MA, 11.2, and IQ, 122. The wide-range achievement test gave a reading level of 2.0, an arithmetic level of 3.0, and a spelling level of 2.0. His Bender-Gestalt drawings were distorted. The psychologist's evaluation showed John to have visual and auditory problems. Glasses were fitted for him. His body image presented a problem as he felt rejected and unhappy. He needed help with phonics and word analysis since he had trouble recognizing: cook, book; cow, how, now, etc. It was recommended that he receive tutoring with the tactile, kinesthetic method to help resolve his problems of reading and perhaps his emotional problems of hostile feelings.

John is now in fifth grade, reads on a second grade level, and still has unresolved emotional problems. His family physician says he is a normal, healthy boy so the parents have decided to let John continue his usual modus operandi. They reinforce him and his teacher feels he is improving.

Thus, children with learning disability are not homogeneous. Usually their intellectual functioning measures near normal, normal, or above normal. They do not always have problems of vision, hearing, and mental retardation.

The implications of physical education on the intellectual functioning and social adjustment of the mentally retarded child and the child with a learning disability will be explored later. Motor patterns and motor proficiency have implications for socialization and recreational activities help these children develop their potential.

Part 1: Mental Retardation

The American Association on Mental Deficiency (AAMD) has published a very useful manual on terminology and classification in mental retardation (158). It represents the collaboration of interested workers in many professional areas. Their definition of mental retardation will find wider acceptance than others so we shall use their concept. The AAMD Adaptive Behavior Scale Manual, revised 1974 and the AAMD Adaptive Behavior Scale for Children and Adults, 1974 revised test booklet can be purchased from the American Association on Mental Deficiency, 5201 Connecticut Avenue, N.W., Washington, D.C. 20015.

Mental retardation refers to the significantly sub-average general intellectual functioning existing concurrently with deficits in adaptive behavior, and is manifested during the developmental period. Mental retardation is a state of impairment recognized in the behavior of the person. It is not a disease or symptom. This definition of mental retardation is changed from the 1968 definition to reflect the deletion of the borderline category. Figure 4-1 (88) represents the distribution of IQ's as determined by Terman (178A). The lower left-hand part of the curve shows that the children with an IQ below 70 constitute the percentage of the population studied and represent the group labeled mentally retarded.

Figure 4-2 illustrates the 1974 AAMD definition of mental retardation, in which the upper limit of retardation in measured intelligence is two standard deviations below the mean. The AAMD staff suggest borderline intelligence for the group between one and two standard deviations below the mean. To determine who fits into the category of sub-average intellectual functioning an individual standardized general intelligence test should be given by an examiner trained for this and also trained in working with retarded individuals. The most frequently used tests are the revised Stanford-Binet and the Wechsler Scales. The preceding levels describe the equivalents of terms commonly used: the educable, the trainable, dependent retarded, and the life support group. These levels are not static but are used as a criterion for planning the service needed by the individual.

The standardized intelligence tests used by the AAMD are Stan-

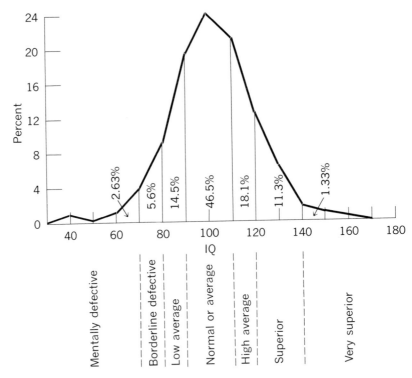

FIG. 4-1. Distribution of composite IQ's (Form L–M). (Adapted from Terman, L. M., and Merrill, M. A.: *Stanford-Binet Intelligence Scale, Manual for the Third Revision Form L–M.* Boston, Houghton Mifflin Company, 1960, p. 18.)

ford-Binet and Cattell with a sigma score (standard deviation) of 16 or the Wechsler Scales with a sigma of 15. The classifications using the Stanford-Binet as a guide are as follows:

1. Profoundly retarded, IQ 19 and below, individual needs complete custodial care, five Standard Deviations below normal.
2. Severely retarded, IQ 35–20, may be trained for bodily needs

Levels	Obtained Intelligence Quotient	
	Stanford Binet and Cattell	*Wechsler Scales*
	(s.d. 16)	(s.d. 15)
MILD	67–52	69–55
MODERATE	51–36	54–40
SEVERE	35–20	39–25 (Extrapolated)
PROFOUND	19 & below	24 & below (157)

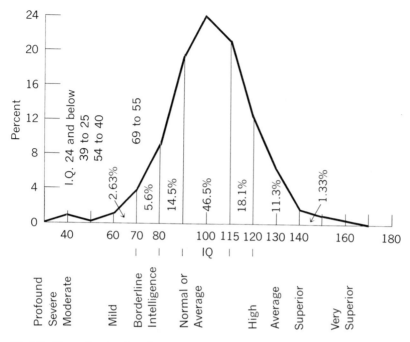

FIG. 4-2. The author has translated the IQ values as shown here using the AAMD definition.

such as self-feeding, some dressing and undressing, bathing, partially toilet trained; develop some language; social and occupational difficulties, four to five Standard Deviations below the normal.

3. Moderately retarded, IQ 51–36, academic skill problems, activities of daily living routines can be trained; may perform in a sheltered workshop, three to four Standard Deviations below normal.

4. Mildly retarded, IQ 68–52, may read and write satisfactorily; is educable in socialization and occupational competence, IQ scores two to three Standard Deviations below the normal. Stanford-Binet 52–68 and the Wechsler IQ score is 55–59.

The borderline intelligence group of children may be included in the regular classroom. The current trend in legislation seems to favor regular instruction and conventional teaching methods. The open classroom favored by some public school systems may create problems for the student one standard deviation below the mean as a structured program seems to favor their learning potential.

Samuel A. Kirk (88) states that the prevalence rate of mental retardation in the United States involves 2 to 3 per cent of the school

Incidence of Retardation per 1,000 School-age Children

Level of Community	Totally Dependent	Trainable	Educable
Low	1	4	50
Middle	1	4	25
High	1	4	10

population. In general, a small percentage of these are identified at the pre-school level, a higher percentage at the middle school level, and only a few at the post-school period.

The terms used in the definition of mental retardation are explained:

1. Sub-average intellectual functioning indicates performance that is more than two standard deviations below the population mean of the age group measured on a standard IQ test.

2. Developmental period refers to six or nine months prior to conception to 18 years.

3. Adaptive behavior means the individual's ability to cope with the natural and social demands of the environment. Impaired adaptive behavior may be reflected in maturation, learning, and socialization.

4. Maturation applies to the rate of development in infancy and early childhood, for example, the self-help skills such as sitting, crawling, standing, walking, habit training, speech and language, and social skills in interaction with peers. In the early years of life adaptive behavior is assessed in terms of the preceding and other sensory motor developments. Delay in the development of early skills is of prime importance as a criterion of adaptive behavior during the pre-school years.

5. Learning ability involves the process by which knowledge is acquired and retained as a function of the experiences of the individual. The skills for adaptation during childhood and early adolescence involve more than the learning processes. Difficulties usually arise in the academic situation but in evaluation of adaptive behavior, attention should focus also on skills essential to cope with the environment. This includes concepts of time and money, self-directed behaviors, social responsiveness and interactive skills.

6. Socialization during late adolescence and adult life relates to the mental retardate through vocational performance and social responsibilities. The degree to which the individual can maintain himself independently in the community and in gainful employ-

ment is assessed by his ability to cope with the standards set by the community. The deficiencies in adaptive behavior usually determine his needs for programs, services, or legal action. At present, clinical judgment is the measurement used for a diagnosis.

Both the intellectual level and adaptive behavior level should be considered for classifying individuals. Separate measures are warranted due to the variability in individuals. Figure 4-3 illustrates that those individuals who demonstrate deficits in measured intelligence and adaptive behavior are considered mentally retarded.

Figure 4-3 shows that a person may change status as a result of changes in his intellectual functioning, changes in his adaptive behavior, changes in the expectations of society, or for known or unknown reasons. If the person's status changes the decisions for the change are made in relation to behavior standards and norms of his chronological age group.

Adaptive behavior for the mentally retarded as well as the so-called normal child concerns the individual's environment. If the child's behavior is invisible and the intellectual functioning is low, the AAMD feels he cannot be categorized as mentally retarded (Fig. 4-3). Some tests available for evaluating adaptive behavior are the Vineland Social Maturity Scale and the AAMD Adaptive Behavior Scale, which includes Independent Functioning, Physical Development, Language Development, Social Behavior, Number and Time Use, Economic Activity, etc.

Decisions relating to the test data should include clinical observation and information of each person's everyday behavior.

The AAMD Adaptive Behavior Scale provides scores that measure a number of separate aspects of adaptive as well as maladaptive behavior. The Scale's Manual offers the procedure by which some of the scores can be combined to derive an individual's overall level of adaptive behavior. For younger children, the adaptive behavior level is determined by a composite of measures

INTELLECTUAL FUNCTIONING

		Retarded	Not Retarded
ADAPTIVE BEHAVIOR	Retarded	Mentally Retarded	Not Mentally Retarded
	Not Retarded	Not Mentally Retarded	Not Mentally Retarded

FIG. 4-3. (From *Manual on Terminology and Classification in Mental Retardation.* Revised, 1974.) (157.)

that include the degree of self-sufficiency, sensori-motor development, language development, and socialization. For older children, the adaptive behavior level is determined by the same composite of measures of domestic skill, vocational potential, and responsibility. At the present time, the value of a SINGLE score for adaptive behavior level classification is limited largely to certain administrative purposes and has little diagnostic or program planning input for the individual. Assessment of performance in SPECIFIC DOMAINS of behavior, however, can be very useful in *identifying deficits* and *training needs.* As with IQ scores, individuals who are classified at the same overall level of adaptive behavior may not be "clinically equivalent" in that they may vary significantly in the various domains of behavior that comprise the overall rating.

Since the concept of adaptive behavior is of a tentative nature, reconsideration of each individual's level should be checked at frequent intervals. Training and environmental changes help the individual to function at a higher level. The adaptive behavior scales are not fully satisfactory, so clinical judgment is very important. As Henry Leland says, the child with an IQ of 70 to 84 may never learn in the regular manner or at the regular rate when he is in a special room. If a child lacks the ability to enter a situation, social inferences may be made. Deficit in adaptive behavior implies the child is unable to cope with the natural and social demands of his environment. His cognitive skills have been modified or neglected as he is unable to adapt. Adaptive behavior needs independent functioning as well as personal responsibility. How does society view the child? Does he throw names? Rocks? What is his visibility? The child is identified by his observed behavior. What does our society request? It calls for: 1. mobility; as adults we must go where the job is, 2. grouping; we must work together, 3. need personal interaction, ability to be quiet, listen; 4. must read, i.e., union rules, bulletin boards, and 5. know unwritten behavior, have tolerance and like each other. Thus the mentally retarded must fit or they are moved out.° So we realize a deficit in adaptive behavior is concerned with how the person copes in his environment. The AAMD change in the mental retardation definition relates to a person's ability to cope in his community—to unlabel the individual as M. R.

The following pages illustrate the pertinent parts of the Adaptive Behavior Scale Manual and the Adaptive Behavior Scale to give one some idea of its scope, content, and its graphic representation of the scores.

The AAMD committee suggests that it has values to help the mentally retarded, the emotionally maladjusted, and the developmentally disabled and other handicapped persons. It is designed to provide objective descriptions and evaluations of an individual's behavior.

° Psychology 857, Henry Leland, Nisonger Center, Ohio State University

The IQ, which was used to identify and classify in the past, is inadequate and often misleading when used as the only basis for evaluation. IQ provides neither a description of the way an individual maintains his or her personal independence in daily living nor how he or she meets the social expectations of his or her environment. This information is most crucial for training and rehabilitation.

As a part of current research the AAMD is very much interested in any information of your projected or ongoing work within the scope of their manual and test booklet.

Part One of the Adaptive Behavior Scale is organized along developmental lines, and is designed to evaluate an individual's skills and habits in ten behavior domains (coherent groups of related activities) considered important to the development of personal independence in daily living. The ten behavior domains (indicated by Roman numerals) and twenty-one subdomains (indicated by letters) are as follows:

I. INDEPENDENT FUNCTIONING

    A. Eating
    B. Toilet Use
    C. Cleanliness
    D. Appearance
    E. Care of Clothing
    F. Dressing and Undressing
    G. Travel
    H. General Independent Functioning

II. PHYSICAL DEVELOPMENT

    A. Sensory Development
    B. Motor Development

III. ECONOMIC ACTIVITY

    A. Money Handling and Budgeting
    B. Shopping Skills

IV. LANGUAGE DEVELOPMENT

    A. Expression
    B. Comprehension
    C. Social Language Development

V. NUMBERS AND TIME

VI. DOMESTIC ACTIVITY

  A. Cleaning
  B. Kitchen Duties
  C. Other Domestic Activities

VII. VOCATIONAL ACTIVITY

VIII. SELF-DIRECTION

  A. Initiative
  B. Perseverence
  C. Leisure Time

IX. RESPONSIBILITY

X. SOCIALIZATION

Part Two of the Scale (158) is the product of extensive survey of the social expectations placed upon retarded persons, both in residential institutions and in the community. The description of these social expectations was obtained empirically from an analysis of a large number of "critical incident" reports provided by ward personnel in residential institutions, by day-care instructors, and by special education teachers in public school systems.

Part Two is designed to provide measures of maladaptive behavior related to personality and behavior domain and information about a person's adaptation to the world. Part Two consists of the following fourteen domains:

  I. *VIOLENT AND DESTRUCTIVE BEHAVIOR*

  II. *ANTISOCIAL BEHAVIOR*

  III. *REBELLIOUS BEHAVIOR*

  IV. *UNTRUSTWORTHY BEHAVIOR*

  V. *WITHDRAWAL*

  VI. *STEREOTYPED BEHAVIOR AND ODD MANNERISMS*

  VII. *INAPPROPRIATE INTERPERSONAL MANNERS*

  VIII. *UNACCEPTABLE VOCAL HABITS*

  IX. *UNACCEPTABLE OR ECCENTRIC HABITS*

  X. *SELF-ABUSIVE BEHAVIOR*

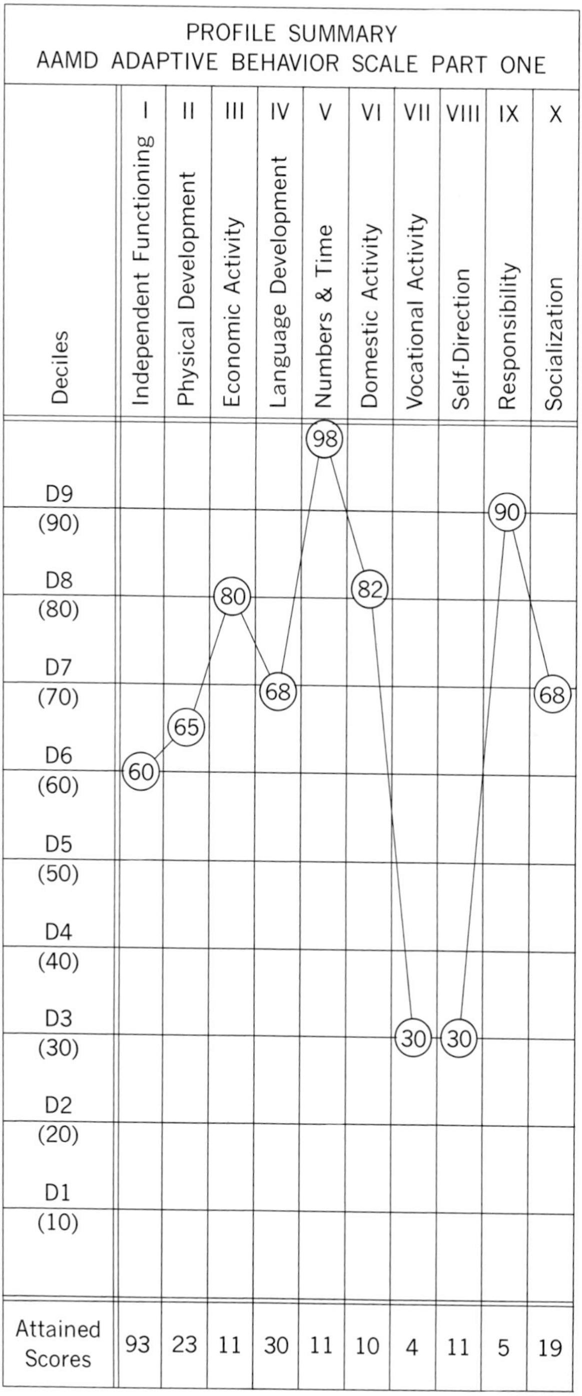

PROFILE SUMMARY
AAMD ADAPTIVE BEHAVIOR SCALE PART ONE

Deciles	I Independent Functioning	II Physical Development	III Economic Activity	IV Language Development	V Numbers & Time	VI Domestic Activity	VII Vocational Activity	VIII Self-Direction	IX Responsibility	X Socialization
					98					
D9 (90)									90	
D8 (80)			80			82				
D7 (70)				68						68
		65								
D6 (60)	60									
D5 (50)										
D4 (40)										
D3 (30)							30	30		
D2 (20)										
D1 (10)										
Attained Scores	93	23	11	30	11	10	4	11	5	19

FIG. 4-4.

FIG. 4-5.

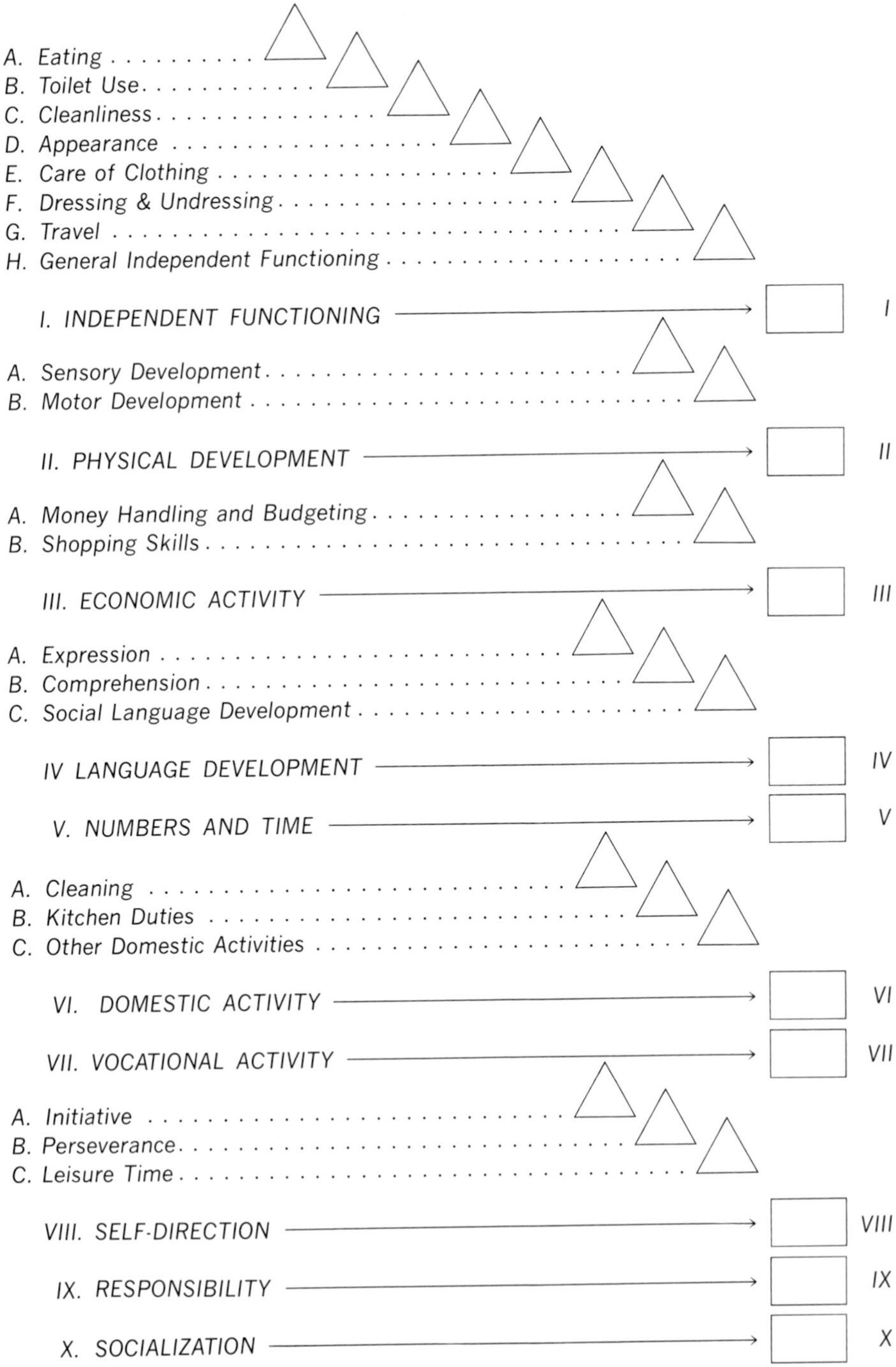

A. Eating . . . .
B. Toilet Use. . . . .
C. Cleanliness. . . . .
D. Appearance . . . .
E. Care of Clothing . . . .
F. Dressing & Undressing. . . . .
G. Travel . . . .
H. General Independent Functioning . . . .

I. INDEPENDENT FUNCTIONING ——————————————————→ ☐   I

A. Sensory Development. . . . .
B. Motor Development . . . .

II. PHYSICAL DEVELOPMENT ——————————————→ ☐   II

A. Money Handling and Budgeting. . . . .
B. Shopping Skills. . . . .

III. ECONOMIC ACTIVITY ————————————————→ ☐   III

A. Expression . . . .
B. Comprehension. . . . .
C. Social Language Development . . . .

IV LANGUAGE DEVELOPMENT ——————————————→ ☐   IV

V. NUMBERS AND TIME ————————————————————→ ☐   V

A. Cleaning . . . .
B. Kitchen Duties . . . .
C. Other Domestic Activities . . . .

VI. DOMESTIC ACTIVITY ————————————————→ ☐   VI

VII. VOCATIONAL ACTIVITY ————————————————→ ☐   VII

A. Initiative . . . .
B. Perseverance. . . . .
C. Leisure Time. . . . .

VIII. SELF-DIRECTION ——————————————————→ ☐   VIII

IX. RESPONSIBILITY ————————————————————→ ☐   IX

X. SOCIALIZATION ——————————————————————→ ☐   X

XI. *HYPERACTIVE TENDENCIES*

XII. *SEXUALLY ABERRANT BEHAVIOR*

XIII. *PSYCHOLOGICAL DISTURBANCES*

XIV. *USE OF MEDICATIONS*

The Adaptive Behavior Scale is an instrument that can serve many purposes. While specific examples of its uses and directions for its application and interpretation will appear later, you should know that some general possible uses of the Scale are:

1. To identify areas of deficiency that individuals or groups have, in order to facilitate proper and useful assignment of curricula and placement in training programs;
2. To provide an objective basis for the comparison of an individual's ratings over a period of time in order to evaluate the suitability of his or her current curriculum or training program.

Implications for Physical Education with the Mentally Retarded Individual

The physical education programs should be based on the nature and need of the learner so that he can achieve his maximal potential. The IQ has an educational expediency for the child's school placement but for the mentally retarded the differential diagnosis should help to understand the individual's needs. These areas may include the following: 1. the etiology, such as organic, genetic, neurotic, and/or psychotic or social neglect; 2. associated disorders such as sensori-motor impairment or cognitive impairment; 3. neurological assessment such as E.E.G. and neuromuscular reflexes; 4. psycho-motor evaluations of motor efficiency such as reaction time, dexterity, and accuracy; 5. perceptual development, as these disorders may be disruptive in learning motor skills (Kephart Perceptual-Motor Survey); 6. physical fitness tests such as AAHPER test, Physical Fitness for the M.R. (Frank J. Hayden) (67); 7. motor fitness test that measures the basic motor skills and explores movement; 8. adaptive behavior scales as mentioned earlier.

A combination of diagnostic entities may be seen in the child, not a unified set of behaviors. Henry Leland says that a diagnosis, in order to serve the child, must reveal the behavior areas that are actually deficient; we must start with the problem that needs correcting and use the best available information as a basis for the correction.

The physical educator's scope has great possibilities for giving the mentally retarded child success with leisure time activities and improved socialization through performances in specific motor skills. Children who are mentally retarded learn through experience and participation, but there are some guidelines the physical education instructor must keep in mind when working with them. 1. The environment should be pleasant and the child should enjoy the motor learning skills. 2. The child may

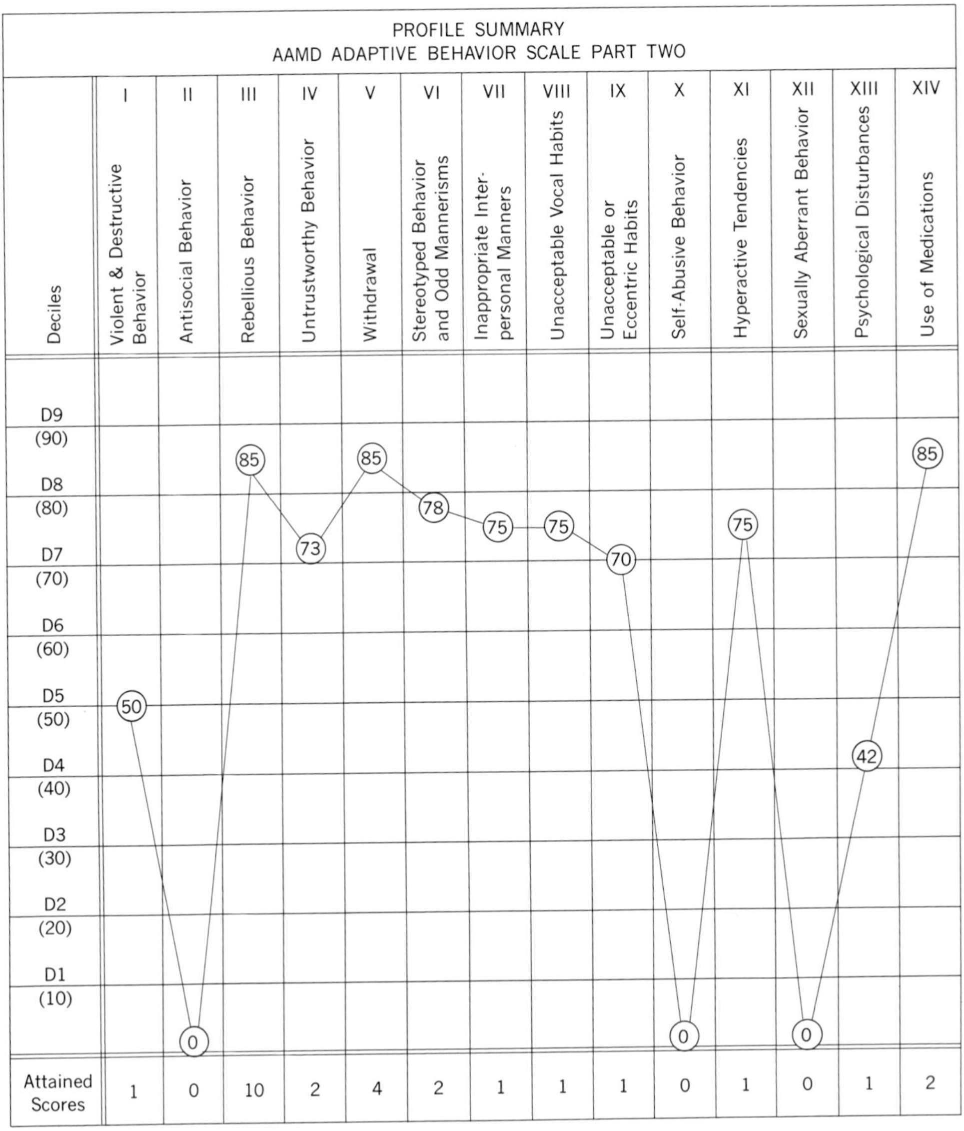

PROFILE SUMMARY
AAMD ADAPTIVE BEHAVIOR SCALE PART TWO

Deciles	I Violent & Destructive Behavior	II Antisocial Behavior	III Rebellious Behavior	IV Untrustworthy Behavior	V Withdrawal	VI Stereotyped Behavior and Odd Mannerisms	VII Inappropriate Inter-personal Manners	VIII Unacceptable Vocal Habits	IX Unacceptable or Eccentric Habits	X Self-Abusive Behavior	XI Hyperactive Tendencies	XII Sexually Aberrant Behavior	XIII Psychological Disturbances	XIV Use of Medications
D9 (90)			(85)		(85)									(85)
D8 (80)				(73)		(78)	(75)	(75)			(75)			
D7 (70)									(70)					
D6 (60)														
D5 (50)	(50)													
D4 (40)													(42)	
D3 (30)														
D2 (20)														
D1 (10)		(0)								(0)		(0)		
Attained Scores	1	0	10	2	4	2	1	1	1	0	1	0	1	2

FIG. 4-6.

I. VIOLENT AND DESTRUCTIVE BEHAVIOR ☐ *I*

II. ANTISOCIAL BEHAVIOR ☐ *II*

III. REBELLIOUS BEHAVIOR ☐ *III*

IV. UNTRUSTWORTHY BEHAVIOR ☐ *IV*

V. WITHDRAWAL ☐ *V*

VI. STEREOTYPED BEHAVIOR AND ODD MANNERISMS ☐ *VI*

VII. INAPPROPRIATE INTERPERSONAL MANNERS ☐ *VII*

VIII. UNACCEPTABLE VOCAL HABITS ☐ *VIII*

IX. UNACCEPTABLE OR ECCENTRIC HABITS ☐ *IX*

X. SELF-ABUSIVE BEHAVIOR ☐ *X*

XI. HYPERACTIVE TENDENCIES ☐ *XI*

XII. SEXUALLY ABERRANT BEHAVIOR ☐ *XII*

XIII. PSYCHOLOGICAL DISTURBANCES ☐ *XIII*

XIV. USE OF MEDICATIONS ☐ *XIV*

FIG. 4-7.

learn slowly so that repeated demonstrations are needed and sometimes patterning (actual movement of the body parts) aids the success of the movement. 3. The games should have simple structures such as circles, lines, and stations with challenges that give him success. 4. Often using stationary objects will present more success for the child. 5. Small group activities or a 1 to 1 ratio for specific motor skills learning are often useful. 6. Individual differences are always important for motor activities and many games can be used for differences in abilities. 7. Verbal directions should be kept at a minimum, and visual and auditory stimuli used with demonstrations. 8. Reinforcement should be given frequently for their strengths. 9. The play environment should always be safe and realistic progressions in skill development followed. 10. Many activities should be available as the attention span of the child is short. 11. All motor skill activities should be presented for recreational and social benefits as well as for improved neuromuscular efficiency. 12. Often individual success is more important than team success so both types of activities should be presented. 13. Be very patient but persistent in getting success in motor learning for carry-over values—at home and community environments.

The Causes of Mental Retardation

There are many etiological factors of mental retardation. We shall discuss some of the more common syndromes. It is estimated that of the 200,000 babies born each year, every five minutes one is born who is mentally retarded. The best generalization as to the prevalence rate tells us that 2 to 3 per cent of school children are mentally retarded. The incidence of mental retardation seems to be higher during the early school years, among children of six to eight years of age. The identification is determined by the sub-average intellectual functioning and the adaptive behavior. What causes this?

The genetic factors; the physical environmental factors such as the prenatal, perinatal, and postnatal; and the psychological environmental factors will be explored.

Genetic Causes

Recent discoveries in genetics and biochemistry have delineated some of the genetic causes of mental retardation formerly classified as unknown. A defect in some gene which controls a certain enzyme necessary for the normal function of a body tissue underlines the significance of biochemistry and genetics in mental deficiency. The great steps in research in genetics this past decade have improved our understanding of the ways the genes direct and control many of the processes of human growth and development. The complex biochemical processes determine how the genes form proteins, which act as enzymes, the basic substances that direct and control most of the chemical reactions that occur in the living cell. The process of genetic control involves the following: 1. each of the thousands of genes distributed unevenly among the forty-six chromosomes is responsible for producing one of the thousands of enzymes; 2. each enzyme is responsible for the rate at which one of the hundreds of different chemical processes take place within the cells; and 3. the living cell is the basic unit of life because it is within the cell that all life processes occur. Recent advances in research establish a genetic code even though genes are too small to be seen through the electronic microscope.

Genetic factors may influence behavior and are sometimes responsible for biological conditions which damage the proper functioning of the central nervous system. Sometimes disorders such as hereditary deafness and blindness may cause intellectual retardation because there is interference with the person's ability to function fully. The degree of the handicap may depend on the technical and medical care available to the child. Hereditary factors also may determine intellectual behavior through the mechanism of social typings. Intellectual opportunities in most cultures are influenced by heredity and environment. The recent advances for the Negroes in the United States can be related to social influences and educational opportunities. Striving for achievement with active and passive modes of adjustment should help to develop higher intelligence, so the more indirect the hereditary influences the greater the opportunities for interaction with other hereditary and environmental factors.

Phenylketonuria (PKU) is a genetic disorder in which the central nervous system is damaged by the improper metabolism of amino acids after birth, when the infant must function without the mother's metabolic, excretory, or hormonal systems. Phenylketonuria accounts for 1 per cent of older patients in institutions and for 1 case for 1,000 live births with 1 in 700 mentally retarded.Its identification and treatment were dramatic breakthroughs in modern genetics and medicine, which have more ways to prevent severe damage. There is breakdown in the metabolic transformation of the protein substance phenylalanine, which is present in most foods. With this breakdown, phenylpyruvic acid collects in the blood and prevents the brain from developing through demyelinization. Fölling (44A) of Norway discovered the phenylpyruvic acid in the musty, odorous urine of two young brothers and identified its recessive mode of transmission. It is estimated that when each parent has this recessive gene, one out of four children may have PKU. The physical characteristics of the PKU infant are a small head (microcephally), usually blonde with blue eyes and with a strong musty smell. The child with such a condition shows a normal appearance the first three months after birth; then, listlessness appears and motor skills such as sitting and rolling may not develop. Without treatment severe mental retardation develops. The treated infant has a good prognosis of a normal or a near normal life. The older child who is retarded due to PKU often becomes more manageable when diet control is followed. The diagnosis involves the Gutherie test at birth, in which the heel is pricked and the blood checked, and often the fluorometric tests and urinanalysis taken to determine the phenylalanine percentage. With 6 per cent phenylalanine present, dietary treatment is started with special *"Lo fenlac formula"* as a substitute for meat and milk. This is continued until the child is six years of age. The metabolic deficiency may not disappear but its effects are not harmful to the nervous system and the emotional development of the child. Most all the states in the United States provide a screening program for all newborn infants so that those with PKU can be given treatment. Carriers and the maternal PKU can also be identified by tests that check a phenylalanine of 6 per cent.

GALACTOSEMIA

A child suffering from galactosemia will be retarded only if he is fed milk since his hereditary defect is the inability to metabolize the galactose contained in milk due to the absence of the enzyme needed for the conversion. The genetic factor causes damage when combined with a particular environmental factor. This is an inherited recessive gene. At birth the infant is in good condition, but after a milk diet he soon shows jaundice, vomiting, cataracts, symptoms of feeding problems, and malnutrition. Early removal of milk from the diet results in disappearance of the symptoms. However, a large variability in clinical symptoms may show as minor manifestation to severe mental retardation from this inability to metabolize carbohydrates. Early treatment consists of a soybean milk to replace regular milk. Late treatment cannot rectify the damage to the central nervous system and ocular system. The child is severely retarded, may lose his eyesight, and has the motor learning problems of the mentally retarded.

CHROMOSOMAL ABNORMALITIES

Normal human cells, except the ova and sperm, contain 46 chromosomes in their nuclei. However, errors have occurred during cell division and if this happens the cell nuclei will end up with more or less than their normal 46 chromosomes. All chromosomes are necessary for life. Most chromosomal aberrations identified in man occur as a trisomy (triplet) of the chromosome #21, with Down's syndrome or mongolism evident or as an abnormal combination of sex chromosomes. Figure 4-8 and Figure 4-9 from Smith and Wilson, *The Child with Down's Syndrome* (153) show the cell division with normal chromosome distribution and the abnormal trisomy 21, the most common Down's syndrome aberration. The symptoms of Down's syndrome are usually clear-cut. The normal child receives 46 chromosomes from his parents. Each chromosome is made of thousands of genes. This genetic material is critical for growth and development, and the genes program the code the body uses to develop and function. An altered gene may program the wrong code, producing an alteration in development. In trisomy 21, Down's syndrome (Fig. 4-10), because there are three sets of number 21 genes in the child and not the usual two, the genetic balance is upset so alterations in development are produced. A mistake in chromosome distribution

NORMAL DEVELOPMENT

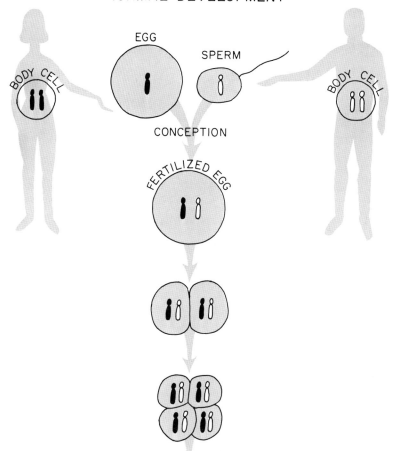

DEVELOPMENT TOWARD A NORMAL BABY

FIG. 4-8. (From Smith, D. W., and Wilson, A. A.: *The Child with Down's Syndrome* [*Mongolism*]. Philadelphia, W. B. Saunders Co., 1973, p. 8.)

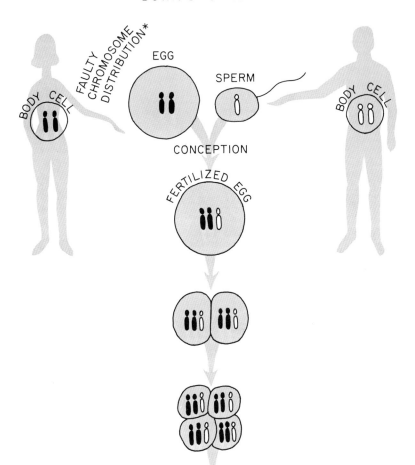

DEVELOPMENT TOWARD A BABY WITH DOWN'S SYNDROME

FIG. 4-9.   (From Smith, D. W., and Wilson, A. A.: *The Child with Down's Syndrome [Mongolism]*. Philadelphia, W. B. Saunders Co., 1973, p. 9.)

FIG. 4-10. A child with Down's syndrome develops when faulty chromosome number 21 distribution occurs. (From Cleveland Riding Center for Handicapped, Sarah Kinzie, *Pegasus*, Novelty, Ohio.)

occurs in the early cell division and may show up in the development of the egg or the sperm or in the first cell division of the fertilized egg.

From 10 to 20 per cent of moderately and severely retarded children are mongoloid. Their birth rate is 1 in 600 to 900 live births. Having a child with Down's syndrome varies with the age of the mother. The cultural level of the family does not affect the frequency of pathological conditions such as Down's syndrome. The Mikkelsen study (120B) indicates how the age of the mother relates to the Down's syndrome.

Mother under age 30	30 to 34	35 to 39	40 to 44	over 45
Incidence 1–1500 of births	1 to 750	1 to 280	1 to 130	1 to 65

Now with the physician's technique of amniocentesis the Down's syndrome can be detected prenatally. The symptoms indicate that in facial and body structure mongoloid children resemble each other.

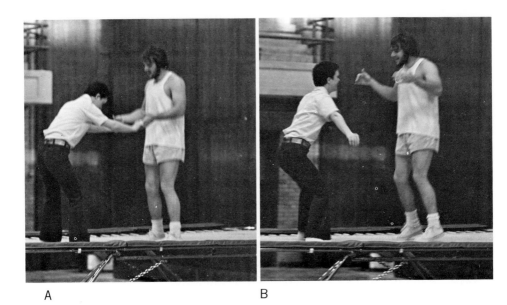

A   B

FIGS. 4-11A, B. These illustrations show a child with Down's syndrome with his physical education instructor.

Some symptoms which occur are listed but all are rarely found in a given child.

1. Intellectual impairment which is usually severe or moderate.
2. The skull is flattened and shorter than it is wide, there are underdevelopment of the nasal bones with a flat bridge, small egg-shaped eye sockets, with the eyes slanting in appearance, and small chin and ears that may look distorted.

It has been stated that most mongoloid children develop to the mental age of four or five years and their life span may be late teens. With recent advances in medical and educational programs the child with Down's syndrome has a good chance for a long life with personal and vocational worth. Motor skills are most important for helping the child to develop. Individual activities are more popular with the child but group activities also should be included for his peer relations and socialization.

ABERRATIONS IN SEX CHROMOSOMES

Clinical examination of the individual will determine the presence or absence of the Y chromosome. Regardless of the number of X chromosomes the individual with the Y chromosome will be a male. Without the Y chromosome the individual will be female. Some aberrations in the sex constitution have been clinically identified. Some males are found with XXY combinations instead of the normal XY, and some females are found with XO,XXX rather than the normal XX.

Turner's syndrome (gonadal dysgenesis) occurs in females and is discovered when menstruation or secondary sex characteristics do not develop at puberty. (Learning problems may be evident and around 20 per cent of the children are mentally retarded.) About 80 per cent of the persons with Turner's syndrome have one X chromosome. The symptoms frequently include small stature, webbed neck, bowleggedness, sometimes coarctation of the aorta (a congenital condition), sexual infantilism, low posterior hair line, and broad chest.

Klinefelter's syndrome seems to be the most frequent sex-chromosome aberration. It occurs exclusively in males. Mild mental retardation may be the only clinical manifestation during childhood. Klinefelter's syndrome accounts for around 1 per cent of institutionalized male defectives. At puberty, boys begin to develop feminine breasts. Their beards and pubic hair are sparse, their testes and penis are small with hyalinized tubules which render them sterile. The chromosome pattern in "true" Klinefelter's syndrome includes an extra X chromosome (XXY). Sometimes rare cases are reported as XXXY accompanying Down's syndrome. The degree of mental retardation increases with the number of additional X chromosomes. Ferguson-Smith (41A) states that mothers of boys with true Klinefelter's syndrome tend to be older than most mothers but younger than mothers of mongoloids, indicating nondisjunction during meiosis (cell division of ova and sperm) possibly caused by the aging process of the mother. Meiosis determines the precise genetic inheritance for the next generation. The incidence of Klinefelter's syndrome is 1 to 500 births and it has been estimated that 15 per cent of those with the syndrome are mentally retarded.

Prenatal Causes of Mental Retardation

Some of the prenatal causes of mental retardation may be nutritional, psychological, or due to the physical environment. Others are more specific and we shall cover some of the more frequent ones. Research indicates that a number of viruses which produce either no clinical condition in the mother or only mild symptoms can harm the fetus.

RUBELLA

Rubella (German measles) has been given much attention since the early 1940's when Gregg (57A) discovered that children of mothers with this disease were often born with congenital cataracts. Infection of the mother during the first trimester (one to three months) of pregnancy increases the possibility of a variety of abnormalities. Studies indicate a sharp gradient in the time of susceptibility. Michaels and Mellin (120A) found that 47 per cent of infants born to mothers infected in the first month of pregnancy were abnormal, 22 per cent when the infection occurred in the second month, and 7 per cent in the third month. Fraser (45A) feels that when the mother has had rubella during first trimester, 17 to 24 per cent of the children are defective. The defects include cataracts, deafness, heart disease, microcephaly and mental retardation. The rubella virus has been isolated and a vaccine developed. This medical advance should decrease or eliminate rubella as a cause of mental retardation.

SYPHILIS

In the past, syphilis was a cause of mental deficiency but medical advances in its treatment and compulsory blood tests in pregnant women in prenatal clinics have reduced its incidence. Congenital syphilis, with the transmission of the disease from the mother to the child, exists in half of the children infected. It involves a central nervous system impairment resulting in mental retardation. Untreated syphilis results in paresis, in which symptoms are delayed and boys between the age of eight and ten and girls between the age of ten and twelve develop neurological and speech disturbances with a variety of psychotic manifestations. Progressive intellectual deterioration seems to be the principal disability.

THE RH FACTOR

Maternal sensitization occurs when the mother is allergic to biochemical substances in her fetus, and the antigens produced by her body to combat the foreign substances may harm the fetus. The Rh factor in the blood is one well-known reaction of maternal sensitization. It occurs in about 5 per cent of Rh negative mothers. When the blood of the rhesus monkey is injected into live rabbits, a serum is produced that will cause a reaction in the blood of approximately 86 per cent of the white population. This is called the Rh factor and these persons are Rh positive. Those in whom the reaction does not occur are Rh negative. This reaction is inherited and the genes producing the Rh factor are dominant. The mother with Rh negative blood may have an Rh positive fetus because this dominant gene comes from the father. Difficulties develop when the red blood cells from the Rh positive fetus escape into the mother's Rh negative blood. To combat this antigen, the mother produces an antibody which can be absorbed through the placenta, into the bloodstream of the fetus, and cause destruction of the fetal red blood cells so that oxygen deprivation occurs in the fetus. When the mother has developed these antibodies in a previous pregnancy, the dangers are greater. The blood systems of the mother and the fetus are separate and the escape of the Rh particles is unusual. The firstborn child is less likely to be affected than subsequent children. If the fetus inherits an Rh factor incompatible with that of the mother he may be mentally retarded so that this possibility should be medically checked.

The Rh incompatibility may cause abortion or death of the fetus. Erythroblastosis fetalis, a condition with permanent brain damage and paralysis, may result. Other blood-group incompatibilities may cause erythroblastosis but the greatest incidence occurs with the Rh factor.

Jaundice occurs in the newborn due to the presence in the bloodstream of bilirubin, which is deposited in the body and brain. A condition known as kernicterus develops with vomiting, diarrhea, respiratory difficulties, and rigidity. When it is left untreated, brain damage, mental retardation, speech difficulties, deafness, and sometimes cerebral palsy develop when the bilirubin level is 20 to 25 milligrams per 100 cubic centimeters of blood. Now, medical advances such as complete blood transfusions during the first day or two of life have been successful so that most children recover completely. Anoxia is insufficiency of oxygen to the fetus which results in cell death and severe damage to the brain. Vaginal bleeding, heart disorders, and other factors may cause this condition.

Perinatal Causes

Perinatal refers to the period during birth or immediately preceding birth. Birth injuries, asphyxia, and prematurity may be included among problems occurring during this time.

The diagnosis of brain injury in children is made retrospectively. When labor is prolonged or difficult, when forceps are used in delivery, if there is a breech presentation, or if other mechanical difficulties occur, a general diagnosis of brain injury may be made.

Asphyxia (caused by lack of oxygen to the brain at birth) may cause mental retardation from a condition called "cerebral anoxia." When the oxygen supply to the brain is blocked more than a few minutes, damage to the brain cells results with the impairment of intellectual functioning and adaptive behavior.

PREMATURITY

Various studies indicate that there is a relationship between prematurity and mental retardation. The Alm study (2A) shows more children born prematurely were mentally retarded, had cerebral palsy, or were epileptic than children of normal birth. The incidence of prematurity seems to be greater in the lower socioeconomic areas. Wortis (192A) reported that in New York the rate of premature births was 9.4 per 100 births and 16 per 100 in the poorer districts. He also reported that in the Soviet Union, the city of Kiev had an incidence of prematurity of 4.7 per 100 births. The usual criterion for prematurity has come to be a birth weight of less than 2,500 grams, or 5.5 pounds. Robinson and Robinson (144) feel that prematurity itself is not a cause of mental retardation or personality disorders since the research does not trace the interrelationship of many other variables.

Postnatal Causes

Head injuries, brain tumors, toxins, epilepsy, and infectious conditions may account for some of the cases of mental retardation when they have an effect on the central nervous system. The earlier the postnatal brain damage occurs, the more severe the results, but generally the consequences are relatively mild.

Encephalitis or sleeping sickness is an inflammation of the central nervous system caused by one of several viruses. It refers to a variety of disorders which occur in early childhood. "Encephalitis lethargica" occurs sometimes in epidemics. It may be fatal and may sometimes result in mental retardation. Sometimes, it develops after other illnesses such as measles, scarlet fever, chicken pox, whooping cough, meningitis, or pneumonia.

The chronic type of encephalitis is important, since permanent patterns of psychological disturbances may follow the disease. Sometimes the disturbances may be delayed by as many as nine years. Greenbaum and Lurie (57A) report that of 78 children who had encephalitis, some had delayed behavioral changes.

Meningitis, inflammation of the meninges, the protective covering of the brain, seems to be a childhood disease. Cerebrospinal meningitis, caused by the meningococcus bacteria, has a high survival rate but a consequential problem of mental retardation. With retardation, residual symptoms such as deafness, paralysis, and epilepsy may be present. Now, as a treatment, antibiotics help keep many children alive, but sometimes with significant impairments.

Toxins or poisons such as lead, arsenic, carbon monoxide, and others can produce severe inflammations of the brain. These occurrences are rare but very dangerous. Kanner (80A) reported 199 cases of children under 5 years of age with lead poisoning. He stated that only one patient developed into a normal, well-adjusted person. Thus, the dangers of toxins cannot be understated.

Some congenital anomalies of the skull and brain are associated with severe mental retardation. Microcephaly, small skull, is a common anomaly. The size of the head is out of proportion with the rest of the body, and the child may appear monkey-like. The causative gene is recessive. Most children with microcephaly are severely retarded, with no speech development. They require feeding and toilet care.

HYDROCEPHALY

Hydrocephaly, a skull malformation, occurs due to an increased volume of cerebrospinal fluid within the ventricular and subarachnoid spaces. Its incidence is 1 to 3 per 1,000 births and it is known to be related to maternal age, but its cause has not been found. Hydrocephaly may result from prenatal factors, birth trauma, or postnatal injury, tumors, or infection. Communicating hydrocephalus implies free communication between ventricles and the spinal theca or sheath and obstructive hydrocephalus, a block to the passage of fluid. Internal hydrocephalus and external hydrocephalus indicate the site of the greatest enlargement of cerebrospinal spaces, whether ventricular or subarachnoid. Sometimes the cranium has a globular shape, the eyes become widespread, and the bridge of the nose is flattened. Other disorders such as visual impairment, epilepsy, and spastic paralysis of the lower limbs may accompany this condition. Symptoms vary widely and some of the children affected may have mild intellectual handicaps. The defect is sometimes operable, for example, by the Arnold Cury shunt and other techniques before permanent intellectual damage occurs.

Another disorder resulting in mental retardation is cerebral palsy. It is a common syndrome. Most investigators report that 50 per cent of those affected have an IQ below 70, about 25 per cent have an IQ between 70 and 90, and the remainder attain the normal range. Mental retardation seems to appear when the dominant cerebral hemisphere (usually, the left) is injured. Nationally, the population of cerebral palsy is staggering and it is estimated ten thousand new babies are born with it every year.

Psychological Environmental Factors

The psychological factors leading to mental retardation present evidence that is speculative, difficult to interpret, and controversial. The retardation may follow a psychosis or disorder when there is no evidence of cerebral pathology. Adverse environmental conditions may affect the intellectual functioning of the child when he manifests no significant organic disease or pathology.

The psychosocial disadvantage usually is related to some subnormal intellectual functioning in at least one of the parents. The environments may be impoverished but no single entity contributes to the slow or retarded development. Sensory deprivation includes atypical parental-child interactions such as maternal deprivation or severe environmental restrictions.

The cultural heritage and the genetic heritage are both indispensable to human existence. The language the child hears and the clothing he wears influence the standards and values he absorbs. His goals for work, expressions of anger, love, and fear are determined to a large extent by the culture to which he is exposed. His subculture in society consists of his social class, his school, his father's occupation, and the neighborhood membership he occupies along with the psychological climate in his home.

Three reflexive behaviors help us to cognize: 1. the defensive or avoidance for protection, such as touching a hot stove; 2. the adaptive, which involves eye-blink and the functioning of organs; and 3. the orienting reflex, which includes knowledge of the environment and adaptations and adjustments for coping. What factors of the psychosocial environmental areas cause mental retardation? Many sources state that children from the low socioeconomic class score lower on the intelligence tests than children from the so-called higher class. It is known that "mothering," warm, maternal care of infants, is basic to normal development. Indifferent maternal care may include sensory deprivation, with resulting retardation from the effects of minimal stimulation. Rejection of the unwanted or disliked child may set up tension and conflict that does not permit maximal intellectual growth. Family size, with its intricate relationships, is thought to correlate sometimes with intelligence. We speak of "sensory inundation," which may occur in small living areas and in which the child "tunes out" to adjust to the environment and to reduce anxiety. Research suggests that anxiety interferes with a high level of cognitive behavior. Cratty (27) tells of a study in which children exerted 50 per cent of maximum pressure on a hand grip preceding memorizing word lists and verbal cognitive skills. In some cases, the muscular tension levels were increased. The study showed better performance by the persons when the tension level was not changed. Does anxiety contribute to subnormal intellectual functioning? Can it be decreased? In a study of children six to ten years of age, McClelland and co-workers (118A) found that the active, striving children have an increase in the IQ scores compared with the IQ scores of the passive and fearful children. Skeels and Dye (151A) studied 13 children taken from an orphanage and placed in an institution for mental retardates. These children were less than three years of age, and their range of IQ's was 35 to 89, average IQ, 64. The children were placed with older patients for daily care. One and one-half years later, these children were given the Kuhlman Test of Mental Development and showed an increase of 27.5 points on the test. A group of orphanage children in a nonstimulating environment were given the same test; they showed a drop in scores of 26.2 points. This points out that a stimulating, warm environment may contribute to intellectual functioning. What does an individual need to function normally? He needs mobility, grouping, and the cognitive skills of reading, writing, and arithmetic. He needs goals of 1. self-realization, 2. good human relationships, 3. economic efficiency, and 4. civic responsibility. The psychological environmental factors should contribute to develop and improve his intellectual functioning and so-called normal behavior.

In addition to the causes of mental retardation already discussed, the authors should like to include the classification system of the American Association of Mental Deficiency:

1. Infections and intoxications.
2. Trauma or physical agents.
3. Metabolism or nutrition.
4. Gross brain disease (postnatal).
5. Prenatal influence.
6. Chromosomal abnormality.
7. Gestational disorders.
8. Psychiatric disorders.
9. Environmental influences.
10. Other conditions.

Each of these ten etiological categories may be linked with any of the following supplementary conditions:

1. Genetic component
2. Secondary cranial anomaly.
3. Impairment of special senses.
4. Disorders of perception and expression.
5. Convulsive disorders.
6. Psychiatric impairment.
7. Motor dysfunction.

Further, we will have a behavioral classification based on measured intelligence (IQ) and adaptive behavior (Grossman, 57B). According to Leland the past-used cause of "cultural-familial" implied an undemonstrated genetic tie so this category now relates to deprivation, malnutrition, improper disease control, and poor environmental support. Behavioral and learning deficits growing out of poor environmental relationships show individuals who cannot cope appropriately within their own subgroup or among their peers.

Activities of motor learning for the mentally retarded will be discussed later.

Part II: Learning Disabilities

Background and Definition

According to Samuel A. Kirk (88), the National Advisory Committee on Handicapped Children of the U.S. Office of Education proposed a definition of learning disability which was used in the congressional bill entitled The Learning Disabilities Act of 1969. It states: "Children, with special (specific) learning disabilities exhibit a disorder in one or more of the basic psychological processes involved in understanding or in using spoken or written language. These may be manifested in disorders of listening, thinking, talking, reading, writing, spelling, or arithmetic. They include learning conditions which have been referred to as perceptual handicaps, brain injury, minimal brain dysfunction, dyslexia, developmental aphasia, etc. They do not include learning problems which are due primarily to visual, hearing, or motor handicaps, to mental retardation, emotional disturbance, or to environmental disadvantage."

The term learning disabilities is confusing to some persons but the preceding definition relates to specific developmental problems. Other definitions vary somewhat from this one, but the common areas of agreement among authors are as follows:

1. The learning problem should be specific and not a correlation of such other primary handicapping conditions as general mental retardation, sensory handicaps, emotional disturbance, and environmental disadvantage.
2. The children must have discrepancies in their own growth (intraindividual differences) with abilities as well as disabilities.
3. The deficits found in a child must be of a behavioral nature such as thinking, conceptualization, memory, speech, language, perception, reading, writing, spelling, arithmetic, and related abilities.
4. The primary focus of identification should be psychoeducational.

Many children with learning disabilities who are excluded by the definition as stated in the Learning Disabilities Act often are included in this program but if they are mentally retarded and have a specific problem they are generally not included. The mentally retarded do have special programs. The learning disability programs are designed to be remedial. Their goal is to return the child to the regular class environment.

Children with learning disorders do manifest some common characteristics, but they also display many disparate problems. For meaningful learning, their instructional program needs to be individualized, especially in motor skill experiences. The common characteristics are as follows: 1. they must have average or above average intelligence; 2. they must have adequate sensory acuity; and, 3. they should be achieving considerably less than the composite of their IQ, their age, and their educational opportunity would predict. Some of the other characteristics sometimes found in these children may contradict the ones just mentioned. 1. *Hyperactivity.* The child with this brain insult may be described as restless, fidgety, unable to sit still, and unable to concentrate on a task. It is theorized that he cannot screen out those stimuli that do not contribute to the task at hand. 2. *Hypoactivity.* This is the opposite of hyperactivity. The child seems to have an earthboundness. This characteristic is less common than the first one but it is found often enough to mention. 3. *Dissociation.* This involves the inability to see or to complete a task as a whole. The child can do isolated skills but cannot develop meaningful patterns. Modifying skills and forming new patterns are difficult for him. 4. *Lack of motivation and inattention.* 5. *Overattention.* This disorder sometimes is called attention fixation and may relate to figure-ground problems, in which a significant element cannot be detected from the background due to extraneous sensory stimuli. 6. *Perseveration.* The child may repeat persistently, in any behavior area, but usually in writing or in an oral response. 7. *Perceptual disorders.* These are usually problems of visual, auditory, tactual, or kinesthetic perception. Sensory acuity may be normal, but the possibility of a perception disorder should be considered. 8. *Lack of coordination.* The child with a learning disability may exhibit clumsiness or show his inability to position his body in space, to maintain his balance, or both. A well-coordinated child may have learning problems with other characteristics. 9. *Memory disorders.* These disorders may be visual or auditory, such as forgetting on which side of the room the window is or the inability to repeat a sequence of three words. These problems seriously affect learning. 10. *Equivocal neurological signs and electroencephalographic irregularities.* These characteristics are determined by special laboratory tests. The preceding characteristics are sometimes called the Strauss Syndrome.

The psychoeducational identification of the child with a learning disability should include a medical evaluation, and an assessment of his academic history, a psychological evaluation, and an evaluation of his abilities in reading, mathematics, spelling, and writing.

Education Procedures, An Overview

Some special educators feel that *Dr. Alfred Strauss* and his co-workers at Cove Schools clearly identified the behavior associated today with children with learning disabilities. In 1947, Strauss and Lehtinen (177A) wrote about the child with a pathology of perception, pathology of language, pathology of concept formation, and pathology of behavior. Then they related these behaviors to the problems of education. Strauss' work with brain-injured adults in neuropathy studies convinced him that brain damage during the perinatal period caused small diffuse hemorrhages scattered throughout the brain and that their effect was a disturbance of the total brain function, with expressed behavioral and learning problems, not specific neurological signs. He differentiated the neurotic child with symptoms such as telling lies, nail biting and manifesting anxieties from the typical child with brain injury. Great attention was paid to the characteristic distractibility of these children. His approach included knowledge of the normal child's development since some of these symptoms may occur in the normal young child. He felt that sensitive observation of each child's performances could give analysis of his failures for use in appropriate procedures to improve his performance or to direct creative guides to learning. The criteria Strauss followed to identify the "brain-injured" child included: a. the medical history, b. the presence of slight neurological signs, c. the family history if the psychological disturbance is severe, and d. the use of qualitative tests to determine perceptual and conceptual disturbances. His educational measures were attempts to overcome specific obstreperous symptoms by the following: 1. remove extraneous sights and sounds to eliminate distractibility; 2. paint lower windows; 3. put desks to the wall to remove visual stimuli; 4. use screens to help the child become tractable; 5. use small portions of a printed page; 6. direct learning with dark to outline the figure area of materials or color clues to attract attention; 7. avoid commercial instruction materials as they are too detailed and complex; 8. have each child assist the teacher in the construction of materials; 9. use repetition through varying experiences for insight and analysis (drill was contraindicated because of perseveration); 10. teach rhythm and manual training; 11. have speech training taught by a specialist; 12. place child in a sheltered environment, as interims for remedial or therapeutic help them return to the regular classroom; and 13. channel motor activity to reduce disinhibition and distractibility. Strauss emphasized motor activity but through the work of Kephart and Barsch, the values of motor activity were greatly enhanced and more fully appreciated. Strauss developed the first innovative work on the subject of educating brain-injured children, now part of a group of children with learning disabilities. According to Leland and Smith (102), a child with the Strauss Syndrome needs psychological counseling to explain and understand his problems, and the parents and teachers need counseling to work out the difficult aspects of the child's behavior to help him develop control as he grows older. They feel psychotherapy should be used when his relationship with his peers prevent his interacting with them; it should be a type of therapy that will provide interactions from which he can learn.

Raymond Barsch (4A) is director of Teacher Preparation Program for Teachers of The Physically Handicapped and Neurologically Impaired at the University of Wisconsin. His theory of movement states that perceptual motor training is effective as shown by clinical observation and by subjectively observed improvement in the child's performance.

Barsch tells us that a curriculum for children with learning disabilities should have one objective, to "correct whatever impediments stand in the way so the child can take full advantage of the offerings in the regular curriculum." The child is a sensory-perceptual-motor organism and needs a variety of experiences for success. When the usual curriculum fails the unusual curriculum is required.

Movigenics (Latin *movere*, meaning to move, and *genesis*, meaning origin and development) is the study of the origin and development of movement patterns leading to learning efficiency. The movigenics theory is the basis of Barsch's physiologic curriculum. It consists of ten constructs. 1. Movement efficiency is the principle underlying the design of the human organism. 2. The primary objective of movement efficiency is to promote the survival of the organism economically. 3. Movement efficiency is derived from the ability to survive in an energy surround. Radiant, mechanical, and thermal energies are constant companions throughout life. Survival depends upon the person's ability to move through time and space. 4. The percepto-cognitive system of the man develops energy forms of information. The six senses are the channels for obtaining data which are passed to the brain. Barsch's view states that man has a "cognition sequence" with four stages of activity. 1. The receiving surface of any modal channel is energized. 2. Perception converts this channel into meaning. 3. Perceptual meanings are transformed to symbols for further processing and storage. 4. The concepts using the symbols in stage 3 are developed. These sequences are in constant use when the person learns well. 5. The terrain of movement is space. In order to adapt to daily demands each person must organize a visual space volume, an auditory space volume, a tactual space volume, and a kinesthetic space volume. Failure to organize each spatial volume reduces survival efficiency. 6. Developmental momentum is a constant forward thrust toward maturity and demands equilibrium to maintain direction. This developmental momentum goes on to middle life (50 years more or less), and then a slow descent may take place. 7. Movement efficiency is developed in a climate of stress. There are necessary stress and adverse stress; coordination is developed by each individual as he moves to the gravity pull and energy surround. Adverse stress in an educational setting might be improper lighting, unclear print and other such factors. The less efficient the performer, the more the adverse stress. 8. The adequacy of the feedback system is necessary for movement efficiency. Developmental disorders result if the feedback is short-circuited. 9. Movement efficiency occurs in segments of sequential expansion. From the simple to the complex movement efficiency develops. 10. Language is a visual-spatial phenomenon, that is, one's space world leads to communication. Statements such as "the way I see it" or "my point of view is" express the speaker's perception. The space world gives language fluency from one's totality of experiences.

Barsch agreed with Strauss about the environment of the classroom. He too removed extraneous stimuli by removing desks, blackening windows, painting lines on the floor for the positioning of the child, carpeting an area for crawling and rolling, placing "alignment targets" on vertical and horizontal surfaces, and having children participate in stockings or in bare feet. His program was flexible and carefully planned so as to help the children get a variation in learning. Visual information, auditory information, the tachistoscope, walking and balancing rails, tracing templates, scooter and teeter boards, plastic balls (all sizes), a metronome, Cuisenaire rods, a geometric symbol system for reading a stereoscope, and a tape recorder were a regular part of the program.

CURRICULUM GUIDELINES

1. The teacher records the child's movement patterns as efficient/inefficient, not as success or failure.
2. The teacher estimates the degree of the child's ability as a result of learning. Focus on the six channels such as visual, tactual, kinesthetic, auditory, olfactory, and gestatory, as well as reading and spelling.
3. The teacher should provide exploration of the balance of muscular relationships and body relationship in time and space.
4. All six perceptual modes need exercise in the school framework.
5. Explore and process information from sources in near, mid, and far space.
6. After the child has learned a task, provide a variety of settings and contexts in which to perform it with slowness, fastness, forward, and backward.
7. Each learner must develop his movement efficiency and discover his limitations.
8. Plan movement to achieve goals so that movement is cognitively-directed.

9. Performance is spatially-oriented and should be spatially-defined.
10. The space orientation approach can be integrated with activities.

The intersensory approach gives the children exposure to all curricular activities and their level of performance is noted. Progress is measured by their improvement. Barsch's technique was to develop orientation to learning, including degrees of freedom as bilaterality, flexibility, rhythm, and motor planning.

Dr. Newell C. Kephart (86) was director of the Glen Haven Achievement Center at Fort Collins, Colorado. He was a professor of psychology at Purdue University and established The Perceptual Achievement Center for Children in La Fayette, Indiana. Also, with Dr. Eugene G. Roach of the Indiana University Medical Center, he wrote *The Purdue Perceptual-Motor Survey,* a direct-action approach to non-achiever problems. In his book *The Slow Learner in the Classroom,* Kephart identifies and attempts to solve the problems of children with inept classroom performance. His thesis is that a child's readiness for the learning experience required in the school situation is the result of a long series of gross motor experiences which the physically normal child will naturally acquire in the process of antogenesis.

Kephart believes in motor activity. Movement is the basis of learning. School problems are symptoms of a lack of early integration of perceptual skills which are learned through visual, motor, speech, and language skills. The Kephart curriculum stresses the effects of movement on perception and the effects of perception on the higher thought processes. The motor bases that Kephart believes effect efficient higher thought processes through motor generalizations are as follows: 1. Posture and the maintenance of balance, through which the child learns to resist the force of gravity in order to right himself, then to play one set of muscles against an antagonistic set of muscles in order to maintain balance and move in a controlled, purposeful manner. 2. Laterality is the awareness of left and right within one's own body; it is also differentiating between one's left side and one's right side. Kephart believes that laterality permits the child to recognize the difference between symbols such as b and d. 2. (a) Directionality is the awareness of left, right, front, back, up, and down in the world around you. This awareness stems from the internal sense of direction developed earlier, laterality. 2. (b) Body image includes the child's identification of body parts, the relationship of these parts to each other and to other objects in space. 2. (c) Locomotion, in which the child generalizes his patterns of walking so as to adapt to rough surfaces, intervening objects, and restraining clothes. 3. Contact includes the experience of reaching, grasping, and other skills to develop patterns for new generalizations. 4. Receipt and propulsion, the fourth motor generalization, refers to activities the child interacts with such as catching, throwing, pushing, or batting. These are elaborations of an integrated body schema and they are dependent upon an awareness of self. Kephart emphasizes that these motor generalizations develop space and time perception. Perceptual-motor match is developed through a feedback system in which the child receives information from his own output, monitoring the accuracy or inaccuracy of his own perceptions and actions.

Perceptual-motor training includes the use of (1) the walking board, (2) the balance board, (3) the trampoline, (4) the angels-in-the-snow, (5) a variety of stunts and games, and (6) certain rhythm activities. The perceptual-motor match training uses (1) gross motor activities, (2) fine motor activities, (3) visualization, and (4) auditory motor match. Multisensory stimulation is used to get the child to respond to numerous data, such as tactual and kinesthetic, to develop and promote problem-solving learning.

Kephart uses training for ocular control through visual fixation, chalkboard techniques, and games and sports. Then he works on form perception through matching, symbol recognition, figure-ground relationships, cutting and pasting, and scanning activities. He prefers to test children in their basic skills and to use their natural order of development.

The Purdue Perceptual-Motor Survey

The object of this survey is to assess qualitatively the perceptual-motor abilities of children in the early grades, to detect their errors in perceptual development, and to set up the needed areas for remediation. It is not a diagnostic instrument but should be used to observe the child's behavior. The survey form shows the range of scoring to be from four to one. Four indicates a prompt and decisive performance duplicating the movements of the examiner, three indicates some deviating in the performance, two points out a hesitancy or lack of certainty, and one shows more than one error in the movement behavior.

This survey has 22 scorable items with 11 subtests. Each item of the survey identifies a perceptual-motor development. The *walking board* is used to measure dynamic balance and postural flexibility. Does the child use both sides appropriately? The *jumping* points out children with problems in laterality, body image, rhythm, and neuromuscular control. The *identification of the body parts* denotes space localization. Piaget

(135A) says spatial development is a basic necessity for an adequate body image. The *imitation of movement* with semiphore movements measures neuromuscular control and the translation of visual clues for motor learning. Parallel movements show that the child has a sophisticated spacial awareness and mirroring may indicate weak sense of laterality. The *obstacle course* tells the examiner how the child reacts to objects in his environment. Clumsiness—is it a spacial error or a problem in motor control? The *chalkboard* requires precise matching and can detect confusion in laterality, directionality, and a midline deficiency. The *angels-in-the-snow* tasks show problems of neuromuscular differentiation and specific problems of right- and left-sidedness. The examiner checks for overflow movements, bilateral movements, and cross lateral movements through visual clues by pointing to the limb or limbs. The *ocular pursuits* reveal the extent of the child's control. The *rhythmic writing* tasks show splinter skills in reproduction and directionality problems. The *visual achievement forms* determine the child's basic form perception and his method of organization on the page. The best organization of drawings is left to right. Top to bottom and circular organizations are acceptable. The examiner should note the child's behavior when he is using the survey to detect perceptual-motor deficiencies.

In physical education laboratory setups, we use Kephart's motor-oriented tasks to aid the children who are mentally retarded and those with learning disorders to improve their skills. The essence of Kephart's theory is a sequence of learning stages through which the child progresses.

Carl Delacato (30A) is co-director with Glen Doman of the Institutes for the Achievement of Human Potential in Philadelphia, Pennsylvania. The Institutes include a section for neurological organization for children with brain damage, a division for language disability for youngsters with speech and reading problems, and a reading clinic and psychological services. The Doman-Delacato Rehabilitation Center perceptual-motor approach is different from the previous systems reviewed.

The neurological organization concept as Delacato states is: "that physiological optimum condition which exists uniquely and most completely in man and is the result of a total and uninterrupted ontogenetic neural development. This development recapitulates the phylogenetic neural development of man, begins during the first trimester of gestation and ends at about six and one-half years of age in normal humans." Delacato indicates that the right or left cortical hemisphere must become dominant in neurological development, and if the higher level of development is not functional, lower levels become operative and dominant (Fig 4-13). He believes that communication and mobility problems result

Name _____   Date of birth _____

Address _____   Sex _____ Grade _____

_____   School _____

Examiner _____   Date of examination _____

Score

	4	3	2	1	
Walking Board: Forward					Balance and Posture
Backward					
Sidewise					
Jumping					
Identification of Body Parts					Body Image and Differentiation
Imitation of Movement					
Obstacle Course					
Kraus-Weber					
Angels-in-the-snow					
Chalkboard Circle					Perceptual-Motor Match
Double Circle					
Lateral Line					
Vertical Line					
Rhythmic writing Rhythm					
Reproduction					
Orientation					
Ocular Pursuits Both eyes					Ocular Control
Right eye					
Left eye					
Convergence					
Visual Achievement Forms Form					Form Perception
Organization					

FIG. 4-12. (From Roach, E. G., and Kephart, N. C.: *The Purdue Perceptual-Motor Survey.* Columbus, Ohio, Charles E. Merrill Books, Inc., 1966.)

from abnormal neurological organization. The individual should be evaluated to locate the abnormal area of organization. Then, he feels, by *passively* applying this concept of neurological organization to the nervous system of those persons with mobility, speech, and reading problems, the incomplete organization of the nervous system may be helped.

Delacato strongly believes ontogeny recapitulates phylogeny—that the individual organism repeats the pattern of development of the species. Men such as Orton, Gesell, Getman, Hebb, and Dr. Temple Tay, a neurologist who worked with Delacato, have worked with this concept. Delacato's neurological organization relates to phylogeny in this manner.

1. The lowest forms of vertebrates live in water and move by undulating the spine or vertically moving the fins. These movements are controlled through the spinal cord and the medulla oblongata. They are the functional neural area.
2. Amphibians are the next highest class of vertebrates. To achieve the transition of living on land and in water required a more specialized neurological system. The amphibians function at the pons and midbrain level. Homolateral movements, alternate right foreleg and hindleg on one side and then on the other side, are used in the water. This is a pons movement. On land the amphibian uses a cross-pattern movement such as the right foreleg and left hindleg simultaneously. This is controlled by the midbrain.
3. Reptiles make up the next evolutionary level. As land animals they always move in a cross pattern, which is a midbrain function.
4. Mammals are next on the evolutionary level. Mammals have a brain cortex, and walk in a cross pattern. Man, the highest primate, has characteristics not found in the lower primates.

Cortical hemisphere dominance develops handedness and eyedness, which are promoted through sequential neurological organization. Delacato feels that speech is controlled in the dominant hemisphere, and subsequently is a step toward reading. Readiness to read begins at birth, with spinal cord and medulla control, then the pons—an alternating one-sidedness control to the midbrain—a two-sidedness control, and finally to the level of the cortex and the development of complete cortical hemisphere dominance. This organization evolves the human perceptual abilities and each level develops completely ending with cortical dominance for normal neurological development. Reading problems and behavior problems pose the question: What is the child's level of neurological organization? Delacato uses a battery of tests to determine if the organization is incomplete in his pons, midbrain, lower cortical, and cortical hemisphere. When the child is unsuccessful at one of the levels, remedial treatment begins at this level.

FIG. 4-13. Doman-Delacato Developmental Profile

		Column A	Column B	Column C		Column D		Column E		Column F
Brain Stage	Time Frame	Mobility	Language	Manual Competence		Visual Competence		Auditory Competence		Tactile Competence
VII	Superior 36 Mon. Average 72 Mon. Slow 96 Mon.	Using a leg in a skilled role which is consistent with the dominant hemisphere	Complete vocabulary and proper sentence structure	Using a hand to write which is consistent with the dominant hemisphere		Reading words using a dominant eye consistent with the dominant hemisphere		Understanding of tactile vocabulary and proper sentence with proper care		Tactile identification of objects using a hand consistent with hemisphere dominance
VI	Superior 22 Mon. Average 46 Mon. Slow 67 Mon.	Walking and running in complete cross pattern	2000 words of language and short sentences	Bimanual function with one hand in a dominant role		Identification of visual symbols and letters within experience		Understanding of 2000 words and simple sentences		Description of objects by tactile means
V	Superior 13 Mon. Average 28 Mon. Slow 45 Mon.	Walking with arms freed from the primary balance role	10 to 25 words of language and two work couplets	Cortical opposition bilaterally and simultaneously	Stereopsis	Differentiation of similar but unlike simple visual symbols	Stereopsis	Understanding 10 to 25 words and two couplets	Stereopsis	Tactile differentiation of similar but unlike objects
IV	Superior 8 Mon. Average 16 Mon. Slow 26 Mon.	Walking with arms used in a primary balance role most frequently at or above shoulder height	Two words of speech used spontaneously and meaningfully	Cortical opposition in either hand		Convergence of vision resulting in simple depth perception		Understanding of two words of speech		Tactile understanding of the third dimension in objects which appear be flat

Level		Creeping on hands and knees culminating in cross pattern	Creation of meaningful sounds	Prehensile grasp	Appreciation of detail within a configuration	Appreciation of meaningful sounds	Appreciation of gnostic sensation
III Midbrain	Superior 4 Mon. Average 8 Mon. Slow 13 Mon.						
II Pons	Superior 1 Mon. Average 2.5 Mon. Slow 4.5 Mon.	Crawling in the prone position culminating in cross pattern crawling	Vital crying in response to threats to life	Vital release	Outline perception	Vital response to threatening sounds	Perception of vital sensation
Medulla and Cord Birth		Movement of arms and legs without bodily movement	Birth cry and crying	Grasp reflex	Light reflex	Startle reflex	Babinski reflex

FIG. 4-13. (From Delacato, C.: *The Diagnosis and Treatment of Speech and Reading Problems*. Springfield, Charles C Thomas, 1965 and Glenn Doman, The Institutes for the Achievement of Human Potential, Philadelphia, Pa.)

Mental retardation is a symptom shown by children who have the following characteristics:

  A. Deficient—or have a substandard brain—i.e., do not have the same color or convolutions of a normal brain;

  B. Psychotic—or seem to have a normal brain but are not using it in the normal manner;

  C. Brain-injured—those to whom something happened before or after birth to damage a normal brain.

What matters is where the damage is, how much injury is in the brain, and what can be done.

The Institutes classify children in the following categories: 1. severely brain-injured—a child who cannot move or make a sound; 2. moderately brain-injured—a child who cannot walk or talk; 3. mildly brain-injured—the child who walks and talks poorly; 4. Strauss Syndrome—a youngster who is hyperactive, uncoordinated, unable to concentrate, and who has learning problems; 5. average with reading problems—a child who can't learn to read; 6. above average with reading problems—a child who has high scores in math and who gets by with not reading well; 7. superior physically and mentally; and 8. ideal or genius mentality.

Delacato has become well known by some of his evaluations. Midbrain level—1. small, rhythmical cross-pattern creeping, position of hands with fingers straight and palms flat on the floor. 2. Vision—follow an object held in his hand as he moves it to arms length; pons level. (1) Sleep position; Right-sided dominance shows child lying on abdomen with head turned toward left with left arm and leg flexed and right arm and leg extended. This position is used most. If it is not, the parents are to turn the child's head; if this passive movement is permitted, pons level organization is poor. The childs turning back to the first position with body adjustments is acceptable. (2) Vision is evaluated one eye at a time as he moves an object. Smoothness of the eye movement indicates organization.

The treatment is to stimulate the brain centers, not the symptoms. The normal human brain contains ten billion brain cells. Dead brain cells cannot be regenerated but stimulating other neurons by patterns of activity which help develop the brain may show a transfer of brain function and help solve learning problems.

Delacato feels that children deficient at the spinal cord and medulla level of neurological organization should express the primitive movements by being placed on the floor and experiencing basic mobility. If the child cannot perform these movements, passive imposition of body movement should be undertaken.

Children who have normal mobility skills but do not sleep in the proper position need to learn the acceptable sleep pattern and work on crawling prone and in the homolateral pattern. Visual treatment at this level needs the monocular visual pursuit training with a flashlight.

At the midbrain level, bilaterality is the developmental objective. Mobility problems are important so the cross-creep pattern, rotating the head to the forward hand and following with the eyes should be practiced ten minutes to one hour each day.

The development of the higher stages of the brain are advanced and some activities were used by Kephart and Getman. Delacato feels that (1) the sensory touch environment is augmented by increasing the intensity frequency duration in the auditory, visual, thermal, and tactile (motor response), (2) the cerebral blood flow should be increased through a rebreathing mask over the nose for 30 to 60 seconds every waking hour, (3) the visual function should be encouraged—reading to develop cortical functions such as speech and establishing cortical dominance through the eye, ear, hand, and foot.

To get the uninjured collateral brain cells to function Delacato uses patterning of the child by a team of three to five people four times a day. One person is at head position and one is at each limb. He believes that of the ten billion nerve cells in the brain the uninjured cells can be activated to function for the dead cells. Criticisms of Delacato's theory have been made so some will be mentioned.

1. There are statistical defects in studies that purportedly prove the value of his method.
2. His program makes parents "therapists" and often blames poor therapy if the program is not successful.
3. His program assumes that the recommended methods directly treat the brain.
4. Does the test instrument—Doman Delacato Neurological Developmental Profile—test?

We do examine the strengths and weaknesses of the programs and feel that many methodologies are useful for helping children with problems in learning so that using the knowledge of the various educators may get beneficial and worthwhile end results.

Dr. Bryant J. Cratty (27) has been working in the perceptual-motor area. He is director of the Perceptual-Motor Learning Laboratory at the University of California at Los Angeles. Cratty states that "movement games may help children with learning problems, aid active normal children to learn better, and improve the academic progress of the culturally deprived and retarded child." This is a simple quotation and does not explain Cratty's writings, which are well-documented and done in a scholarly manner. Cratty states the following:

1. Movement accuracy is necessary to express the intellect.
   a. Concrete steps are needed to improve visual-manual skills.
   b. Alternate methods of expression should be open to children.
      1. Typing can be taught for the time attribute.
      2. The fluid movements of handwriting may be difficult.
      3. Verbal testing is necessary at times. Accurate hand movements are needed to express the intellect in academic performance.
2. Motor tasks can elicit optimal levels of arousal, alertness, and activation. Performance needs arousal. The level determines the best performance. It has been demonstrated that 50 per cent of maximal hand pressure applied to hand grips by individuals increased their performance level in memorizing word lists and in verbal-cognitive skills. The tension seemed to raise the level of activation for mental skills.
3. Game participation can be used as reinforcement for concept acquisition. Success in games and the high motivation state indirectly contribute to intellectual endeavors.
4. Self-control should be increased and lengthening attention span lengthened. Vigorous, active games arouse children. The child must attend for a period of time and focus on the materials. He must place himself under his own control. The task should be gradually lengthened to increase the child's concentration.
5. The satisfaction gained in physical efforts contributes to a success syndrome. Self-concept may be vague through participation. Failure in games sometimes may cause withdrawal to academics. Yes and no.
6. Gross movement can be a learning modality through sensory input of the visual, kinesthetic, and tactile for moving through space. Playground modifications of gross movement patterns may enhance serial memory ability, pattern recognition, and spelling and number manipulations. Grids, six feet by six feet, painted with one-foot squares can be used. Some squares have numbers, and some have letters. Thus, a child hopping or jumping from square to square can improve his agility and his numbers and spelling. This modality may help the child with reduced input stimuli. Lines, squares, and zig zag may improve his ability to order a series of events correctly. Pattern recognition practice through the use of triangles, rectangles, and half circles can be taught on the playground and in the classroom to develop basic concepts for letters, words, and reading.

7. Problem solving can be aided through movement. Muska Mosston (124A) has a framework in which a child responds to commands and then can be led in problem-solving activities which are helpful for motor-mental relations. The mental, physical, emotional, and social channels should enter into learning situations. "Response generalization" for mongoloids should include engagement in choice-making behavior. Problem solving through gross motor movements is direct; it should not be confined only to the classrooms.

DEFINITIONS OF CRATTY:

1. Motor educability is the capacity to learn and relate to one's general athletic ability.
2. Movement behavior is overt movements of skeletal muscles.
3. Motor learning should develop a permanent change in motor ability through practice performance.
4. Motor skills are reasonably complex motor performances.
5. Motor performance is short-term movement in an identifiable task.
6. Motor fitness is the capacity to perform a task.

Cratty says that motor skills are placed on a continuum, from those that are considered "gross" to those that may be termed "fine." Motor output seems to be the first aspect of a performance to get the attention of the researchers. How sensory cues influence the performance and the formation of the meaning of sensory experiences are now studied in greater detail. Thus sensory-motor and perceptual-motor terms of the performance are used to point out the influence of these processes upon the motor act.

Dr. Gerald N. Getman (53A), an optometrist, and his associates have developed a program of visuo-motor training based upon the belief that visual perception is learned. He has coauthored publications with Gesell and has worked at the Child Development Clinic at Yale University to develop learning readiness programs. Getman has some points in common with Kephart and Barsch although he stresses ocular mechanisms and visual perception for the child with learning problems.

His developmental learning readiness program refers to the four learning arts: the art of movement, the art of orientation, the art of identification, and the art of communication. Getman believes that the developmental stages of perception and cognition of the pre-school child follow in sequence and overlap. These are as follows: 1. general motor patterns when the child learns by moving as he uses the eyes as the guidance system; 2. special movement patterns which include eye-hand coordination and other neuromuscular skills; 3. eye-movement patterns when vision starts to replace the hand in exploration of movement; 4. visual language patterns are acquired, so that gesturing may be replaced by oral language; 5. visualization patterns (visual memory) or the recall of other learning and the interpretation of new learning. He maintains that the total involvement of the child requires that two or more information systems function at the same time. One is movement and the others are visual, auditory, tactile, gustatory, olfactory, or kinesthetic; and the process of making a decision.

Getman has six programs which are easy to understand and which are well-packaged for the teachers' use. A description of the programs follows. 1. Practice in General Coordination to develop movement without thinking. Some exercises are different types of head, arm, and leg movements, rolling, races, crawling, jumping, hopping, and skipping. 2. Practice in Balance for the children to explore the right and left sides of the body, to direct their movement with their eyes, and improve balance through the walking beam. 3. Practice in Eye-Hand Coordination with visual and motor systems exercises developed at the chalkboard, circles, and lines. 4. Practice in Eye Movements to develop control and accuracy through ocular sweep span, and sweep exercises. 5. Practice in Form Recognition to develop the form perception necessary in learning to read words. Templates and then free hand drawings are used to begin visual memory training. 6. Practice in Visual Memory (Imagery), a visuo-motor complex using a tachistoscope which projects circles, squares, and other shapes on the wall. The child closes his eyes and names the shape or traces it in the air, identifies a picture or draws the picture from memory. From the simple to the complex forms, development of visual memory is learned through Getman's six programs.

Dr. Marianne Frostig's (46A) materials have focused on children with learning disabilities primarily through the assessment and remediation techniques in the area of visual perception. She is well known for the Developmental Test of Visual Perception (DTVP), which is sometimes called The Frostig and the Marianne Frostig Center of Educational Therapy in Los Angeles, California, whose slogan is "Return to Reading—Return to Normal Life." The Frostig Center has a multi-disciplinary approach, with four types of services provided; psychiatric, psychotherapy and counseling, psychological evaluation, and educational. It offers four basic types of educational programs. The first is a full-time educational program for children in the elementary grades whose needs are remediated through a special program designed for them. The second program is for junior high school children and is coordinated with the public schools. The third program is for pre-school children with a pre-academic design. The fourth is a tutoring program to develop ability in specific academic subjects and remediate other problems.

At the Frostig Center many instruments are used to evaluate learning problems. Four tests are used to individualize the remedial programs. They are 1. The Frostig (DTVP) for visual perception, 2. the Wepman Test of Auditory Discrimination, 3. the Wechsler Intelligence Scale for Children, and 4. the Illinois Test of Psycholinguistic Abilities. Other tests may be used for sensory-motor abilities, perception, emotional development, and social development problems.

The Frostig (DTVP) measures five areas of visual perception: eye-motor coordination (draw curve, straight line), figure-ground perception (children cannot find words in the dictionary), constancy of shapes (circles and squares, large numbers from small), condition in space (figures identical), and spatial relationships (linked space through dots and lines, also peg boards).

The philosophy of the Frostig Center for development and improvement in children points out the influences of many well-known persons such as Hebb (67A) (cell assembly theory), Skinner (151B, 151C), (operant conditioning), Montessori, and Kephart in her design of special programs. Basically Frostig's programs are concerned with visual-perceptual skills, and like Dr. Getman, she has made instructional material available.

There are many other persons, educators, and psychologists who have excellent contributions for children with learning disabilities. The authors include some of their names for the student's further personal research. The Orton-Gellingham system uses a linguistic approach for the child with learning disabilities. The multisensory approach of Grace Fernald (41B) has also been called the "kinesthetic" or "tracing" method. Johnson and Myklebust (78A) use the language development approach for children with problems. William Cruickshank's (26A) approach to educating the brain-injured child is similar to the Strauss/Lehtinen ideas and program. Barbara Bateman and Douglas Wiseman (191A) seem to follow the linguistic approach for these children. We include Maria Montessori, the Italian physician, as she started the work with problem children. Also included is Jean Piaget (135A), whose discovery method of teaching children supposedly enables adults to approach children with more sensitivity.

For the child with learning problems, an effective form of learning that parallels a special educational method is behavior modification. Ullman and Krasner (179A) demonstrate through their research that positive reinforcement of the child with behavior modification techniques often shows modified behavior that is less visible. Children have coping strategies or behaviorial patterns, and behavior modification, through reward and punishment, can reshape those patterns into acceptable forms. As a result, the status of the child will improve in his own concept of self, his social abilities, and his learning.

This chapter focused on the mentally retarded child, and diagnosis and etiology as set up by the American Association of Mental Deficiency. The various systems established for the child with learning disabilities were reviewed, with a discussion of the work of specific authorities in this area. Our primary concerns are in the motor learning dichotomy to improve the children's total learning potential. An overview of mental retardation and the available educational systems to help children with problems point out the many benefits of motor learning.

CHAPTER

Mechanical
and Muscular
Efficiency

The physical education teacher has many aids in helping students to coordinate body movements and to develop psychologically healthy body images. Exercise is one of the tools. The person with slight or marked divergencies in body structure can apply specific exercises to maintain or to improve the body function of movement. This chapter contains analyses of posture from the side and back views; descriptions of essential tests and exercises for flexibility, muscle strength, and specific body segment conditioning; and analyses of movement patterns, including questionable or debatable exercises. It is our hope to provide basic information to help prevent or to correct alignment faults and muscle imbalances.

During the history of mankind, many systems of exercise have been developed. Now it is generally recognized that the history of therapeutic exercise is a long and complex one. Adumbrated physical education has been traced by historians to early civilizations. Survival of man's primitive ancestors depended on their ability to develop physical skills and strength and endurance of the body to maintain the effective living of the hunter and family provider. Because modern living shows an increase in sedentary pursuits, physical education activities are basic for the development and maintenance of the body. National concern for fitness and personal needs in ego satisfaction have motivated many persons to seek exercise programs. In 1962, the late President John F. Kennedy delivered a school address on fitness, in which he said:

The strength of our democracy is no greater than the collective well-being of our people. The vigor of our country is no stronger than the vitality and will of our countrymen. . . . It is of great importance then, that we take immediate steps to ensure that every American child be given the opportunity to make and keep himself physically fit, fit to learn, fit to understand, to grow in grace and stature, to fully live (155).

The Youth Fitness program has enlarged in scope through the efforts of many physical educators and the national concern of the President's Council on Youth Fitness. Its role has been to place physical fitness in the proper place in our American culture.

Scientific investigation, along with traditional beliefs and practices, shows that body movement patterns, exercises, and recreation need to be a regular part of the daily living routine to maintain positively the optimal health of our bodies. Health includes not only concern for acute accidents and illnesses, but the lessening of the incidence of chronic diseases present in this age (188).

Exercises have been set up to enable each person to choose a pattern for a personal program to suit individual needs. Are these needs for sports conditioning, figure control, lessening of tension, improved posture, the building of muscle tone, or the development of more strength? The HOW, the WHY, and the WHAT are presented in this chapter as guidelines for a personal program. It is our belief, regardless of individual purpose, that everyone should seek physical activity for the sake of getting more out of life and putting more life into living.

What Is Fitness?

To be "fit" is the parrot-like reiteration expressed by many persons who are interested in the condition of the body. A plethora has been written on this concept.

The following is a résumé of some concepts to clarify the term "fitness."

1. Fitness is described as "that state which characterizes the degree to which the person is able to function. It implies a dynamic homeostasis, the ability to respond to life's physical, emotional, and social ongoing demands; the ability of each person to live most effectively within his potentialities (44, p. 8) (11, p. 1)."

2. "Fitness is the functional capacity of an individual for a task."[*]

3. "Physical fitness denotes adaptability or suitability to some specified muscle stress (81, p. 244)."

---

[*] Darling, R. C., *et al.*, *Physical Fitness.* J.A.M.A., *137*: 764, 1948.

4. "Physical fitness is the capacity of a person to perform a task without undue fatigue and with a reserve of strength to meet the unexpected (81, p. 244)."

5. "Fitness, whether it is physical, mental or social, is a reflection of competence of the total person to risk a task and the physical, psychological, social, even spiritual factors, cannot be dissociated when one is seeking to develop or evaluate the quality of one's life or his fitness for a task."°

6. ". . . each person, in order to satisfy his own needs and, at the same time, contribute his share to the welfare of society must possess:

   a. Optimum organic health consistent with heredity and the application of present health knowledge;
   b. Sufficient coordination, strength and vitality to meet emergencies as well as the requirements of daily living;
   c. Emotional stability to meet the stresses and strains of modern life;
   d. Social consciousness and adaptability with respect to the requirements of group living;
   e. Sufficient knowledge and insight to make suitable decisions and arrive at feasible solutions to problems;
   f. Attitudes, values and skills which stimulate satisfactory participation in a full range of daily activities;
   g. Spiritual and moral qualities which contribute to the fullest extent to effective living in a democratic society."†

7. "Total fitness for modern living means:

   a. A body free from disease;
   b. Muscles, heart, lungs developed to give strength, speed, agility and endurance to do the tasks of each day easily;
   c. An alert mind, free from worry, fear, or tension, that can relax completely with the moment of opportunity and as quickly be engrossed in the next challenging task;
   d. A spirit that feels itself unselfishly part of an important venture and important to that occasion (174, p. 3)."

Currently many recommend that fitness be incorporated as a regular, daily part of the physical education program. Some programs for increasing strength employ mechanical devices, such as the Universal Hercules.

° *Fit for College:* Report of the National College Physical Education Association for Men. 1959, p. 9. American Association for Health, Physical Education and Recreation.
† Darling, R. C., *et al., Physical Fitness.* J.A.M.A., 137: 764, 1948.

Purposes of an Exercise Program

The teacher plans activities to give each person an understanding of his particular problems in body mechanics and a knowledge of exercises to achieve efficient body dynamics through improved muscle balance and posture.

The teacher of body mechanics must motivate the student to become involved in:

1. Normal range joint movements.

2. Stretching tight muscle groups and tightening stretched muscle groups.

3. Posture dynamics with checkpoint alignment of the body segments in walking, sitting, standing, reaching, lifting, pushing, pulling, jumping and landing, ascending stairs, descending stairs, and getting into a car.

4. Kinesthetic awareness (knowing the position of one's body parts in space) for balanced body segment control.

5. Relaxation to relieve tension.

6. The development of a program of exercises in a sequential circuit for one's needs.

7. The assessment of physiologic needs determined by a minimal screening test of strength, flexibility, cardiorespiratory index, anatomical measurements, and a posture evaluation.

Graceful, efficient movement is the motivational purpose of a program of body mechanics in our society.

Values of Correct Body Mechanics

The mechanics of balance and alignment of the body segments permit free and controlled movement, lessen strain and insure conservation of energy. Since posture is primarily reflex movement, the formation of habits and the reconditioning of formed habits present a motivating challenge to the individual. "Static" posture pertains to the fixed positions of the body. "Dynamic" posture is defined as the body segment positions during the variety of movements in work and play.

Why are good body mechanics important?

Aesthetic Value

To look better is to present an aspect of confidence, alertness, and poise which may be lacking in the person with poor posture. Physical poise is an asset in any situation and adds a desirable impression in the professional and social world. Good carriage is an asset for personal appearance. Clothes look better.

Psychological Value

To feel better is closely related to the aesthetic, as well as to the psychological. Psychologists study the behavior and movement patterns of the individual. They are interested in his attitude toward himself—perception, body image, identification, expression, communication—and his attitudes toward life. We associate moods—joy, courage, hope, fear, and indifference—with specific postures. For years, performing artists have shown physiological and chronological age in stage and motion picture productions through posture as well as makeup. Poise of an individual depends upon the development and maintenance of physical bearing. Justly or unjustly, posture influences the concept others have of one's personality in social and business worlds. "Keep your chin up" is a sound principle of mental health.

Health Value

To be well is a justifiable reason for paying attention to the mechanics of the body. In part, body efficiency is affected by musculo-skeletal structure and functioning. An example can be found in lessened heart and lung function if the thorax or chest is restricted and inflexible because of a habitual rounded back. Although unsubstantiated, the following two hypotheses are thought by many to lessen health level: the sagging abdomen, which affects organs of the abdominal and pelvic regions, and trauma in joint articulation and hypokinetic activities, which puts strain on the feet, lower limbs, and lower back. "Knowing how and what to do for correct body mechanics during the habit-forming years is pertinent for the individual's fitness capacity and organic development."[*]

Efficiency Value

To conserve energy contributes to movement efficiency. The beautiful coordination of the dancer, diver, gymnast, and others has developed through continuous practice on specific movements until energy conservation has been achieved or conditioned. Poise in movement is free, smooth, well-controlled, and conditioned through good body alignment

[*] Rasch, Philip J., and Burke, Roger K.: *Kinesiology and Applied Anatomy*, 5th Ed., Philadelphia, Lea & Febiger, 1974.

and well-balanced muscular structures. In the upright posture, the anti-gravity or extensor muscles reflexly maintain tonus when the body segments are in balance.

Personal Testing and Assessment Program

A self-inventory should enable one to see, understand, analyze, and correct his postural problems. The following tests should be checked on the analysis chart for such an assessment. CHECK THE FAULTS.

I. Posture Test

Use a gravity line or plumb line.

Stand with the feet parallel, 2 to 3 inches apart in the back view and side view.

A picture or silhouette of the body back view and side view can be examined objectively.

Without a picture a partner can check the gravity line posture test, or this can be individually checked at the mirror.

General postural faults included on the analysis chart are explained below:

Back and Front View Faults (Figs. 5-1 and 5-2 illustrate some of these faults.)

1. Toeing in and toeing out when standing may indicate the person will walk in the same manner.

2. Pronated ankles indicate a lowering of the inner ankle bone. The outflaring of the tendon of Achilles (Helbing sign) also indicates pronation.

3. Knees: bowlegs (genu varum) or knock-knees (genu valgus). In a long sit (knees straight) the person with bowlegs can bring the ankles together but not the knees. If knock-knees are present, the knees will come together but not the ankle bones.

4. Hips: high or prominent. The hips should be even in contour. When the arms are relaxed at the sides, the space there should be symmetrical. A habit of standing on one leg may cause this fault.

5. Scoliosis or lateral curvature of the spine is a *medical* problem to be checked by the physician. When the spine deviates from the gravity line, this fault can be further examined in a prone lying position, suspension from a bar position, or the Adam's position. The curve is named from the location of its convexity.

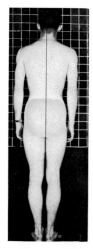 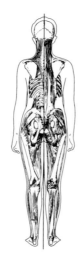 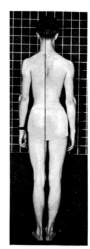

FIG. 5-1. Posture, back view. *Good.* Head straight (as in drawing), not tilted to one side (as in photographs). Shoulders level. Shoulder blades flat against upper back, not far apart or close together, and not "winged." Spine straight. Hips level. Arms hanging easily at sides, palms of hands facing toward body. Legs straight, not bowed or knock-kneed. In relation to plumb line, body weight is equally distributed between right and left sides. *Faulty.* Right shoulder low. Shoulder blades too close together. Spine curves slightly toward left. Right hip higher than left. In relation to plumb line, body weight is too far toward right. (From Kendall, Kendall and Boynton, *Posture and Pain,* Courtesy of The Williams & Wilkins Co.)

  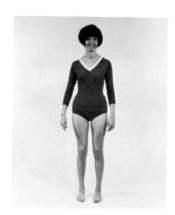

FIG. 5-2. Posture, front view. *Good.* Legs straight, not bowed or knock-kneed. Knees "easy," not stiff or bent. Kneecaps face straight ahead. Ankles straight, not rolled inward or outward. Feet pointing straight ahead or toeing out slightly. *Faulty.* As demonstrated by this subject, legs can appear to be bowed as a result of the following faulty positions of the feet and knees: knees pushed back, legs rotated so kneecaps face somewhat inward, ankles rolled inward, and weight on inner sides of feet. Correction of the faulty foot and knee positions will correct this type of apparent bowing. FOOTPRINTS. A wet footprint should show a normal arch like the top illustration not a flatfoot, like the bottom illustration. In standing or walking, feet should point straight ahead or toe out slightly. Note the low right shoulder, which may indicate a left C lateral curve or right handedness since the hip line seems even.

If present in the rib cage area of the spine, it is called a dorsal curve; in the low back region it is called a lumbar curve. In both regions it is called a "dorsolumbar curve" with the convexity named as Right Dorsal Left Lumbar. A Left Total indicates a left convexity of the complete spine. Scoliosis clinics are found at most children's hospitals, so this deviation should have medical diagnosis and treatment prescribed by the physiatrist or orthopaedic surgeon.

6. Scapulae. If the scapulae are not flat on the ribs along the vertebral borders, this is a clue to the fault of round shoulders (kyphosis). The vertebrae should normally be 2 to $2\frac{1}{2}$ inches from the shoulder blades. A common fault of adolescence shows a winging of the low or inferior angle of the scapulae.

7. Shoulder high. This fault may be occupational owing to right-hand dominance or left-hand dominance. The asymmetry of the shoulders in front of a mirror or a grid or the position of the hands alongside the thighs quickly shows this fault of muscle imbalance.

8. Head tilt. The head should be balanced evenly on the spine. Tilting may be a clue to handedness or imperfect hearing or vision, indicating that medical examinations are needed.

Side View Faults (Figs. 5-3 and 5-4)

1. Feet and ankles. The body weight is on the heel area, and the medial or inner border of the foot is flat or low to the floor.

2. Hyperextended knees (genu recurvatum). The knee joint is locked and stiff with possible backward bowing or is a straight line without the natural curve.

3. Pelvic tilt. The increased tilt shows a swayback or lordosis, which is an accentuated curve in the low back. A decreased tilt of the pelvis gives a flat-back appearance.

4. Abdomen relaxed. An exaggerated rounding of the abdomen may accompany swayback and hyperextended knee faults.

5. Kyphosis. This means a rounding of the upper back, a common postural fault accompanied by spreading of the scapulae with some limitation in muscle strength and flexibility.

6. Chest low. This fault is also associated with kyphosis.

7. Shoulders. Shoulders are forward, hunched, and not aligned over the hip joint.

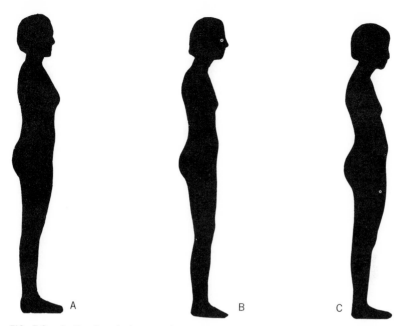

FIG. 5-3. A. Excellent balance and alignment; B. General "slump." No increase in lower back curve; C. Poor alignment, increased hollow in lower back. (Frost, *Posture and Body Mechanics*, State University of Iowa Extension Bulletin.)

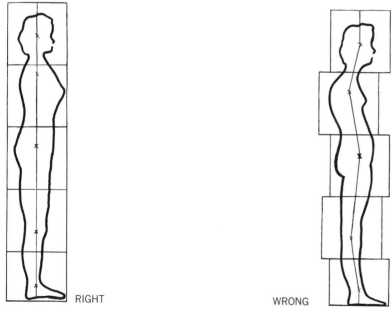

RIGHT   WRONG

FIG. 5-4. (Adapted from Lee and Wagner, *Fundamentals of Body Mechanics and Condition*, Courtesy of W. B. Saunders Co.)

8. Head. A forward head with an imbalance of the posterior neck muscles and anterior neck muscles shows stretched posterior neck muscles. A chin out position presents tight posterior neck muscles.

9. Weight distribution or body balance. The gravity line should

POSTURE ANALYSIS CHART*

Test No. 1. _____ Test No. 2. _____

Posture Grade ___ A A– B B– C C– ___   ___ A A– B B– C C– ___

Circle: A indicates excellent, with all five body segments on the checkpoints.
  A– indicates that one body segment has a fault.
  B identifies several body segment faults.
  B– indicates three body segments have deviations.
  C indicates four body segments have faults.
  C– identifies all five body segments with deviations.

Height _____ Weight _____

Back view or lateral deviations

Body segments:

	ANALYSIS			
	RIGHT		LEFT	
	I	II	I	II
1. Feet				
Pronation				
Toeing out				
Toeing in				
2. Knees				
Bowlegs				
Knock-knees				
Spine				
Lateral curves				
Dorsal				
Lumbar				
3. Hips				
High				
Prominent				
Scapulae				
Spread				
Winged				
4. Shoulders				
High				
5. Head tilt				

Side view or anteroposterior deviations*

Body segments:	ANALYSIS I		ANALYSIS II	
1. Feet and ankles				
Longitudinal arch				
2. Knees				
Hyperextended				
3. Pelvic tilt				
Increased				
Decreased				
Relaxed abdomen				
4. Shoulders				
Forward				
Chest low				
Kyphosis				
5. Head				
Forward				
Chin out				
Weight distribution				
Forward				
Backward				

Key: SL means slight deviations.　　　　　　　　*Check only the faults or deviations.
     M means moderate deviations or faults.

bisect the body at the checkpoints illustrated at the five body segments; feet, knees, hips, shoulders, and head. Forward or backward weight distribution faults may be checked through body lean at the ankles or at one of the five body segments.

II. Comparative Performance Tests

Take these next three tests; the cardiorespiratory, the Kraus-Weber minimum fitness test of the trunk muscles and the flexibility tests. Along with the posture analysis these tests help you assess your needs in stamina, muscular strength, and flexibility for the development of a personal individual program. Record the scores on the score charts. Watch for improvement, then retest, and tally the score.

A. Cardiorespiratory Test

This modified Harvard Step Test estimates the individual's response to moderately strenuous exercise. His recovery index test or cardiorespiratory index is measured by the pulse count after completing the test. This is only one aspect of evaluating a person's response to exertion and does not replace the periodic medical examination and other fitness tests.°

FIG. 5-5.

POSITION: Stand in front of a 16-inch bench.

MOVEMENT: Continuous for two minutes.

On a signal step up on the bench with the left foot and rise to an erect position with the right foot next to the left on the bench. Step down to the floor with the left foot, then the right foot. THIS IS ONE STEP.

REPEAT this four-step routine (up left, right; down left, right) at a speed of 30 per minute for 2 minutes. Sit or rest on the bench for 1 minute.

SCORE: Then count the pulse for 30 seconds following the one-minute rest. The pulse count is your score; record it.

The carotid artery pulse in the neck is very pronounced following exercise. This or the radial pulse at the base of the thumb are the preferred pulse spots. Use the index, or second, finger to get the pulse.

Cardiorespiratory Index	Test I	Test II
Date:	_____	_____
	_____	_____

B. Kraus-Weber Minimum Fitness Test

This test estimates the minimum fitness of the trunk muscles. See illustrations (Fig. 5-6).

	Test I	Test II
a. or abdominals plus	_____	_____
b. or abdominal minus psoas	_____	_____
c. or iliopsoas	_____	_____
d. or upper back	_____	_____
e. or low back	_____	_____
f. or hamstrings	_____	_____

Score a plus for passing and a minus for not passing

° *AMA Recommends an Exercise Test:* J. Amer. Phys. Therap. Assoc. 45: 1100, 1965.

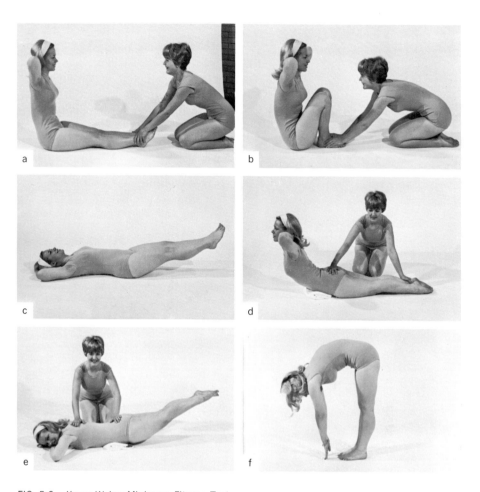

FIG. 5-6.   Kraus-Weber Minimum Fitness Test.

Test a. With your hands behind your neck roll up into the sitting position.

Test b. With knees bent and hands behind neck roll up into sitting position.

Test c. With hands behind neck and knees straight, raise your heels 10 inches from the floor. Hold this ten seconds. Keep the back flat.

Test d. Lie face down with a pillow under your abdomen. With hands behind neck, raise head, chest, and shoulders off floor. Hold this ten seconds.

Test e. Place your hands under your head and with pillow still under your abdomen, raise your legs off the floor. Keep the knees straight. Hold this ten seconds.

Test f. With feet together slowly bend forward and see how nearly you can come to touching the floor with your finger tips. Do not bend your knees and do not "bounce" down. If you can touch the floor for three seconds you pass this test.

C. Flexibility Tests

These tests are planned to help one evaluate his own joint flexibility, so that he may have a better understanding of the type of exercises of greatest value to him. Flexibility and extensibility comparisons can be made with estimates of the body in single effort positions as follows:

a. TRUNK: With the legs in a long sit position, estimate the distance between the forehead and floor upon trunk flexion. Seven inches is normal.

Correct

b. HIPS: Knee-chest hug in the supine position allows an estimate of the distance between back of the opposite knee and floor. Tightness of the hip flexors will limit the leg from the floor touch.

b

c. TENDON ACHILLES: Forced dorsiflexion in the long sit position or reverse Adam's position shows comparison of the heel cord flexibility less than, equal to, or greater than a 90-degree range of motion.

c   Correct

d. SHOULDERS: Hook lying position with the arms extended overhead permits estimating the distance of the elbows to the floor to show limitation of tight anterior shoulder structures.

Correct

d

	Test I	Test II
a. Trunk (*inches*)	_____	_____
b. Hips	_____	_____
c. Tendon achilles	_____	_____
d. Shoulders	_____	_____

FIG. 5-7.   Flexibility tests.

D. Anatomical or Body Measurements

Measurements show how the weight of the body can be adjusted and redistributed through exercise. Take the anatomical measurements at five-to six-week intervals.

Record the measurements on this chart, using a tape measure at the following body sites:

1. Waist—narrowest point of the mid-trunk.
2. Hips—pubic bone landmark—largest hip area.
3. Bust, chest—nipple level.
4. Thighs—7 inches below the anterior superior iliac spine (the bone felt at the mid-abdominal area on each side).
5. Calves—largest point between the knee and ankle.
6. Ankles—just above the ankle bones (malleoli), or smallest area.
7. Arms—mid-biceps with static contraction.
8. Wrists—just above the radial tuberosity—smallest area.

	Test I		*Test II*	
WAIST				
HIPS				
BUST/CHEST				
	RIGHT	LEFT	RIGHT	LEFT
THIGHS				
CALVES				
ANKLES				
ARMS				
WRISTS				

To be well-proportioned, according to current dress sizes, a woman should have a waist 8 to 10 inches smaller than the bust circumference. The hip measurements should usually be 1 to 4 inches larger than the bust. The calf should be 4 to 5 inches larger than the ankle, and the thigh about 10 to 13 inches larger than the ankle.

For the male adult the waist should be 6 to 9 inches smaller than the chest circumference. The hip measurement should be 2 to 4 inches larger than the chest measurement.

A gain or loss of 12 to 15 pounds usually indicates a change in size. For example, a woman wearing a size 10, who gains 12 pounds, will need a size 12; with a loss of weight the reverse is indicated.

Judging Body Mechanics

Judging the so-called normal body mechanics requires evaluation of individual factors of each body structure—body type, age, flexibility, and anomalies.

Somatotype or Body Type

The basic figure type is estimated by three components: the amount of fat, the size of the muscles, and the size of the bones. Body build is hereditary, and the three types are endomorph, or stocky, mesomorph, or average, and ectomorph, or the slender type. Few people fall into one clearly discerned type, but the dominant component usually identifies our figure type. Dysplasia refers to several dominant components— as ectomorph for the upper trunk and endomorph of the lower body.

The endomorphs have excess fat pads distributed throughout the body. Skin-fold caliphers can measure fat deposits at the abdomen, hips, arms, or midriff. An easier way is to pinch at these sites. If the pinch between the thumb and forefinger is more than an inch, some weight watching and an exercise program are advised.

The mesomorphs have sturdy muscles. Measurement of muscle strength requires special equipment, but for an estimate we suggest having the individual tighten his muscle groups—abdominals, hip, legs, —and with your fist punch or push on the tightened muscle group. If there is considerable give (softness), physical activities are recommended, usually specific activities for the particular area. The mesomorph presents less body flexibility and a larger bone size than does the slender type.

The ectomorphs have long, thin bones with long muscle structure.

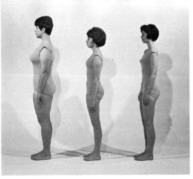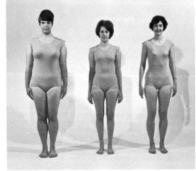

FIG. 5-8.　Basic figure types.

They are prone to posture faults because of weaker muscles and more flexible ligament structure. Fatigue problems are more common with the ectomorph than with the average and stocky body types.

Height and weight charts for women follow the bone size for somatotyping. This is important for figure analysis of the body frame. The wrist measurements are the guide lines. For the small bone structure the wrist may measure 4.6 to 5.5 inches; for the average or medium bone structure 5.6 to 6.2 inches; and for the large frame the wrist measurements are 6.3 to 6.8 inches. Men use a trunk index that is more difficult to assess.

Age, Flexibility, Anomalies

The young child has the normal growth line of prominent abdomen and winged scapula. Body segment balance should be achieved through natural, dynamic activities of games, climbing, creeping, and hanging. Flexibility decreases with age, or some restricted flexibility may be due to such anomalies as short clavicles or low back spine articulations. When the balance of the body segments and the muscle tone is poor, the physician should be consulted.

How to Correct Faulty Posture in Standing

Although some posture problems are beyond the scope of the physical educator and the student and fall under the physician's purview, many of the common problems can be improved by the individual. The following are some ways of combatting posture problems. The gravity line test is the criteria for body segment alignment.

A. The body weight should be on both feet.
B. The center of the hips, trunk at the shoulders, and head are in a direct line over the center of the arch or weight-bearing part of the foot.
C. The <u>feet</u> point forward; a vertical or gravity line extends from the center side point of the foot, upward behind the <u>patella</u>, through the center of the <u>hip</u>, and through the middle of the <u>shoulder</u>, to the center of the <u>head</u> or ear lobe.
These five points are called "body segment *checkpoints.*"

FIG. 5-9. The gravity line test.

Hints for Improving Posture

FIG. 5-10. The mirror test.

1. Use a mirror to appraise your personal posture problems.

2. Stand tall with side to mirror.

3. Keep feet parallel, with more weight on the outer border to avoid pronation.

4. Hold the knees easy. A 5° angle provides for a straight articulation between the femur and the tibia.

5. Tuck hips under, decreasing the pelvic tilt, and maintain a normal lumbar curve. The back wall test or phantom chair may help get this position.

6. Keep the lower abdomen flat so that the lower end of the sternum (breast bone) is more prominent (forward) than the pubic bone. This is the key to good mechanics.

7. Let the upper back have some roundness; keep the chest high and the shoulders low (not hunched) with the arms at the sides not forward.

8. Hold the head erect, well-balanced above the shoulders, with the lines of the chin and neck at a right angle.

9. Relax; repeat; see and feel these body positions.

Asymmetrical standing is acceptable and harmless if the elements of good balance and line are maintained. Avoid allowing the body weight to sink on the weight-bearing side and keep the body segments vertically aligned. The body is never absolutely immobile; there is a sway, investigated by Hellebrandt in 1938, called "movement on a stationary base." Tucker found that people stood asymmetrically four times as often as symmetrically, each stance being held about thirty seconds.°

Developing a Personal Program

The individualized exercise program is set up to meet specific needs. These needs are to maintain and improve organic tone, muscle strength,

° Tucker, W. E.: *Active Alerted Posture*, Edinburgh, E. & S. Livingstone Ltd., 1960, p. 18.

flexibility, cardiorespiratory endurance, posture control or kinesthetic awareness, and alteration of the body shape or contour. The attainment of these goals requires the application of principles and the selection of exercises relating to that particular goal.°

Does the exercise program provide:

1. General all-round development, as well as the development of specific muscle groups?

2. Development of a physiologically, anatomically, biologically, dynamically, and kinesthetically aware individual?

3. Prevention of deviations and aid in the correction of minor weaknesses?

4. Adaptation to the needs of the individual?

5. Improvement of definite muscle imbalances through exercises which lend themselves to the prevention of possible injuries?

6. Preparation for strenuous participation in activities?

7. Development of increased postural control and stability through improvement of muscle tone and organic efficiency?

8. Activities that may be used by the individual to maintain fitness (109, p. 197)?

Guidelines for Checking the Program

1. Is the sequence of exercises good?

2. What does the movement do for the individual?

3. Are the patterns exercising the right muscles or muscle groups?

4. Does the exercise lend itself to a progressive circuit program and a modified interval training type program?

5. Will a six-weeks' or two-months' follow-up show kinesthetic learning, as well as a change in muscle balance?

6. Does the individual like the exercise patterns; does he look and feel better?

7. Are the starting positions and movement positions in sitting and standing correct so that the student will maintain improved alignment for later life activities?

° Margaret A. Hukill, Department of Physical Education, Women's Division, The Ohio State University, assisted in this plan for a personalized program, 1967.

What to Include?

Choose a variety of exercises with a logical sequence relative to the starting positions. The common starting positions are supine or prone lying, sitting, and standing. See Figures 5-27 through 5-43. The body parts include the head, neck, trunk, arms, legs, ankles, and feet. Alternation of the movement patterns of the body segments will lessen fatigue and increase the effectiveness of the exercise. Balanced activities are necessary.

How Many to Do?

Repetitions progress daily for conditioning or reconditioning. A sixty-second period for each exercise or a starting number of 25 times for young adults will prevent the overdosage that develops soreness of the muscles. When soreness of the muscle or muscle group develops, several repetitions of the movement that caused this help alleviate this condition.

How Fast?

The correct, accurate movement pattern is essential. Increasing the speed (intensity) uses more energy. The movement should be smooth, rhythmic, and as fast as possible without disturbing the normal range of joint motions.

When and How Often?

When the exercise or activity session is performed varies with each individual's daily living routine or habits. Like the coffee break, the exercise break has great value for the individual with sedentary activities. Regularity of the exercises, daily or 3 times a week for 15 minutes, will reveal greater goal gains than one hour once a week.

The following charts by Hettinger report the gains in strength with exercise training sessions. Figure 5-11 illustrates the effect of regular training sessions of resistive type exercises on muscle strength. The upper segment shows a rapid increase in muscle strength with daily training and a decline in muscle strength when training is discontinued. The middle segment points out the increase in muscle strength starting with a daily training session. Changing to the weekly training session shows a slower rate of the decline of muscle strength, and muscle strength also declines more slowly after training is discontinued. The lower segment shows once-a-week training sessions for fifty weeks produce a slow increase in muscle strength and also a slower loss in muscle strength after the training is stopped, compared with the result of the daily training. Three examples of the decrease in muscle strength after a period of daily training are shown in Figure 5-12. In the upper curve, the

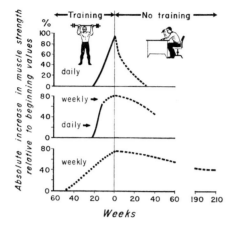

FIG. 5-11. Variation in muscle strength during and after training in relation to frequency of training stimuli. (From Hettinger, T., *Physiology of Strength*, Courtesy of Charles C Thomas, 1961.)

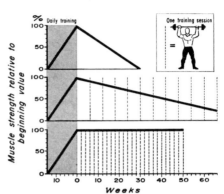

FIG. 5-12. Effect of infrequent stimuli following daily training. (From Hettinger, T., *Physiology of Strength*, Courtesy of Charles C Thomas, 1961.)

change in muscle strength is illustrated without further training stimuli. The center curve shows the decline of strength after daily training, followed by one training session every six weeks. The lower curve points out the results when the daily training session is followed by a two-week rhythm training session.

Hettinger's charts show that the retention of neuromuscular strength is analogous with other fitness components such as flexibility and cardio-respiratory endurance. They illustrate the need for regular training and follow-up.

Summary of Rules of Exercise

1. Find a comfortable and stable position to avoid tissue injury or exertion soreness.

2. Use smooth motions.

3. Prevent overdosage. Use a levels system, and progress to tolerance.

4. Keep the exercise period short with even progressions.

5. Exercise regularly; exertion soreness indicates a reduction in the number of repetitions, not complete elimination of the exercise.

6. Make the exercise activities fun.

Exercise and Weight Control

For a person who is obese, medical guidance and supervision are important to maintain organic fitness. For the individual who wants to maintain his present weight or lose a few pounds, activity and diet should be synchronized. Can a person lose weight by exercising? The problem is concerned with how much activity the person does in relation to how much food he eats. Exercise uses calories; eating adds or replenishes calories. Body weight can be lost by using more calories through activity than the body consumes. The factors that influence the body weight are (1) somatotype or the body build (2) the food or caloric intake, and (3) the energy expended or the activity performed.

Keep in mind that it takes 3500 calories to produce a pound of body fat. Approximately 15 to 17 calories are needed to maintain each pound of fat the body contains. If 1 pound a week is lost, the caloric intake must be reduced 500 calories each day or the energy expended must be increased by 500 calories each day and the same food intake maintained. For weight control old habits should be changed and new habits formed. A coordinated program of exercise and diet will do much to improve body build and maintain fitness. The fat and muscle components can be changed, but the bone component remains the same.

Every action, even sleeping and thinking, uses metabolic and caloric energy. The energy used and the calories needed depend upon:

1. The amount of large muscle activity.

2. The number of muscles involved.

3. The speed (intensity) of the muscle contraction movements or the range of the joint movements.

4. The duration or time for the muscle activity.

5. The restless or nervous habits.

The total cost of these five components determines the energy expenditure in relation to age and body size.

The recommended daily dietary allowances of the Food and Nutrition Board of the National Academy of Sciences are intended for persons normally active in a temperate climate. Energy costs of manual labor activities and the caloric requirements for various activities are presented. This information for those working with students to improve the figure is basic to the coordinated program of activities and balanced diet.

Food and Nutrition Board, National Academy of Sciences—National Research Council, Recommended Daily Dietary Allowances (Revised 1968)

	Age[2] Years From - Up to	Weight Kg	Weight (lbs)	Height cm	Height (in)	K calories	Protein gm	Fat Soluble Vitamins — Vitamin A Activity I.U.	Vitamin D I.U.	Vitamin E Activity I.U.	Water Soluble Vitamins — Ascorbic Acid mg	Folacin[4] mg	Niacin mg equiv[5]	Riboflavin mg	Thiamine mg	Vitamin B₆ mg	Vitamin B₁₂ µg	Minerals — Calcium gm	Phosphorus gm	Iodine µg	Iron mg	Magnesium mg
Infants	0 - 1/6	4	9	55	22	kg × 120	kg × 2.2[3]	1500	400	5	35	0.05	5	0.4	0.2	0.2	1.0	0.4	0.2	25	6	40
	1/6 - 1/2	7	15	63	25	kg × 110	kg × 2.0[3]	1500	400	5	35	0.05	7	0.5	0.4	0.3	1.5	0.5	0.4	40	10	60
	1/2 - 1	9	20	72	28	kg × 100	kg × 1	1500	400	5	35	0.1	8	0.6	0.5	0.4	2.0	0.6	0.5	45	15	70
Children	1 - 2	12	26	81	32	1100	25	2000	400	10	40	0.1	8	0.6	0.6	0.5	2.0	0.7	0.7	55	15	100
	2 - 3	14	31	91	36	1250	25	2000	400	10	40	0.2	8	0.7	0.6	0.6	2.5	0.8	0.8	60	15	150
	3 - 4	16	35	100	39	1400	30	2500	400	10	40	0.2	9	0.8	0.7	0.7	3	0.8	0.8	70	10	200
	4 - 6	19	42	110	43	1600	30	2500	400	10	40	0.2	11	0.9	0.8	0.9	4	0.8	0.8	80	10	200
	6 - 8	23	51	121	48	2000	35	3500	400	15	40	0.2	13	1.1	1.0	1.0	4	0.9	0.9	100	10	250
	8 - 10	28	62	131	52	2200	40	3500	400	15	40	0.3	15	1.2	1.1	1.2	5	1.0	1.0	110	10	250
Males	10 - 12	35	77	140	55	2500	45	4500	400	20	40	0.4	17	1.3	1.3	1.4	5	1.2	1.2	125	10	300
	12 - 14	43	95	151	59	2700	50	5000	400	20	45	0.4	18	1.4	1.4	1.6	5	1.4	1.4	135	18	350
	14 - 18	59	130	170	67	3000	60	5000	400	25	55	0.4	20	1.5	1.5	1.8	5	1.4	1.4	150	18	400
	18 - 22	67	147	175	69	2800	60	5000	—	30	60	0.4	18	1.6	1.4	2.0	5	0.8	0.8	140	10	400
	22 - 35	70	154	175	69	2800	65	5000	—	30	60	0.4	18	1.7	1.4	2.0	5	0.8	0.8	140	10	350
	35 - 55	70	154	173	68	2600	65	5000	—	30	60	0.4	17	1.7	1.3	2.0	5	0.8	0.8	125	10	350
	55 - 75+	70	154	171	67	2400	65	5000	—	30	60	0.4	14	1.7	1.2	2.0	6	0.8	0.8	110	10	350
Females	10 - 12	35	77	142	56	2250	50	4500	400	20	40	0.4	15	1.3	1.1	1.4	5	1.2	1.2	110	18	300
	12 - 14	44	97	154	61	2300	50	5000	400	20	45	0.4	15	1.4	1.2	1.6	5	1.3	1.3	115	18	350
	14 - 16	52	114	157	62	2400	55	5000	400	25	50	0.4	16	1.4	1.2	1.8	5	1.3	1.3	120	18	350
	16 - 18	54	119	160	63	2300	55	5000	400	25	50	0.4	15	1.5	1.2	2.0	5	1.3	1.3	115	18	350
	18 - 22	58	128	163	64	2000	55	5000	—	25	55	0.4	13	1.5	1.0	2.0	5	0.8	0.8	100	18	350
	22 - 35	58	128	163	64	2000	55	5000	—	25	55	0.4	13	1.5	1.0	2.0	5	0.8	0.8	100	18	300
	35 - 55	58	128	160	63	1850	55	5000	—	25	55	0.4	12	1.5	0.9	2.0	5	0.8	0.8	90	18	300
	55 - 75+	58	128	157	62	1700	55	5000	—	25	55	0.4	10	1.5	0.9	2.0	6	0.8	0.8	80	10	300
Pregnancy						+200	65	6000	400	30	60	0.8	15	1.8	+0.1	2.5	8	+0.4	+0.4	125	18	450
Lactation						+1000	75	8000	400	30	60	0.5	20	2.0	+0.5	2.5	6	+0.5	+0.5	150	18	450

[1] The allowance levels are intended to cover individual variations among most normal persons as they live in the United States under usual environmental stresses. The recommended allowances can be attained with a variety of common foods, providing other nutrients for which human requirements have been less well defined.

[2] Entries on lines for age range 22-35 years represent the reference man and woman at age 22. All other entries represent allowances for the mid-point of the specified age range.

[3] Assumes protein equivalent to human milk. For proteins not 100 percent utilized factors should be increased proportionately.

[4] The folacin allowances refer to dietary sources as determined by Lactobacillus casei assay. Pure forms of folacin may be effective in doses less than 1/4 of the RDA.

[5] Niacin equivalents include dietary sources of the vitamin itself plus 1 mg equivalent for each 60 mg of dietary tryptophan.

METABOLIC COST OF MANUAL LABOR ACTIVITIES*

Activity	Kilocalories used per minute
Metal working	3.50
House painting	3.50
Carpentry	3.84
Farming chores	3.84
Plastering walls	4.10
Truck and automobile repair	4.17
Farming, planting, hoeing, raking	4.67
Repaving roads	5.00
Gardening, weeding	5.60
Stacking lumber	5.83
Stone, masonry	6.33
Pick and shovel work	6.67
Shoveling, miners	6.80
Chopping wood	7.50
Gardening, digging	8.60

*Modified from C. Frank Consolazio *et al.* (p. 24, 330), from data of Benedict and Cathcart, Lusk, Pollack *et al.*

METABOLIC COST OF VARIOUS ACTIVITIES

Activity	Kilocalories used per minute
Sleeping	1.17
Resting in bed	1.26
Sitting normally	1.29
Sitting, reading	1.29
Lying quietly	1.33
Sitting, eating	1.49
Sitting, playing cards	1.52
Standing normally	1.50
Classwork lecture	1.67
Conversing	1.83
Personal toilet	2.02
Sitting, writing	2.20
Standing, light activity	2.60
Washing and dressing	2.60
Washing and shaving	2.60
Driving a car	2.80
Washing clothes	3.13
Walking indoors	3.11
Making a bed	3.38
Showering	3.40
Cleaning windows	3.70

Activity	*Kilocalories used per minute*
Sweeping floors	3.91
Ironing clothes	4.20
Mopping floors	4.86
Walking downstairs	7.13
Walking upstairs	18.58

This energy cost was calculated by time and motion studies. Although the body weight of the male used in these tasks varied, it was estimated for the average male of approximately 150 pounds, or 68 to 73 kilograms.

The average individual's energy expenditure per minute for general living activities approximates 2.50 calories.

CALORIC REQUIREMENTS FOR VARIOUS ACTIVITIES

Physical Exercise	*Kilocalories per hour*
Walking	2 mph, 200; 3 mph, 270; 4 mph, 350.
Running	800–1,000
Cycling	5 mph, 250; 10 mph, 450; 14 mph, 700.
Horseback riding	walk, 150; trot, 500; gallop, 600.
Dancing	200–400
Gymnastics	200–500
Golf	300
Tennis	400–500
Soccer	550
Canoeing	2.5 mph, 180; 4.0 mph, 420
Sculling	50 str/min, 420; 97 str/min, 670
Rowing, peak effort	1,200
Swimming	Breast and back str, 300–650; crawl, 700–900.
Squash	600–700
Climbing	700–900
Skiing	600–700
Skating fast	300–700
Wrestling	900–1,000

Mathews, Donald K., *Beginning Conditioning;* Wadsworth Publishing Company, Inc., Belmont, California, 1965, p. 35. Modified and summarized from J. B. Orr and I. Leitch and from R. Passmore and J. G. A. Durnin as it appears in Chapter 12 by J. Mayer, *Exercise and Fitness;* Washington D.C., National Education Association, 1960.

Here is a practical assignment of personal interest to you as a student or as a teacher; use the tables on the preceding pages to complete this assignment. Estimate your caloric intake and your energy output; determine your body movement pattern; then set up a program of exercises, using the following chart. Body movements, starting positions, and exercises are described in the next section, "Selecting Exercises." Name the exercise from the movement; give the starting position; then record your repetitions. State the specific purpose for each exercise on the program.

INDIVIDUAL EXERCISE SHEET*

Exercises:	Starting Position	Repetitions	Purpose†
1.			
2.			
3.			
4.			
5.			
6.			
7.			
8.			
9.			
10.			
11.			
12.			

*Check your health status with your physician.
†To develop strength, flexibility, stamina or endurance, figure improvement, and posture control.

Consolazio (24, p. 328) has studied the average time devoted by military personnel to various activities during the day. His findings are applied here as a point of reference for young adults. He found that approximately 88 per cent of the day was spent in sedentary activities; 10 per cent of the day consisted of light-to-medium work activities; and 2 per cent of the day was spent in moderate or heavy work activities. The breakdown for the time spent in each activity shows in the following table.

When similar studies are made, we believe the lack of movement activities of youngsters, young adults, adults, and senior citizens will be just as appalling. Should this pattern be correlated with dietary problems of the general population, the need for the medical obesity specialist and the endocrinologist will be many times multiplied.

Time Spent in Daily Activities	Per Cent of 24-Hour Day
Sleeping	33.59
Sitting	34.03
Lying down (excluding sleep)	16.47
Standing normally	4.36
Walking around normally	3.73
Morning and evening personal activities	3.15
Standing light activity	2.28
Physical fitness training and sports	1.97
Miscellaneous activities	.42

Selecting Exercises

Types of Exercises

Exercise and calisthenics have a relative connotation. There are numerous types with different values connotated.

1. Passive: the person is relaxed; a partner moves the limb through the desired range of motion. Passive exercise with a partner is used for neuromuscular relaxation. The physical therapist uses passive exercise to restore the normal range of motion.

2. Active assistive: the partner moves the limb at the start and end of the normal range, assisting at the difficult exertion points.

3. Active: the individual performs without help. Isotonic exercise is a term which means free, normal range motion.

4. Active resistive (or progressive resistive or overload): resistance is provided by manual or mechanical devices. Resistive exercise is strength developer and sometimes is called "isometrics" when joint movement is nil.

5. General exercises: free physical activity as sports, dance, and aquatics are included in this type.

6. Therapeutic or remedial exercise: specific exercises are medically prescribed for a particular condition; developmental and/or conditioning implies attainment of strength through vigorous large muscle group activity.

MUSCLES (FRONT VIEW)

This surface anatomy chart identifies some of the muscles and groups of muscles used in exercises and physical activities. Since muscles come in pairs, each one has a partner on the other side.

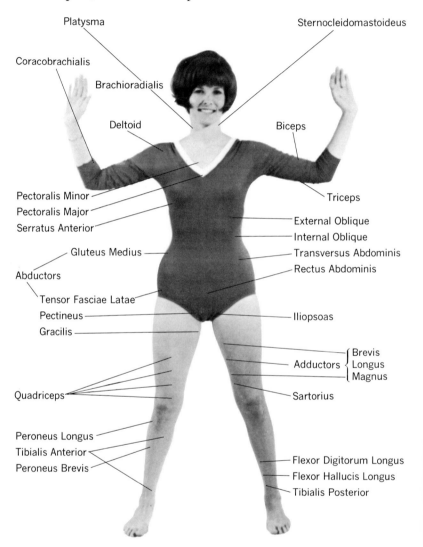

Platysma

Sternocleidomastoideus

Coracobrachialis

Brachioradialis

Deltoid

Biceps

Pectoralis Minor
Pectoralis Major
Serratus Anterior

Triceps

External Oblique
Internal Oblique

Gluteus Medius

Transversus Abdominis

Abductors

Rectus Abdominis

Tensor Fasciae Latae
Pectineus
Gracilis

Iliopsoas

Adductors { Brevis
Longus
Magnus

Quadriceps

Sartorius

Peroneus Longus
Tibialis Anterior
Peroneus Brevis

Flexor Digitorum Longus
Flexor Hallucis Longus
Tibialis Posterior

FIG. 5-13.   Front view of the surface anatomy of the human body.

MUSCLES (BACK VIEW)

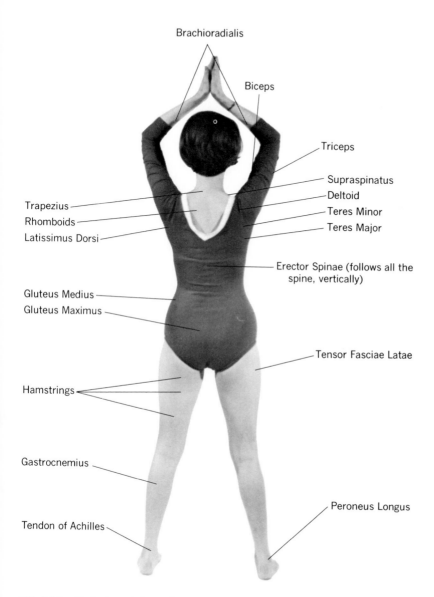

Brachioradialis

Biceps

Triceps

Supraspinatus

Deltoid

Trapezius

Teres Minor

Rhomboids

Teres Major

Latissimus Dorsi

Erector Spinae (follows all the spine, vertically)

Gluteus Medius

Gluteus Maximus

Tensor Fasciae Latae

Hamstrings

Gastrocnemius

Peroneus Longus

Tendon of Achilles

FIG. 5-14.   Back view of the surface anatomy of the human body.

Body Movements

Since movement occurs at the body joint, muscles are attached above and below the moving joint. Joint movements illustrated are flexion, extension, hyperextension, abduction, adduction, outward and inward rotation of the limbs, and circumduction or circling of the body parts.

Trunk flexion.

a. Hip flexion, knee flexion; b. hip flexion, knee extension; c. standing, side bending with arm overhead.

Leg abduction, inward rotation shoulder.

Trunk extension.

Hip flexion, knee flexion, foot dorsiflexion.

Arm abduction, elbow extension.

Trunk hyperextension.

Lower extremity; leg hyperextension, foot plantar flexion.

Arm forward flexion.

Outward rotation of trunk, outward rotation of shoulders.

Outward rotation of shoulders, flexion of elbow.

Arm extension, shoulder blades abducted, hip flexion, knee extension, foot dorsiflexion.

Starting Positions

Accuracy of the starting position affects the exercise routine. Frequently used starting positions are included in the illustrations.

Standing erect, arms rotated outward.   Stride stand.

Hook sitting, upper extremity forward flexion.   Kneeling.

Long, stride sitting, arms abducted.   Triangle sit.

Half-kneeling.

Adams position.

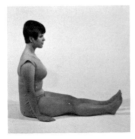

Long sit, arms
adducted.

Prone lying, arms
outward rotated.

Reverse Adams, feet
dorsiflexed, neck grasp.

Supine lying, arms
inward rotation.

Hook lying.

Side lying.

Modified Yoga
sitting.

Modified tailor
sit. (cross)

All fours position.

Inclined sitting.

Tuck sit.

Knee-chest position.

Half side lying.

Cross or tailor sitting.

The preceding pages have explained and illustrated how to assess objectively the body needs. To fulfill your program, choose one exercise from each of the following classifications. What you want and need to achieve is posssible. Be accurate, be regular, be specific. When taking exercises, keep the foot relaxed, avoid pointing the toes (plantar flexion is a stronger position than dorsiflexion).

Total Body Exercises

Total body exercises are designed to place demands over all the body areas. The warm-up is used to develop and maintain endurance and stamina: the cardiorespiratory endurance should be improved.

In the directions for exercises *reps* is used as an abbreviation for *repetitions*.

1. The squat thrust or Burpee: standing: reps, 10 times or 30 seconds.

Squat, then place the hands on the floor under the shoulders, extend the body, return to the squat, and stand. Keep a fast rhythm. Gradually increase the number of times you perform this exercise each day.

2. Flexions: supine, finger tips at the shoulders; reps, 25 times or 60 seconds.

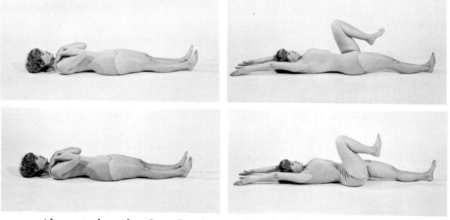

Alternate knee bend to the chest with a double arm fling over the head. This exercise is used for persons that have contraindications such as obesity and some knee conditions, for the more strenuous weight-bearing exercises.

3. Running in place with 10 cut steps: standing; reps, 50 times or 60 seconds.

This exercise can be made more difficult by replacing the 10 cut steps with 10 jumps, squats, or 5 hops on each foot.

4. Vertical skip: standing; reps, 30 to 60 seconds.

Use a high, alternate arm swing; keep the feet straight; step hop in place. When the right knee comes up, the left hand swings to head height. This exercise is good for improving coordination.

5. Skip rope: standing; reps, 25 times or 30 seconds.

This exercise can be performed with or without a rope. Using the feet alternately is less strenuous than using both feet together.

6. Jumping jack: standing; reps, 25 times or 30 seconds.

Begin with feet together and arms at the sides; jump to a stride position as the hands comes together over the head. Get a good fast rhythm. Clapping the hands at the thighs and over the head takes more energy. Variations can be used by hands together forward, hands together behind the body, or all three hand positions coordinated with the stride jump.

Many activities such as bicycling, swimming, track events, skiing, hockey, soccer, handball, tennis, and dance—contribute to the increase of endurance. A progressive, graduated exercise circuit striving for top capacity of intensity should produce significant results in two to four weeks.

Flexibility Exercises

Most body movement depends upon the degree of flexibility found in the joint structures. Flexibility is needed, because (1) the range of motion improves most activity performances, (2) good flexibility helps prevent damage to muscle fibers and joint structures and provides some insurance against muscle pain and strain. Hypokinetic living habits and habitual static positions as well as body type and aging may cause restricted flexibility.

Flexibility of all the body joints can be improved with effort. The flexibility exercises can be used when a restriction of the body segment is present. These exercises help achieve normal range of motion of the spine and limbs through improved muscle balance and development of suppleness of the soft tissues. Bend, twist, and stretch for easy warm-ups before heavier activity. Then use the normal range movements for each specific flexibility problem, such as maximum bending and stretching.

Passive flexibility exercises employ a stretch-sustained movement. Active flexibility exercises use rapid, repeated, quick normal range movements.

1. Trunk pendulum: standing arms overhead; reps, 10 times or 30 seconds.

Forward bend at the hips with an easy bob to the floor; repeat. Stretch to the ceiling and repeat. (Also done in a supine position or at a gym bar.)

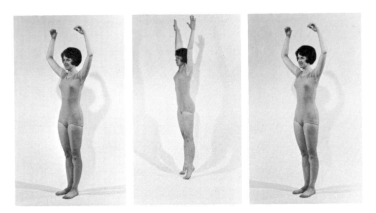

2. Passive chest lift with a partner: cross sitting or stool; reps, person's tolerance.

Fingers at the neck or forehead, the partner stands at the person's back with the hip or knee at the shoulder blade level. A slow easy pull backward of the elbows will stretch the anterior chest muscles; release the pull and repeat.

3. Airplane: stride stand arms shoulder height; reps, 25 times. Alternate toe touch.

Feet straight, twist to the left and bend at the hips to touch the outside left heel with the right hand; come to the erect standing and repeat to the right side. This exercise stretches the muscles of the shoulders, back, hips, and legs.

4. Hook lying on a narrow table with arms stretched at right angles will ease pectoral tightness. Arms stretched overhead will ease latissimus dorsi tightness, providing passive stretch to anterior chest muscles. Both of these muscles tightened promote forward shoulders.

5. Trunk bounce: stride long sitting; reps, person's tolerance.

Arm position varies; bounce easy to get the head toward the floor between the knees.

This exercise can be performed with the knees together, hands at the ankles, and easy bounces toward the knee with the head.

In the stride long sitting, easy bounces to the right knee with the head and then to the left knee with the head present an easier flexibility workout and use the side muscle groups of the trunk.

6. Double knee pull: hook lying; reps, 5-second holds, then repeat.

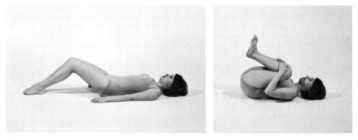

Hug the knees at the chest tightly; then return to starting position and repeat. Keep the chin in. This exercise is good for low back stretching.

7. Nose to knee exercise: all fours position; reps, 10 to 20 times each leg.

Touch the knee to the nose; then extend the head and the leg. The performance varies, as this exercise can be done 5 times with the right knee, then 5 times with the left knee or alternated first with the right and then with the left. Both ways are equally beneficial for hip and neck flexibility.

8. Prone rocking: prone lying, knee apart, hands at the ankles; reps, person's tolerance.

Separate the knees and bend them; grasp the ankles firmly. This may be the beginning for several days; then extend the head and upper trunk and rock forward and back. This gives maximum stretching of the anterior body muscles and contraction of the back muscles. The rock or pummeling affects the fat pads over the abdominals. This exercise is contraindicated for persons with low back problems.

Strength Exercises

The ability to do work against resistance indicates the strength of the muscle or muscle group. The overload, or resistance, principle builds and maintains muscle strength. The gradual increase of the resistance develops firmness of muscles.

1. Curl sit-ups: supine lying; reps, 60 seconds.

This curl sit-up with the knees straight is controversial. The supine position can be used for a 45 degree sit-up. The hands are on the thighs, the head and shoulders are curled toward the hips as the hands slide to the knees; return to the floor and repeat the head and shoulder curl with the hands sliding to the knees. This exercise promotes abdominal strength. The supine and the hook lying positions for sit-ups are often indicated when there is a predisposing factor of low back problems. The Williams' routine.

2. Alternate toe touch: supine position; reps, 25 times or 60 seconds.

Touching the right hand to the left toe, then the left hand to the right toe with gravity and with the head and shoulder weight as resistance uses the anterior trunk muscles, especially the abdominal obliques with the rectus abdominus and transversus strongly contracting.

3. Double leg raising: hook or supine lying; reps, 30 to 60 seconds.

The hook lying position prevents arching of the back. Bring the legs to a tuck position, straighten the knees, and dorsiflex the feet; then lower the legs until a back arch starts; tuck the legs and lower the feet to the floor. The extension of the knees and dorsiflexion of the feet stretches the low back muscles, the hamstrings, and the tendon of Achilles.

The supine position uses the hip flexors (iliopsoas), see Kraus-Weber No. 3, the first 10 inches of movement; then the abdominal muscles contract. The contraction of the low back muscles increases the pelvic tilt, and the abdominals are stretched.

4. Push ups: prone lying; reps, to tolerance.

The first push-up sometimes is called the girl's push-up and is not as strenuous as the second. Arm and shoulder strength is developed through both types.

In both push-up positions applying pressure with the hands is a modification and can be classified as an isometric exercise. Applying pressure four to six seconds and then relaxing, with no body elevation will contract the muscles of the shoulder girdle.

5. Pull ups: standing at a gym bar; reps, 20 times.

The pull ups develop shoulder and arm strength. Stand with the hands in an underhand grip on the bar at shoulder height and shoulder distance apart. Bring the chest to the bar with complete elbow flexion; then extend.

The pull up, or chinning with the bar overhead, is more strenuous, as the full body weight and gravity present more resistance. The optimum number is 3 to 6 reps. Progress gradually on the reps.

6. Back curls: prone lying; reps, 10 to 20 times.

Clasp the hands below the buttocks; then stretch and reach down toward the heels as the head and shoulder raise slightly from the floor. A chin-in position improves the head and shoulder alignment. The feet should be on the floor.

Modifications, such as placing the fingers behind the neck or on the forehead, are often used.

This exercise strengthens the muscles of the upper back and should improve head and shoulder posture.

7. Double leg raising: side lying; reps, 60 seconds each side.

Straight body alignment on the side is important. Avoid bending at the hips. The hand in front of the chest maintains equilibrium of the body. With the head down, raise both lower limbs, using a heel lead position toward the ceiling. A sandbag placed over the feet increases the resistance, thus developing muscle tone and strength.

This exercise contracts the abductors (gluteus medius and tensor fascia latae) of the thigh. Keeping the legs together, contract the adductors of the bottom leg. The trunk muscles stabilize the position.

Single leg raising is used to strengthen the abductors, to a lesser degree. When the double leg raising is too difficult, start with the single leg raising.

Isometrics or Isometric Contraction

Iso means same; *metric* means length. A muscle remains unchanged in length when it produces tension (contraction) against an immovable object, such as pushing or lifting an object that will not move or pushing or pulling one muscle group against another. Isometric contraction of the muscle was investigated by the German physiologists, Mueller and Hettinger, in the 1940's. Their findings show muscle strength development with a six-second maximum contraction. Using these exercises daily for a week, the young men averaged a gain in strength of 4 to 5 per cent; in women the average increase in strength showed about 3 per cent for the specific muscle group involved in isometric contractions (173, p. 59).

Isometric contraction is synonymous with Svoboda's "conscious evolution," with Charles Atlas's "dynamic tension," and the physical medicine terms of "muscle setting" and "static contractions" of the muscle or muscle groups.

On page 181 are seven isometric exercises which require little or no equipment.

1. Hip tightening: prone position; reps, 6-second hold. This can be done standing, also.
2. Hand press: standing, kneeling, or sitting; 6-second hold.
3. Hand press: kneeling.
4. Posterior towel stretch: standing or sitting; 6 seconds.
5. Anterior towel stretch: standing or sitting; 6 seconds.
6. Leg push against an object, chair, or wall: standing, lying, or sitting; 6 seconds.
7. Leg push against the hand of the same side: standing or sitting; 6 seconds.

These exercises develop strength in the hip joint muscles, the chest, arm, and abdomen muscles, the back muscles, the leg abductors, and the anterior thigh muscles.

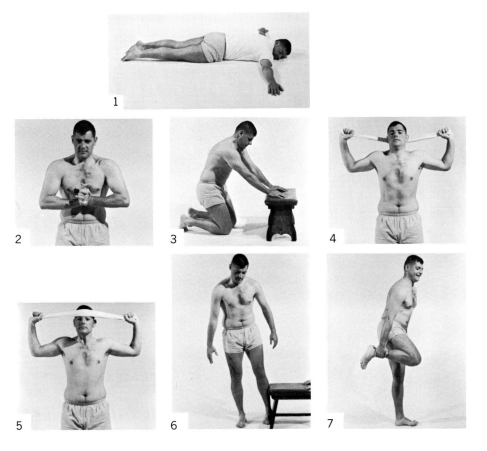

Controlled Movement Patterns

Posture Control with Kinesthetic Awareness

Posture is an individual matter. The values of aesthetics, psychology, and movement efficiency on the job may overshadow the health and organic values. To attain effective daily living, each person should do the best in the positioning of his body.

Learning the coordination necessary for good posture requires concentrated work in remembering, registering, and applying the basic gravity line checkpoints. For the best body mechanics, rechecking and repetition are necessary to reeducate the kinesthetic sense and change habits. Some of the following exercises should be practiced.

1. Abdominal retraction with neck retraction: hook lying; reps, 60 seconds.

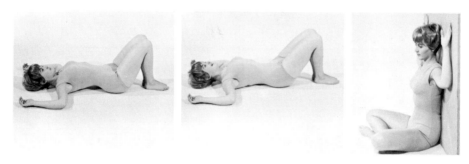

Flatten the back to the floor by contracting the abdominals and the neck muscles, so that the back arch disappears. Breath normally. This helps promote the hip tuck position and feeling of abdominal tightening, as well as the high chest position. Follow up this same movement in a sitting and in a standing position.

2. Wall test: standing at a wall; reps, 60 seconds.

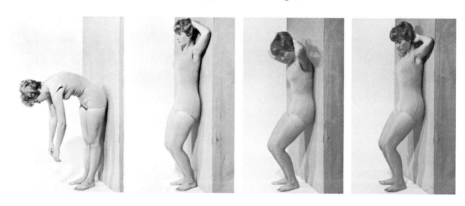

This exaggerated knee flexion wall test helps achieve the feel of the pelvic and abdominal control necessary for good trunk position. The curling and uncurling at the wall promotes trunk alignment.

3. Door knob check. This is applied by standing at the door frame opposite the knob. Pull the door closed so the door will touch the feet and not the abdomen or chest body segment. The squeezing-through-the-small-space feeling tucks the hips and chin in to further the awareness of the hip control.

4. The gravity line tests explained earlier in the chapter.

Foot Exercises

Using the feet correctly at all times and wearing proper shoes for the occasion promotes strong, flexible feet. A straight foot and ankle is esthetically more attractive and provides a balanced soft tissue support for the bones. A foot exercise in the personal physical fitness program will help to maintain strength and flexibility.

1. Correct walking with the feet parallel. Abducted walking with the weight on the outer border of the foot.

2. Foot circling: lying or sitting; reps, 10 times, slowly.

Circle the right foot clockwise and the left foot counterclockwise, as the tibialis anterior which aids the support of the long, inner arch has a stronger contraction. The three-point base sit for foot circling also develops trunk and shoulder muscles.

3. Toe curls with a towel or sheet: sitting; reps, 60 seconds.

Keep the heels stationary and bunch the sheet under the foot, using the intrinsic foot muscles to maintain the muscle strength.

4. Golf ball roll under anterior foot: sitting; reps, 1 to 2 minutes each foot.

Roll the ball slowly under the ball of the foot. This strengthens the anterior or metatarsal arch.

5. Stretching the tendon of Achilles: supine, long sitting; reps, 10 times.

Dorsiflexion of the foot with the knee straight or bent stretches the tendon. A towel or sheet pull of the anterior foot arch stretches the Achilles tendon, along with the hamstrings, used in a long sit. See minimal program.

Waistline and Midriff Exercises

The following exercises will help tone the midriff and the waist.

1. Trunk circling: standing or sitting; reps, 60 seconds, 30 right-
   30 left.

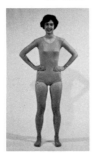

   Place hands on the hips; then circle forward, sideward, backward, sideward, and foreward. This exercise uses all the trunk
   muscles. Circle to the right for 30 seconds; then to the left for
   30 seconds.

2. Lateral or side bending: standing or half kneeling; reps, 30 seconds right, then left.

   With hands on the hips, bend sideward to the right; then change
   the half kneel position and bend sideward to the left. When bending laterally to the right the right trunk muscles tighten and the
   left stretch; the reverse happens on the left lateral bending.

3. Trunk twist with knee left and cross-over: long sitting; reps,
   30 seconds each side.

With palms on the floor for support, bring the right knee up and twist to the left side of the left knee; then return to the starting position. Repeat this movement with the left knee going to the right side of the right knee. Using the full range of movement, increase the tempo and keep the hands on the floor. Twisting motions are using the middle trunk muscles. Keep the chest high by having the hands near the hips.

4. Hip raising: half side lying; reps, 30 seconds each side.

The supporting elbow should be directly under the shoulder; the other hand should be close to the abdominal region for best equilibrium in performing this exercise. Raise and lower the hips quickly for 30 seconds; repeat on the other side. All trunk muscles are contracted and there is some pummeling of the side hip muscles (tensor fascia latae).

5. Trunk twist: sitting position; reps, 30 to 50 each side.

Place the fingers on the neck. Sustain the hold position on both sides. Very good for the waistline and midriff.

Hip and Thigh Exercises

Some effective exercises for the toning of the hips and thighs are double knee roll, scissors, hip walk, hip roll, and side lying-double leg raising.

1. Double knee roll: hook lying; reps, 60 seconds.

With arms extended at shoulder height or with hands holding onto a sofa or a mat to hold the position and knees together and above the hips, roll to the right and then to the left with vigorous movements for 60 seconds. Keep the shoulders on the floor.

2. Scissors: side lying; reps, 30 seconds each side; progress slowly to 60 seconds each side.

With balanced side lying and support from the hand in front of the chest, keep both knees straight, raise the legs, and scissor vigorously forward and back for 30 seconds. Repeat on the other side. A sheet under the hip will help eliminate the friction between the hip and the mat or floor. Check on keeping the knees straight and getting good extension of the bottom leg. This exercise is strenuous and uses the thigh muscles and hip abductors (gluteus medius) with pummeling of the high thigh regions.

3. Hip walk: long sitting; reps, 30 seconds forward and 30 seconds backward.

Forward flexion of the arms, keep the knees straight, then walk forward with a hip wiggle and a heel push from each limb. Walk backward with a hip wiggle while the knees are kept straight. Hip and thigh muscles are used.

4. Hip roll: modified Yoga sit (feet together); reps, 60 seconds.

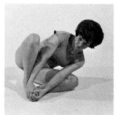

With hands grasping the ankles, chest high, and forward trunk lean at the hips for maintaining equilibrium, rock as far to the right as possible; then to the left, performing a continuous rock right and left. Hip and thigh muscles are well pummeled.

5. Side lying-double leg raising: See exercise for developing muscle tone.

Upper Back Exercises, Head and Shoulder Exercises

Upper trunk alignment depends upon the upper back muscle strength and the head and shoulder movements. Some exercises to improve the strength and tone of the trapezius, teres, rhomboids, and erector spinae are illustrated.

1. Trunk stretching: hook lying; reps, 30 to 60 seconds.

With the arms overhead and chin in, retract the neck as the arms are stretched and the spine is kept flat on the floor.

2. Wand exercise: sitting or standing; reps, 10 times with a 4-second hold in outward rotation of the shoulders.

Stretch the wand overhead; lower behind the head to the shoulder blades; bring the elbows forward in outward rotation of the shoulders; hold for 4 seconds; relax and stretch high; then repeat. When standing, check the pelvic tilt to prevent lordosis or a swayback position.

3. Cross sit at the wall: reps, 60 seconds.

   This exercise stresses a chin in position, arms in outward rotation, using a pull and push of the arms against the wall to raise the chest and tighten the upper back muscles.

4. Head push with partner: kneeling; reps, 4-second hold, 10 times.

   Resistance from a partner tightens the upper back muscles. This tightening adds strength to these muscles. Check the low back to prevent increased pelvic tilting.

Exercises for Menstrual Problems

Menstrual difficulties are a medical problem that should be checked by the physician. The individual's capacities and limitations should be considered. Mild physical activity may relieve congestion during menstruation.

1. Billig Exercises.

Harvey Billig, Jr., M.D., set up exercises for painful menstruation. His hypothesis was based on the correction of faulty low back posture (9).

With shoes removed, feet parallel, arm on the supporting side at shoulder height, and the other hand at the greater trochanter in the thigh, tighten the abdominals and the hip muscles; then push the hips forward obliquely toward the wall, getting a pull in the lower abdomen on the side near the wall.

Starting position, front view.

Starting position, side view.

Pelvis forward and toward wall, front view.

Pelvis forward and toward wall, side view.

Repeat three times on the right side; then three times on the left side. This should be done three times a day for two to three months.

Eighty per cent of the women who followed the preceding exercises in the Billig study group reported improvement of menstrual pain.

2. Golub Exercises.

Leib J. Golub, M.D., of Philadelphia studied over 15,000 girls with primary dysmenorrhea and found that using the airplane exercise for improved flexibility and good body stretching helped decrease menstrual pain (56).

Reps: 4 times twice a day, gradually progressing to 10 times twice a day for three months.

Standing in a stride position with arms abducted to shoulder level, twist to the right and touch the right foot with the left hand; return to the erect position; then twist left and touch the left foot with the right hand; repeat 4 times, twice a day.

3. Mosher Exercises.

Many years ago Celia Mosher, M.D., developed exercises for dysmenorrhea. Illustrated is the knee-chest position which is combined with gentle abdominal pumping. It is recommended at bedtime, daily, for several months.

With knees apart and arms spread pull the abdominal muscles in; relax; then push out. Repeat for 60 seconds. Hold this position for 3 to 5 minutes.

Williams' Routine for Low Back Conditions

These exercises are designed to increase the flexibility of the low back extensors and strengthen the flexor muscles. They are to be performed daily, starting with ten repetitions for each exercise and progressively increasing to as many as forty repetitions. These exercises are best performed on a firm, flat surface.

The first exercise can be made more strenuous by progressing from one step to the next, as each becomes easier to perform.

1. Purpose: to strengthen the abdominal muscles; position: hook lying.

   Come to a sitting position: *a.* reaching the hands past the knees; *b.* with the arms folded across the chest; *c.* with the hands clasped behind the head.

a   b   c

2. Purpose: to strengthen the hip muscles; position: hook lying.

   Roll the pelvis backward, flattening the low back curve; pinch the buttocks together and raise the tailbone slightly upward.

3. Purpose: to stretch the low back muscles; position: hook lying.

   Stretch the back by pulling the knees to the chest. Curve the back by ducking the head forward.

4. Purpose: to stretch the low back and hamstring muscles; position: supine lying.

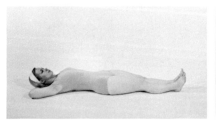 

Come to a sitting position. Keep the knees straight. Bend the head toward the knees to stretch the low back and hip muscles.

5. Purpose: to stretch the hip flexor muscles; position: standing.

    Place one foot forward. Lean forward on that leg, keeping the back leg straight. Bend the trunk forward so that a stretch is felt along the front of the hip and thigh.

6. Purpose: to stretch the low back and to strengthen the thigh muscles; position: standing.

    Squat as far as possible; then stand. Keep the feet *flat* on the floor. Curve the back to keep balanced and stretch the low back and hip muscles.

Relaxation

Neuromuscular relaxation, a positive type of exercise with a partner putting the limbs and head through normal range movements is relaxing, but wiggling, bobbing, and circling of the body segments can also release muscular tension for improved relaxation and rest. Deep breathing and rhythmical, even breathing contributes to relaxation of the body. A change of pace, or a new and different activity, provides a diversional relaxor for the person. Yoga, a Hindu method of relaxation which developed in the ancient cultures, offers a change of concentration with physical activity. Yoga means "to yoke" and was developed by Hatha Yoga, who used a system of body postures and conscious attention to breathing during these postures to rest the mind. The practitioners of Yoga apply meditation and the physical poses (asanas) for long periods—sometimes five minutes to thirty minutes. The few poses illustrated have some modifications from the orthodox yoga. They contribute to the achievement of muscle strength and body flexibility.

When even breathing is used between each pose, these modified poses contribute to relaxation. Begin with a 30-count hold.

1. Lotus sit: spine erect, hands on knees, soles of the feet upward. Breathe evenly.

2. Plough pose: supine. Lift the legs over the head and touch the floor. Keep the knees straight. Hold the pose and relax. Breathe slowly and evenly.

3. Locust pose: prone. Arms at the side of the hips, knees together, raise (hyperextend) the legs as high as possible. Even breathing.

4. Jackknife pose: supine. Lift the head, arms and feet at the same time. Balance on the buttocks. Even breathing.

5. Cobra pose: prone. Elbows bent, hands at the shoulders, on the floor. Raise the head and shoulders upward as far as possible.

6. Neck stand, bicycle position: supine. Bring the legs upward to the ceiling, body weight on the elbows, neck, and shoulders. Hold and breathe evenly; slowly uncurl to the supine.

7. Modified fish pose: sitting. Place right foot against the left thigh with a full right knee bend. Hold 30 seconds; repeat with the left foot. Bend forward slowly or to the foot on the thigh; sit erect; repeat once to the other reverse position. Hands on hips; even breathing.

8. Bow pose: prone. Knees bent, grasp feet with both hands. Arch the back as much as possible. Breathe evenly and hold 30 counts.

9. Twisted pose, modified: sitting. Hands on hips. Try to place sole of the right foot against the inner left thigh and bend the left knee. Place the left foot on the outside of the right thigh. Twist right and then bring the trunk back to starting. Repeat in reverse. Even breathing.

10. Upside down at the bars or wall hand stand. Hands on bars, lower head with back to bars. Kick the legs upward to a head stand. Hold. Breath evenly.

DO THESE POSES DAILY:
INCREASE THE COUNT OR HOLD.

Analysis of Questionable Movement Patterns

The physical education teacher and others who work with young people have the opportunity to detect the beginning of deviations. Contraindications for some exercises, as well as the need for special exercises, are identified through the minimal screening test and a functional test observed by the teacher. The functional test for judging efficiency in action situations consists of a designed movement to apprise normal or abnormal incoordinated movement patterns.

Some questionable or debatable movement patterns are discussed below.

Feet

Since foot and leg deviations have a high incidence, the following positions should be scrutinized:

1. Activities with *toe out stances*, as this position may increase pronation and increase the tendency to lengthen and flatten the longitudinal arch. Proper foot position will improve movement performance as the muscles and joints can function correctly.

2. Activities which have continual or static *rising on the toes*. The gastrocnemius and soleus muscles are many times stronger than the foot dorsiflexors, so this position furthers this strength and throws added stress on the balls of the feet; also the elongated plantar structures stretch further. If this movement is needed, inversion of the feet should be stressed. With foot weaknesses, rope skipping should be done on mats to eliminate the jar stress.

3. *Rising-on-the heel* activities tighten the anterior tibial and anterior leg muscles, so in congenital flatfoot or flexible flatfoot, it should be contraindicated. Walking with the feet in abduction is often prescribed for flatfoot.

4. *Toe curling* exercises are inclined to thrust the distal end of the first metatarsal (base of great toe) upward. It should remain down in a depressed position as the anterior bony support.

5. *Improper weight bearing* will produce foot faults, since the pelvic position may be forward and cause stress on the forefoot and plantar structures; muscle laxity may accentuate tibial torsion. The piriformis muscle is the only muscle which crosses the sacro-iliac joint, and, as an outward rotator of the hip, it helps protect the added stress placed on this joint by weight bearing. When the feet pronate, the leg will rotate in giving a tension pull to the upper end of the sacrum—downward and forward. Correct foot position will help keep the sacro-iliac joint in good alignment and reduce the stress on the ligaments.

6. *Lunging activities*, if prolonged, may easily injure weak feet or feet that present slight malalignment conditions. Warm-up movements should precede the activity of weight-bearing stress when the lunging movement is a part of the planned program.

Deep Knee Bends

Deep knee bends—the duck walk, full squat position, and the Russian bounce—place undue stress on the ligaments of the knee. The extensors (quadriceps) are completely stretched, and the front surface of the knee is pushed forward, placing full body support on the knee flexors and the anterior surface of the feet. Lead-up progressions for tendon Achilles stretching should be developed preceding the knee-bend positions.

Supine Leg Raising

It seems to be a common belief that this movement will strengthen the abdominals; it actually strengthens the strong hip flexors (iliopsoas). The abdominals may tense to stabilize the pelvis—a very difficult movement—as normally the back will arch showing abdominal lengthening and back muscle tightening, increasing the pelvic tilt (lordosis). Since the incidence of lordosis is high in postural deviations, this movement should be modified by bringing the knees to the chest, then straightening the legs toward the ceiling and lowering while the back remains flat. When the back starts to arch, the knee-bend position should be used to return the heels to the mat.

Prone Leg Raising

When the body is prone, it is in an extended position. To strengthen the trunk extensors, the leg raisings will go into a hyperextension position and increase lordosis with resultant abdominal muscle stretching. To improve back muscles and not increase lordosis, one should start from the Adam's position over a table or plinth; then alternate leg raisings progressed to double leg raising, progressed with resistance to achieve better back muscle development. Another position on all fours with knee touching the nose and then followed by leg extension will achieve a better therapeutic exercise technique.

Sit-ups

Many variations of the sit-ups are to be found, but, to receive maximum abdominal strengthening, the curling movements are recommended. The back muscles have to give hip stability but may be hyperactive with some students who use a straight back posture in sit-ups.

1. Supine position with hands on the thighs. The movement pattern should have a curling of the head and shoulders while the hands reach toward the knee. *A 45 degree sit-up.* Lower slowly; repeat to tolerance (10 times at first).

2. Supine position with the back of the fingers on the forehead (to help keep the chin in). Raise the head and shoulder as the knees bend to the chest; then lower to starting position.

3. Supine position with a partner holding the feet. Arms are folded on chest with hands at the elbows; curling to a sitting position, twist and touch left elbow to the right knee; return to the supine and repeat with right elbow to the left knee.

4. Hook lying position with feet stabilized. With arms as in (3) (this position rules out the hip flexors in isotonic contractions) rise to a sitting position and return to the hook lying; then repeat.°

5. The sit-up from a stall bar bench or long stool sit with the feet anchored under the stall bars. The teacher should check the upper positions of the rectus abdominal for a diastasis (an interspace) to prevent the possibilities of ventral hernia (umbilical). The breathing should be stressed to prevent interabdominal pressure. Arm position same as 3. The sitting position places tension on all trunk muscles, and the forward movement tightens the abdominal muscles.

6. Same position as above with a slight knee bend. Lower the trunk until the trunk (shoulders and head) is approximately 4 inches from the floor in hyperextension; return to the sitting position; then repeat. The degree of difficulty or increased resistance can be achieved by changing the upper extremity positions to the wing, or by placing the hands overhead and adding weight on the chest or arms.

7. A balanced "V" position of leg and trunk. For the well-developed person, a sit-up in this position achieves maximum strength for the abdominal group. Another more strenuous sit-up may be done with a continuous lower extremity bicycle movement coordinated with head and shoulder raising. To insure against interabdominal pressure hazards, counting aloud or singing softly is an adjunct because when the breath is held closing the windpipe, the downward thrust of the diaphragm on the fixed abdominal wall may provoke a hernia.

° The authors have found approximately 33 per cent of young adults cannot perform this movement.

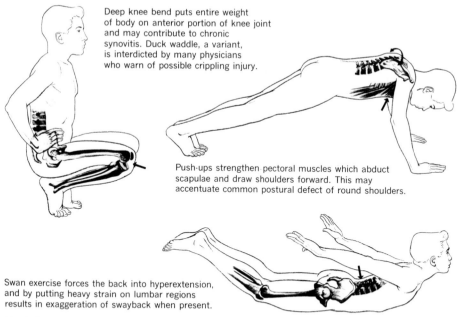

Deep knee bend puts entire weight of body on anterior portion of knee joint and may contribute to chronic synovitis. Duck waddle, a variant, is interdicted by many physicians who warn of possible crippling injury.

Push-ups strengthen pectoral muscles which abduct scapulae and draw shoulders forward. This may accentuate common postural defect of round shoulders.

Swan exercise forces the back into hyperextension, and by putting heavy strain on lumbar regions results in exaggeration of swayback when present.

Youth fitness: a medical view. (Courtesy of Roche Medical Image-Lou Barlow; Roche Laboratories, Nutley, N.J.) *Muscle-building exercises may injure joints and muscles.* These exercises are considered potentially harmful by Dr. C. L. Lowman, Los Angeles orthopaedist, and M. Marilyn Flint, Ph.D., Santa Barbara physical educator.

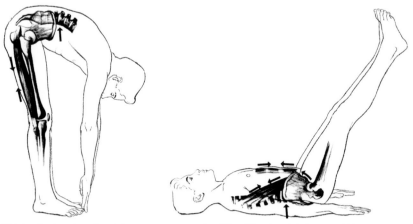

Toe touch, done by a forceful bouncing motion to reach foot, is blamed for low-back pain as well as damage to joints.

Leg lift, achieved mainly by use of hip flexors, puts great strain on iliopsoas and tends to increase degree of spinal curvature in lordosis.

Toe Touches. At particular ages—usually prepuberty or puberty—the child has long legs and a short trunk as a result of the normal growth increment. Inability to touch the toes does not necessarily mean tight hamstrings. (Courtesy of Roche Medical Image-Lou Barlow; Roche Laboratories, Nutley, N.J.)

We have seen the sit-up exercise abused by many young adults, with a resultant increase in the prevalent swayback deviation leading to a potential low back syndrome.°

Chinning, Dips, or Push-ups

Overdevelopment of the pectoral muscles means that they are in a chronically shortened position with the shoulders forward and the shoulder blades spread apart. This may develop into a compensatory curve in the thoracic region of the spine, such as round back or kyphosis. Occupational positions, as well as fatigue slump, show this position as a common malposture. The posterior muscle groups need good development so there can be muscle balance of the upper trunk and shoulder girdle in direct ratio to muscle strength and flexibility.

When *chinning* for improved muscle strength (the underhand grip with the fingers toward the face), good pectoral muscle action is evident. With the overhand grip, palms facing outward, the biceps and brachioradialis have greater activation; the shoulders are in the inward rotation position so that the antagonist action of scapular adductors and outward rotators is insufficient.

The *dips* or *push-ups* do develop the pectorals and upper fibers of the serratus because the body weight is the resistance. When relaxed shoulders, fatigue slump, round back, or kypholordosis is present, this movement should be contraindicated and alternate movements should be used. Wall sitting with isometric hand pushes and finger pulls can improve muscle strength. Prone lying with the hands at the side of the shoulders accompanied by isometric pushing on the mat without body elevation adds to the shoulder girdle strength. Tailor sitting eliminates lordosis and with isotonic rhythmical Danish shoulder movements adds stamina and flexibility to the shoulder region.

Discrimination should be focused on all activity programs. The teacher must be able to assess and evaluate quickly an exercise program as to its principle of specificity, as well as to its contribution to general, all-round development.

Minimal Exercise Programs

It is often claimed that in the busy daily life of the average person, little attention can be directed toward completion of an optimal exercise program. However, everyone should find time for at least a minimal

---

° July and August of 1965, Wheeler did clinical physical therapy observing that the majority of low back pain conditions had negative findings and the age variable ranged from 18 upward for these patients.

effort. Two such programs are presented here, one for women, one for men.

When previous activity has been limited, start easy with 30 seconds for each exercise; then progress to 60 seconds; and then to 90 seconds daily or three times a week.

WOMEN'S MINIMAL PROGRAM
Purpose of the exercise and repetitions

FLEXIBILITY

ABDOMINAL STRENGTH   60 sec.

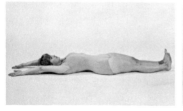

BACK STRENGTH   60 sec.

ARM STRENGTH   60 sec.

WOMEN'S MINIMAL PROGRAM (CONT.)

Purpose of the exercise and repetitions

CARDIORESPIRATORY   60 sec.   10 jumps

FOOT   4 sec.   5 times

BACK FLATTENER and POSTURE CONTROL   1 min. to 5 min.

MEN'S MINIMAL PROGRAM
Purpose of the exercise and repetitions

FLEXIBILITY   60 sec.

ABDOMINAL STRENGTH   60 sec.

BACK STRENGTH   60 sec.

ARM STRENGTH   60 sec.

MEN'S MINIMAL PROGRAM (CONT.)
Purpose of the exercise and repetitions

CARDIORESPIRATORY   60 sec.   10 squats with a jump

Summary

Adapted physical education can promote mechanical and muscular efficiency through personalized programs for posture improvement, figure conditioning, and fitness. Correct body mechanics have aesthetic, psychological, health, and efficiency values. Screening tests aid in appraising back view and side view posture faults. Posture tests combined with medical examination and comparative performance tests to determine fitness enable the physical education teacher to develop the personal individualized exercise program.

A variety of exercises for posture improvement of the neck, upper back, shoulders, low back and abdomen, hips, and feet are available. In weight control, caloric intake and energy expenditure are other factors to consider. In programs for women special attention must be given to functional menstrual problems and functional low back pain. Frequently, relaxation and modified Yoga exercises may achieve relaxation, as well as strength and flexibility. In planning any exercise program, it must be remembered that some movement patterns are debatable and must be performed with caution. The minimum exercise programs described in the chapter illustrate the type of program that will contribute to total body development.

THE BASIC MOVEMENT SKILLS IN SPORTS AND GAMES*

(A Valuable Guide of Activities for the Handicapped)

Standing	Walking	Running and Stepping	Jumping, Leaping, Hopping, etc.	Landing and Falling	Sitting	Pushing and Pulling	Holding, Lifting, Carrying	Throwing and Catching	Striking
All activities except	All activities except	Badminton	Apparatus	Apparatus	Canoeing	Archery	Canoeing	Apparatus (spotting-catching)	Badminton
Canoeing	Archery	Baseball	Basketball	Baseball	Crew	Canoeing	Dance	Baseball	Baseball
Crew	Canoeing	Softball	Dance	Softball	Modern dance	Crew	Tumbling	Softball	Softball
Riding	Crew	Basketball	Diving	Basketball	Riding	Dance	Weight lifting	Basketball	Basketball
Swimming	Riding	Dance	Skiing	Dance		Fencing	Wrestling	Bowling	Boxing
	Shuffleboard	Football	Track and Field	Football		Riding		(throwing)	Football
	Weight lifting	Handball	Tumbling	Skiing		Shot Put	Also, carrying equipment for many activities such as	Deck Tennis	Handball
		Hockey	Volleyball	Tumbling		Shuffleboard		Football	Hockey
	Note: use of walking coordination in crawl, kick in swimming	Lacrosse		Track and Field		Swimming	Golf	Lacrosse	Squash Raquets
		Soccer		Volleyball		Wrestling	Skiing	Track and Field	Soccer
		Speedball		Wrestling				Tumbling (spotting-catching)	Speed-a-way
		Speed-a-way						Speed-a-way	Speedball
		Squash Raquets						Speedball	Table Tennis
		Tennis						Some application of throwing to	Tennis
		Track and Field						Hockey (Roll-in)	Volleyball
								Soccer (Goalie)	

*Adapted from Broer, Marion: *Efficiency of Human Movement.* Philadelphia, W. B. Saunders Company, 1960.

Daily Tasks and Body Mechanics

Alignment in motion focuses attention on the daily tasks. Daily activity skills may be defined as all physical movements that occur when carrying on the routine activities of living. The forms of locomotion used include walking, running, jumping, sitting, climbing stairs, stooping, lifting, carrying, pulling, pushing, reaching, and getting in and out of cars. Each of these activities should be performed with the basic mechanical principles of movement in mind. The teacher and the student should know the importance of the principles of balance, force production, and control. The application of these principles will develop graceful and poised movements and prevent physical harm, pain, and disability. Correct body mechanics of movement must be applied in the home, office, and factory. This means the physical educator must teach how to use the body in daily tasks, as well as in the special skills and exercises, so that the individual learns to use his body to the best advantage.

Strong muscles will not assure efficient motion as the body moves through the daily routines. Efficient body movements are a form of posture exercises. To improve the body mechanics, the person must have the desire to practice correct body segment alignment until the neuromuscular system takes over the new or changed position as a new habit. This feel and perception of the right alignment in space and motion produce less stress on the joint articulations of the body. Sedentary positions when prolonged tend to result in adaptive shortening of some muscles and stretching of the antagonists. Consequently, the kinesthetic feel must be reinforced through repetitive movements which tend to balance the strength of the muscle groups.

The body size, shape, and strength are factors that help determine the success attainable in body movement performance. The degree to which an individual can approach his potential depends upon the way he uses his physical, emotional, and mental faculties. Morehouse and Cooper state:

"The degree of success in most physical activities is determined by the manner in which forces are applied. Through more effective use of available forces, a small man can outwrestle a larger man, a short-statured golfer can outdrive a taller golfer, a person with a short arm can throw farther than another with a long arm and a weak-muscled person can move a heavier load than a strong-muscled person." °

Correct Positions of Dynamic Posture

The basic knowledge of the correct body alignment used in most daily tasks is illustrated on the following pages. These illustrations provide the correct positions of dynamic posture and specific errors to be avoided. The cliché "every little movement has a meaning all its own" is an analogous implication for the human movement concept.

For efficiency and graceful movement in everyday tasks throughout the day attention to body segment alignment may need specific assessment of the situation through a problem-solving approach. New situations should be appraised by a (1) pause, (2) quick assessment, and then (3) controlled movement.

° Morehouse, Laurence E. and Cooper, John M: *Kinesiology*, St. Louis, The C. V. Mosby Co., 1950, p. 117.

How funny animals would look if they walked like man

How man would look if he walked like animals

FIG. 6-1. A pictorial, phylogenetic analogy used on The Mayo Clinic posture sheets in the Physical Medicine Clinics, Rochester, Minnesota.

Walking, Running, and Jumping

CORRECT POSITION—WALKING

1. Walk tall.
2. Easy leg swing from the hips and natural arm swing.
3. Keep the feet straight and close together—1 to 2 inches—push off with the toes and roll from the heel to the toes on outer border of the foot.

ERRORS

1. Forward body lean with a drop on the front foot.
2. Toes turned outward—results in a rocking motion of the buttocks.
3. Too long a stride—mannish walk.
4. Too short a stride—bouncy walk.
5. Exaggerated arm swing—ungraceful.

CORRECT POSITION—RUNNING

1. Arms close to the body with elbows bent.
2. Chest high and the trunk inclined forward.
3. Push off with the balls of the feet.
4. Take long strides and use more knee action than used in walking.

ERRORS

1. Short steps with a straight body lessens efficiency.
2. Landing on or taking off with the whole foot presents a jerky run.
3. Running in high heels is not graceful.

CORRECT POSITION—JUMPING

ERRORS

1. Jump from one foot or both feet.
2. Land on both feet in a crouch position with the body weight forward.

1. Trunk too straight.
2. Landing with feet too far apart.
3. Landing on the whole foot or heels presents too great a jolt for the body.

Sitting

CORRECT POSITION

ERRORS

1. Sit tall, hips against the back of the chair, spine and head erect.
2. Place feet close together on the floor, one slightly ahead of the other, or ankles crossed with feet straight and knees together.
3. When writing, eating at a table, incline the body forward from the hips.
4. When seated in an easy chair, maintain good trunk alignment, with a graceful straight leg position.

1. Sitting on the tail bone, abdomen relaxed, head forward.
2. Feet turned out or in, knees apart.
3. Hands supporting the shoulders on the chair.
4. Restless hands.
5. Short persons should avoid perching and dangling legs.

Sitting Down and Rising from a Chair

CORRECT POSITION

1. Stand close to the chair with one foot in front of the other.
2. Keep the trunk and head erect as the knee and hips bend to lower the hips to the chair.
3. Keep the arms relaxed.
4. Push up with the rear foot when rising.

ERRORS

1. "Jack-knifing"—buttocks prominent.
2. Dropping or bouncing into the chair.
3. Lifting self from the chair using the arms.
4. Sliding or wiggling into the chair.
5. Crossing or sitting on the legs may retard the circulation.

Sitting on the Floor

CORRECT MOVEMENT

1. Keep the spine straight.
2. Squat and place the hand on the floor for support.
3. Kneel on one or both knees, knees together.
4. Sit to one side with hand support.
5. To change positions, use the hand to raise the hips and move from left to right.
6. To rise, reverse 1 to 3 and push with the hand.

ERRORS

1. Knees apart.
2. Too much trunk lean, forward.
3. Slump of the middle torso.
4. Knees straight.
5. A push-up type rise with both hands in front of the knees.

Climbing Stairs

CORRECT POSITION

ASCENDING

1. Keep the body erect.
2. Place the entire foot on the step.
3. Straight push up from the ankle and knee.
4. Smooth, continuous movement.

DESCENDING

1. Keep the trunk tall and the head high.
2. Reach for the next step with the foot extended.
3. Lower the body weight slowly to the forward foot.

ERRORS

1. Looking at the feet.
2. Pulling self up, rather than lifting.
3. Feet turned outward, with side to side rock.
4. Forward lean at the hip.
5. Perching on the ball of the foot.

1. Falling or dropping from step to step.
2. Eyes on the feet.
3. Toes turned out like a duck.

Stooping, Lifting, Carrying

CORRECT POSITION

1. Place one foot slightly ahead (forward stride).
2. Bend the hips, knees and ankles so the leg muscles support the weight.
3. Keep the spine erect, the weight on both feet.
4. Lift by straightening hips and knees and pushing the toes to the floor.
5. Keep the object to be lifted or carried close to the body.
6. In carrying, use the arm muscles for support and make a body weight adjustment to the opposite side for balance.

ERRORS

1. Bending at the hips and waist only.
2. Keeping the knees straight, straining the back muscles.
3. Sagging to the side the weight is carried on, or same side head tilt.
4. Carrying objects habitually on the same side.
5. Facing object to be lifted.
6. Standing too far from the object to be lifted.

Pulling, Pushing, Reaching

CORRECT POSITION

1. Brace feet firmly in a forward stride position, spine straight.
2. Crouch with a knee bend to use leg muscles and body weight.
3. Grasp the object firmly.
4. Push, rather than pull, heavy objects.
5. When reaching, stand close to the object, stride stand, rise on the toes with good body balance, stretch the arms and side toward the object.

ERRORS

1. Using arms and upper back muscles.
2. Bending only at the hips, knees straight.
3. Arching the low back.
4. Standing too far from the object.

Automobiles

Getting into a car gracefully usually requires individual problem-solving techniques. To sit on the rear seat, put one foot into the car first; use the hands to assist in the body weight shifts on the seat; think about your skirt line and knee position and move as gracefully as possible. To sit on the front seat, place the hips on the seat and slowly swing the legs around into the car. To get out of a car, reverse the sequence. Keep knees together.

ERRORS

1. Entering and leaving with a bend at the waist or hips.
2. Knees too high.
3. Knees too far apart.
4. Entering head first.
5. Leaving with the hips first.

The type of skirt the person is wearing will affect the entrance and exit techniques for getting seated in a car. When with an escort, use his hand or arm for balance.

To improve the activities of daily living and body image we are confronted constantly, through the media, with products for developing the body beautiful. One such product (used by the Astronauts) to maintain muscle tone and strength is the EXER-GENIE* exerciser. The principles of friction for resistance are used in this apparatus. Each person sets his own degree of resistance when using the Exer-Genie. It is an inexpensive, portable type of apparatus that should have many benefits for those persons desiring to improve neuromuscular strength and muscle tone for the body. See illustrations.

Exercise for abductors and adductors of the thigh (Copyright © 1970, EXER-GENIE, Inc. U.S.A.)

Static contraction of the thigh muscles to strengthen and tone them. Partner controls the resistance (Copyright © 1970, EXER-GENIE, Inc. U.S.A.)

*EXER-GENIE, Inc., P.O. Box 3320, Fullerton, Ca. 92634

Summary

The rationale of this chapter is concerned with daily tasks and body mechanics. Many persons are not efficient in body movement and use incorrect movements to the point of doing physical harm to themselves.

The values of correct alignment in motion and everyday tasks cannot be overemphasized. The effect of normal stress upon the articulation of the body joints is measured in terms of a person's ability to perform and endure optimum physical activity and freedom from pain and disability. This chapter also photographically illustrates and provides cues to practice for improved body dynamics.

Common
Deviations
of Posture

The physical educator should be aware of the basic physiologic and biomechanic principles affecting posture. As one who prescribes exercises for specific postural conditions, the teacher must be cognizant of all factors involved; otherwise the effort tends to be unproductive.

"Good" posture is an individual concept which is related to the somatotype. In the analysis and evaluation of faults and defects, the examiner and examinee should consider the basic body build—the characteristics of the endomorph, mesomorph, and ectomorph. Predispositions of each body type have been established, but to date the findings have not been scientifically investigated (54).

Correct posture is the body alignment for the maximum physiologic and biomechanic efficiency (105). "Posture is usually defined as the relative arrangement of the parts of the body. It is that state of muscular and skeletal balance which protects the supportive structures of the body against injury or progressive deformity irrespective of the attitude (erect, lying, squatting, stooping) in which these structures are working or resting. Under such conditions the muscles will function most efficiently, and the optimum positions are afforded for the thoracic and abdominal organs. Poor posture is a faulty relationship of the various parts of the body which produces increased strain on the supportive structures and there is less efficient balance of the body over its base of support (85)." Persistent faults may cause discomfort, pain, or deformity, and the range of effect is related to the severity of the fault.

The applied mechanics of posture involves the static and dynamic stances retained or altered by stimuli through the neuromuscular mechanism to the muscles that need activation. Posture is the product of the coordination of the nerve impulses coming from (1) the eyes, (2) the labyrinth of the inner ear, and (3) the proprioceptive nerve endings in the muscles, joints, and tendons. The tonic neck reflexes (which operate at a subcortical, involuntary level) provide the individual with the ability to maintain an antigravity position with no conscious effort. The "stretch" or myotatic reflex gives tonus to the antigravity muscles:

1. Sole of the foot and inner border of the foot and lower leg.

2. Calf

3. Front of the thigh.

4. Buttocks.

5. Up the back to the head.

6. Abdominal wall.

7. Between the shoulder blades.

These muscles are the extensors of the spine, hip joints, knee joints, and ankle joints; the abdominal muscles; the retractors of the shoulder girdle; and intrinsic-extrinsic muscles of the foot. Because of their function, they have been given the group designation, *antigravity muscles*.

When the strength and the endurance of the antigravity muscles are insufficient or unbalanced, deviations of skeletal alignment occur. Other deviations occur through "postural strain," which pertains to those conditions involving joints and their supporting structures, the so-called static stress rather than the sudden acute strains (109, p. 96). This entity conveys a definite picture with a gradual onset occurring in any part of the body. A *postural fault* or *deviation* is the incorrect alignment of a body segment resulting from an undesirable habit pattern which is immediately correctible; a *defect* is a skeletal or muscle imbalance that the individual cannot correct immediately. The incidence of postural deviations, stated by Lowman and Young, shows that at least 75 per cent of the school children have faults of total or segmental deviations in the body alignment shown through gross screening tests given in the schools. "An orthopaedic specialist might add another 5 or 10 per cent to this figure, for it is common knowledge that a majority of children have some postural fault or growth divergence (109)."

After a gross screen test or class inventory, the time element obviously will not permit individual class organization in attempting to correct postural defects. The program potentials should be studied and evaluated in terms of the needed therapeutic development possibilities.

Assessment of all activities and exercises should be made for the student to avoid fatigue factors or overdevelopment of muscle groups that are promoting deviations. Therefore, postural fitness of students should be checked through (1) the physical education gross screen test (followed by refined appraisal), (2) action tests for judging movement efficiency such as checking specific basic skills, for example, stair climbing, (3) silhouettes on a grid background or polaroid prints (side view, back view) on a grid screen, and (4) medical examinations.

When the program includes *special classes* for posture control and conditioning with students chosen from the analysis and evaluation of such a battery of tests, better cooperation between student and teacher accrues when the assignment is made with the full consent of the student and the parent.

Reappraisal on a continuing basis is necessary for the student in a special class to achieve return to the regular activity program and to correct the deviation. The teacher's responsibilities include (1) understanding of the student's static and dynamic postural need, (2) planning and checking a progressive exercise circuit for the individual's needs (individual personal program), (3) regular examinations (reappraisals), (4) regular student consultations, and (5) good record keeping of each student's analysis, personal program, and evaluation. (See charts in Chapter Five.)

The special class for developmental purposes of "posture control and conditioning" is a worthy adjunct to the total physical education program. Passive, assistive, active, and resistive exercises are used to achieve good habit formations of the neuromuscular system and eliminate poor habits established by the individual.

Postural adjustments the individual makes to the force of gravity are classified as functional, postural, or physiologic divergencies and structural or pathological divergencies. The functional divergency involves the soft tissues (muscles and ligaments) and should disappear when the effect of gravity is eliminated. Functional deviations may be tested (1) from the prone position, (2) by suspension by the hands from a stall bar or gym bar, or (3) from the Adams' position (forward bend position). In the structural divergency, bony change has occurred; therefore, the positions just mentioned will not correct the deviation. Another classification frequently used is the transitional divergency; here, the applied functional tests may show incomplete correction of the deviation. The structural and transitional divergencies are medical problems that need to be pointed out to the parent so that medical diagnosis and recommendations will be available to the physical educator for developmental procedures.

Postural appraisals are considered from the anteroposterior plane (side view), the lateral plane (back view), and the back sagittal view (looking from the top of head down back) (85). Here we are concerned with postural faults and defects. Since the common procedure applies the "gravity line" from the feet to the tragus of the ear, the feet will be considered first. In case of imbalance at either the ankle or the pelvis, compensation corrections are accomplished by muscle contractions. When contraction is sustained, fatigue, immobilization, a less dynamic body, and ischemia may develop. Although teachers and therapists do not diagnose pathological conditions, for referral purposes they should be able to recognize the more serious faults (109). The role of various parts of the body in the individual's overall posture is discussed below:

Feet

The foot, consisting of 26 bones, many ligaments, and muscles, serves as a locomotor organ for body movement and functions as the base of support for the upright position. It has two arches: the longitudinal, which extends from the heel to the base of the great toe, and the transverse or metatarsal, which extends across the ball of the foot.

The Functions of the Foot and Ankle are to:	
Bear weight	Kick
Grasp the ground	Propel
Walk	Push objects
Run	Touch
Spring from the ground	Feel

FIG. 7-1. (From Lewin, *The Foot and Ankle.* Courtesy of Lea & Febiger.)

The foot develops so that between the ages of four and seven complete bone ossification occurs for the 26 bones. To understand the foot, the physical educator should understand the following terms:

1. *Talipes* means foot deformities.

2. *Pes* refers to the word *foot*.

3. *Equinus* is the term used when the toes are lower than heel level (Fig. 7-2).

4. *Calcaneus* means the heel is lower than the toes (Fig. 7-3).

5. *Varus* describes the position with the toes turned in.

6. *Metatarsus varus* means pigeon toes.

7. *Valgus* refers to position with toes out.

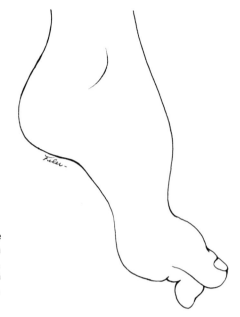

FIG. 7-2. Talipes equinus. The contraction of the calf muscle group causes the foot to assume a position of acute flexion. As the term indicates, the foot is held in a position similar to that of a horse's hoof. (From Giannestras, *Foot Disorders*, Lea & Febiger.)

8. *Hallux valgus* is an abnormal abduction of the great toe (bunion, Fig. 7-4).

9. *Pes cavus* means hollow foot (Fig. 7-5).

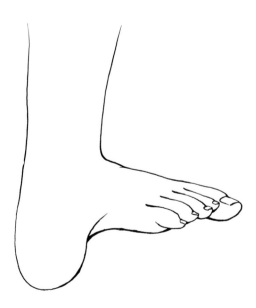

FIG. 7-3. Talipes calcaneus. Malposition of the heel bone in relation to the ankle bone is the cause of this deformity. (From Giannestras, *Foot Disorders*, Lea & Febiger.)

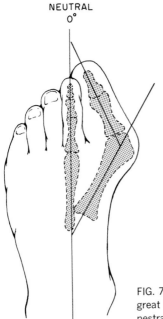

FIG. 7-4.   Hallux valgus. The deformity consists of abduction of the great toe in relation to the metatarsal shaft and head. (From Giannestras, *Foot Disorders*, Lea & Febiger.)

10.   *Pes planus* means flatfoot (See Figs. 7-6 and 7-7).

11.   *Hammer toe* refers to continuous contraction of the second toe.

12.   *Pronation* means the weight is borne on the inner side of the foot: eversion or valgus (navicular deviation, Fig. 7-8) (Helbing sign, Fig. 7-9B).

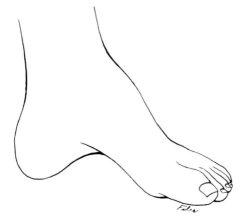

FIG. 7-5.   Pes cavus. This deformity produces a foot with a higher than normal arch and may or may not be accompanied by flexion (cock-up) deformity of the toes. (From Giannestras, *Foot Disorders*, Lea & Febiger.)

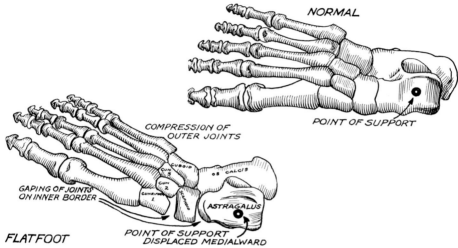

FIG. 7-6. The bones of the foot seen from above in the normal and in the flatfoot position. Looking at the top, you see that the point of support in the normal foot bears a definite relation to the astragalus. This spot takes the weight of the whole body. In the flatfoot you see that the point of weight-bearing is shifted downward medially and the astragalus is turned. Notice the gap that occurs between scaphoid and cuneiform 1 and between scaphoid and cuneiform 2. On the outer border there is compression. Pain may occur on both sides. (Lewin, Amer. J. Dis. Child., 31:704, 1926.)

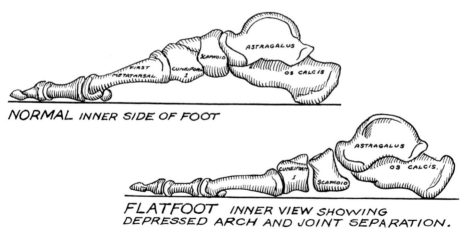

FIG. 7-7. The bones of the foot seen from the inner side in the normal and in the flatfoot. At the top you see a view of the normal inner border of the foot; the astragalus, scaphoid, cuneiform, first metatarsal, sesamoid, first and second phalanges. In the flatfoot there is an arch depression; the bones become separated. You can visualize what happens to the ligaments. With the foot on the ground there is no strain on it. When a person who has at one time had a normal arch experiences strain, he suffers pain because the ligaments are stretched and the muscles are weakened. When the muscles weaken, strain is thrown on the ligaments so that in addition to muscle pain he has ligament stress and strain. (Lewin, Amer. J. Dis. Child., 31:704, 1926.)

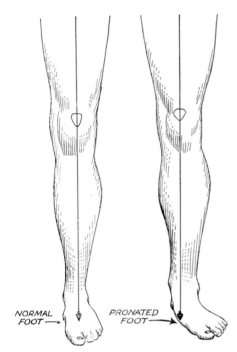

FIG. 7-8.   Showing the position of a plumb line dropped from the middle of the patella in the normal and flatfoot. (Lewin, Amer. J. Dis. Child., *31*:704, 1926.)

If you drop a plumb line from the middle of the patella, it should bisect the tibia and the astragalus and follow toward a point where a line drawn from the crotch of the first and second toes would meet that line. The pronated foot line is the one you see on the right. That throws one off balance. The astragalus receives a glancing blow instead of a straight on blow.

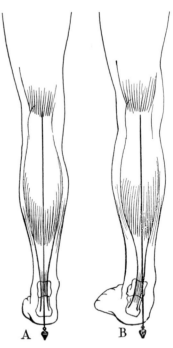

FIG. 7-9.   The position of a plumb line dropped from the middle of the popliteal space in the normal *A*, and in the flatfoot *B*. (Lewin, Amer. J. Dis. Child., *31*:704, 1926.)

In the rear view, the line bisects the calf, is parallel with and bisects the astragalus and the Achilles tendon. This is the flatfoot from the rear. The astragalus is tilted. Very often you get an accurate impression of the mechanical trouble from the posterior as well as from an anterior view. (Helbing sign) (104, p. 87).

13.   *Supination* refers to a position in which the weight is borne on the outer side of the foot: inversion or varus.

In the biomechanics of the foot when standing, the foot is supported mainly by ligaments; in action patterns, the foot is supported chiefly by the muscles.

The feet perform a Herculean task for the body. Small in proportion to the rest of the body, they propel the body through millions of steps and years of standing. About 90 per cent of infants are born with well-formed feet, but when adulthood is reached, this percentage has been reduced by acquired defects. Lewin's illustration amplifies the etiology (Fig. 7-10). In 1962, the American Podiatry Association estimated that 70 per cent of all Americans either have foot trouble or will develop foot ills during their lifetimes (106). More than half of all school children are affected (11). This incidence of foot problems in the United States may be caused by (a) ill-fitted shoes, (b) city pavements, (c) occupational standing, (d) lack of walking, and (e) poor posture.

The well-fitted shoe for daily use should have (a) flexible shank, (b) a combination last which gives a snug heel fit, (c) toe space when standing, approximately ½ inch longer than the foot, (d) heel height

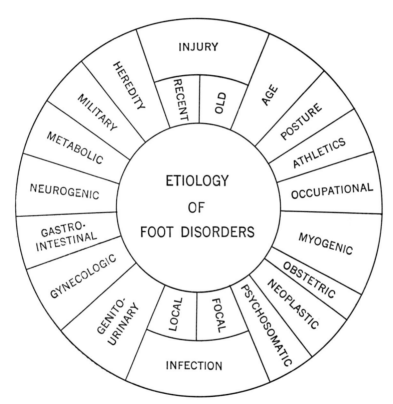

FIG. 7-10. Lewin stated the causes of foot and ankle troubles include race, age, sex, hereditary, congenital, traumatic, infectious, neurogenic, myogenic, circulatory, metabolic, arthritic, nutritional, endocrine, dermatologic, allergic, climatic, geographic, and neoplastic factors. For example, in cases of clubfoot, it is necessary to consider congenital factors; in syphilis, hereditary sources; in fractures, trauma; in infection, tuberculosis; in poliomyelitis, neurogenic damage; in thrombophlebitis, circulatory disturbances; in osteoarthritis, metabolic causes; and in rickets, nutritional deficiencies. Various etiological factors may produce similar symptoms and pathological changes. (Lewin, *The Foot and Ankle*, Lea & Febiger.)

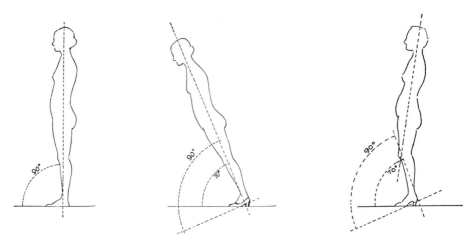

FIG. 7-11. Avoid high heels. When high heels are worn, adjustments must be made to maintain the body equilibrium. The hips and abdomen may become prominent, swayback develops, and the leg and calf muscles are shortened, as the knees are kept bent to preserve balance.

from $\frac{1}{2}$ to 1 inch (a 1-inch heel places the foot in 10 degrees of plantar flexion, Fig. 7-11), and (*e*) leather or material that permits ventilation (patent leather and reptile skins do not permit this). The saddle-type shoe gives good support for the feet. The tennis shoe is popular and does permit good usage for the normal foot.

With pes planus conditions, the orthopaedist and physiatrist sometimes prescribe a stiff shank and a Thomas heel (Fig. 7-12). The congenital flatfoot (Figs. 7-6, 7-7) usually has no pain but may give a "pedestal gait."

People with abnormalities of the foot often show compensatory faults at the ankle, leg, and hip. Some further abnormalities are:

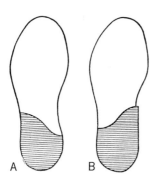

FIG. 7-12.   Thomas heels built on shoes correct pronation. A. Reversed Thomas heel. B. H. O. Thomas heel—inner border prolonged and elevated. (From Lewin, *The Foot and Ankle*, Lea & Febiger.)

1. *Abducted foot*—weight on the outer border.

2. *Talipes equinovarus*—clubfoot, a congenital defect.

3. *Morton's toe*—a short first metatarsal described by Dr. Dudley Morton (Fig. 7-13B).

4. *Morton's metatarsalgia* or *syndrome*—pain on weight-bearing due to short first metatarsal bone.

5. *Metatarsalgia*—pain at the heads of the metatarsals, may be caused by poorly fitted shoes, high heels or osteochondritis (trauma to the epithyses interfering with circulation and growth).

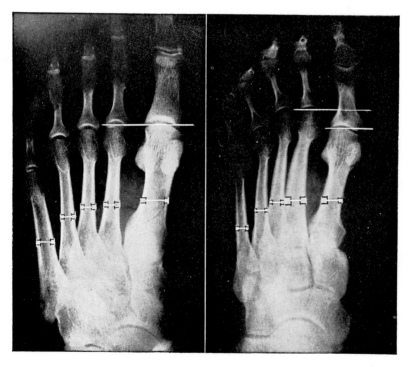

A   B

FIG. 7-13. In the ideally designed foot, A, metatarsal I and II extend forward the same distance, and the first is twice as wide as the second. Also, all four outer metatarsals are the same width. The influence of weight-bearing upon the development of these bones is indicated (1) in their comparative width and (2) in the strength of their walls—represented in "square of the wall's thickness" (small white squares). In the foot B, with a short metatarsal I, weight stresses are concentrated on metatarsal II. Consequently, metatarsal II becomes greatly widened and its walls greatly thickened. (From Morton, D. J.: *The Human Foot.* New York, Columbia University Press, 1935.)

6. *Subluxation of the ankle*—partial dislocation due to severe sprain.

Other faults, defects and injuries of the feet are:

1. Overbone—a prominence over the dorsum of the foot found in persons with high longitudinal arches.

2. Exostoses or spurs—bony outgrowths found chiefly on the head of the first metatarsal, calcaneous and phalanges (Policeman's heel).

3. Bursitis of the calcaneus (tendon Achilles)—due to irritation of the shoe.

4. Muscle spasms or cramps at arch of foot or great toe due to over-activity, fatigue, foot weakness (pronation), lack of salt.

5. Golfer's big toe—a hallux rigidus which may be due to excess pivoting aggravated by fatigue, overactivity, and muscle imbalance.

6. Tennis leg—rupture of the plantaris muscle and sometimes the tendon Achilles (Lewin felt this may be due to a spiral twist of muscle) presents a sudden pain as if hit by a stone.

7. Tendinitis—inflammation of the tendon Achilles or anterior tibial due to overactivity.

8. Shin splints—myositis of the anterior tibial and toe extensor muscles with periostitis due to trauma or repeated sudden starts and stops; dull pain over lower third of the leg and difficulty raising the heel.

9. Causalgia—a burning pain due to a wound or injury of the peripheral nerve.

10. Charley horse—muscle spasm due to overactivity (calf frequently).

11. Peroneal nerve injury—due to crossing legs applying pressure to the nerve, accompanied by a foot drop.

12. Restless legs—a syndrome that may occur with nutritional deficiency and may show up more at night.

13. Corns, calluses—irritations from pressure which need shoe correction and/or podiatrist treatment.

14. Ingrown toenails—may need a podiatrist or better fitting shoes.

15. Tight tendon Achilles—a short heel cord caused by injury or high heels worn too frequently.

The physical educator should be alert to the need for correct foot postures in static and dynamic patterns, and should set up progressive activity for normal development and report suspected weaknesses to the student, his parents, and his physician. Specific exercises are important for maintaining good foot muscle strength and flexibility and correct body alignment posture for specific activities. In long, slender, rapidly growing feet (especially in girls) a definite type of weak, pronated or flatfoot may appear in adolescence (104). A good chiropodist or podiatrist is a valuable member of society from the standpoint of foot hygiene and comfort. One should exercise good judgment in the selection of a podiatrist—particularly a person with diabetes, arteriosclerosis, peripheral vascular lesions, and neurological lesions (104).

Since the foot is the final shock absorber for the body, shoes should be well fitted and kept in good condition for correct weight-bearing. (See Figs. 7-14, 7-15.)

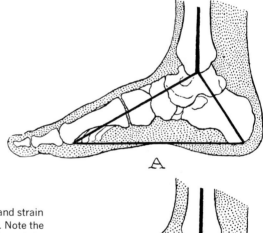

FIG. 7-14. *A*, illustrating lines of stress and strain on normal foot. *B*, in a case of pes cavus. Note the components of weight-bearing; the heights of the longitudinal arches; the distances from each os calcis to the head of the first metatarsal. (Lewin, *The Foot and Ankle*, Lea & Febiger.)

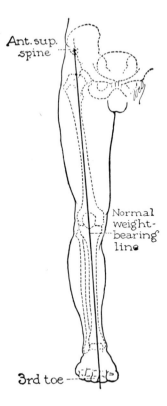

Ant. sup.
spine

Normal
weight-
bearing
line

3rd toe

FIG. 7-15. Weight-bearing line of leg.
(Magnuson and Stack, *Fractures,* Courtesy of J. B. Lippincott Co.)

Knees

Knee defects develop from poor habits of body mechanics with resulting muscle imbalances. The most common are (1) hyperextended
knee or genu recurvatum (Fig. 7-16) caused by static stress over a
period of time, (2) overflexion of the knee, (3) tibial torsion, and (4) iliotibial band tightness.

Hyperextended knee results in undue compression of the knee joint
in front and undue tension on the ligaments and muscles posteriorly
(85). Pain in the popliteal space may develop. Also, if not given correct postural alignment (stress a 5 degree knee position on standing
and strengthen hamstrings), growing children may develop the bony
defect of genu recurvatum. Overflexion of the knees prevents good
antigravity muscle balance, as it puts the quadriceps into a state of
exaggerated muscular effort with accompanying hip flexor tightness
and posterior capsular ligament stress (85).

Tibial torsion results from the bad habit of walking with the foot
rotated externally (everted), which, slowly during growth, progressively

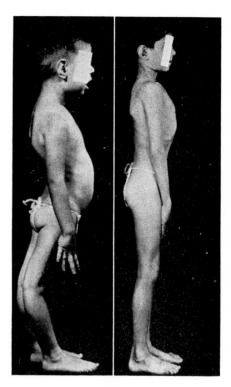

FIG. 7-16. This illustration of advance hyper-extended knees and poor pelvic position is not common. Occasionally it is found in an elementary school student. Ruth Wheeler has seen two comparable cases of a fourth grade student and fifth grade student in the past five years. Specific re-education with improved posture and the growth increment has definitely shown the follow-up improvement which Lowman and Young illustrate. Genu recurvatum. Five-year follow up. (Lowman and Young, *Postural Fitness*, Lea & Febiger.)

rotates the tibia externally. The teacher should check the position of the child's patella in standing and walking. External tibial torsion (knock-knee) places the stress on the lateral side of the knee, with resultant increased mobility of the medial ligaments; internal tibial torsion (bowleg) may arise from exaggerated inversion of the feet (Fig. 7-17). This deformity often develops in children from ages two to ten. Correction of the foot and hip position is important, and referral to an orthopaedist or physiatrist for correct wedging of the child's shoe should be stressed to the parents. This bowing of the knee should be appraised by the physician when the kneecap is not forward in static and dynamic postures. A wedge on the lateral side of the shoe is frequently prescribed by the physiatrist for bowlegs. For knock-knees, a wedge is added to the medial heel surface. Posture habits and muscle weakness should be checked by the teacher.

Iliotibial band tightness is a defect which will bend the knee inward (knock-knee). This band is the tendon of the gluteus maximus and tensor fascia latae which extends down the leg laterally and inserts posterior to the knee joint (head of the fibula). This may show

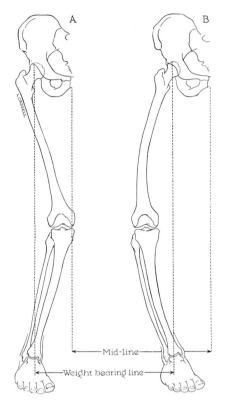

FIG. 7-17.   Diagrammatic representation of knock-knee, *A,* and bowleg, *B.* (Lewin, *The Foot and Ankle,* Lea & Febiger.)

an inversion of the feet and, upon standing, flattening of the pelvis or tightness of the hip flexors. To test the iliotibial band tightness, the student should lie supine and hug one knee to flatten the lumbar spine while the examiner extends and adducts the other extremity. Normally, complete extension of the hip and 30 to 40 degrees of adduction are possible (105). This test, used as an exercise, may help the student in six to eight weeks; if not, the physician should be consulted. A unilateral drop of the pelvis may be due to a short leg, tight iliotibial band, or dislocated hip. Measuring the leg length for a unilateral drop of the pelvis from the anterior superior spine to the medial malleolus in a supine position or from the umbilicus to the medial malleolus in a supine position or from the umbilicus to the medial malleolus should check leg symmetry. If the distances are equal, check for a tight iliotibial band. In hip dislocations the Trendelenburg sign usually shows. This sign may be checked by having the child stand on the affected side, then raise the good limb. The gluteal fold on the good side falls instead of rising as it should in the normal hip condition. The physician will apply these tests, but the teacher should be aware of what techniques are administered. All reports of suspected malpostures should be sent to the parents and the physician.

Trunk

The analysis and evaluation of trunk faults and defects should be appraised generally and refined through the specific body segments (pelvis, abdomen, chest, spine, scapula, shoulders). Common deviations are described.

1. Lumbar Lordosis

In the profile plumb line test (subjective evaluation or objective—picture) frequently there is a compensatory dorsal kyphosis with lordosis. This deviation, which is an exaggerated concave curve of the normal physiological curve of the lumbar spine, involves undue compression on the posterior surface of the vertebral bodies and their articulating facets. Also, undue tension is placed on the anterior vertebral ligaments. The muscle imbalances which develop from this increased pelvic tilt° (Fig. 7-18) are tight low back muscles, weak abdominal muscles (sometimes ptosis), tight hip flexors, and weak hamstring muscles. This defect may be a "weak back" from strong, overdeveloped, short muscles.

The pelvic segment is the key to many postural problems. The adjustment and control of the body mass above and below the pelvis is relevant to the pelvic position. The pelvic region has the center of gravity for the body. In women this point is centered at the level of the second sacral vertebra. The only bony connection between the upper and lower body segments is a small disc of bone about the size of a silver dollar at the lumbosacral joint. This joint is held in place

° Measurement of Pelvic Tilt. Normal anteroposterior tilt or inclination of the pelvis is 54 to 60 degrees in women and 50 to 56 in men, as measured from the lumbosacral junction line to the syymhysis pubis in the upright position. Tension in the iliofemoral or Y ligament causes some variation. For clinical analysis Cyriax states: "the relation of the anterior superior spine to the upper margin of the symphysis should be in the same vertical plane. Roughly speaking, every half inch of deviation of the anterior superior spine from this plane means a corresponding alteration in the pelvic tilt of approximately 9 degrees; the relation of the anterior spine and posterior spine in normal men is horizontal, but in women the posterior process is about $\frac{3}{4}$ of an inch higher. Every $\frac{1}{2}$ inch of deviation indicates a pelvic tilt alteration of 5 degrees (109, p. 120)." Steindler states that the longitudinal axis of the fifth lumbar vertebra and the upper sacral segment should form an angle of 120 to 135 degrees for normal tilt. The smaller the angle, the greater the stress (172). For accurate measurement of the pelvic tilt an X ray of the lower spine in the anteroposterior plane should be used.

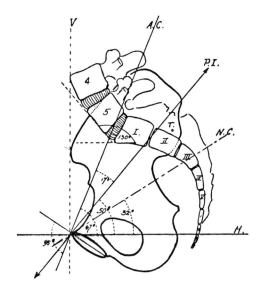

FIG. 7-18. Pelvic tilt. A pelvic angle of 50 to 60 degrees is considered normal. If the upper part of the pelvis is tilted farther forward, the curve of the lumbar spine is forced farther forward also, resulting in hollow back and protruding hips. (After Fick and Morris, *Human Anatomy*, Courtesy of The Blakiston Division, McGraw-Hill Book Company.)

by two small articular processes and the ligaments that bind the last lumbar vertebra to the sacrum. The laws of physics and mechanics state that the stability of the base must be in direct ratio to the load put on the base of the motor action; subsequently, the probabilities of strain or injury are increased in direct proportion; that is, if one increases muscular strength when the segments are out of line, he may increase the malalignment (105). The pelvic region, including the hip ball and socket joint (acetabulum), allow a wide range of movement while at the same time giving good support because of the massive muscles and ligaments—especially the iliofemoral or Y ligaments.

Some individuals have a congenital structure at the lumbosacral joint which may show an exaggeration with a flat curve above this joint. This is called *spondylolisthesis* when the last lumbar vertebra slides forward on the first sacral vertebra due to a neural arch defect accompanied by gradual destruction of the intervertebral discs of L4, L5, and S1. The short, sharp curve lordosis should be watched closely in activities as the stress of weight-bearing is primarily on the ligaments.

2. Weak Abdominal Muscles

The ectomorph and the endomorph often have prominent abdominals. The ectomorph may have muscle laxity and fatigue posture, while the endomorph has an excess of fatty tissue. Weak abdominal conditions may be accompanied by a flexible back or tight back muscles. The flexible back permits pelvic tilt movement, but the tight back musculature (lordosis) may lead to pain symptoms. Abdominal strengthening exercises are needed for the former, and strengthening and flexibility exercises are indicated for the latter. Kyphosis and forward head faults accompany the lordotic-hollow-swayback posture.

3. Flat Back

When the lumbar spine is flattened, presenting a deviant inclination of the pelvis or a decreased pelvic tilt, the flat back is seen. Licht states that this usually occurs with disc derangement and spondylolisthesis (105). The lumbar spine may be in slight kyphosis in standing and sitting, causing undue compression on anterior surfaces of the lumbar vertebrae. Clinically, this posture is associated with back pain when the individual tightens the back extensors and tension on the posterior spinous ligaments when he stretches the extensor muscles. This posterior pelvic tilt or decreased inclination of the pelvis may accompany sacro-iliac sprain, coccygeal neuralgia (coccygodynia), protruded interverted disc, sciatica, and lumbago (back pain). Sciatica may be caused by a stretched piriformis muscle (outward hip rotator) as it follows the sciatic nerve, thus creating pressure and a severe pain syndrome. A shoe correction is suggested (85, pp. 140–141). Relief for this stretch piriformis pressure uses physical medicine modalities or may be achieved through lying with the thighs over an 18-inch bench or chair (knees bent) with the hips elevated 3 or 4 inches then doing back flattening and abdominal retraction very slowly 5 to 10 times. Abdominal tensing and gluteal pinching will decrease this fault. When pain is not present, low back muscle tightening, strengthening, stretching, and flexibility (mobilization) through leg raisings should be programmed.

4. Lateral Pelvic Tilt

Lateral pelvic tilt may be caused by scoliosis, a lateral curvature of the spine which shows asymmetry of the hips from a back or a front view. This is a *medical problem* the teacher should report to the parents or school physician for immediate referral to a physiatrist. The physical educator should know that the functional or postural curve is the "C" and is named after the spinal convexity of the curve. Thus, if the spine curves convexly to the left from the seventh cervical to the lumbar spine, this is called a *"Left C Curve."* The transitional may be a C or an S curve. The S curve indicates the body is compensating in a functional or physiological way. When this is evident from the seventh cervical through the lumbar spine, its convexities determine the name so it would be a *Left Dorsal Right Lumbar Curve*. The transitional phase does not disappear completely in the prone or Adams' position, indicating some bony changes. The structural, or pathological, change means the spine has ossified in an asymmetrical manner usually presenting the S *Left Dorsal Right Lumbar Curvature*. The functional and transitional deviations develop in children of prepubescence, and the

ASYMMETRICAL EXERCISES FOR FUNCTIONAL OR POSTURAL SCOLIOSIS
Used only upon prescription from the physician to maintain stability of the spinal column.

FIG. 7-19. An uncorrected left total curvature of the spinal column.

FIG. 7-20. Correction of a left total curvature of the spinal column when the person is prone.

FIG. 7-21. Correction of a left total curvature when the person is sitting.

FIG. 7-22. Key position for correction of a left total curvature of the spinal column when the person is kneeling.

FIG. 7-23. Key position for correction of a left total curvature when the person is in a crawling position.

FIG. 7-24. Correction of a left total curvature of the spinal column when the individual is standing.

pathological deviations of the spine occur in the pubescent ages. Shoulder positions are usually asymmetrical, and sometimes the scapula prominence and the rib cage show rotation. Figures 7-19 to 7-24 are shown for possible prescription of activities from the physician for the student with a postural curve. The teacher should set up good, general, symmetrical exercises for the student to maintain as normal a muscle strength and trunk flexibility as his tolerance will permit. The all-fours position (on hands and knees) is good, with creeping, for strengthening trunk muscle weaknesses or imbalances. Correct posture dynamics, particularly lifting, should be taught any student with trunk muscle imbalance. Asymmetrical movement patterns must have a *medical* prescription, with regular follow-up reports so that the student, the parent, the physician, and the teacher can evaluate the progress.

Lateral pelvic tilt may show no spine changes but may be due to handedness or heredity. A British study made early in the twentieth century pointed out that few individuals are absolutely symmetrical even though they are sound organically.

Nevertheless, low back pain problems are sometimes associated with lateral pelvic tilt, as well as lordosis or increased pelvic tilt (85, p. 139). Compression over the articulating surface of the fifth lumbar vertebra on the high side may be the spot of the pain syndrome. The majority of people are right-handed, so unilateral lumbosacral strains come with a high position of the right hip. With all acute conditions where pain is manifested, rest (no exercise) is important. Physicians sometimes prescribe muscle relaxants to enable the individual to maintain necessary daily activities. Later, exercises are progressed to include correct body dynamics. The pain syndrome in children should alert teacher and parent to the need for immediate medical care, as this may be an acute condition or a result of chronic stress.

5. Thorax and Scapula

The ectomorph is more prone to (*a*) the *flat chest condition*, which shows a subcostal angle of less than 90 degrees accompanied by short pectorals, and (*b*) the *winged scapula* or stretched rhomboids (flaring of the scapulae). The normal scapular interspace is about 3 inches. When the inferior angle (lowest) of the scapula is protruded, this condition indicates weakness of the lower fibers of the serratus anterior muscle. (*c*) The *funnel chest* with the sunken breastbone and (*d*) the *pigeon chest* with the rounded high breastbone are associated with nutritional deficiencies and early asthma. (*e*) *Pectus excavatum,* a hereditary or developmental condition coming early in life, presents a sunken lower chest with abdominal protrusion and dorsal kyphosis. Deep breathing exercise with specific movement patterns to stretch tight muscles and strengthen stretched muscles should be given, accompanied by the correct trunk position. (*f*) *Sprengel's deformity*, a scapular condition present at birth, is the failure of the scapulae to take their normal position. A fibrous bridge over the dorsal vertebrae prevents the scapulae descent. Surgery is required to correct this condition; otherwise, severe postural defects develop.

6. Kyphosis or Round Back and Round Shoulders

Kyphosis is an exaggerated dorsal curve of the spine and may be acquired or inherited. Infants are born with a side view C spinal curve. When the head movements develop with the neck extensors strengthened, the normal physiological curves develop so that the cervical vertebrae are convex on the anterior surface; as the leg movements develop, the anterior convexity of the lumbar spine is manifested. Frequently kyphosis has an associated lordosis called "kypholordosis." Body adjustments for balance against gravity demand this zigzag position. The ectomorph, due to long, weak muscle structure, needs close watching and help in body mechanics to maintain good muscle balance. Round shoulders accompany the previous deviations and/or may be caused by muscle imbalances due to continuous use of the arms in front of the body. Occasionally a congenital condition of short clavicles may occur.

Other shoulder conditions are tight upper trapezius and levator muscles (shoulder shruggers), which give the appearance of tension and shoulder elevation and low chest position. Children with early allergy conditions may present this fault. An uneven shoulder position as viewed from the back, may be due to handedness or scoliosis. Fatigue slump inevitably presents round shoulders but not always a round back. Well selected gross muscle activities are needed for development of good trunk musculature.

7. Forward Head and Head Tilt

This deviation, which is usually acquired, sometimes is caused by visual problems or eye strain and occupational conditions. Head tilt refers to a back or front view position with the asymmetrical appearance. This is muscle imbalance primarily of the sternocleidomastoid muscles, which give equal support when both have good tonus. Contracting individually, they turn the head to the right and to the left, and pull the ear to the shoulder on the same side. When one side is faulty, the condition of *torticollis* is present. This may be acute or chronic, and when it does not disappear with rest and gentle easy movements, the doctor should be seen. Sleeping in a draft occasionally causes a condition of the neck like torticollis.

The chin forward position has stretched posterior neck muscles and tight anterior neck muscles. The forward head with a chin out position indicates tight posterior muscles and stretched anterior neck muscles. The flabbiness under the chin (double chin) is inherited but can be helped by a program of good head movement exercises.

The head does most of its skeletal growth before birth, so protective positions during early infancy are important to insure good development. The weight of the head, approximately 12 per cent of adult body weight and with 93 per cent of its full growth by age six, requires good skeletal support and trunk muscle strength to maintain body balance. When head alignment deviates, the normal physiological curves also will deviate.

8. Hypokinetic Deviations

Hypokinetic deviations occur when insufficient motion and sub-par motor skill abilities affect good body muscle balance. With minimum muscular efficiency and poor muscle balance the principle of bodily adaptation cannot be met except perhaps to precipitate acute or chronic body derangement when challenged by unusual physical or emotional demands. Underexercised youth needs progressive grading of physical education activities so that each student can reach his potential. Orthopedic instability from tension, as well as emotional instability, is important from the standpoint of physical softness as "Action absorbs anxiety (92)."

The prevalent conditions of low back pain and the unstable knee have replaced the duodenal ulcer status symbol. The teacher of physical education should work diligently to give quality motor development abilities to youngsters and preventive conditioning to all, including adults, through therapeutic exercises, games and sports, recreational activities, and diversional activities.

The prophylactic value of exercises for the improvement of motor skills is being recognized by the medical profession and accepted as a pharmacopoeia for some preventive medical problems. Focusing on the school children, the authors believe that the once-a-week, double period used for physical education activities in many schools is to be much deplored. The daily, shorter class period permits better learning of motor skills and lessens the dangers of chronic strain that may develop through the growth periods. For example, the child participating in a soccer class for two hours once a week may develop foot and leg pain symptoms following each class, while thirty minutes of activity daily may promote better development of the foot and leg muscles for immediate and future total body functioning.

Physical and skeletal maturation are concomitant processes, and the criterion used for the maturational status of a child is the assessment of the skeletal age. While there is a wide range in the ossification centers for any given age, the table of normal standards gives the carpal indices as the usual sign posts. X-ray pictures of the small bones of the wrist indicate whether the skeletal development is normal, delayed, or accelerated—if the physiological age is in proper relation to the chronological age. Normally, by seven to nine years of age the carpal bones have assumed their mature shape, but they continue to grow until the fifteenth to seventeenth year (115). A recent study states that a significant number of children have skeletal age curves that level off or lag behind the medial level during their preadolescent years just as they do in the increment curves for growth in height.

Long bones grow in size and length according to the periods of the growth increments. Their growth plates (epiphyseal lines) may not fuse until the age of twenty-one. The pelvic bones and spine do not completely ossify until around the sixteenth or seventeenth year, and occasionally as late as the twenty-fifth. This knowledge emphasizes the value of continued developmental movement activities through school life. Since skeletal growth is rapid between the ages of ten and fourteen, dynamic, rather than static, tests of coordination and agility should be emphasized to eliminate any possible damage to the epiphyses due to overexertion.

Two laws concern the adaptation potential of bones. Robert Hooke's law (1660) on elasticity and stress resistance of bone, states:

There is a constant arithmetical relationship between force and elongation, one unit of force, one unit of elongation, two units of force, two units of elongation, and so forth (172, p. 11).

In 1870 Julius Wolff interpreted the functional adaptation of bone stating:

. . . that the spongiosa of bone is able to re-orient itself by a process of re-arrangement of its trabecular system to new mechanical tension or pressure stresses (172).

True to good engineering principles, bone reshapes itself both under normal and pathological conditions so as to sustain a maximum of stress with a minimum expense of bone tissue. This reorientation of the architectures is being carried out to a degree of almost mathematical perfection by a process of absorption and apposition. This bone growth principle may be reduced to these simpler terms: *External stress determines internal architecture.* Thus, good developmental movement activities are necessary for best body function.

Planning Activity Programs

Since exercise needs and motor skills vary with physiologic and work requirements of each individual, it is important to keep in mind the capacities of the different age levels. The following age classifications help in planning activity programs (105):

1. Infancy: Birth to two years, during which the balance of the trunk and the extremities is developed. The mother can safely give exercises to a four-month-old baby as play.

2. Childhood: Two to six years, during which speed of movement is developed. Games and group activities which develop speed and rhythm are very important. During these years the child must learn good alignment; muscle imbalances of the shoulders and hips must be prevented. The gait must be controlled; barefoot exercises (walking on the outer edge of the foot) are needed to insure good foot development.

3. Schoolchild period: Seven to fourteen years, during which growth is very rapid. Exercises must be varied with vigorous movement. Speed games stimulate the heart and lungs; strength and endurance activities should be avoided. Big muscle activities such as running, swimming, skating, ball games, and gymnastic exercises on bars, ladder, self-testing activities, movement fundamentals, and rhythms are suitable. Long periods of sitting in school teach children proper working positions. Children must learn to sit, stand, and walk correctly so that these activities become natural for them in later life. Exercises of stooping and lifting are as necessary as other movements. Poor alignment (juvenile kyphosis) should be controlled and corrected. Watch for signs of posture deviations.

4. Puberty: Fifteen to twenty years, when there is a differentiation of the capacity and ability according to sex. At puberty exercises for coordination and skill along with speed should be developed. Training the smaller muscles with such sports as baseball, volleyball, tennis, badminton, basketball, track and field, and dance are necessary. Include rest periods during strenuous activities. Trying academic activities during these years demand relief of body movements. An important aim of motor activities is to teach the individual to perform work with a maximum economy of muscles and the cardiovascular system. Correct body mechanics with exercises for strength, flexibility, stamina, and specific body development can be set up through dance, swimming, or special class work. Boys and girls who

engage in office or sedentary occupations must learn to sit and use their arms and fingers correctly. If manual work is to be done, correct standing and lifting should be stressed. It is essential to know that speed does not lead to accuracy. Well-coordinated movements with the least amount of energy expended will result in the most productive work with the least fatigue; skill depends on practice. Provide a variety of activities with flexible standards.

5. Young adults: Twenty to thirty years, when full growth is accomplished and strength, endurance, skill, and speed predominate and are at their best. These years should witness the richest body development. All motor activities are excellent, but excesses should be avoided. Exercises should prevent unhealthy "hypertrophy" of the heart. Pulse-ratios should be checked. Increasing strength and power should be gradual with a progressive resistive program to improve neuromuscular coordination and muscle capillarization.

6. Full vigor: Thirty to forty years, when speed and skill decline, but strength and endurance are developed with practice. The cardiovascular system begins to show wear; joints and ligaments do not adapt to strenuous exercise, the fibrous changes of the motor units decrease flexibility; intervertebral disc degeneration impedes spine flexibility. Exercises of increased complexities—climbing, swimming, golfing, bicycling—are challenging and help stretch the stiff joints. The heart is trained but not strained, muscle capillarization is maintained with a normal blood pressure. Rhythmical exercises help the reflexes more than power movements. The individual should avoid muscle tension or sustained positions. "Factory gymnastics" have demonstrated increased efficiency and better performance speed for participants of this on-the-job program.

7. Beyond maturity: Forty to sixty years, when speed and strength decline more; heart and lungs are more easily exhausted; endurance is reduced; complicated movements are good but strenuous exercises should be avoided. Such exercises as gymnastics, walking, golfing, riding, tennis (doubles) which train abilities and endurance and keep up body vigor should be encouraged. Daily activities reduce mental stress and improve cardiovascular and joint movement.

8. Old: Sixty years and on, when quiet exercises with rest intervals are indicated. Prescribed exercises are best for this age group. Exercises should establish and maintain general muscle tone including that of the heart; have a favorable effect on the psyche, an antidote for mental strain; aid the digestive system by reducing nervous tension; control obesity; deepen the respirations, which favors gaseous exchange and the state of the pulmonary tissues.

Relaxation is necessary for all, but this does not mean stopping activity. Neuromuscular relaxation is excellent and can be learned with practice. During sleep most people move 20 to 40 times; even this unconscious pattern relieves fatigue.

Postural deviations are either hereditary, congenital, acquired, or developmental. Both slight and severe deviations obviously will affect the body's neuromuscular and other systems. Body growth is quantitative, and its patterns are well established. Body development is qualitative and needs parental, teacher, and medical assistance. The physical educator is a specialist for motor activities, and good movement activities are essential for best body functioning. Keep in mind the law of vulnerability, stressing the fact that during stages of rapid growth, cells and tissues are more likely to be injured by forces applied to them than after growth has been completed. Principles to follow in correcting faults and defects are:

1. Progress exercises from a lying position to the sitting, then to standing positions.

2. Develop strength and flexibility in the trunk muscles. With kypholordosis get pelvic control before strengthening the upper back.

3. Use caution in exercises so that compensatory deviations are not aggravated.

Summary

This chapter focused on many specific postural deviations. The condition of the various body segments—feet, knees, trunk, and head—should be assessed individually from the side view and the back view test, and faulty characteristics noted. Structural and transitional divergencies should be reported to the parent, and medical advice should be sought before planning remedial exercises for the individual.

The capacity of physical activity for different age levels varies. Young people are more suited to activities that involve speed, adults to the activities that need strength, and the older ages to activities requiring less endurance and skill. These factors should be considered when planning the personal activity program. (See Chapter 5.)

Implementation of the Physical Education Program for the Exceptional Child

Attitudes of Those Who Teach

High on the list of "problem children" in the problem-studded modern school is the "handicapped child." In earlier civilizations he was eliminated at birth or became a jester or a beggar. It is only in recent years that educators have seen the handicapped child as a *child*, to be educated with other children, preferably in the same schools. The emphasis is on rehabilitation, not handicap. The Denver *Health Service Department Annual Report*, for example, is interested in "Conditions . . . which would diminish their most effective participation in Educational Activities (32)."

The cardiac, the blind, the deaf, and other atypical students are a relatively small but important group. They need understanding, empathy, and thoughtful help if they are to reach their potential. In dealing with them the teacher needs most of all to follow the command: "Know thyself." What he is (and that includes the attitudes which are an intrinsic part of his personality) affects tremendously the ways in which he behaves as he meets and works with children.

Professional Preparation of Physical Educators in Adapted Programs

In physical education the teacher is tested daily as these children come into gymnasia, swimming pools, exercise and dance rooms. How well is the teacher prepared to meet the challenge involved in teaching these children?

In an effort to find the answer to this question, Hooley recently conducted a survey to identify the certification requirements and course work practices which exist in the various states of the United States. Replies were received from fifty states. In all, only 13 states require a course in adapted physical education while 16 recommend such a course. Field work is included in such course work in 16 states.

Many states alluded to the fact that such concerns are discretionary, that is to say, that the decisions are left up to the educational institutions in the state. The replies indicated that the titles of the courses were also on a local option basis, and ranged through 11 selections. The most popular title was adapted physical education, with second place going to correctives, or corrective physical education. Third place was attained by the title adapted/corrective physical education (71).

While states and teacher-preparation institutions have been slow to answer those who have insisted for years that more attention should be given to the handicapped, commercial organizations, social agencies, and the government have been alert to, and have implemented the requested services. Equipment companies, resorts, travel agencies, and construction firms have planned and carried through many special arrangements which make it possible for the handicapped to "join the mainstream." Social agencies have included the handicapped in swimming, camping, craft and theatre groups, for example, so that they may take advantage of the many opportunities for fun, skill-learning and socialization. Government has passed laws, held hearings, threatened withholding of funds, and provided expertise and dollars to make it possible for the handicapped to use parks, public buildings (such as libraries, concert halls and theatres), and to enjoy the advantages of publicly funded housing. Costs for education can be procured by the handicapped. Retraining following accident or illness is possible. To sum up, there is less and less reason for the positive-minded, but handicapped person to remain an observer. Public attitudes, funding, and creative planning have been upgraded over the past several years, and opportunity is increasingly available to all.

Let us return for a moment to the term "creative planning" mentioned in the last paragraph. Two unique examples come to mind: *Pegasus* and *Guidelines*. *Pegasus* is a riding center for the handicapped in Novelty, Ohio; it is patterned after many such centers in England. In addition to the benefits derived from an activity which stresses rhythm, balance and coordination, riding encourages equal opportunity in competition, for as Heidi Mehring, President, says: "For the handicapped this association means accomplishment, and the ability to cover ground . . . to win the race that otherwise would be lost." °

° From material supplied to Agnes Hooley by Heidi Mehring, 1974.

FIG. 8-1. Mounted up and ready to go. Photo credit Sarah Kinzie, *Pegasus*.

Another example of "creative planning" is a publication, backed and written by prestigious groups, and entitled: *Guidelines for Professional Preparation Programs for Personnel Involved in Physical Education and Recreation for the Handicapped.* Dealing in specific but flexible suggestions, and calling for a joint effort among physical educators and recreation therapists, this publication has already had considerable impact on the training of those who work with the handicapped (170).

But even when that situation has improved among special teachers, not much will have been done for the classroom teacher who is, after all, generally held responsible for the teaching of physical education in the elementary school. Exceptional children who are in regular classes must look to him just as their classmates do. How well is he prepared to solve the problems which will arise? Many of these teachers have had minimal physical education experience or training during their own school years. Few engage in genuinely active hobbies of a physical education nature. And still fewer have had any experience in teaching skills of an active type to exceptional children.

Many writers have stressed the need for physical education instruction and activity in the life of the child. Havighurst (66) earlier underscored the necessity of attainment in age-related tasks if a child is to succeed in becoming a genuinely mature adult. Kephart has said that children learn perceptually—that is, through the combined perceptual-motor tasks which they experience. He emphasizes the need for skill-learning through physical education so that a child can do what he wants to do:

Classroom teaching, therefore, involves attention to both perception and motor ability, and especially to the very important feedback or matching between them. . . . Because of the cyclical nature of the process, physical education becomes a part of reading and the too frequent dichotomy between muscular or motor activities and intellectual activities becomes untenable (86).

Suggestions for Physical Educators

1. Physical education students should be prepared to teach the exceptional person by enrolling in courses in adapted physical education and taking part in as many affiliated laboratory experiences as possible. Actual work with the handicapped seems to be most helpful.
2. Physical education teachers should help others, especially classroom teachers and administrators, to organize and carry through the adapted physical education idea. They can do this best by teaching well, by acting as consultants, and by submitting suggestions to solve problems posed by handicapped children in the school.
3. Teachers and administrators on local, state, and national levels should work together to upgrade certification requirements, improve attitudes, and keep records of successful solutions to problems in the area of adapted physical education.

Physical educators are encouraged by the thought that at one time the idea of schooling for all normal children seemed the "pipe dream" of a theorist. Perhaps in time complete schooling, including physical education, will be available as a reality for all exceptional children. It will take intelligent and dedicated effort by all who work with them.

Methods of Working with the Education Team

Once the physical educator sees the possibilities in the adapted program, he can forward it as quickly as anyone on the education team. But since he is a member of that team, he should remember that he will make maximum progress by working with all who are concerned with solving the problems of the exceptional child.

Eventually this group will include children who are the peers of the exceptional child. But at the start, the group will probably consist of the principal or executive head, the physicians (family and school), the school nurse, and any others whose training or interest indicate that they be included.

These people would be called together by the principal of the school to consider steps in the setting up of a program of adapted physical education. Often it is necessary for such a group to spend considerable time together before policies and procedures can be agreed upon. Usually the early meetings reveal shared interests and produce some tentative procedures and the beginnings of office forms on which records will be kept. Most of all, they introduce everyone to the overall problems of the handicapped and to the unique local problems which exist.

The physical education teacher should make it clear that he depends on the physician for diagnosis, direction, and suggestions relative to the program for the handicapped child. In this way roles are spelled out and responsibilities and limitations are established. This is important for the legal protection of child and teacher and to reassure the physicians that the teacher will remain willingly within the limits established for those without medical degrees or licenses.

Another advantage of such a team approach is that it allows the physician to gain some measure of insight into the knowledge and understanding of the physical educator. At a recent conference of a state health and physical education association a panel of physicians commented on the desirability of their communicating information on child case-findings to physical educators. Most were willing to talk over cases with intelligent, knowledgeable persons as well as to make specific recommendations for the physical education program of children in need of special programming.

Physical educators who are well versed in their field can handle such knowledge and profit from it. But one may have to work harder to prove this to those physicians who do not understand the background of the physical educator, and so tend either to "write off" physical education by means of a negative, all-inclusive "no physical education" note to the teacher, or to assume that he (the physician) has a full knowledge of what the program is.

One of the earlier products of the team conferences could be an easily duplicated form listing all physical education activities in which a child may participate in a particular school.

Space should be provided for the name of the student, home telephone number, grade or year in school, date of the examination, date of the re-examination, condition or disease, signature of the physician, and length of period during which the recommendations are to be operative. The physician indicates which of the activities are permitted or writes *no activity* on the top of the card.

The use of such a form has several advantages:

1. It calls for a decision by the physician and protects everyone: physician, teacher, child, school.
2. It indicates a definite future time when a re-examination will be given. Such a follow-up examination might be overlooked by children who have the non-participating habit, dislike activity, perform badly and so prefer to remain out of action, or are coddled by parents who think of them as "ill."

3. It can be duplicated; ideally the child and his parents should have a copy so that all can follow his progress and take responsibility for it. In addition, it helps him to recognize limitations and develop a healthy, realistic acceptance of temporary or permanent disabilities. Copies of the form are kept on file by the physician and principal for future reference by any school staff member who would find the information professionally useful.

As team conferences become customary during the school year, many advantages accrue to the exceptional child. His case is known by those who should be acquainted with it, and his progress is followed and encouraged by enthusiastic professional people. Children soon reflect the attitudes of their adult leaders and before long the entire school has begun to accept and encourage him.

Whenever one sees handicapped children participating to their full limit in physical education, one can be sure that conferences have taken place and that certain professional agreements have been reached. It may take a year or more before the operation of the conference team is smooth, but the time and effort spent to develop it are well worthwhile. As time goes on, top-level conferences become fewer and problems are settled on a broader base in many classrooms among many teachers and children. But the initial planning must begin "at the top" so that provision is made for the time, facilities, and personnel which will make the program feasible.

Summary

The well-educated physical educator is ready to join the education team. His attitudes result from knowledge, experience, and empathy. His skills are acquired through course work and field work. He is ready to plan with others for the exceptional child so that learning may occur in the best environment possible. He is capable of convincing others, including physicians and administrators, of the necessity for the provision of a modified (or adapted) program for those who cannot participate fully in the regular program. And he is willing to work out the details which ready an individual program for any individual who needs it.

Chapter 9 examines the entire program of physical education, and recommends activities for each of the fifteen common diseases and conditions which may be found in a typical school population.

9

CHAPTER

Processing the Integrated Program of Adapted Physical Education

The name of Homer Allen is well known among those who work with the exceptional. For thirty years following the death of his son in a streetcar accident in 1907, he devoted his life to therapy for the handicapped. Continuous motivation was provided by the many school-aged children who were the victims in that streetcar accident and who grew into crippled adults in Elyria, Ohio.

Gradually the work of "Daddy" Allen, as he came to be called, spread around the world. Treatment, education, and research programs have brought help to millions of handicapped persons. The International Society for the Rehabilitation of the Disabled and the National Society for Crippled Children and Adults, developing from early individual and group efforts, promote programs and research designed to help professional leaders serve the handicapped better.

Since man first began to take seriously the role of The Good Samaritan, individuals and groups have been recording information for those who would follow. One of the newer professions, physical education, has been among the modern leaders in making available for the elementary and the secondary teacher, the parent, and others concerned with the welfare of the exceptional individual information based on observation and research.

Early portions of this book discussed the preparation of the teacher (Chapter 8), and most of the book includes materials and methods used by various members of the rehabilitation team, including the teacher. The regular physical education program, and the activities therein, can, if necessary, be modified to meet the abilities of the exceptional, and to assist them to make the greatest use of the opportunities provided.

One example which occurs throughout the school year is the return to school of a child who can be classified as a convalescent. The intelligence, knowledge, empathy, and planning ability of the teacher are called into play; he must make those decisions which implement the recommendations of the physician regarding exercise and activity for the child. Logan and Dunkelberg summed it up very well when they said:

In planning the program, the teacher must utilize his knowledge of (1) the limitations of the student's condition; (2) the biophysiological characteristics of man; (3) the physiological demands of the various games, sports, rhythms, and aquatic activities, and (4) the principles of exercise (108, p. 280).

To put this into the vernacular, the teacher must know his field so thoroughly that adapted physical education becomes a matter of choosing from a wide range of possible activities. He cannot be versed solely in aquatics or team games. The elementary teacher, for example, must recognize that movement exploration holds great promise for the child and that learnings in this area will help him to develop insights about his ability to move in time and space; these are insights which will go with him when he moves on into other areas of activity. The well-versed teacher will realize too that such activities as relay games can be modified so that all children can take part equally. For example, a wheelchair patient on each team will often equalize the teams, or a "head start" for the only wheelchair patient in the class may accomplish the same goal.

Those who are not permitted the strenuous swings of golf can benefit by being part of a group which tours the golf course or learns the use of short irons and putters. Patients on inner tubes can play water basketball, and leg-amputees can propel a canoe as swiftly as other persons. Wheelchair patients usually are adept at table tennis, and the nuisance of chasing the ball can be minimized if side-boards are attached at an upward angle from the table. Patients on crutches are usually facile at crutch-use; many a punchball or softball game has proceeded excitedly after a sharp rap of the ball with the batter's crutch!

These illustrations show that interest, ingenuity, and intelligence on the part of teacher and student can move the adapted physical education program forward. It is helpful too if (1) the building is on one level, or if ramps, and/or elevators are provided; and (2) toilet rooms, locker rooms, and water fountains are so built that the handicapped may use them easily. This includes such factors as height of furnishings, nonslip floors, and doors which permit passage of those with canes, crutches, walkers, and wheelchairs.

Ways of Modifying Activities

Activities can be modified to enable exceptional persons to take part without apology and with a sense of achievement through equal participation with others.

Guides for Modifying Activities

1. Shorten time periods.

2. Shorten distances.

3. Change the types of signals.

4. Use guide wires, ground surfaces with different sounding textures, hand rails, and similar devices.

5. Soften landing spots with mats.

6. Allow two hands instead of one where accuracy or power are involved.

7. Change the rules so that they do not contain as many limiting conditions which lessen success.

8. Lower nets, baskets.

9. Increase the size of the striking implement and the targets.

10. Increase or decrease the size of the projectile such as the ball, discus, or javelin.

11. Permit body positions such as sitting which increase stability in games usually played in a standing position. (Example—Wheelchair End Ball).

Judicious choices of equipment will also do much to augment the program, particularly for those whose strength, endurance, or coordination limit them to special schools or special classes. There are several devices on the market which are aimed at helping these persons to improve themselves. The Lind Climber, for example, is stable, sturdy, and easily assembled and is a useful piece of equipment for those who need further development and enjoy climbing, swinging, hanging, or crawling (Fig. 9-1).[*]

[*] The Lind Climber Company, 807 Reba Place, Evanston, Illinois 60202.

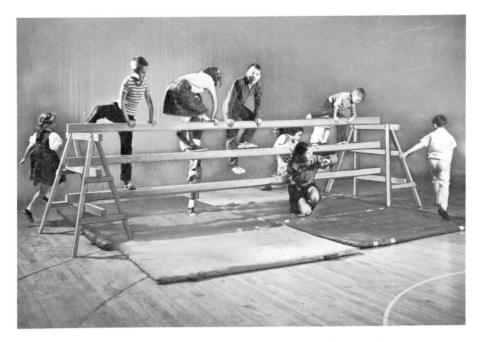

FIG. 9-1.   Commercial Lind climber. (Courtesy of the Lind Climber Company.)

Many in physical education and recreation stress the importance of the communication approach. Foremost among the successful leaders who have used it are Arthur Daniels and Janet Pomeroy, whose books are listed in the bibliography. These people and many others have realized that facilities, equipment, and program cannot succeed where communication has failed.

Cooperation between teacher and student is required for a successful program; they must study the problems together, devise means of handling them, and appraise results. Channels of communication between teacher and student must be maintained. Communication begins in the first conference, and that all-important conference sets the tone for mutual respect, understanding, and cooperation.

The teacher must know the history of the case, understand the directions and recommendations of the physician, and be willing to take time to work with the student. The student may have to be convinced of the desirability of physical education, and he should be taken into the confidence of the teacher with regard to the recommendations of the physician (See Chapters 2, 7, and 8).

The student may need many conferences, and he will certainly need and usually want special help as he improves and is able to take part more fully and equitably with others. Knowing and understanding each other and sharing in the planning and evaluation processes will continue to build respect and rapport between teacher and student. Once that has been accomplished, the program can become operative. Praise, success, and enthusiasm are important, but nothing can replace careful initial and mutual planning.

Planning sets goals, establishes limits, interprets the program, and involves all who must be involved: the rehabilitation team, administrators, teachers, parents, and the handicapped person. Furthermore, it encourages the student to help himself. Exceptional youngsters have been observed modifying games on their own by setting up slalom obstacle courses in gymnasia and handling "car washes" to earn money for such aids as "radar canes" for blind friends.° The latter is a fine example of a way in which the handicapped have begun to take the initiative in solving problems.

Fifteen Handicapping Conditions

In the pages which follow, the reader will find a discussion of the problems and program possibilities for the handicapping conditions found among school children; all occur often enough that the teacher may want to look to this material for help now or at some future time.

The conditions are presented alphabetically as follows:

1. The Allergic

2. The Anemic

3. The Blind and Partially Sighted

4. Cardiac Handicaps

5. The Cerebral Palsied

6. The Deaf and the Hard of Hearing

7. Dermal Disorders

8. The Diabetic

9. The Epileptic

10. Hernial Cases

11. Menstrual Difficulties

12. The Mentally Different: The Retarded and The Gifted (see Chapter 4)

° The cane is an invention of Dr. Thomas A. Benham, a blind physics professor at Haverford College. The cane user knows the size and distance of obstacles through the functioning of radar which "bounces" the information from obstacle to user. It is described in *Journal of Rehabilitation* (133).

13. The Orthopaedically Handicapped

14. The Tuberculous

15. Those with Weight Problems

For each of these conditions there is a presentation of background information and problems. Specific activities are recommended as well; for most of the conditions activities are presented from each of the five areas of the physical education program: (1) dance and other rhythmic activities; (2) individual, dual, and team activities; (3) aquatic activities; (4) body mechanics; (5) movement exploration.

We should like to add a word of encouragement to those who are hesitant about taking those first steps into the adapted program. Once they are taken, the next ones will be comparatively easy, for as Justice Oliver Wendell Holmes wrote many years ago:

. . . the race is worth the running. A man is pretty sure to get his due share of appreciation, for, whether he speaks or is silent, the world generally finds him out. But while it is a delight to get praise that one deserves, the fiercest joy is in the doing. Those who run hardest probably have the least satisfaction with themselves, but they know most of the joy of life when at top speed (63, p. 147).

May we all go forward at top speed to do a job that so badly needs to be done.

1. The Allergic

One of the most miserable conditions which victimize mankind is a reaction to allergens. Sensitivity to a particular substance (which other men can tolerate) ranges from a mild skin rash or swelling of the fingers or toes to violent headache and upset stomach.

Those who suffer from an allergy react adversely to some specific foreign substance (antigen). These substances include foods, drugs, endocrine products, inhalant factors, and matter injected by stinging insects. Technically, allergy-producing agents are of two types:

1. Substances which produce anaphylactic or "serum sickness," such as proteins, polysaccharides, and haptens.

2. Substances which are not related to serum antibody.

With regard to allergy, many things concern the physician, but primary consideration is given to the sensitivity of the patient, the size of the dose of antigen, and the speed with which it is absorbed by the body systems. In general, medical handling of allergy cases involves preventive measures, treatment of symptoms, and therapy toward hyposensitization.

While allergies are not inheritable, a familial predisposition has been observed; as an example of this, one-half of the patients with asthma or hay fever show a family history of allergic reactions. In addition, certain acquired diseases, such as Hodgkin's disease, affect immunologic responsiveness.

Allergy reaction may take a mild or severe form. Mild reaction cases develop temporary skin conditions and demonstrate most of the signs of the common cold: nasal discharge, watery eyes, sneezing. Hives or urticaria may occur; media involved are ingestion, inhalation, injection, or contact with an antigen which happens to be offensive to the subject. Severe reactions may involve the digestive system or may demonstrate the signs of hay fever or asthma.

Hay fever is the name given to the reaction condition which results in difficult breathing because of the swelling of the mucous membranes of the nasal passages. Asthma involves the swelling of the bronchial mucous membranes.

The spring, summer, and autumn of each year bother the hay fever sufferer, while the asthma victim may suffer the year round. Another simple way to divide these two unhappy states is to say that the hay fever victim sneezes often, while the asthmatic wheezes during the attacks. An asthmatic attack may last a few minutes or several hours. Often the sufferer is anxious as he tries to inhale enough air for lungs which seem to be under pressure from within and without the body. Cyanosis (or bluing) of the skin may be noted; often cold hands and feet persist throughout the attack.

The asthmatic may be chronically fatigued from the effects of the attacks which leave him exhausted from the necessity of sitting up (often in a bent forward position) to secure air and from the general state of anxiety and frustration which may accompany this condition.

What Can Be Done

As usual, in dealing with the exceptional there are many who sympathize. Others wish to curtail all activity. Neither of these measures does anything for the victim. Instead, four steps should be undertaken by the victim:

1. Consult an allergist to find the cause through skin testing and other diagnostic procedures.

2. Eliminate as far as possible those substances to which the victim is allergic.

3. Use whatever medical means of prevention and/or treatment are available.

4. Develop a well-rounded life through participation in those areas of activity which are safely open to the victim.

Once the preceding steps are underway, the physical educator and the physician can plan a program for the student. Obviously those who are hypersensitive to dust, grasses, and other elements associated with field games must be restricted from such activities. Often students can enter into certain fall and spring sports indoors while their classmates take part outdoors; for instance, badminton, tennis, and archery become possible where facilities and staff permit.

Swimming is often excluded for those who are allergic to chlorine; however, many pool systems now operate with other chemicals to which students are not allergic. Before an automatic excuse is given, one should determine the sanitation chemicals used; some school systems send such information to physicians who will be responsible for recommendations concerning the physical education program.

The discomfort which follows ingestion of foods to which a person is allergic generally results in his remaining on his diet voluntarily; however, some students may need counseling in this regard. In addition, continued eating of such foods with subsequent reactions should prompt school authorities to seek a conference with the parents; knowledge or funds may need to be supplemented before a change in diet can take place. Chocolate and eggs are known agents of allergic reactions; yet, many are surprised to discover that beef, milk, and wheat are common offenders. Parents are often hesitant to eliminate such important foods from the diet of an allergic child; however, when sensible substitutes are suggested, soy protein for milk, for example, cooperation is usually easy to obtain.

Exceptions may have to be made in clothing requirements for those who are allergic to materials from which sweat shirts, socks, swim suits, or other gymnasium costumes are manufactured. Companies which rent or sell outfits to institutions generally will be helpful in suggesting uniforms which duplicate appearance and functional qualities but eliminate the offensive materials of the standard outfit. As a matter of class and individual morale, the student should be expected to dress for activity, rather than be excused because of an allergy to some substance from which the uniform is made.

The Asthmatic

It must be noted too that students with asthma need exercise as much as others. In the case of mild allergies, and even hay fever, this idea usually does not meet with much resistance. In the case of the asthmatic, however, the teacher may be faced with a serious situation.

Here is a person who needs exercise; yet should he become overactive (with resultant fatigue), he may suffer an attack. Since the student who has suffered from asthma all his life may have avoided exercise for fear of precipitating an attack, he may resist participation in physical education. Such a person is often physically unfit, filled with apprehensions and negative attitudes regarding physical education, and somewhat embarrassed or defensive about his inability to perform the skills which are natural for his years.

The wisest way for the physical educator to work with the student with asthma is to follow closely the recommendations of the physician. Sometimes the latter may contraindicate any activity; in such cases the physical educator should confer with him and make it clear that, with permission from the physician, a very gradual and light program may be started. Subsequent increase in activity should never be sufficient to bring the person to the point of extreme fatigue. Since emotional states such as frustration, anger, and embarrassment may bring on an asthmatic attack, the physical educator should observe the progress of the student and give whatever counsel seems indicated. If the student is aware of the supervision of an interested teacher, he will tend to feel more secure and relaxed. These are important factors if improved health is to result and is to be reflected in performance, fitness, and attitudes.

Guide Lines for the Asthmatic

1. Provide an individual program of challenging activities so that physical fitness and security develop together.

2. Teach the student to recognize his exercise tolerance and to stop before he is unduly fatigued.

3. Encourage the development of skill in activities which allow for rest when needed and which remain interesting even when there is no great stress on winning.

2. The Anemic

The first two letters of the word *anemia* are a Greek word in themselves; translated, *an* means "lack." The remainder of the word *anemia* comes from *haima*, the Greek word meaning "blood." Stated simply, anemia refers to a blood deficiency. Sometimes this is a matter of quality; often it is one of quantity. Anemia can be local or general, mild or severe, curable or incurable, and is often symptomatic of other conditions and diseases.

Anemia is caused by blood loss from the body, as in hemorrhaging, or by problems associated with the manufacture and maintenance of a good blood supply. Many of the problems are biochemical in nature and involve glands and various other "working systems" of the body. In school children, anemia seems to be associated with severe loss of blood from accidents, with various infectious conditions, history of disease, and consistently poor nutrition.

Because of the wide range of causal possibilities, the child with anemia should be programmed with as much care as is any other handicapped child. As always, the recommendations of the physician in charge must be followed exactly.

The name of the condition (anemia) and the undramatic and near normal general appearance of the child may tell little about his state of health. However, the listless attitude toward activity and the typical lack of endurance and power in performance can tell a great deal. Many girls, particularly in adolescence, do not resent the inactivity which anemia makes so easy. Concerned with appearance, popularity and a heterosexual value scheme, many of them would be happy to forego physical education. But to boys, anemia and the limitations which it puts upon energy expenditure may become a threat to the manly role they hope to play. Attempts to curb activity may result in defensive behaviors and actual refusal to follow the recommendations of physician and teacher. Frustration and illness are potential outcomes in these threatening situations.

The key to an understanding of the place of the anemic student in physical education is a genuine appreciation of his lack of energy. There are many activities in which he can participate with no harmful effects. Especially to be recommended are those which permit him to:

1. Observe others as they learn, thus lessening the learning energy which he will expend.

2. Participate and then recuperate before the next outburst of energy is required.

3. Improve his skill with the least amount of energy.

4. Relax in the company of others.

The teacher should bypass activities which call for endurance and strength. Properly supervised activities will tend to improve the health of the student in two ways:

1. Physiologically—by calling for increased oxygen, thereby spurring the production of red blood cells.

2. Mentally and socially—by encouraging him to take part in activities on a maturity level with his own age group.

Suitable Activities

Dance.

Of the many types of dance, the only unsuitable one would seem to be tap dance which requires steady effort. Usually ballroom, folk, square, and modern dance would be appropriate, although they might have to be limited from the point of view of time or space. The most suitable group dances are those which permit periods of rest as part of their total performance, such as "Round and Round the Village," "Oats, Peas, Beans," many reels, "Gustaf's Skoal," "The Girl I Left Behind Me," and "Czardas." Ballroom dances are excellent, since participants can drop out at any time. The anemic student in modern dance should be assigned to such a place and position that his need for rest does not cause embarrassment to him or inconvenience to the other dancers.

Individual, Dual, and Team Activities.

These should be chosen so that the age and needs of the student are reflected in the choices. Circle, couple, relay, and similar activity formations are good, since they provide automatic rest periods without affecting the continuity of the event. Mass activities such as "Midnight," "Catch of Fish," "Triple Dodge Ball," and "Bombardment" are contraindicated, but "Duck, Duck, Goose," "End Ball" and "Stoop Tag," all of which include rest periods, are suitable. A list of activities which would be appropriate for many anemic patients follows:

1. Archery.
2. Bait casting.
3. Billiards.
4. Bowling.
5. Golf (especially short irons and putting).
6. Horseshoes.
7. Ice skating.
8. Paddle tennis.
9. Riflery.
10. Softball (particularly if playing in outfield or on third base).
11. Some stunts, and certain self-testing activities such as simple balance beam work.

12. Table tennis.

13. Some track and field events such as standing broad jump and ball throwing for accuracy.

14. Tumbling (simple).

15. Volleyball.

Aquatics.

These activities should be limited by the endurance of the student; this will automatically exclude skin and scuba diving, life saving, and synchronized swimming. However, salutary effects can be procured through swimming, diving, boating and canoeing, sailing, and a limited amount of water skiing.

Body Mechanics.

The student needs participation in this area of activity, since his energy is limited. Body mechanics is concerned with the proper expenditure of energy in many areas of life. Everyone needs this instruction, but the anemic shows the benefits of such instruction more quickly than others because soon he works longer, more effectively, and with less fatigue.

Movement Exploration.

This area is of particular use and interest in the early grades. The pupil solves problems associated with movement through time and space. Rest should be encouraged where needed, and the resting pupil can be taught to observe others and to learn through the energy they are expending. This does not mean imitation, but intelligent awareness. The evaluation sessions which are a part of the lesson encourage such awareness as a part of the problem-solving technique.

3. The Blind and Partially Sighted

For well over a hundred years the plight of the blind has been of concern to educators throughout the nation, and private and public institutions have initiated testing, treatment, social, and physical education programs. Historically the blind have received much attention because blindness is such a dramatic and total disability. Early efforts at such schools as Perkins Institute in Boston were followed by similar exploratory and remedial work in Cleveland and other large cities. Although leadership has been provided by many groups, one of the foremost groups today is the New York Association for the Blind, known to many as *The Lighthouse*.

The Lighthouse in New York City is a mecca for thousands of patients and the volunteer and professional people who work with them. Modern in every way, the midtown building contains all the service and treatment features which help the blind and partially sighted to help themselves. It includes workrooms, bowling lanes, and stairways with braille numbers and elevators with recorded voices to enable the blind to know their location as they move about the building. During the regular school term, physical education activities are conducted indoors and outdoors (on a walled-in roof); in the summertime camping facilities are provided for sports, games, and aquatics. Here the handicapped participate as noisily and as enthusiastically as children everywhere.

Yet, although much has been done for the blind, considerable progress remains to be made. This is particularly true for the general public which, although interested, knows little about blindness or the problems of the blind.

Daniels and Davies state that there are up to a quarter of a million blind persons in the United States; the partially sighted are twice as numerous (29, p. 261). Generally blindness occurs after birth and is due to disease, accident, or hereditary factors. Fortunate is the person with good sight through a lifetime; less fortunate is the person who enjoys a few years of sight before blindness overcomes him. But most unfortunate of all is the one whose sight is gone before movement, light and dark, and the shapes and colors of objects have been perceived, comprehended, and stored in memory. Loss of sight may happen to very young children whose eyes are injured with sharp toys, or who suffer through early bouts with scarlet fever or ophthalmia.

Visual acuity of between 20/70 and 20/200 in the better eye after correction generally labels the person as partially sighted; less than that figure is considered blindness. Present theory is to include the partially sighted in regular schools wherever possible; those who can benefit from daily learning with normal children are to be placed in regular classes. However, only about one child in ten is so placed; many stay permanently in sight-saving classes, while still others attend schools for the blind.

Examples of partially sighted children are those with common structurally caused deviations: myopia (near-sightedness), hyperopia (far-sightedness), astigmatism (hazy vision), and strabismus (double vision— sometimes known as cross-eye).

The partially seeing and the blind child often share common characteristics:

1. They may favor solitary pursuits which permit them to start and stop, and to move about in space as they will. Such activities as they choose protect them from injury and from the failure which might result from

competition with others, yet provide them with the satisfaction of having moved. Often their choices are sedentary activities in contrast with the usually more active occupations chosen by the normal child. Seldom do they participate in activities which lead to strength, speed, and endurance.

2. They may display symptoms of fear, frustration, concern over the future, worry about social maturity, especially with regard to the opposite sex.

The blind and the partially seeing might be compared to a prisoner who has been kept in solitary confinement for a long time, then suddenly released. It is hard for such a person to understand the relationships of people, places, and events in a free world. It can be seen then that those who teach the blind must communicate verbally with them—informing, explaining, interpreting, and evaluating. As one blind adolescent said, "It's pretty easy to learn how people do things; but it's much harder to find out how they *feel* about things."

Those who teach persons with partial or complete impairment of vision should recognize that there are goals which both teachers and learners should keep before them.

Program Goals for the Visually Impaired

1. Do everything possible to minimize eyestrain and to save vision where present.

2. Seek to improve other senses, especially auditory, kinesthetic, and tactile senses.

3. Concentrate on the accomplishment of tasks which are socially or vocationally useful, and which instill feelings of confidence and purposefulness. In the process, development of discovered talents and aptitudes should be anticipated and encouraged.

4. Seek the development of awareness of all kinds, for awareness brings knowledge of people, space, and time.

It is important, of course, that consideration be given to the cultural, maturational, and intellectual levels of the potential learner. Regarding intelligence, Hunt says:

The median IQ of blind people is only slightly lower than that of normal people; the difference is probably related to central nerve destruction, which causes much blindness (76).

Teachers of the blind should keep this in mind in setting levels of attainment for pupils. However, they should remember that each child should be tested individually, and that some raising of IQ has been shown in some children who were taken from solitary environments and exposed to settings which involved social orientation and community living.

There is no doubt that teachers need to protect from injury the blind or partially seeing person as he begins to move about in the world of seeing people. But overprotection can lead to no activity at all or to such guarded participation that the child learns little except fear. Much advice has been given to those who wish to teach the blind, but the statement of Daniels and Davies is probably the best of all:

A teacher trained in the needs and problems of the blind will see that there are no hazards in the play area; that proper equipment will be used; and that the right type of activities, well organized and controlled, will make up the program (29, p. 268).

It is suggested that a teacher might gradually involve a visually handicapped child in full participation in physical education through the following sequence of steps:

1. Learn the child's name, and address him by name always.

2. Use music whenever possible, sometimes to relax him (the handicapped tend to be tense in learning situations), sometimes to bring beauty into his world, sometimes to signal to him as in dance.

3. Let him work alone for a while if he is used to that. This will let him learn where things are. (It is important, too, that things be kept in an orderly fashion so that the child does not fall over them as might happen if they are left strewn about).

4. Let him progress from the use of stationary equipment to movable objects which he can shape, stop, throw, and carry about.

5. Gradually introduce him to the idea of working with others in formations such as circles and lines, predictable protective formations.

6. Let him begin to take part in open space activities such as walking and skipping, guided by a sighted partner or a wire with which he keeps in contact by a short moving lead to his hand.

7. Permit movement in cleared spaces which warn him of area limits through change in surface, for example, grass to cement to gravel.

Suitable Activities

Many visually handicapped children have favorite activities which they do well. However, most need encouragement to broaden their interests; therefore, they should be introduced to new activities which they might avoid if permitted an all-choice program.

The only physical education activities which are not indicated for the blind or partially sighted are those which might cause injury to the body, or further loss of vision to the partially sighted.

Activities which are especially suitable for the visually handicapped include:

Dance.

Folk, square, ballroom, tap, and modern appropriate to the age and interests of the group may be selected. The use of music and rhythm in dance allows the blind to substitute rhythmic and meaningful movement and gestures for the "blindisms" or nervous mannerisms which they often develop, such as foot tapping, head rolling, and body rocking. Folk and square dances are most useful for beginning dancers because the group is arranged in easily remembered floor patterns. Modern dance, which teaches free movement in unpatterned space, is important in helping the blind to break the habit of moving stiffly with feet close to the floor. While teaching dances, the leader may have all join hands and walk through floor patterns. He may have the dancers gesture instead of using holding movements, since individual work is easier than coordinated work with partners. He may substitute simple steps for complicated ones (*e.g.,* sideward slides for the grapevine). Wherever possible the partially sighted are asked to help the blind. Gradually the leader teaches the blind to execute as nearly as possible the steps and movements which are used by sighted persons. After all, those are the persons with whom the visually handicapped hope one day to dance.

Individual, Dual, and Team Activities.

Games of low organization should be used if appropriate to the group. The following activities of higher organization are suitable for many intermediate and older visually handicapped students.

1. Bait casting.

2. Baseball.

3. Basketball.

4. Billiards.

5. Bowling.

6. Some gymnastics which do not involve work high above the floor by beginners.

7. Horseshoes.

8. Roller skating.

9. Softball.

10. Stunts and self-testing activities.

11. Track and field.

12. Tumbling.

13. Volleyball.

14. Wrestling.

15. Weight lifting.

Often modifications must be introduced to make games suitable: for example, in baseball, if a partially sighted outfielder stops a ball before the runner gets to first base, the runner is out.

It has been said that "rules were made to be bent, if not broken"; this is true for the lowered net in volleyball, the shortened field in softball, and the lowered hoop in basketball. The program is limited only by the imagination, time, and energy of the instructor (190, p. 25). Some of the more common changes which can be introduced include:

1. Use of brightly colored mats, balls, fences, and playground equipment for use with the partially sighted.

2. Use of a bell or rattle inside a ball; such a ball rolled, as in kickball, tells the sightless batsman of its approach. Newcomb can be played satisfactorily with such a ball, and the allowance of one bounce after the ball has crossed the net makes the game even more possible among blind players.

3. Placement of a metal bar from his seat to the foul line helps the bowler to align himself before he rolls the ball.

4. Provision of a guide wire with a moving lead makes it possible for the dash man to run the track without weaving. The lead, held in one hand, makes his progress both straighter and swifter than if he had to depend on his sense of direction alone.

Verbal communication, of course, adds greatly to the performance of the blind players. Teammates and coaches shout directions, and teammates stationed near goals, such as bases, ring bells to help guide the player. While conducting the continuous and necessary supervision, teachers and leaders often think of new ways to aid the blind seeking to emulate their sighted companions.

Some physical education instructors have used successfully both archery and golf. Ingenuity devises stationary markers on a vertical pole with which the archer "lines up" his pulling arm, and friendly partners direct the golfer at the range. Such activities add satisfying experiences to those who are fortunate enough to partake of them. But best of all are those events such as the standing broad jump, the shot put, and wrestling which permit the blind and partially sighted to compete on equal terms with others who are sighted. Whenever the physical educator can include activities with this equalizing factor, he is well advised to do so.

Many low organized games provide an advantage to the blind child; one example is Blind Man's Buff. Sighted players find it difficult to move about when blindfolded and seldom are as successful as the blind child in the use of the tactile sense in trying to recognize players by the feel of clothing. In certain types of recreational games such as Detective, the blind child surpasses others. Common objects are hidden under an inverted box and the players are asked to identify them by touch; the winner is the one who can name the objects correctly and most quickly.

Aquatics.

Aquatics is generally encouraged for the visually handicapped. It is not indicated for the partially sighted whose condition would be aggravated by salt water or impurities in fresh water. But most visually handicapped are permitted to swim, and later to boat, canoe, join crew, perform simple dives, and join other water skiers.

Because of the hazardous nature of unsupervised swimming, care must be taken to prepare the visually handicapped child for a safe experience in the water. Time should be taken to have him become acquainted with the locker room and pool area, and to learn the means by which deep and shallow areas are separated (usually ropes, floating corks on lines, or runways). In addition, while still on land or in shallow water he needs to become used to the effect of splashed water on the breathing cycle.

During instruction periods, gradual immersion should be encouraged. Instructors teach with varying methods, for example:

1. Arm strokes are taught by placing the instructor's hand on the swimmer's hand, then executing the movement.

2. Other instructors have swimmers place their hands on the shoulders of the instructor while he moves his arms through the double arm movement.

3. Often instructors move the feet of the swimmer when teaching the kick movements for a given stroke.

Again verbal communication should be emphasized, for it provides the swimmer with the location of the instructor and the coaching, directions, and praise which mean most when they come from him.

Competitive swimming becomes possible for students when the lane markers used in meets are provided for practice sessions. A sighted competitive swimmer seldom comes near his lane marker since he swims straight by using arms equally. This is as true for the blind or partially sighted experienced swimmer who is thereby able to compete on an equal footing with his sighted friends.

Body Mechanics.

An improvement in body mechanics is especially recommended for the visually handicapped. Stressing efficient handling of body weight, it teaches the blind to execute flowing movements rather than the stilted ones which are common among the untutored blind. Body mechanics programs are particularly useful for the blind and partially sighted when they feature work in static and dynamic posture and then apply this to everyday tasks such as stair climbing and lifting and carrying objects.

Movement Exploration.

This is probably the most useful activity for the sightless young. Stressing movement limited only by imagination and cued by a resourceful teacher, it can help the child to discover how much space his body needs, what he can do in space, and how it feels to move at various levels. Space and time become related, and he learns to explore a bigger world by the development of auditory, tactile, and kinesthetic senses.

As an example, the kinesthetic sense, operating through receptors at the joints of the body, tells him where he is in space and where the body parts are with reference to each other. Gradually the child learns to perform many skills, not merely while standing, but while progressing from foot to foot, or while kneeling, sitting, or jumping through space. Movement exploration cannot give him eyesight but it can help him to become more aware of the world around him than many sighted people are.

4. Cardiac Handicaps

Man has always been intrigued by and concerned about his heart, especially its efficiency, (health). Modern tests of that factor include monitoring of the heart, and the entire cardiovascular system, while walking, jogging, running on a treadmill, pedaling a bicycle, or taking the Master's (step) test. Such measures are processed for the same reasons that a good physical education regime is provided for a person: to prevent deviant heart conditions, and to supply means of rehabilitation, or at least maintenance of present efficiency for those with such deviations.

The heart is a muscle; if normal, it grows larger and stronger and more efficient with use. Despite this simple fact, more people die of heart and circulatory diseases than from any other cause. Perhaps it is because the heart is one of the few machines which never really rests. Perhaps it is the tension-filled environment which puts pressure upon the person and so upon his heart. Perhaps the heart tires because it must provide oxygenated blood to the body, while handling the mechanics of sending blood to the lungs for an exchange of gases. Such a complicated system of mains and moving parts is bound to develop defects.

Thus it is no wonder that organic and functional disturbances affect the heart. The former refers to lesions in the cardiovascular-renal system; the latter refers to atypical functioning of the heart, which results in such symptoms as shortness of breath after exercise, accentuated heart beat, and great anxiety. These terms—*organic* and *functional*—often arise in conversations about so-called "heart murmurs." Some children are said to have *organic* murmurs, which are usually associated with structural deviations—*e.g.*, a faulty valve which permits blood to "leak" past it. Many murmurs are of the *functional* type and disappear as the child develops. Frequently the announcement that a child has a heart murmur causes some alarm; yet the nature and cause of the murmur or "heart sound" is far more important than the simple labeling of all such sounds as murmurs. But in any case such matters should be left to the physician, who is the only one capable of diagnosing abnormalities and making recommendations concerning them.

Although there are numerous kinds of organic heart diseases, the three most common are coronary heart disease, hypertensive heart disease, and rheumatic heart disease. Rheumatic heart disease is responsible for almost all cases of heart disease among minors. Hypertension is generally associated with adulthood and is known as "high blood pressure." Thickening of the arterial walls, or arteriosclerosis, often occurs simultaneously, with resultant severe strain on the heart. The patient now has hypertensive heart disease. Although lack of exercise and cholesterol buildup are suspected causative factors, age is the only known predisposing factor. Coronary heart disease is usually a threat to people of middle and older years. It is caused by occlusion or the rupture of a blood vessel which causes a flow of blood into the muscle tissue of the heart. Coronary heart disease seldom strikes children.

The heart may be affected, too, by such problems as anemia or overactive thyroid gland. Congenital heart disease and acquired diseases such as tuberculosis and diphtheria cause many to become heart victims. Infections which strike the heart muscle (myocarditis), the outer covering of the heart (pericarditis), and the inner covering (endocarditis) raise the number of patients still higher.

Although the causes of heart disease are varied, the problems of the victims are similar:

1. Most have some problem of physical limitation.

2. Many are overweight and in poor physical condition because of a history of limited exercise.

3. Some fill the descriptive phrase, "cardiac cripple," refusing to participate in activity because they fear that they cannot safely do so. Their entire thinking revolves around disability.

4. Many are depressed, feel isolated from others.

5. Many are fearful, and worry that their condition will worsen and that they will become a burden to themselves and to others.

6. Some are so sure that death is imminent that they "take chances" by being overactive despite the warnings of friends and physicians.

Today heart and circulatory diseases are responsible for more deaths among our countrymen than any other cause. Research of all kinds is being advanced to lessen this national catastrophe. Physicians have given educators much assistance in handling children with heart disease. The New York Heart Association Inc. and Heart Fund have devised a classification scheme whereby persons with cardiac diseases are categorized with regard to function or the amount of physical effort which they should expend. The range extends from no restriction to bed rest:

Class I. No restriction of usual activity.
Class II. Slight restriction of physical activity.
Class III. Marked restriction of physical activity.
Class IV. Even at rest, these people are not comfortable. Severe restriction of physical activity.
No heart disease, although predisposing factors exist in the history of patient. Follow-up examinations considered necessary.
Undiagnosed symptoms and signs, uncertain diagnosis of heart disease. Follow-up of the case is undertaken by the physician.

We are concerned primarily with the first four classes: people who are so listed by their physicians must follow advice given or they experience undue fatigue, palpitation, anginal pain, or dyspnea.

The physical educator who is to be responsible for a cardiac pupil should proceed through five steps:

1. Read the health history and whatever other records are available concerning the past activity and academic experience of the child.

2. Discover the interests and attitudes of the child by a conference with him.

3. Discover, by a personal interview with the physician, the classification of the child, as well as the exact activities in which he may participate and to what degree. The teacher should inquire about unusual symptoms or other aspects of the case which might be of help to him in working with the child.

4. Get to know the child further through apparently casual interviews, by watching him in action, and from reports which parents, physicians, or teachers may submit.

5. Encourage the child in the health practices which are particularly beneficial to him (*e.g.*, rest, exercise, and recreation).

Points to remember when setting up the programs for most cardiac participants include the following (generally these do not apply to Class I).

Program Guides for Cardiac Cases

1. Plan well to avoid useless moving about which expends limited energy of heart cases.

2. Perform generally on flat surfaces; go to grades and levels gradually.

3. Teach some activities while students are lying down or sitting; then change body positions slowly, from lying to sitting to standing.

4. Do most things slowly, allowing for as much rest time as for activity time.

5. Avoid tensing, enduring, sustaining kinds of movement, (*e.g.*, permit no isometric exercises).

6. Include mild activity, performed in short periods of time.

7. Avoid movement performed to a strong commanding "beat."

8. Teach the students that rest is part of the lesson and that shortness of breath means "stop." A good "rule of thumb" is that open-mouthed breathing usually means that the heart is working harder than it should for the cardiac on limited activity, and that it is time to rest.

9. Work in areas with stable temperatures and sufficient ventilation.

10. In cold weather or water, go indoors with the first sign of chilling, such as shivering.

11. Avoid competitive activities or any others which bring emotional stress to participants.

12. Try to "sell" the right amount of exercise to the cardiac cases on the basis that it brings them four satisfying results: (1) better circulation, (2) better condition, as weight is reduced and muscles developed, (3) better coordination, and (4) more confidence as they come closer to living normal lives through activity.

Suitable Activities

As in other handicapping conditions the physician is the final arbiter of the amount and kind of exercise and activity to include for the student. Nevertheless, the physical educator can help by providing the physician with a list of available activities and by discovering exactly what amount of energy output is permissible. Usually the doctor will classify the child and then tell the teacher what activities are specifically allowed. Usual activities permitted for each classification are described, but they should be reviewed by physician and teacher with each cardiac case in mind.

Class I—No Restriction of Usual Activity

The pupil may perform any activity which is included for others in physical education. Hopefully this would mean dance of all types; games of low or high organization; appropriate individual, dual, and team activities; body mechanics; and movement exploration as appropriate. Stress should not be placed upon "winning above all else." Since both competition and endurance sports tend to place strain upon the heart, they should be avoided.

Class II—Slight Restriction of Physical Activity

The cardiac victim in this class should not engage in any activities which involve great emotional tension. This restriction would eliminate competition in hard-fought tournaments and matches and would indicate that such games as table tennis should be supervised carefully because the competitive strain appears early for these performers. In addition, care should be exercised to shorten or narrow courts and lessen time periods in games played by those who show symptoms of fatigue. An easy application of this principle is the limitation to doubles in badminton with 11-point games instead of 15.

These students might be allowed to pitch in softball for a limited time, but not in baseball, since underhand throwing is less strenuous than overhand. Activities which demand an explosive expenditure of energy, such as pole vault, are contraindicated as are activities which call for heavy lifting, such as weight training and wrestling.

Cold weather and water further limit the cardiac who earlier than others may need to retreat indoors to warmer air. Thus swimming in warm water with others is permitted, but games such as water polo should be postponed until the cardiac group has left the area. While the others are playing this exciting game, he can take a warm shower and dress at the leisurely pace he needs.

The program, having been agreed upon, is evaluated constantly by the observant teacher and the intelligent participant who heed signs of fatigue and respect the power of rest. Activities for Class II victims can include the following:

Dance. Rhythmic games and folk dances which permit some to stand while some dance are indicated; an example is "Round and Round the Village." Contraindicated are such dances as "Captain Jinks," which call for continuous action by all, with as many repetitions as the performers can endure.

Tap dance is acceptable if the "breaks" are as long as the steps. Square dance demands more energy than these people should be asked to use. Modern dance, possibly in stationary positions and at various levels can be a satisfying and creative experience. Ballroom dance is acceptable, since it includes rest as a part of the social amenities with which it is surrounded. Such steps as the waltz and a reasonable amount of such steps as the rumba are fine, but recent novelty steps which demand jumping and twisting at a fast pace should be excluded. Generally, however, these are no problem as they are not taught to any great extent in school classes.

Individual, Dual, and Team Activities. Games of low organization are generally permitted if they allow the participant to be a spectator for part of the time. Examples include Three Deep and Sitting Soccer. In the latter game two rows of sitting players face each other. When the whistle sounds, players try to kick the ball over the heads of their opponents. Each successful try brings one point. Obviously, choice of game activities should be made with age and interest of the participants in mind.

Activities of an individual, dual, or team nature which are most suitable include:

1. Archery.

2. Badminton (doubles, using single court boundaries only).

3. Bait casting.

4. Basket shooting games, using lowered basket.

5. Billiards.

6. Bowling with light balls, as in candle pin bowling, or bocce.

7. Darts.

8. Deck tennis on a narrow court, played as a team game.

9. Golf; short irons and putting only.

10. Hiking.

11. Horseshoes.

12. Ice skating, in limited time periods, no competition, and generally indoors.

13. Paddle tennis.

14. Riflery.

15. Shuffleboard.

16. Table tennis, limited time only.

17. Volleyball, limited time only.

Aquatics. Activity here depends a great deal on the environmental controls exerted: temperature of the water and pool area and availability of dry towels and clothing between short swim periods.

If conditions are correct, the student may take part in swimming (limited time only); diving, if capable of doing it without tension; boating; canoeing; sailing.

Body Mechanics. This area provides instruction on how to manage typical weights. Efficient handling of weights saves energy and thus reduces heart strain. Practical applications of theory as in stair climbing, carrying suitcases, and moving light furniture are the usual procedure in this area. In addition, instruction in the attainment of balanced posture through remedial exercises and relaxation techniques is of special value to the cardiac child.

Movement Exploration. Although this area of activity is generally limited to the elementary grades, it might be blended with limited modern dance for all with cardiac conditions. It permits individual movement through space and can be limited as desired. It is a great relaxant and confidence-builder.

The student, instructed and cued by the teacher, becomes aware of people, time, and space. He learns to use his energy wisely as he solves movement problems and builds as much fitness as is indicated for him.

Class III—Marked Restriction of Physical Activity

Activity for this group should be very limited in time, distance, and type. Even ordinary activities tire these people. Many will benefit by individual exercise programs rounded out by relatively sedentary activities such as archery, walking, shuffleboard, riflery, and bait casting.

Sometimes such students can fulfill tasks which add to the efforts of the group. Care should be taken not to permit them to assume managerial posts with varsity teams in whose competitive atmosphere they become unduly fatigued; neither should they be relegated to handing out towels and suits, monitor-tasks which further isolate them from their peers. As scorekeepers in physical education class games and as record keepers in the necessary paper work of class tournaments they have positions of recognized value and will tend to be included by their classmates in plans and discussions. We remember a Class III student who was an excellent fire-builder and chef for class outings. Driven to the camp-site with the rest of the "cooking crew," she helped prepare the meal which awaited the hungry hikers. Part of the success of the venture was her joy in filling a role which anyone, not merely the cardiac, might fill!

Class IV—Severe Restriction of Physical Activity

These students are usually home-bound, or if in school are not the responsibility of the physical education teacher. Therefore, no program need be planned for them. They spend most of their time in bed where limited exercise is sometimes programmed for them by the attending physician.

5. The Cerebral Palsied

Cerebral palsy was recognized in 1863 by William John Little, M.D. and was known as Little's disease for many years. Cerebral palsy still has something of the mystique about it. The multiplicity of the signs and problems associated with it and the inability to predict exact success or failure for the sufferers probably account in part for the endurance of this quality. It is hoped that as greater knowledge of cerebral lesions becomes available some of the mystique will disappear. Consequently the victim should find greater acceptance as well as greater provision for his education and guidance.

Causes

Prenatal conditions and birth injuries account for approximately 90 per cent of the cases. Causes of prenatal cases (30 per cent of the total) involve such factors as metabolic disturbances of the mother and such biochemical difficulties as differences between the Rh factor in mother and child. Sixty per cent of the cases develop at birth; most are linked to anoxia (oxygen-starvation), or cerebral hemorrhage in the newborn. The latter results from such conditions as weakness in the blood vessels of the premature baby or quick delivery of full-term infants with consequent requirement of quicker accommodation to pressure changes than the body can handle. The remaining 10 per cent of the cases occur after the birth process has been completed and may be due to injury, anoxia, or infection.

General Problems of the Cerebral Palsied

The problems are suggested in the definition of cerebral palsy:

Paralysis due to an intracranial lesion; any one of a group of cerebral diseases of children marked by paralysis (33, p. 701).

In common parlance this means that the person cannot control muscular movements. Depending upon the severity, a victim may be confined to a wheelchair or he may take part in regular school activities. Deformities and sight, speech, and hearing difficulties are often noticed. Lassitude may be present due in part to weakness or experiences of failure. Since the central nervous system is involved, one is not surprised when some victims evidence lower IQ's than their age-mates.

Because of their condition many cerebral palsied show signs of social isolation. Some who might work well with others are under such nervous strain and so fearful of failing that they cannot take full advantage of opportunities offered to them.

Table 9-1 is presented with the hope that it will further an understanding of the common characteristics of each type of cerebral palsy. While it represents only a summary, it can be useful to those who wish to plan programs for the cerebral palsied.

Although most persons fit into one classification of cerebral palsy, there are differences among the cases within each category. For example, some cases of rigidity are not mentally retarded although this is common for that group. Muscle malfunction may vary in degree among a group of patients who suffer from the same type of cerebral palsy; some may prove to be educable, some may not.

While attempting to achieve his professional goals, the physical educator should be realistic about the possibilities of success with those who come into his program. The following figures acquaint one with predictions on a number basis:

1. About 25 per cent of all cases with cerebral palsy have an intelligence quotient of between 70 and 90.
2. About 50 per cent of all cases score below 70 on a standard intelligence test.
3. The remainder of the cases, or 25 per cent, show "normal range" scores, and can be expected to do as well as the average person in academically-oriented tasks.

Since low intelligence is a problem associated with some of those afflicted with cerebral palsy, the reader is reminded that Chapter 4 of this text includes many insights and suggestions with regard to programming for retarded persons.

TABLE 9-1 CHARACTERISTICS OF TYPES OF CEREBRAL PALSY

Types of Cerebral Palsy	Per cent (Physician's Estimate)	Usual Characteristics and Marks of the Various Types
Ataxic	5–8%	Tends to be overweight. Severe problems are coordination, balance. Usually extroverted, unselfconscious about his appearance. Somewhat unstable emotionally; likes or dislikes people thoroughly.
Athetoid	19–45%	Continuous involuntary muscle action. Usually extroverted, unselfconscious about his appearance. Somewhat unstable emotionally; likes or dislikes people thoroughly.
Rigidity	4–5%	Tends to be overweight. Hypertense (or rigid) musculature. Mental retardation common. May be introverted or extroverted.
Spastic	40–66%	Tends to be overweight. Strong involuntary muscle contractions and hypertonicity. Stiffness. Stretch reflex; results in flexion at many joints; may cause "scissors" gait in walking. Often lower IQ than agemates. Often introverted; needs individual or small group work.
Tremor	2–5%	Rhythmic motion patterns; may occur when person tries to move (intention tremor) or continuously (non-intention tremor). May be introverted or extroverted.
More than 1 type	1%	Each case depends on the causalities.

In general, it can be said that the physical educator is, or should be, concerned with all cerebral palsied children who attend school, whether they are retarded or not. In addition, beyond school hours, many physical educators come into contact with cerebral palsied of all ages, as they take part in leisure-time programs associated with camps, recreation centers, senior citizen centers, and other non-school areas. Success can be expected for all of these persons if instruction and opportunities for success are presented wisely.

The Bobath Concept

Recent years have shown an increased interest in the field of neurological disorders of children and have led to closer studies of the earlier stages of child development. The neurodevelopmental approach to children with cerebral palsy has been profoundly developed by Karel and Berta Bobath.° The use of automatic postural responses present at an early age in the child help keep the learning of voluntary movement in persons with central nervous system lesions. The Bobaths' idea of very early treatment of infants under the age of one year, before disordered postures and movements are established, suggests the exciting possibility that some disorders may be prevented.

Many procedures and techniques have been developed by the Bobaths for the child with cerebral palsy to get better voluntary motor results. These techniques have gained world-wide acceptance. They assess which normal postural and movement patterns the child has and which he lacks and what abnormal postural positions block or distort movement and so interfere with good function.

Normal motor development proceeds in an orderly sequence of events. To understand the nature of the motor handicap of a child with brain damage, it is necessary to study the normal development of the automatic postural reactions of a child's functional activities. The two sets of processes which are closely interwoven and dependent upon each other are as follows: 1. The normal postural reflex mechanisms (not present at birth). The righting reflex, the equilibrium and tonic neck reflexes, and other adaptive reactions fall into this group. The development of these highly complex reactions is associated with postural tone, which gives maintenance of position against gravity, and normal movements. 2. The inhibition of some of the responses of a new born baby (neonate) may be associated with the maturation of the brain. Examples

° Bobath, K.: The motor deficit in patients with cerebral palsy, *Spastic International Medical Publications.* (2nd ed., Chapter 8). With William Heinemann, Medical Books Ltd., The Lavenham Press Ltd., Lavenham, Suffolk, England, 1969.

are primary standing and walking, the startle reflex, and the tonic finger flexion response.

Cerebral palsy interferes with normal orderly development. 1. An insufficiently developed postural reflex results in poor head control, lack of rotation within the body axis, lack of balance, and other adaptive reactions. 2. A lack of inhibition results in prolonged retention of primitive total patterns of earliest childhood.

The Bobath techniques are very helpful. They have established basic postural patterns, sensory patterns, and sensory motor learning for babies to help prevent the development of abnormal patterns in movement.

Positioning the child with cerebral palsy so as to change the abnormal movement patterns to normal postural reactions includes designated "key-points." The most effective key-points are those which involve movements of the head, neck, shoulder girdle, trunk, and pelvis. Bobaths think that a feedback from the joint receptors to the vestibular and the midbrain nuclei may lay down the basic patterns of movements by using proximal joints as key-points of control.°

Since the techniques of treatment by Dr. Karel Bobath and Berta Bobath are extremely complex, interested persons should be trained in their special workshops. The physical educator working with children with the neurological or cerebral palsy disorder should incorporate perceptual motor learnings and follow the levels of motor integration. To increase the speed, agility, and reliability of the postural adjustments and to make activity as automatic as possible, the child should be placed in play activity. Specific movements such as stamping, lunging, stepping backward, balancing on the affected leg, and heel-toe pivot may contribute to the child's improvement in postural adjustment and physical education activities.

The implications for physical education are dependent upon the child's interests and physical motor capacities. Often physical education activities with rest intervals will accomplish good results. Light muscle tapping may help get relaxation in the tight muscle group.°

The Program

Goals of the Program

The school program is intended to supplement the therapy supplied to the child. Insofar as possible, the physical educator should help the child to attain his motor potential, and to take his place as a social

° Semans, S.: "The Bobath concept in treatment of neurological disorders, a neuro-development treatment. Am. J. Phys. Med., 46:732–785, 1967.

° Research material supplied by Marian F. Chase Allied Medical School, The Ohio State University.

being in a world where he will be respected in part for whatever independence he may have gained.

Generally the cerebral palsied should be provided with programs which:

1. Call for challenging free movement activities performed in free space. Instruction is important, but perfection should not be expected.

2. Help them to attain neuromuscular habits in tasks of daily living. These require such components as skill and endurance.

3. Avoid continuously competitive situations. Relaxation is an important factor in a program which seeks in part to teach voluntary muscle control.

4. Insures some success, even if in such simple tasks that normal children would find them nonchallenging. Hitting a 5-foot target with a 5-inch ball from a distance of 5 feet may be a great accomplishment to a child who could not even hold the ball a month earlier. One such achievement is worth far more to the child than promises of future success in complicated activities.

As always with other handicapped, activities for the cerebral palsied are chosen with the advice and under the direction of the medical team. The physical educator may be asked to suggest specific areas or activities for an individual case. In this difficult and dual role some guidelines are needed; therefore, the activities which follow are based on the severity rather than the cause of the handicap.

The student needs no particular care and may attend a regular school. His walk may not be perfect but is adequate for locomotion. He can use his arms, although not as skillfully perhaps as a normal child. His speech is understood by everyone, but perhaps with difficulty.

Dance. This student can perform all forms of dance but may need a slower tempo than others. The music should contain an easily heard beat so that he tends to perform as well as he can, keeping time with others in the group, although he may not always be able to dance as quickly as the others.

Individual, Dual, and Team Games. The student should take part in the activities of his age-group insofar as he is able. Sometimes he will learn with more effort, and all competition should be kept at a low level for him. The following activities are generally suited to mild cases:

1. Badminton (especially doubles).
2. Baseball and softball (sometimes played as kickball, one o' cat and other modified games).
3. Bowling.
4. Croquet.
5. Football (flag).
6. Golf (sometimes as clock golf, and with whatever clubs he can use best).
7. Horseshoes.
8. Paddle tennis.
9. Shuffleboard.
10. Soccer (defensive positions such as halfback, not goalie).
11. Some self-testing activities and stunts (such as chinning, kick for distance).
12. Table tennis.
13. Tennis (especially doubles).
14. Tumbling (simple).
15. Volleyball (and Newcomb).

Aquatics.

1. Swimming (Learning should be done in water which is kept at a comfortable temperature. At first the student should learn any strokes he chooses. Buoyancy devices help during the learning process. Play, such as fish imitation, induces relaxation. Some claim merit for the backstroke since it overcomes flexion tendencies of most cases, but this is debatable, for it may bring hypertension and anxiety. Floating should not be stressed as one of the first skills; it can follow stroke learning.)
2. Diving.
3. Boating.
4. Canoeing.

5. Sailing.

Body Mechanics. All those which the student can perform eventually should be included.

Movement Exploration. Because of the nature of this area, there can be few mistakes. This is salutary for the cerebral palsied who may feel penalized in other areas because of his level of skill and speed. In addition this area allows him to solve space and time problems which pertain to him, his body, and his needs. Properly taught movement exploration improves other areas of activity.

Cases of Moderate Handicap

The moderately handicapped person has problems which pertain to day-to-day living tasks, such as speech and locomotion. He may need help in various ways but is not so disabled that he cannot attend some school, perhaps a school for exceptional children. Often such cases are in wheelchairs which they can maneuver.

Dance.

1. Folk dance (often simplified).

2. Square dance (often simplified).

3. Modern dance (sometimes in a stationary place in the room).

Steps, time, formations, and space must be modified in many cases so that success is possible. It is better to modify dances for the age-level of the student than to select and perform unmodified dances intended for younger age-levels. The patient likes to feel that he is being offered material which measures up to a model in terms of the greatest potential to be hoped for; moreover, he resents being treated as younger than he is in terms of interests, and even needs.

Individual, Dual, and Team Activities. The child should take part in big muscle activities and in free, vigorous play. Perhaps he needs help in holding and placing objects and in extending and flexing the arm at will. There are many activities which will appeal. Nevertheless, he and his teacher must be patient as his attention span may prove to be short and distractions frequent.

Program Guides for the Cerebral Palsied

1. Plan for activity and for rest.

2. Modify activities as needed; modify equipment so that it is easier to handle, to hold, to catch and to throw. Semi-inflated balls and extra

long shuffleboard cues are examples; the latter can improve the game when it is played from a wheelchair.

3. Include games whose equipment is controlled without the necessity of continual retrieving by those not in the activity; bowling and box hockey are examples.

4. Provide for some quiet games which involve many players in social situations such as table games and checkers (the "men" are set into grooves on the board rather than being placed on the squares).

Activities which are suitable in tempo, socialization, and interest for many of these cases include the following:

1. Archery.

2. Bowling (light balls).

3. Croquet.

4. Horseshoes.

5. Some self-testing activities such as kicking for distance, running, or wheelchair relays which involve carrying objects and returning them to the starting point, and target throws.

Here, as in all adapted physical education programs, the instructional background, experience, and motivation of the learner are the important clues to the selection of appropriate activities.

Aquatics. The same general directions as were given for relatively mild cases of cerebral palsy hold for the moderately handicapped child. In addition, more time should be allowed for overcoming fear, and more individual help should be given as the teacher and the child experiment with suitable strokes. Boating, canoeing, and sailing are permissible if care is taken to be sure that the child can swim, that buoyancy equipment is in place on the child, and that alert adults are nearby to provide help in case of an accident.

Body Mechanics. This area is very suitable, especially if it provides instruction and repetition of skills which are difficult for the child. Care should be taken to explain the rationale of certain ways of performing tasks so that they are "easy," and save the energy of the person who must expend so much energy to perform even simple tasks.

Movement Exploration. This area provides freedom in space and in investigating ways to join space and time in the performance of satisfactory movement. Movement exploration is ideal as an activity, for all sincere effort is acceptable, and individual problems are more important than any group problems. Creativity, ingenuity, and imagination are rewarded by solutions, an important result to those whose lives are filled with unsolved problems.

The Severely Handicapped Cerebral Palsied

This is usually a person who must spend a lifetime in a wheelchair propelled by others, or in bed. Any play which leads to control is advised. Motivation toward learning is often induced by the use of colors, sounds, and opportunities to touch and feel objects. Most of these people cannot hold, release, or place objects at will; sometimes magnetic devices are used to hold placed objects steady. Peg boards, rhythm band instruments, and heavy plastic balloons which can be pushed over only to return upright are some of the equipment which appeals and often teaches.

A severe cerebral palsied child of ten years, for example, was taught over a period of several weeks to throw suction darts onto a large target with rings of different values marked upon it. Later a "child's set" of archery was brought to the room and the child taught to use it. Strength, accuracy, and real interest in improvement were noticed. Eventually and after many months the youngster was able to handle a regulation bow fitted with suction arrows and to shoot many a round with visitors, few of whom could equal his scores.

Many other ideas for activities, as well as the names of companies which manufacture suitable equipment for use with severely handicapped children are mentioned in a handbook called *Recreation for the Homebound Person with Cerebral Palsy*. It is available for a small fee from United Cerebral Palsy Associations, Inc.°

6. The Deaf and the Hard of Hearing

The school population of any community includes the deaf and the hard of hearing. This is true for all grades—kindergarten through adult education. Although these persons are generally normal in appearance and behavior, the defect tends to isolate them more completely than many conditions considered to be far more serious.

Those who teach classes which include deaf or hard of hearing members may not be aware that the condition is present, or knowing, may forget. The result may be an impatient teacher, and many impatient fellow learners who compound the errors made by the handicapped person by adding tension to the learning climate. Thus, it is imperative that all teachers be provided with information and recommendations which will increase the opportunities for successful learning among those who are deaf or hard of hearing.

° United Cerebral Palsy Associations, Inc., 321 W. 44th St., New York, N.Y. 10036.

There is great variance among these persons. Some have been handicapped since birth and have never heard spoken words. As a result of injury, infection, or gradual deterioration, many have lost some or all of their hearing but retain a recollection of what words mean, how they sound, and how they must be said to be effective. Others have been taught to lip read, wear hearing aids, and pronounce a normal vocabulary. Some speak but do so in monotonous voices and unpredictable volume.

Many of the deaf and hard of hearing have fallen behind in activities which are suitable to their years because they have not been able to perceive cues such as words, gestures, or the whistle of the referee at an athletic contest.

It is helpful to the teacher to know the type and degree of deafness for each pupil so that the usual prognosis for the condition can be related to him and his education. It is known, for example, that conduction deafness "which is caused by a physical obstruction to the conduction of sound waves to the inner ear" generally leaves at least a residue of hearing (40, p. 64). On the other hand, so-called nerve deafness usually does not respond to treatment, and the subject may receive no benefit from a hearing aid. This condition results from the inability of sensory cells or nerve fibers to carry sound impulses. While cases of nerve deafness are sometimes linked to senility, many cases are congenital; a child who is congenitally nerve deaf will probably remain at that level of handicap and will benefit from lip reading, speech training, rhythm development, and similar constructive methods.

It can be seen that the permanently deaf, the temporarily deaf, and the hard of hearing should not be taught alike. This does not invalidate the idea that they share certain characteristics:

1. Balance is often poor, especially if the condition involves the semicircular canal of the ear. Starting and stopping quickly as well as changes in direction are performed with some difficulty.

2. There may be anxiety and frustration, due in part to past errors or lack of participation, and in part to impatience with lengthy explanation, demonstration, and the setting of special signals before activity can begin.

3. There may be lack of ability to cooperate with others in game, dance, and other activity situations. Those who hear poorly or not at all often retreat from communication with others and become depressed in a world with little or no sound. This leads to many problems including an excess of energy (expended by typical individuals as they react in movement to sound-stimuli), and to social immaturity among those whose age-group has begun to mature socially. One does not develop by living outside the world of one's peers.

Generally those children who are hard of hearing will learn at about the rate normal children do. Often, with help from those around them and with positions where they can see and hear, they present few problems. Although the following suggestions are intended for those who teach the deaf, the first four apply to teaching the hard of hearing as well.

Suggestions for the Teacher

1. Speak slowly, facing the class, and be exact in choice of words.

2. Speak in a normal tone; do not whisper or shout.

3. Speak in a medium pitch if teaching older persons; remember that generally older men do not hear high-pitched sounds, nor do older women hear low-pitched sounds.

4. Sit down so that teacher and pupils are near the same level; then talk and show signals.

5. Demonstrate activities, use chalk-board to diagram plans, establish signals such as raised hand, blinking light, foot-stamping, bell ringing—messages which come to the brain through the eye and through impulses picked up as vibrations.

Suitable Activities

Activities suitable for the acoustically handicapped include:

Dance. Folk, square, ballroom, tap, and modern dance as appropriate to the age and interests of the group should be included. Tap dance is especially useful for this group, since it helps in the concept of a rhythmic pattern. Unable to hear music easily, if at all, the deaf and hard of hearing need ways to develop a sense of beat, or rhythmic understanding. The vibratory repetition which can be established through tap, folk, and square dance particularly is an important medium for such learning. Moreover, in following a communal beat, they develop a sense of unity and belonging, an important adjunct to those who have felt alone so often.

Simple hand-clapping, and the use of drums, bells, and various rhythmic instruments are most valuable in establishing a sense of time. Before long the handicapped person will be keeping good time; music is not needed, since singing, clapping, heel-clicking, foot-stamping, and the use of percussion instruments set the "time." To this group tempo may become meaningful through the palms of the hands and the soles of the feet as time is "felt."

Individual, Dual, and Team Activities.

Games of low organization should be used if appropriate to the age of the group. This holds true for individual, dual, and team activities with the following exceptions:

1. Boxing is usually contraindicated, since blows to the head may aggravate ear damage. (However, bag-punching and rope-skipping used by many boxers are satisfying skills which develop strength, balance, and endurance. These should be encouraged.)

2. Golf, acceptable in itself, may be contraindicated for the deaf who cannot hear oncoming players who shout "fore." If playing in a twosome or a foursome on a well-regulated course, this disadvantage can be overcome by teaming the handicapped person with someone who stays near him and can warn him.

3. Rebound tumbling (trampoline), suitable for those whose balance is normal, tends to create serious problems for those with semicircular canal involvement. Such an activity can be responsible for nausea and for serious accidents.

4. Any tumbling which would bring on the difficulties mentioned in number 3 should be avoided. Stunts can be employed to teach balance, followed by an exploration into simple tumbling, especially those activities which permit the body to remain fairly vertical.

Aquatics.

Swimming is generally encouraged for the deaf, especially if means can be found to protect the ears of those with faulty or easily infected middle and inner ears. Contraindicated for most auditory cases are diving, skin and scuba diving, and lifesaving (except for extension rescues and others which do not require sub-surface swimming).

Body Mechanics and Movement Exploration.

These two areas are usually included among activities for the acoustically handicapped. Their potential for fitness is obvious; further, both lead to an understanding and efficient use of movement. Teachers have found, too, that both areas stress balance and the development of kinesthetic sense to attain it.

The deaf are often made insecure or despondent by the smiles or sudden laughter of those around them, because they fail to understand the cause. Sometimes the skill of a teacher can help the deaf or the hard of hearing to become part of the joy at such a time. A deaf boy who became an expert soccer player said that half of the pleasure he had from playing well was due to the sheer joy of successful activity, and half to his knowledge that the cheers, shouts, and hand-clapping of a crowd which he could see but could not hear were urging him on and not deriding him.

7. Dermal Disorders

One of the toughest yet most resilient organs of man's body is the skin. Exposed to irritation, infection, and growth processes from within and without, the skin manages rejuvenation and many other functions which are its special province. "Skin condition" is the composite term assigned to abnormalities of the skin; not all of these require the attention of physical educators since many are neither severe nor contagious.

All persons experience occasional skin disorders such as calluses, pimples, small cuts, and chapping; which are considered mild nuisances but certainly not handicapping conditions. The alert teacher will, of course, recommend to a student whose skin condition is apparent but not severe that he see a physician. Such help may locate the cause and provide a cure. Severe conditions become of real concern to the teacher who may be called upon to provide adapted activities for the victims.

Physical educators should know the symptoms of most skin conditions, especially those which may be contagious or which have a detrimental effect on the sufferer. Most skin conditions result from irritation, infection, or faulty metabolism.

Irritation may result in:

1. Blisters. Rubbing or other pressure causes the space between the dermal and epidermal layers of the skin to fill with water or blood; the result is a water or a blood blister.

2. Calluses, corns. Thickened layers of skin build up because of pressure on the area; while corns are confined to the feet, calluses may appear on feet, hands, or any areas under pressure.

3. Eczema. Cracked skin over joints, or raw and red skin, or itchy, burning skin sores are present. Most eczema is caused by irritants such as dust or smoke, the ingestion of certain foods, or fungus-linked infections.

Infection may result in:

1. Athlete's foot, a form of ringworm. Communicability is still a controversial question. Any portion of the body may be affected by fungus-caused infections.

2. Boils which result from a staphylococcus-produced infection in

the hair follicle or in a sebaceous gland. Boils may spread from one part of the body to another.

3. Pediculosis, scabies, and impetigo. Communicability is extensive and victims are generally excluded from school until cured beyond the contagious stage. Pediculosis victims harbor lice while those with scabies are infected by a skin mite. The "weeping," crusty blisters of impetigo reflect a form of dermatitis.

Faulty metabolism may result in:

1. Acne. Linked to adolescence, it usually requires maturity, change of diet, and a dermatologist's aid. The overactive oil glands produce sebum in such amounts that the body processes cannot handle it. The physiologic discord appears as whiteheads or blackheads. The condition is aggravated by chocolate, fatty fried meats, rich desserts, and other favorite foods of the adolescent.

Suitable Activities

The conditions previously cited, as well as others which appear occasionally in the school-age population, generally need medical advice and treatment. Through cooperation between physical educator and physician, the student may be retained in physical education classes but excluded from those activities which will aggravate the condition and/or cause it to spread to others. As an example, a student with a serious skin condition which affects the feet might take part in archery, bait casting, and horseshoes, and other activities which can be performed in a standing or a sitting position and require no running.

Eczema sufferers should be programmed so that specific irritants are absent from their environment. Those with dust-related symptoms, for example, should not be programmed in such activities as field hockey and soccer, which are played at seasons of the year when playing fields may be particularly dusty. Some victims of eczema must be excluded from swimming since the sun and water aggravate their skin condition. Inability to swim would, in turn, exclude them from small craft activities such as canoeing.

Besides programming recreational activities for such students, the physical education teacher can work with them by:

1. Stressing the importance of personal cleanliness. The idea of a daily shower can be re-enforced most effectively if time for it is provided as part of the physical education class.

2. Emphasizing the importance of exercise which can (*a*) help to excrete through the skin some of the waste products which often become building blocks of skin lesions and abnormalities, and (*b*) teach the student to relax and build self-confidence through physical education and recreation.

3. Counseling them about the need to work with a dermatologist, rather than depending on the advice of friends, quacks, or advertisements.

The physical education teacher is in a position to help prevent or control unhealthy skin conditions. He should be able to advise students on diet and exercise. He can handle such departmental matters as outfitting students so that only clean, properly fitting suits are worn, a measure which will eradicate corns resulting from badly fitting footwear, and impetigo from the sharing of used gym suits. Such examples can be multiplied. The teacher can stress the importance of gradual "toughening" in seasonal games such as touch football and lacrosse, thereby reducing the number of foot blisters. And he should make it his business to report any cases of skin disorders which show symptoms of impetigo, scabies, or other contagious conditions. To protect the uninfected, students with contagious disorders should be excluded from class until the physician says that they are no longer contagious.

8. The Diabetic (Diabetes Mellitus)

One of the most worrisome conditions confronting teachers is *diabetes mellitus*. Although only one of every ten persons affected is a child, still the dramatic possibilities of "shock" and "coma" which are associated with it cause real trepidation among many who are responsible for school children.

It would be well if everyone understood this disease. Campaigns for early detection, sponsored by such groups as the American Diabetic Association, have uncovered many cases which years ago would have gone untreated. The increase in numbers of cases among middle-aged persons merely reflects an increase in the number of persons within a group which has always been victimized by the condition.

There are several forms and modifications of diabetes, but the one which is most apt to be found in the school child is *diabetes mellitus*. The cause seems to be biochemical and functional rather than organic; it can be summarized as a failure of the pancreas (gland) to oxidize carbohydrates. In a normal person the production of insulin in the pancreas is regulated so that sugar is used or absorbed for future use; in the diabetic person, sugar is wasted by being expelled into the urine, thereby robbing the body of needed energy and heat. Before the synthetic production of insulin, patients often died of coma or from an overload of sugar in the blood. On the other hand, an oversupply of insulin can result in so-called insulin shock in which glucose is digested so quickly that hunger, weakness, and perspiration result. A quick swallowing of sugar will alleviate the condition. A physician should be procured if either of these conditions occurs.

The disease seems to be hereditary and, among older persons, linked with obesity. Victims generally exhibit a low energy level, are continuously hungry and thirsty, and suffer from the following conditions which are associated with imbalance in the handling of carbohydrates by the body:

1. Hyperglycemia: oversupply of sugar (glucose) in the blood.

2. Glycosuria: excessively high proportion of sugar in the urine.

3. Polyuria: discharge of large amounts of urine.

Treatment is implemented through diet, a regimen of rest and exercise, and insulin taken either by injection or by mouth. Because of the solicitude of family and friends and the anxiety on the part of the patient, many diabetics have been overprotected and underactive. The physician may recommend exercise which can take the place of insulin in the digestion of sugar; however, it is important for such plans to be made carefully so that the patient does not overdo or become unduly concerned with performance. Because of inadequate skill, muscle tone, or other conditions, his entry into the world of activity may be a harrowing experience. A coach would not send a player into the first varsity game of the season without instruction, practice, equipment, and proof of ability to absorb the physical and emotional bruising of such an encounter. Neither should the physical education teacher direct a child with diabetes to take part in a program without adequate knowledge of his motor background and attitudes and the advice and agreement of the physician.

The physician who understands the purposes and program of physical education will tend to be enthusiastic about patient participation, provided that precautionary measures are taken. Contraindicated are activities which demand team effort and permit little rest on the part of any player unless all are resting. Power volley ball is an example of a contraindicated activity.

Fatigue can be brought on by physical and emotional causes; it is controlled best by permitting participation in areas which balance activity with rest and which avoid emotional involvement in the outcome of a contest. Bowling, dance, and sailing are good examples. Sometimes

individual sports which are highly competitive in nature, such as badminton and tennis, are permitted because the controlled individual can
stop when necessary without affecting the activity of more than one or
two other persons.

Early in the diagnostic period of the disease, the physician and physical educator can work out an exploratory plan for the student. In time
this may be modified to permit greater energy output. Meanwhile, the
student, through medication, diet, exercise, and rest, learns the best
means of attaining the proper amount of sugar for his needs. In addition, he should learn ways of avoiding infection, which has always been
high among this group; antibiotics have reduced but not removed the
seriousness of this peripheral hazard of *diabetes mellitus.*

Unlike many other handicapped persons, the diabetic enjoys the advantages of being normal in appearance. The teacher and physician can
do much to help him maintain and increase his feelings of normalcy by
helping him toward success in as nearly normal a program as he can
adapt to. Gradually the diabetic person can participate in almost all
physical education activities which involve no body contact and which
permit rest when needed; these should be selected from the five areas
of dance, sports, aquatics, body mechanics, and movement exploration,
with final choices being those which suit the age, needs, and health
condition of the student. The physical educator can protect himself and
the student in this regard by being sure that:

1. The student is under a physician's care.

2. The student knows how to provide whatever medication in whatever
   amounts he may need. Emphasis should be put upon the necessity of
   having sugar with him in some form at all times in case of emergency
   (to offset the symptoms of insulin shock).

3. The student knows and lives within his limitations through an active-
   passive program (which includes both exercise and rest).

4. The student knows the importance of regular meals despite schedule
   changes which may make irregular eating seem more attractive.

5. The student knows the value of sunshine and soap in the prevention of
   infection and takes a shower after activity. Prevention of irritation is
   especially important in his selection of sock and shoe sizes.

A correlation is apparent between age at onset of the disease and
ability to adapt easily to the regimen which it requires. Surely children
who give their own injections of insulin deserve the programs for which
they prepare so eagerly and so regularly every day.

9. The Epileptic

An old expression says: "The Greeks had a word for it," and this is true for epilepsy as for many other words which are with us today. Two Greek words were joined to form the word *epilepsy*, which can be translated as seizure: *epi*, meaning *upon*, and *lambano* which means *seize*. But until recently many people used other names for this disease, the most common being *fit*. Epilepsy has always been surrounded by secrecy and sorcery, which have helped to create a vague fear of the afflicted. Some considered them mentally retarded, while others thought that they had the power to talk to the departed. All the ignorance and myths have created a great social isolation for the epileptic.

What do we know of epilepsy? Basically, it is a brain-centered malfunction or lack of function of unknown cause. Epileptic parents have a greater number of epileptic children than do non-epileptic parents, so there seems to be some truth in the idea of the hereditary tendency of the disease. Those with such a predisposition as heredity often develop the condition following brain damage from tumors, infection, or accident. It is known, too, that emotion-linked behavior and metabolic imbalance trigger seizures among those with a history of epilepsy.

Fortunately for the sufferers there is often a warning of a seizure through a so-called "aura;" Hunt describes this as follows:

(there are) vague emotional feelings of discomfort or depressions, hallucinations, muscle twitchings or weakness, or sensory clues through flashes of light, sounds, or tastes (76).

Some sufferers report warning signs of nausea, shivering and pains in arms or legs. When an aura occurs, the patient knows that he has only a few seconds before the seizure will begin. During a seizure the victim may experience unconsciousness or convulsions, or both. Each of these is linked to certain categories of seizures as follows:

1. *Grand mal*, from the French for great illness. During the seizure the victim loses consciousness, may fall, tends to become rigid and often bites his tongue. Jaw contraction is so strong that teeth have been broken and the tongue actually bitten through. Moans and frothing at the mouth are seen in some cases. The person will usually sleep for hours following the seizure.

2. *Petit mal*, from the French for little illness. During this type of seizure the victim may stare straight ahead, show severe muscle twitching, or blink his eyes continuously. Some students have actually experienced such seizures without the teacher or classmates being aware of them. The attack is over quickly and completely, but during its tenure the student can learn nothing, since mental action stops.

3. *Psychomotor.* This type of attack may cause the person to drop things, stumble about, and show anger, uncertainty, and amnesia. Such a person is conscious but not responsible for his behavior, which may be detrimental to others. Some of these patients are psychotic; many suffer *grand* or *petit mal* attacks as well. Often, when psychomotor attacks become severe, the patient is placed in an institution as a protection to others, as well as to himself.

4. *Jacksonian.* The victim usually remains conscious while suffering muscular seizure on one side of the body; occasionally the seizure involves the entire body and the person becomes unconscious. These seizures have been associated causally with damage of some type to the cortex of the brain.

Unlike certain other handicapping or limiting conditions, epilepsy generally becomes evident during the early years. Thus most epileptics have had the first attack before they attend school. Where cooperation exists among physician, parents, and school authorities, the information is passed on when the child registers for nursery school or kindergarten. Aided by chemotherapy (anticonvulsant drugs and other medication which help to ward off seizures) most children can attain an education which fits them to live equally with others in a society designed for normal persons.

The physical educator is foremost among those who can help design the educational experience for the epileptic. Since first aid training usually is required of those in physical education, this teacher is in a strong position to handle and to help others handle any emergency which may arise regarding the epileptic student. He can help, too, in building favorable and acceptable attitudes among teachers and pupils toward the epileptic and to prepare them to carry out the usual and simple first aid measures in case of seizure.

First Aid Measures for Epileptics

1. Make sure that the person is lying down and away from objects with which he might injure himself.

2. Loosen clothing at neck and waist.

3. Place an object, wrapped in soft material, between the jaws to prevent him from biting the tongue or breaking his teeth as he brings the jaws together.

4. Be sure he has sufficient air but is not chilled.

5. Inform a physician and the parents.

6. Provide a place for the patient to sleep if the physician cannot come immediately.

Planning for the Epileptic Student

The epileptic student needs physical education as a release from tension, as a way of building skills which make him more acceptable to his fellows, and as a means of warding off seizures through the salutary chemical effect which exercise has upon the body processes. The student should be permitted to enroll in most activities of his age group, according to interest and need, but the following precautionary measures should be kept in mind:

1. Participation in aquatics is indicated only if supervision is close and continuous.

2. A follow-up should be instituted after participation in competitive or emotionally charged situations; if seizure has occurred, these should be lessened or removed from the program of the student. Some students benefit, some suffer from such situations. This is true for vigorous exercise also; if a seizure follows the activity, modification should take place in the amount of time and/or activity permitted. Cross-country run, soccer, lacrosse, and basketball are examples of such vigorous events.

3. Activities which involve heights are to be avoided; there is always the possibility that the student might suffer a seizure when on apparatus or equipment from which he could fall. Trampoline, parallel bars, and flying rings are examples of such contraindicated activities.

4. Contact sports are not indicated either, since head injuries may aggravate the already serious condition of the epileptic and may bring on an increase in the incidence of seizures. Thus, football, ice hockey, and such games as bull-in-the-ring for elementary boys should not be scheduled for the epileptic student.

At first it may seem that such precautionary statements modify the program greatly, but a further examination will prove that this is not necessarily so. All of the five usual areas of physical education are open to the student, but certain activities within some of the areas are contraindicated. For instance, all dance and aquatic activities are permitted. Individual and dual sports are certainly acceptable, but many contact games should be eliminated. Body mechanics and movement exploration should be included, dependent on age, interest, and need.

The socializing effect of most physical education activities is of special benefit to this student. People who are learning or recreating together tend to forget individual differences; the resulting socialization brings the acceptance, security, and shared laughter which are very important to the epileptic. Such participation helps him to see the reasons behind the health regimen which his physician wishes him to follow through diet, rest, exercise, and medication, and often helps him to make progress in the psychotherapy which is part of the medical team effort to remove causes of his condition. The epileptic is still somewhat limited. However, with the strides which are being made in neurology and chemotherapy, one can foresee the day when these persons will participate in an unrestricted physical education program.

10. Hernial Cases

Although hernia or rupture is a common complaint and is often regarded casually, it can become a serious problem—especially old hernias whose surrounding tissues have lost their elasticity and whose continued presence threatens strangulation and other major consequences.

A hernia is simply a protrusion of some bodily tissue or organ into a foreign area. Such an effect involves an abnormal opening through which the material passes; thus, the part is out of position as it goes through the opening. Incomplete hernias are those in which only a part of the affected organ has passed through the orifice; the term "complete" is given to those in which the process has been accomplished (33, pp. 443-444).

Hernias have been seen in many body areas including the abdomen, brain, and bladder. Abdominal hernias, which occur most frequently, are primarily of three types: umbilical, inguinal, and femoral. The umbilical (or navel) hernia occurs most often in male infants. Males of all ages seem to be more prone to inguinal hernias than are females. This type of hernia is present in the inguinal canal at the groin. Females are subject more often to the femoral hernia which is located in the femoral canal in the thigh region. Not all hernias are visible to the examining physician; some can be seen only when the subject is standing or sitting, while others are visible even when the subject assumes a horizontal position.

One possible explanation for the greater prevalence of abdominal hernias among men is that they tend to volunteer or agree to lift objects which are considered too heavy for women to handle. Perhaps the outmoded cultural association of male virility and brute strength is at fault. Nevertheless, it is considered both chivalrous and masculine for any man, fit or unfit, to lift almost any weight. The irony is that women are generally the ones who are taught how to handle weight in such courses as body mechanics, modern dance, and movement exploration. Except for the small number of men who receive instruction in weight lifting, few learn to handle weight safely and easily. This thought brings us to the causes of hernia in which lifting certainly plays a prominent part. Most hernias are linked to one or more of the following causes:

1. Pre-natal or natal conditions; these bring about umbilical hernias in infants.
2. Lifting objects without breathing.
3. Lifting objects for which body strength is not sufficient.
4. Lifting objects without "setting" or contracting the lifting muscles slightly before moving the object.
5. Lifting heavy objects when overweight.
6. Injury due to a blow or quick deep pressure at or near the site of the hernia.

The dangers of hernia often are unknown to the victims, especially to those who have not consulted a physician since the discovery of the condition. Sometimes friends are successful in getting such a person to see a doctor; often the pressure and feeling of constriction of a hernia are the motivators. The physician will be on guard against further constriction which tends to diminish the blood supply and can actually lead to gangrene in certain body areas. In addition, he will recommend certain procedures which he thinks will be helpful; these may include rest, special exercises as part of an adapted physical education program, and/or surgery. In most cases, particularly with adults, he will be specific about the dangers of weight increase and may even indicate the need for a weight loss.

Suitable Activities

The person may participate generally in all areas of physical education. Discomfort in the area of the hernia will usually act as a deterrent when the patient is eager to continue although fatigued, or when poor choices of activities have been made. Often the physician will indicate a few activities which should not be included and will counsel the physical education instructor generally on choice of activities for the patient. A choice of such favorable activities can be made among those which:

1. Tire, but do not exhaust the participant. Dances which are repeated endlessly (for example, the Virginia Reel and the Hully Gully) and games in which rest periods are few are examples of activities which should be omitted. Another is field hockey, which calls for periods of play of thirty minutes, with modification to twenty minutes for young players. More appropriate for the student with hernia are work on the low balance beam, captain ball, archery with medium or light bow, and relays. Suitable dances would include many such as the waltz, various mixers, most folk dances and modern dance.
2. Encourage ordinary starts and stops rather than those done at great

speed; thus basketball would be contraindicated if played at varsity speed, but golf (with clubs mounted on a cart, not slung over the shoulder) would be satisfactory. Badminton doubles, Newcomb and mild games of volleyball and most recreational children's games would be well within the range of possibility. Square dances would be excellent, especially those in which rest is alternated with action.

3. Include activities in which danger of rough body handling (or abdominal blows) are neither rewarded nor the natural result of participation. Trampoline, certain gymnastic activities such as uneven parallel bars, and boxing would be contraindicated. Diving should be omitted because of the possibility that the diver might land on the water in a horizontal position. However, recreational swimming, synchronized swimming, and usual small craft activities would be suitable.

4. Include only normal amounts of weight lifting, such as pitching horseshoes, swinging a bat, or learning to move light furniture in body mechanics. Certainly the hernia victim should never act as the human stabilizer in such activities as pyramid building, tumbling (including "spotting"), or stunts.

5. Include exercises, some to be done while lying down and some while standing, which will strengthen the abdominal wall in preparation for a hernial operation, or in an effort to recover muscle tone after such an operation. The physician is the source for these but the physical educator should feel free to suggest to him further exercises to increase effort as the patient performs the first ones with a lessening of effort and an increase in strength, muscle tone, and general endurance. During the exercise period emphasis should be placed upon relaxation and proper breathing.

6. Foster good posture as an antidote to the tendency toward ptosis, (falling of abdominal contents) which often accompanies hernia, especially in the overweight. Exercise, proper breathing, good carriage, and avoidance of undue fatigue lessen the possibility of ptosis.

11. Menstrual Difficulties

Few subjects have been fraught with more anxiety, taboos, folklore, misinformation, and bad advice than menstruation. In recent decades physicians, psychologists, and sociologists have studied the problems which are associated with this natural phenomenon, adding facts and theories to the confusing files left to them by their predecessors.

The term *menstruation* derives from some Latin and some Old English words which mean *"month"*: *mensis,* and *mona,* or *moath* respectively. Very simply, menstruation is a periodic flow of blood from the uterus of the female mammal; this menstrual flow takes place in most women approximately once in twenty-eight days.

From menarche, the beginning of the menstrual phenomenon, to menopause, when it ceases, the female discharges an ovum from the ovary each month and, if conditions are normal, is capable of producing offspring if intercourse takes place. Generally menstruation takes place over a period of about thirty-five years.

Since the beginning of menstruation occurs during the years when girls are in school, the physical educator may be asked to increase or decrease activity for these students. Especially is this true for those who:

1. Fail to menstruate at an age when their classmates have begun the cycle.

2. Menstruate in excess.

3. Menstruate with accompanying severe pain.

These and other conditions may be due to organic or functional causes, and may be related to problems of posture and body mechanics. They may reflect physiologic adjustment to the many internal changes which are associated with adolescence. Sometimes they are reported falsely to mask pregnancy or other unusual conditions which the student wishes to hide.

It should be noted here that there has been considerable lessening of the tendency of physicians to brand painful menstruation as psychosomatic. This change is related to the work of such men as Leib J. Golub, a gynecologist who has pointed to possible linkage between menstruation and pain in the peculiar characteristics of the female nervous system. Golub wrote the following after performing autopsies on males and females:

This study revealed that the iliohypogastric and ilioinguinal nerves in the female may have a number of different relationships to muscles and connective tissue bundles near the vertebral column. From some of these relationships it can be inferred that nerve irritation could result from constriction when tension is applied to an overlying muscle bundle or connective tissue band (55, p. 59).

It has been said that oversolicitousness on the part of parents, teachers, and friends has made acceptance and adjustment to menstruation a difficult thing for many girls. Nevertheless, the teacher should be alert to notice such symptoms as painful cramps, anxiety, and changes in body temperature which make the menstrual cycle a difficult and dreaded time for some women.

In most instances exercise is helpful; certain exercises have become well known for use in cases of dysmenorrhea, or painful menstruation. During normal menstruation, exercise aids circulation and digestion and thereby reduces the incidence of pain, nausea, and fatigue. In addition it encourages the young woman to live normally during the period, and thus to consider menstruation a normal part of life. The latter is important in helping her to adjust to the decades ahead of her when menstruation is a normal part of her life as a woman.

However, a word of caution should be inserted here. Since exercise tends to increase blood flow, it should be suspended in cases of excess bleeding or menorrhagia.

The physical educator should keep records of menstruation occurrence as reported by students; gradually it will be seen that the majority of those girls who menstruate go through the cycle at about the same time each month. One of us (Hooley) kept such records over a period of ten years and found this phenomenon to be true. Such information is important when planning events which involve tension and demand the most of each girl. Examples might include tournaments, demonstrations, and productions, and practical tests from which grades are to be ascertained. These events may be placed on the calendar at times when the menstrual cycle is not imminent for the majority of the girls in the school population. It might be remarked, too, that many physicians warn that the most difficult days for many women occur two days before, and on the first day or two of the cycle.

For most girls who experience no real difficulty during menstruation, the physical educator should encourage:

1. The wearing of loose clothing.

2. Relaxation, rest, and sleep.

3. Diet which builds and re-builds the body and helps avoid constipation; the latter has been proven to induce tension and resulting pain during menstruation.

Activity during menstruation need not be curtailed for most girls. The girl who experiences difficulty may need a physician's diagnosis to discover the cause. She may need more exercise or counseling concerning the place of menstruation in the entire framework of womanhood. Many will need help in learning the specific exercises which have been designed for dysmenorrheics. A few may need psychiatry or surgery.

When considering any case of difficult menstruation, the physical educator should work closely with the physician, reporting symptoms and recommendations.

12. The Mentally Different: The Retarded and the Gifted

The education of the boy or girl who is less gifted or more gifted mentally than his peers poses a real problem for society. It is assumed generally that he should be educated. But how shall it be done? Does he belong in a regular classroom, or in a special class within a regular school? Should he be sent to a special school or tutored at home? The answers are being sought on a wide front, and physical educators, among others, await these answers eagerly; it is felt that they will help to assign the role which physical education may play in guiding the forward progress of the mentally retarded and the gifted.

The Mentally Retarded (The reader is referred to Chapter 4 of this text for a complete discussion of this topic.)

National figures show that three of every 100 children born are mentally retarded. At present there are six million such persons in the United States. For years the enormity of the problem was unknown because the total count was hidden as were the victims in backrooms, attics, and institutions. Recently the spotlight of research has been beamed toward mental retardation. Very simply this is a condition which lessens the mental ability and potential of a person. Spelling it out more fully, one source reports:

... the brain is prevented from reaching full development, limiting the victim's ability to learn, and put learning to use, retarding social adjustment. It is a lifetime handicap that ranges from slightly impaired development to complete disability (130, p. 2).

Despite widespread research and professional therapy programs, it is realistic to state that investigation is so new that little proven information has yet been garnered. On the "known facts" list are 100 causes of mental retardation which account for about 25 per cent of identified cases (129, p. 7). These causes may be summarized with reference to the periods within which they occur:

1. Before birth. Examples include poor medical care of the mother, infectious conditions and diseases of the mother, and various genetic irregularities.

2. During birth. Examples include any birth conditions which bring great stress, or which lessen the oxygen supply to the brain of the child.

3. After birth. Some examples are diseases, accidents, impaired body chemistry, and any social, economic, or cultural deprivations during the first two or three years of childhood.

Much is being done to impress on adults the necessity for good medical care before, during, and after the birth of the child. The retarded are burdens to themselves and, unless they are at least trainable, to society. It is advocated now that all retardates be given as much education as they can handle; such a plan is humane and lessens the economic liability which exists in any society which supports those who might support themselves.

It has been estimated that each institutionalized retardate costs the public approximately $50,000. How much wiser, more civilized, and economical it is to prepare the person to provide for himself, thereby making it possible for him to win his own self-respect and the respect of his neighbors. Such an independent person will be a happier person and will be able to do his share to promote the common good by his contributions of service, taxes, and whatever volunteer contributions he wishes to make to causes of his choosing.

The road from dependence to independence is a long one, even for the normal child; for the retardate it is especially long and often frustrating, with no promise of success for the small percentage who will never attain more than token independence. To understand the problems presented by retardates, it is necessary to recognize that they differ widely from one another in tastes, interests, and degrees of learning ability. The National Association for Retarded Children, Inc., has set up four categories which encompass all cases of retardation: mild, moderate, severe, and profound. Educators favor three categories, as follows:

1. Educable mentally retarded. These children develop (and progress academically) at about one-half the speed of the normal child. When they are ready to leave school, they have attained success in work of about the fourth grade level and usually have learned some vocational skills. Most are capable of meeting agemates on a social basis, although recognition of an inferior status in our society sometimes brings about defensive and anti-social behavior.

2. Trainable mentally retarded. These children learn best those tasks which call for simple directions, repetition of performance of a few simple skills, and a protected and known environment. Many of them can learn about one-fourth to one-half the knowledge of a normal child but they cannot think ideationally or in concepts. All of them will require guidance, care, and some economic assistance during their lives.

3. Totally dependent. These children will always need protection, support, and care. They can learn, at best, only a few habits. They cannot be expected to mix with others or even to communicate with them. Thus, they will never become even partially self-supporting.

Physical Education for the Mentally Retarded

Physical education and recreation offer much to the educational program for these children. Both areas utilize play, the "work of childhood," at a time when children find other ways of learning less attractive. Play helps people to adjust to others; this is an important opportunity for the retarded who have generally experienced little contact with others beyond the immediate family. Putting this thought to practical use, certain leaders have advocated bringing the retarded into physical education classes with normal children. Pilch did this at Wooster, Ohio, with a group of children who were retarded but possessed "reasonable motor ability." She reported success and acceptance by both groups of one another. Children who were less able to adjust to such a situation because of physical, mental, or social limitations were taught in separate classes (136, pp. 173–174).

Schreiber has said that "children learn to live with others only through experience." He calls attention to the need to solve the "segregation-integration" issue with regard to the retardate. Since children who are moderately retarded will eventually live with normal people, should their experience with normal people begin with situations which are planned by the school, or should they be taught separately but expected to make the transition to integrated living later (148, pp. 194–203)?

From these and similar writings, one may conclude that the retardate should be moved into normal groups when such contacts can benefit him without lessening the achievement of normal children. Even the mildly retarded child may need some help with motor ability to ready him for such integrated grouping. The greatly retarded will need considerable help so that socially and physically he can perform well enough to be accepted by others and to experience some success and pleasure in their company.

The selection of activities for the mentally retarded is difficult because of the range of learning ability represented in any group.

Program Guides for the Mentally Retarded

1. The retarded learn slowly.

2. They learn in part from the voice, manner, gestures, and repeated demonstrations of the instructor.

3. They do best when simple activities are taught: that is, the activities should be governed by simple rules, include repetition of the same skill by all, and should be done slowly in structured formations such as circles or lines.

4. The retarded do best in those activities which require the manipulation of no objects, or of only stationary objects.

5. They do best in activities which can be performed alone or with few other people.

6. They appreciate playing in a group but tend to work for individual over team success.

The program can include activities from the five activity areas: dance, games (individual, dual, and team activities), aquatic activities, body mechanics, and movement exploration. Selection depends on the motor ability and motor potential of the retardate, as well as his capacity to understand directions and his desire to socialize.

For most retardates body mechanics and movement exploration are the most salutary of the activity areas. Both concentrate on individual skill instruction and remedial activities which these children need. Examples of the material which might be covered include posture work, corrective exercises for low vitality and fitness, and learning to move the body in space. For most retardates these involve heretofore untried skills which must be mastered before further motor experience can prove useful or successful. It is difficult for normal people to realize that walking, hopping, and running on a narrow track may be difficult skills for a child to accomplish. For the retardate they may seem impossibly difficult. Time and patience are required if the balance, laterality, strength, agility, and other components of such simple activities are to be learned.

Tests are being developed for discovery of the achievement level of retarded children in physical education activities. Donald Kupfer reports success in adapting items from some Kephart tests (86, pp. 137–219). Kupfer added test items which measure manipulative ability through the use of tennis balls and basketballs (99, p. 2). These tests, as well as various tests of motor educability, are devised to discover the ability of the subject to hold and handle objects; to use the legs in walking, running, and jumping; and to throw or catch objects. Visual and hearing tests should be given by professional personnel so that sensory capacities can be known.

It is important to remember that these children need enjoyment, and so should not be limited to difficult or impossible tasks, such as maintaining good posture or learning to gallop. Whenever possible their abilities should be used in activities which are fun to do, which bring them into contact with others, and which motivate them to seek further success.

Activities for the Mentally Retarded

Presented below are a variety of activities under each of the five program categories. All have been used with retarded children, the more advanced skills being reserved at first for those with greater mental and coordination ability. In time and with instruction most educable retarded can perform all of these activities and many more. It should be remembered that these are presented as examples of activities, and are not intended to limit the program which is possible under the leadership of creative and ingenious teachers.

Dance.

1. Ballroom: waltz, fox-trot, and other simple traditional dances, as well as current "fad" dances, particularly those which can be performed alone.

2. Folk dances and singing games: "Muffin Man," "Farmer in the Dell," "Danish Dance of Greeting," "Jolly is the Miller," "Paw Paw Patch."

3. Modern dance: especially when done alone or in small groups.

4. Square dance: "Shoo Fly," "Bow Belinda," "Brown-eyed Mary."

5. Tap dance: especially that performed to clearly marked rhythms, and dances which do not involve fancy breaks.

Games of Low Organization, Individual, Dual, and Team Activities.

1. Passing objects in a circle formation.

2. Rolling objects to one another, while seated in a circle.

3. Bowling with rubber balls on a track which is curbed on each side.

4. Stride dodge ball, a great favorite with these children.

5. Bouncing balls to others while standing in a circle.

6. Throwing and catching, in line or circle formation.

7. Hide and seek games.

8. Relay games.

9. Newcomb, modified volleyball.

10. Captain ball, other modified forms of basketball.

11. Kickball, punchball, other modified forms of softball, soccer.

12. Flag and touch football, other modified forms of football.

13. Weight lifting.

14. Punching the bag.

15. Simple track events, such as short dashes.

16. Simple gymnastics, such as walking a wide line, walking a low balance beam, mounting a horse or buck by climbing onto it, hanging from a low horizontal bar, doing stunts and simple tumbling.

17. Trampoline.

Aquatics.

1. Swimming, which at first may be merely going into the water, learning to keep balance with feet on the bottom. Gradually and with instruction the children learn to float, take a few hesitant "dog paddle" strokes, and begin to swim the crawl stroke.

2. Boating, which can be accomplished after children can swim, and in boats which provide for shallow water rowing by children wearing life jackets.

Body Mechanics.

1. Warm-up, developmental and balance exercises.

2. Posture work.

3. Everyday tasks such as lifting, carrying, pushing, pulling, stair-climbing.

4. Relaxation techniques.

Movement Exploration. This area is especially necessary for retardates who are confused by time, space, and the need to coordinate their body parts so that they can move well through both elements. At first work should be on an individual basis, but gradually partners, small groups, and eventually many children can be involved.

This type of activity permits the individual to move independently of others, but requires him to be aware of others in order to move safely. This awareness is important if the child is to learn to take part in more complex group work on a higher plane at a later date.

With normal children the ideational phase of problem-solving is important in movement exploration. They explain how and why they performed in a certain way or modified their earlier performance. Retardates should be taught to focus on the solution rather than on the study of the process involved in solving the problem. The solution may be presented to them or they may help in developing it.

The difference in the way the two sets of children are directed can be illustrated as follows:

Directions to the *Retarded Child*	*Directions to the* *Normal Child*
Let's try to go to the windows over there (pointing) by walking very quietly (or on tiptoes, or on heels, or by taking very big steps).	Let's try to go to the windows on the other side of the room in as many different ways as you can.
	Questions afterward: why is it easier to run than to walk on your toes? (or how did you keep your balance when walking on your heels? etc.)

In developing the program the physical educator should create and explore, while watching for certain signs that modification in activity is indicated, *e.g.:*

1. Failure seems to be the lot of the children despite the passage of time, and the continued presentation of instructional material.

2. Embarrassment, fear, aggression, and/or inattention are noticed.

Such signs call for a change of pace, activity, child-groupings, and, occasionally, leadership personnel.

Some mentally retarded children may not learn well through imitation; it seems they must receive direct training in the skills they are to acquire. A three-step progression is suggested for the training program when the imitation techniques are not satisfactory. The first step includes a demonstration and provides assistance through manipulation of the body parts while giving verbal cues. The second step includes a demonstration (no assistance) and verbal cues. The third step provides just verbal cues (36).

Many materials are available for those who want to provide good programs for the retarded; several examples of these are listed in the bibliography. With such aids and a desire to help these children, the physical educator can contribute a great deal to the lives of the retarded.

The teacher or teachers of persons with subaverage intellectual functioning and/or adaptive behavior need to assess and develop motor skills. The following structured plans should help the teacher learn movement limitations and help plan the individual or group motor skills to improve the child's neuromuscular efficiency.

Materials we include here are suggested as a gross motor screening appraisal.

Kraus Weber Test

Purpose: Test of minimum strength of the trunk muscles.

Test 1.   With your hands behind your neck roll up into the sitting position.

Test 2. With knees bent and hands behind neck roll up into sitting position.

Test 3. With hands behind neck and knees straight, raise your heels 10 inches from the floor. Hold this 10 seconds.

Test 4. Lie face down with a pillow under your abdomen. With hands behind neck, raise head, chest, and shoulders off floor. Hold for 10 seconds.

Test 5. Place your hands under your head and with pillow still under your abdomen, raise your legs off the floor. Keep knees straight. Hold for 10 seconds.

Test 6. With feet together slowly bend forward and see how nearly you can come to touching the floor with your finger tips. Do not bend your knees and do not bounce down. If you can touch the floor for three seconds you pass this test.

This test is scored with a plus for successful movement and a minus for unsuccessful performance.

PHYSICAL FITNESS SCORE SHEET

Name_____   Date_____

Date of Birth_____ month 19___   Test I_____

IQ_____   Test II_____

1. Physique   Test I   Test II

    Height   _____ in.   _____ in.

    Weight   _____ in.   _____ in.

    Predicted weight (tables)   _____ in.   _____ in.

COMMENTS: _____

2. Muscular Fitness   Standard Score   Standard Score

    Hang Times   _____ sec _____   _____ sec _____

    Medicine Ball Throw   _____ ft _____   _____ ft _____

    Speed Back Lifts (30 sec)   _____   _____   _____   _____

    Speed Sit Ups (30 sec)   _____   _____   _____   _____

    Vertical Jump & Reach   _____ in.   _____ in.

    Standing Reach   _____ in.   _____ in.

    Vertical Jump   _____ in. _____   _____ in. _____

    Floor Touch   _____   _____   _____   _____

    Back Extensions   _____ in. _____   _____ in. _____

3. Organic Fitness

    300 yard run   _____ sec _____   _____ sec _____

COMMENTS: _____

_____

_____

RANGE OF MOTION APPRAISAL FORM

The following joints of the body should be appraised in terms of the degree of movement present in a joint as executed without assistance by the student. The degree of movement should be evaluated on the present scale:

0-no movement
1-¼ range of motion
2-½ range of motion

3-¾ range of motion
4-full range of motion

Right Left Total

NECK

Right	Left	Total	
			1 Bend head forward and touch chin to chest, keeping mouth closed.
			2 Bend head backward.
			3 Bend head toward left shoulder and try to touch ear to shoulder (do not raise shoulder). Straighten.
			4 Bend head toward right shoulder and try to touch ear to shoulder (do not raise shoulder). Straighten.
			5 Turn face to left side. Straighten.
			6 Turn face to right side. Straighten.
			7 Move head in circles.

TRUNK

Right	Left	Total	
			1 Bend body forward. Straighten.
			2 Bend body backward. Straighten.
			3 With hands on hips bend body to left and then to right.
			4 With hands on hips twist body to face first left and then right, without moving the feet.

SHOULDER

Right	Left	Total	
			1 Raise arm forward and straight above the head.
			2 Raise arm sideways and straight above head.
			3 Place palm of hand on back of neck; then bring hand forward, down, under the arm and back, touching back of hand to shoulder blades (do not allow elbows to drop).

RANGE OF MOTION APPRAISAL FORM (continued)

Right	Left	Total	ELBOW
			1 Bend arm until fingertips touch shoulder, then straighten it out completely.
			2 Bend elbow to right angle. Turn palm up, then down.

WRIST

Right	Left	Total	
			1 Rest forearm on table with palm down. Move hand and wrist to left and then to right without moving forearm.
			2 Rest forearm on table with palm down. Lift hand up off table as far as possible without moving forearm.
			3 Rest forearm on table with palm up. Lift hand up off table as far as possible without moving forearm.

FINGERS AND THUMB

Right	Left	Total	
			1 Make a tight fist, then straighten fingers completely.
			2 With fingers straight, spread wide apart, then bring together.
			3 Bend thumb and make it lie in center of palm.
			4 Rest forearm on table with palm up. Place thumb over base of index finger, then lift it straight up.
			5 Touch tip of thumb to fingerprint of little finger, then open hand wide and do this with each of the other fingers.

RANGE OF MOTION APPRAISAL FORM (continued)

Right	Left	Total	HIP
			1 Lying on back, bend hips and touch knees to chest.
			2 Lying on back, move legs sideways as far as possible, keeping knees straight and toes pointed straight ahead. Return to starting position.
			3 Lying on abdomen, move leg up and back as far as possible, keeping knee straight. Do first with right and then with left leg.
			4 Sitting on edge of bed, move lower leg and foot from left to right like a pendulum.

KNEE

Right	Left	Total	
			1 Bend knee so that calf touches thigh. Then straighten knee completely.

ANKLE

Right	Left	Total	
			1 Bend foot up.
			2 Bend foot down.
			3 Turn foot out.
			4 Turn foot in.
			5 Make circles with foot.

TOES

Right	Left	Total	
			1 Curl toes down.
			2 Curl toes up.

BODY MECHANICS SCREENING CARD

Name _____ Age _____ Height _____ Weight _____

Scoring—Slight—Marked (R., L., Bilateral)

STANDING			Date						
Lateral Imbalances-Anterior									
Overweight									
Underweight									
Lateral Head Tilt									
Pigeon Breast									
Shoulders Uneven									
Hips Uneven									
Pes Planus									
Pes Cavus									
Knock Knees									
Bow Legs									
Foot Pronation									
Toe Deformity									
Lateral Imbalances-Posterior									
Shoulders Uneven									
Scoliosis									
Winged Scapula									
High Hip									
Achilles Deviation									

BODY MECHANICS SCREENING CARD (continued)

Name _____ Age _____ Height _____ Weight _____

A. P. Imbalances

Forward Head									
Flat Chest									
Round Shoulders									
Kyphosis									
Round Back									
Lordosis									
Kypholordosis									
Abdominal Ptosis									
Hyperextended Knees									
WALKING		Date							
Lateral Imbalance									
A. P. Imbalance									
Pelvic Oscillation									
Foot Placement									
Toeing Out									
Toeing In									
Forward Lean									
Back Lean									
Tension									

DEVELOPMENTAL GROSS AND PERCEPTUAL MOTOR SURVEY

NAME _____ AGE _____ SEX _____

TEST PERIODS

	1-Date:				2-Date:		
	Passed	Inade-quate	Failed		Passed	Inade-quate	Failed
Body Image and M. O. 1. Parts identification							
2. Independent movement							
3. Bilateral movement							
4. Homolateral movement							
5. Cross pattern movement							
Movement Patterns 1. Jump-both							
2. Jump-right							
3. Jump-left							
4. Hop-right							
5. Hop-left							
6. Gallops							
Balance 1. Forward walk							
2. Backward walk							
3. Slide left							
4. Slide right							
5. Slide left, cross r.							
6. Slide right, cross l.							

	1-Date			2-Date		
	Passed	Inade-quate	Failed	Passed	Inade-quate	Failed
Motor Coordination—Body Image Problems						
1. Hop right on line						
2. Hop left on line						
3. Double hop-l. and r.						
4. Double hop r., one l.						
5. Double hop l., one r.						
6. Steps over object						
7. Steps under object						
8. Steps through object						

GENERAL DIRECTIONS

This is merely one battery of a series to determine any developmental deficiencies and to provide remediation through an activity program. Provide verbal instruction first and if child does not appear to understand, demonstrate, then have child do test. The tester should observe the degree of tonicity in student and record anecdotal remarks so that programs can be more individualized.

DEVELOPMENTAL GROSS AND PERCEPTUAL MOTOR SURVEY

A. Body Image and M. O.

Item 1 Parts Identification

Method: Instruct child to face you and have him touch the following:
1. Shoulders
2. Hips
3. Knees
4. Ankles
5. Ears
6. Feet
7. Elbows
8. Eyes
9. Nose
10. Mouth

Scoring: Passed—Child performs adequately.
Inadequate—Hesitates or shows confusion on one or more parts.
Failed—Unable to identify one or more.

Item 2, 3, 4 & 5 Extremity Movements (Angels-in-Snow)

Method: Instruct, point, or touch the part of arms or legs to be moved.
Provide brief explanation as to what is expected. Order of movements is:
2. Independent: arms and legs singly.
3. Bilateral: arms and legs together.
4. Homolateral: one arm and one leg on one side, then other side.
5. Cross pattern: opposite arm and leg and repeat.

Scoring: Passed—Performs adequately.
Inadequate—Shows slight hesitancy, restricted movement, or overflow.
Failed—If child cannot perform task.

Observational Keys:
1. Can he visually identify part?
   a. May need to verify identification with tactual or kinesthetic clues. Child will "bang" or "tense" limb.
2. The nature of limb movement identified
   a. Difficulty in starting—abortive and excessive tones.
   b. May be jerky and explosive.
   c. May tense other limb.
3. Prevention of overflow

B. Movement Patterns

Items 1, 2, 3, 4, 5 & 6

Method: Instruct child verbally (additional help may be given on difficult task) on the following tasks for thirty seconds.

DEVELOPMENTAL GROSS AND PERCEPTUAL MOTOR SURVEY (continued)

Item 1. Jump in place, both feet
Item 2. Jump on right foot
Item 3. Jump on left foot
Item 4. Hop on right foot
Item 5. Hop on left foot
Item 6. Gallop

Scoring: Passed—Performs task easily.
Inadequate—Performs task with difficulty.
Failed—Cannot perform.

Observational Keys:

1. Can he maintain balance?
2. Can he get off the ground?
3. Are the patterns rhythmically executed?

C. Balance

Items 1, 2, 3, 4, 5 & 6

Method: The examiner simply instructs, verbally describes, demonstrates or manipulates the child in the following task:
Item 1. Forward walk
Item 2. Backward walk
Item 3. Sidewise walk—left
Item 4. Sidewise walk—right
Item 5. Sidewise left, crossover right
Item 6. Sidewise right, crossover left

Scoring: Passed—Walks easily and maintains dynamic balance.
Inadequate—Occasional balance difficulty, but retains control.
Failed—Steps off more than once, pauses frequently, difficulty in regaining balance, performs more than one-quarter out of balance.

Observational Keys:

1. Steps off board.
2. Pauses.
3. Uses one side more than other.
4. Avoids balance, runs, long steps, feet crosswise.
5. Rigid posture.

D. Motor Coordination—Body Image—Differentiation Problems

Items 1 through 8

Method: Instruct child verbally (additional help may be given on tasks 1 through 5 only) on the following:
Item 1. Hop with right foot on line 10 feet long.

DEVELOPMENTAL GROSS AND PERCEPTUAL MOTOR SURVEY (continued)

Item 2. Hop with left foot on line 10 feet long.
Item 3. Hop twice on left and twice on right for 30 seconds.
Item 4. Hop twice on right, single hop left.
Item 5. Hop twice on left, single on right.
Item 6. Step over stick.
Item 7. Duck under stick.
Item 8. Go between objects without touching.

Scoring: Passed—Completes task adequately.
　　　　Inadequate—Task performed unrhythmically, balance difficulty, slightly over or underestimates object (soft touch), corrects after one repetition.
　　　　Failed—Cannot perform, overestimates, cannot correct after one repetition.

Observational Keys

1. Judges body movements with respect to objects in space.
2. Over- or underestimation of spatial relationships.
3. Does child make allowance for objects which are not within his visual fields?

　　The remediation needed for the student as shown on the screening test should be incorporated in the child's program along with the activities mentioned earlier. Some special exercises are included here to improve perceptual motor problems common to the mentally retarded.

　　Laterality: The two main errors we see in the child's performance which are problems in laterality are: using both sides together, simultaneously, when only one is needed, and using one side to the exclusion of the other. In either case the development of laterality has been avoided, the first by making both the same, the second by needing only one side and not both. Thus, the child will have difficulty in learning activities requiring different actions of both sides at the same time or activities requiring alternate use in a similar manner of both sides or the performance of either side. These exercises often improve the laterality problem. Windmill, trunk twist, leg raising in side lying, trunk bending sideways, log roll—left and right, coffee grinder, chopping wood, and windshield wiper.

　　Exercises that help rhythm of movement from side to front, side to back, to help children who cannot make a smooth transition are: front lunge to side lunge, trunk bending forward—backward—sideward, straddle hop-forward and sideward, and front squat stride to side squat stride.

Exercises for balance to pinpoint the center of gravity within the body are as follows: V-sit, flying "V," hip raising with balance in the side support position, and balance stand. Exercises for improving adjustment and reaction to gravity include standing, sitting, walking, running, rolling, crawling and creeping, jumping, climbing, hopping, skipping and sliding, pushing, pulling, catching, hitting, and kicking.

Exercises which give a fast release of energy in a short period of time are as follows: seal walk, push-ups, sit ups; two man see-saw, and three man see-saw. These should be alternated with periods of relaxation.

Exercises which would give one an idea of coordination of the hands and feet in a vertical position are as follows: cat walk, lame dog walk, crab walk, inch worm.

Exercises which would give one an idea of coordination of the hands and feet in a horizontal position are as follows: heel slap, heel click, ball pick-up, side straddle hop.

Exercises which would provide a better awareness of lower and upper extremities: flying, inch worm, single leg-raising, balance stand, crab walk, rocker, bend and stretch, front lunge, side lunge, windshield wiper, swaying tree, lame dog walk, cat walk.

Mimic exercises or imitation exercises: flying, climbing a rope, inch worm, seal walk, climbing ladder, windmill, cat walk, swan, crab walk, snake walk, airplane, jack-in-the-box, indian stand, lame dog walk, coffee grinder.

Increase attention and concentration span—keep head up—eyes on visual target: balance stand, flying, swinging "L," front lunge, side lunge, indian stand, trunk bending—sideways and forward.

Neuromuscular relaxation also has a place in the physical education program. The hyperactive and/or Strauss syndrome child should receive daily instruction to relax tension. Dr. Edmund Jacobson° started relaxation programs. The child is taught to identify tensions of the various muscle groups so that he can internalize the true meaning of relaxation. Lying supine and sitting are the basic positions. With the eyes closed, feet apart, hands from the body, be a rag doll, then alternate, tensing body or one limb, etc. The child feels the tenseness and then the relaxation. These techniques should start with a several minute session and increase to a 10- or 15-minute session.

The exercises presented here should provide performance objectives such as the following: 1. fast release of energy; 2. create a high level of interest and motivation; 3. provide a better body concept; 4. develop directionality and laterality; 5. pinpoint the center of gravity; 6. improve

---

° Jacobson, Edmund, M.D., *You Must Relax*, McGraw Hill Book Company, Inc., New York, 4th edition, 1962.

coordination between the arms and legs; 7. teach fuller use of the body and a better understanding of the body; 8. increase attention and concentration span; 9. provide better awareness of the lower and upper extremities; 10. help get physical control of emotional patterns; 11. provide fun, enjoyment, and pleasure; and 12. develop better social relations with their peers.

The Mentally Gifted

In contrast to the problems of the retarded, those of the mentally gifted seem miniscule. But this impression fades away as more thought is given to the problems of the gifted, particularly when they are considered on an individual basis.

The stereotype of the bright boy or girl is that of a person who wears large glasses, who has little concern for appearances or popularity, and who has a greater interest in books and unfinished experiments than anyone else in the school. He is supposed to outdistance his teachers in the pursuit of knowledge and to understand difficult concepts which baffle all of his agemates.

Actually few gifted students can be so described. Many are healthier, larger, and possessed of more stamina than others of their age. Most have the same general interests, as well as a deep and lasting interest in some special field of study. Usually, they are recognizable by their flair for investigation, their mental curiosity; they want to know the "why" of things, and they have the intelligence to locate and perceive the answers. By definition the gifted are those who attain a score of 130 to 140 in the standard intelligence test. While their scholarly interests may place them among older students, their ability in motor tasks tends to be average for their age-group. Thus it seems that there should be no problems with regard to physical education; the problem where it exists is bound up with "success." A child who is praised for doing better than others intellectually, who finds enjoyment and satisfaction in the consideration of facts and ideas among older people who can supply him with information, materials, facilities, and praise, tends to divorce himself from younger people who do not seem to understand him or his pursuit of knowledge. Gradually he seems "different," both to himself and to them. Unless his parents make sure that he takes part in instructional and intramural programs of physical education, he may fall so far behind in motor ability that his classmates will not want him to join them. If a few of them envy him or are defensive about his classroom progress, they may make it uncomfortable for him in the gymnasium, swimming pool, or locker room.

Therefore, it is easy to see that as such a child gains in scholarship and apparently recedes in motor ability, he may begin to avoid situations which test the latter. Parents and administrators who permit the gifted student to omit physical education do him a real disservice. Instead they should do all they can to help him develop his talents, including potential leadership ability, through physical education.

To do this, the gifted student should be encouraged to use his ability to think in the abstract, to judge critically, to perceive quickly, and to write and speak clearly. Student positions such as managers, team statisticians, team strategists, game officials, and publicity department speakers and writers are always open to those who can function on a high level. These positions present challenging opportunities, and all of them motivate their personnel to take part in activity in and around the physical education complex. Such activity may not make a "star player" of a person who is an average performer, but it makes participation readily available and tends to prevent the gifted child from becoming a shy, defensive failure in physical education.

The teacher should remember, too, that modern leaders in democracies have diverse skills, including favorite and often strenuous hobbies which take them out of doors. These men and women are usually more stable than the introverted or self-centered leader whose perspective is as narrow as his interests, the person to whom power, control, and serious contemplation of self is seldom relieved by a humble, good-humored smile. Modern civilization needs the leadership services of the best men and women; those who are fortunate enough to be able to solve problems, to think critically, to plan wisely with and for others must be encouraged to develop all of their talents.

It has been observed by many that, given a choice, the gifted often prefer the individual pursuits in physical education: hiking, aquatics, gymnastics, the racquet sports. These are fine activities, but they need to be supplemented by others. Most of the gifted need to learn to mix easily with others who are less brilliant and are quite satisfied to be so. The gifted child needs to learn the attitudes of the average person at the various socioeconomic levels. He must learn patience, tolerance, and graciousness when dealing with others whose pace and motivation in intellectual tasks is average. Such contacts generally prove relaxing to the gifted person once he or she has made friends in the group. And such contacts can encourage participation in the physical education and recreational activities which are so natural to man. While the higher development of his intellectual powers is of relatively recent date, man has always needed and enjoyed movement. The intellectually oriented person needs movement experiences, for he is first of all a person, and then a gifted one.

13. The Orthopaedically Handicapped

Throughout history the orthopaedically handicapped or "crippled" have been a source of ridicule, distrust, concern, and consideration. Many stories include the cripple who is cast in the role of evildoer or witch, with strange and often occult powers attributed to him. The lame and deformed are found in art of all centuries, even in the present age. Ben Shahn's "The Red Stairway," painted in 1944, features a one-legged man climbing a long and tortuous staircase.

During the past decade crippling conditions have become less frequent among the school age population. Orthopaedically handicapped children total about two million in the United States; while this is high, it represents a significant drop in percentage of cases. Vaccines, various forms of medical treatment, including surgery, and improved prenatal and postnatal care, have accounted in part for this reduction. But the gradual cessation has only served to dramatize the more serious crippling conditions which are seen and which less than ever act as deterrents to school attendance. We must meet the needs of a group which years ago would not have attended school, certainly not with typical children.

Programming activities for orthopaedic patients is a challenging assignment. A group which is similar in appearance may need very different kinds of activities; even those who are programmed into the same activities may vary in amount and degree of participation permitted. It is important that the physical educator do all in his power to understand the cause, movement problems and prognosis of each person with whom he works. In this way and with the continuing advice and evaluation of the medical team, he can provide the right physical education for each person in the group.

Causes of Orthopaedic Disabilities

Orthopaedic handicaps result from conditions or diseases which may affect the spine and joints, and often interfere with proper function of body systems and proper movement of body parts. Usually they are seen as paralysis, limited joint range, or amputation. The great majority of cases can be attributed to one of the following causes:

1. Congenital as in scoliosis, clubfoot, spina bifida, and dislocation at shoulder or hip.

2. Osteochondrosis (as in Morquio's disease) which tends to render insufficient the functioning of the ossification centers of the body. It is seen most frequently as Perthes' hip in which the head of the femur undergoes dystrophy, then recalcification.

3. Injury resulting in the loss of function of all or part of a limb, and pressure on a portion of the nervous system. Amputation is a frequent result in such injury cases.

4. Diseases such as tuberculosis of the bone, osteomyelitis, and, despite the availability of vaccines, poliomyelitis.

Physical Education for the Orthopaedically Handicapped

Goals of the Program

The physical educator, working with the medical team, hopes to provide a program of exercises and other activities which will protect the person and help him to attain the maximum physical level of which he is capable. While leaving to the therapists the treatment which is indicated for the condition involved, the physical educator strives to provide the patient with approved big muscle exercise which leads to accomplishment in the areas of motor skill and leisure time activities. Often he is working with people who have never known or have forgotten how to perform motor tasks. The teacher can do much through careful progression and presentation to help a person to become a proficient performer.

Further, he can help the learner to improve in body mechanics so that he uses well the substitutes for body parts, whether crutches, wheelchairs, or prosthetic devices; this results in the greatest amount of work with the least expenditure of energy. Thus good body mechanics puts off the onset of fatigue, the time when such a person becomes less coordinated.

Problems in Planning the Program

Planning for these individuals is difficult for many reasons. Since nearly every limb, joint, or muscle may be the site of an orthopaedic handicap, each child's limitations must be handled individually. The physical educator must follow some plan or he will become lost in the maze of varieties of causes, limitations, and activity indices. At the beginning, he should recognize that most orthopaedically handicapped share the following similarities:

1. Most have some problem with body mechanics, especially balance.

2. Most are dependent upon some sort of supportive device or equipment as they move from place to place.

3. Most experience some embarrassment, some frustration, some hesitancy in attempts to duplicate motor tasks accomplished by ordinary people.

4. Many avoid situations where appearance is important; this can be seen, for example, in refusal to take part in aquatics and other activities which require (a) dressing at places other than at home, (b) appearing in costumes which display a deformed limb, (c) appearing without supportive or cosmetic prostheses or other normalizing equipment.

Despite the similarities, the differences are many and are related to:

1. The cause of the handicap.

2. The specific area of the body affected by the condition or disease.

3. The present age of the person.

4. The age of the person when the handicap occurred.

5. The intelligence of the person, especially in relation to aspirational levels, in his personal and professional, business, or vocational life.

6. The effectiveness of any instruction which he has received relative to handling the handicap.

7. The general health of the person.

Thus it can be seen that the physical educator must know and understand the particular student before he begins to plan his program. Also, he should be aware of:

1. Cause of the handicapping condition.

2. Limitations, including those imposed by the medical team. One example of a question which must be answered is: Can he bear weight on the lower limbs?

3. Degree to which the patient is dependent upon artificial means of support at rest and in motion.

4. Knowledge of individual differences related to age (at present and when handicap appeared), intelligence, general health, desire to live normally, and lifetime goals.

Perhaps a few examples are in order. A teacher faced with the problems posed by one student with an atrophied leg and another with a prosthetic limb recognizes that neither student will tend to equal the efficiency in gait, balance, and endurance of the normal person. Perhaps the student with the atrophied leg will function better than his classmate, but if the fit and weight of the prosthetic limb are correct, and the student gains experience in using it, the reverse may soon be true.

Continuing case evaluations, the teacher may find a great difference between amputees with below-knee and above-knee amputations, or with below-elbow and above-elbow amputations. Usually the fewer the joints which have been removed the more readily will the person show improvement in skill performance. This is related to movement patterns, balance, limb weight, and weight-bearing.

Further complicating the picture is the fact that there may be some cases for whom no program should be planned. Typical of these (and of course the physician is the final judge) are cases of active osteomyelitis, knee and shoulder injuries which are mobilized or are being prepared for surgery, and some cases of tuberculosis of the joints.

For those who are permitted to participate, the program develops within the framework of permissiveness allowed by the physician, and the imagination and ingenuity of teacher and pupil. Perhaps most important is the recognition of the need of a sense of adventure and exploration. The teacher, while empathetic, cannot physically duplicate most of the limitations of these cases, and so the students must contribute ideationally. In addition the teacher must stress the abilities, real or potential, of the student. Everything, even crutches and wheelchairs, must be considered as contributing to the success of the activities undertaken.

Selecting the Activities

Over the years authors of articles and books have suggested many ways of typing orthopaedically handicapped students so that activities might be chosen on a rational basis. Some have suggested activities according to age, causal factors, and mode of locomotion. Time has brought a continuous improvement in prosthetic devices which have made the handicapped more equal to the nonhandicapped. It seems to us that the most logical presentation is on the basis of limb involvement.

One Arm Affected

Hopefully the affected limb is the nondominant one. The activities which are suitable generally include the following:

Dance. Folk, square, ballroom, tap, and modern appropriate to the age and interests of the group may be included. A cosmetic hand and an empathetic partner can lessen the fears of the ballroom dancer.

Individual, Dual, and Team Activities. Games of low organization should be used if appropriate to the age of the group; among individual, dual, and team activities the following are best:

1. Badminton.

2. Bait casting.

3. Baseball and softball. Some difficulty may be experienced in catching; this can be remedied by attaching a device or a second glove to the noncatching hand to cover the caught ball.

4. Basketball.

5. Bowling.

6. Croquet.

7. Deck tennis.

8. Fencing.

9. Field hockey.

10. Football (modified as flag football, for example).

11. Golf (Golfer Ed Furgol is a good example of what can be done, despite a withered arm).

12. Gymnastics.

13. Handball.

14. Horseshoes.

15. Ice skating.

16. Lacrosse.

17. Roller skating.

18. Skiing.

19. Soccer.

20. Speedball.

21. Some stunts.

22. Some self-testing activities.

23. Shuffleboard.

24. Table tennis.

25. Tennis.

26. Track and field, except certain events such as pole vault.

Aquatics. All are possible, although the student may need the use of a floating weight on the handicapped arm to help him maintain balance while learning standard strokes. Other activities need no modification.

Body Mechanics. All activities are possible.

Movement Exploration. Movement exploration may be used with real benefit.

Two Arms Affected

The activities which are suitable generally, include the following:

Dance. Folk, square, tap, and modern dance as appropriate to the age and interests of the group may be selected. In addition, ballroom dance might be included for those who care to take part, and whose cosmetic prostheses and empathetic partner make it a relaxed experience.

Games of Low Organization, Individual, Dual, and Team Activities. Age and interests dictate the program in part; in addition activities should involve motor tasks which the performer can handle successfully. Those with atrophied or prosthetic arms find it difficult to control objects, to handle many movements in sequence; they should be taught at first through activities which require only one reaction, for example, punt kicking from behind a line, rather than a kicking relay which requires running, changing direction, and getting the ball to a teammate. The following are some suggested activities for this group:

1. Football-type activities, including kicking over a goal and kicking for distance.

2. Ice skating.

3. Roller skating.

4. Some self-testing activities such as the low balance beam (about 8 inches from the floor).

5. Shuffleboard, using the hands or feet to propel discs on a regular court.

6. Soccer.

7. Track, especially such activities as cross-country running which develops balance by placing the runner on various and uneven surfaces. In addition endurance is built without tension.

8. Volleyball or volley-handball, using any part of the body, such as feet, head, knees to move the ball forward. This can be played over a 3 or 4 foot net, against a wall or several walls. It is indicated for boys, not recommended for girls.

Aquatics. Aquatic activities for this group would include swimming (beginning in the supine position for those who do not swim), diving, skin and scuba diving.

Body Mechanics. Such exercises are important for this group.

Movement Exploration. These activities are appropriate if developed for the age of the participants.

One Leg Affected

It is assumed that the person can get about with the aid of a crutch, cane, or prosthetic device, or that the atrophied leg is able to contribute at least as a support though it may cause unevenness in gait. Those in the latter category may not be able to accomplish as much as those who wear prosthetic devices; in any case choices must be made among activities which are suitable generally for those with one affected leg.

Dance. Ballroom, folk, modern, and square dance are indicated for those who can move about rather easily. Steps may be simplified, sudden stops and turns omitted and the dances done to a slower tempo than usual. Older students often enter regular square dance sets with the understanding that they will stand through, instead of dancing through, certain difficult maneuvers. When done to music, dance often helps to improve the gait of those who have poor locomotor rhythm.

Games of Low Organization, Individual, Dual, and Team Activities. As always age and interests help to determine selection; in addition activities should be chosen which allow for locomotion difficulties. A participant should be taught to depend on poles, tables, or even his braced crutches for balance during such stationary activities as bait casting and shuffleboard. Rules such as that which penalizes table contact by the hands during table tennis should be overlooked and distances to be covered in locomotion activities such as relays should be lessened. The following are some suggested activities for this group:

1. Archery.

2. Badminton (serves, clears and drives only, singles court).

3. Bait casting.

4. Basketball (shooting).

5. Billiards.

6. Boxing (punching the bag).

7. Bowling.

8. Golf (short iron game and putting only, if distance or uneven surfaces contraindicate course play).

9. Gymnastics.

10. Horseshoes.

11. Riflery.

12. Shuffleboard.

13. Softball and baseball (with someone to run bases if needed, and reservation of such positions as first base and third base for the handicapped students).

14. Some stunts and self-testing activities.

15. Table tennis.

16. Volleyball (or Newcomb).

Aquatics. No restriction in aquatic activities is required. The student may take part in swimming, diving, life saving, scuba and skin diving, synchronized swimming, boating, canoeing, crew, sailing, water skiing.

Beginning swimmers may need help in development of ability to balance if the affected leg is not as heavy as the other leg, or if they swim without the prosthetic device. Sometimes a buoyant weight attached to the affected limb is helpful until the person has mastered the rudiments of swimming; if this is not done, he must handle the dual problem of keeping his balance while learning strokes.

Body Mechanics. All are permitted; indeed, most are necessary for these students, since they generally have problems related to balance and to weight handling.

Movement Exploration. This is a useful part of the program for these people, as it aids in their orientation to space, time, and the levels on which humans move.

Two Legs Affected: Ambulatory

If able to get about on crutches or prosthetic limbs, the person can perform many of the skills listed for those with only one leg affected. If able to get about on crutches but with difficulty, the student can perform certain activities in a seated position for a part of the time. Activities which seem suitable for most of the group in this category follow:

Dance. Ballroom, folk, square, and modern dance are entirely possible, especially if the tempo is slowed and the distances lessened. Tap dance is generally not suitable. Some who cannot move readily enjoy modern dance at various levels but performed with the body stationary.

Games of Low Organization, Individual, Dual, or Team Games. These should be chosen on the basis of age, interests, and success potential for those who have difficulty in locomotion. Activities which can be slowed down or simplified without spoiling them for the players are best. Some of the more suitable ones follow:

1. Archery.

2. Badminton on a narrow court.

3. Bait casting.

4. Basketball (shooting to a lowered basket).

5. Billiards.

6. Boxing (punching the bag).

7. Bowling (sometimes from a chair).

8. Croquet.

9. Golf (short iron game and putting only, if distance or uneven surfaces contraindicate course play).

10. Gymnastics (rings, for example).

11. Horseshoes.

12. Riflery.

13. Shuffleboard.

14. Softball or baseball (batting, primarily).

15. Table tennis (often played on rolling chairs around an anchored table).

16. Volleyball (or Newcomb).

Aquatics. Outside of diving or water skiing, these people can perform all aquatic activities.

Body Mechanics. Such exercises definitely should be included.

Movement Exploration. This is important to these people.

Two Legs Affected: Wheelchair

Exercise and social recreational types of activities are indicated for most of these patients. For those who have strong torsos, exercise is necessary for maintenance of physical condition; for others it is a way to attain it. Many wheelchair patients need help in learning to move their chairs swiftly, turn corners at a good speed, and perform other movement patterns which are used in activity. Once these are learned, the number and types of activities expand from those used during their first days of cautious participation in the physical education setting.

The following are typical of activities which have been performed successfully by wheelchair patients:

Dance. Folk, square, and modern dance are possible with modifications. Steps are eliminated, modified, or changed outright; movement patterns which distinguish a particular dance are maintained. Distances are no problem to the wheelchair patient but providing enough room for circles and similar formations must be considered ahead of time.

Games of Low Organization, Individual, Dual, and Team Activities. Even with older patients, the game of low organization provides learning and practice periods. Circles provide learning experience as patients learn by watching others; relays permit individuals to have the room which they need while learning to perform a skill such as ball bouncing while moving in the chair. Advanced activities include the following:

1. Archery.

2. Bait casting.

3. Basketball (with padded walls to protect the players).

4. Baseball or softball (sometimes a partly deflated ball is introduced, since it travels slower, hits with less force, and permits learning fielders to retrieve it and to judge force and distance of moving objects).

5. Billiards (often with short-legged table).

6. Bowling.

7. Deck tennis (played as a team game).

8. Horseshoes.

9. Riflery.

10. Table tennis (played around a fixed table).

11. Track events such as dashes, slalom, and field events such as javelin, discus, shot put.

12. Volleyball (and Newcomb).

13. Weight lifting.

Aquatics. Swimming is especially beneficial as it permits freedom, and (with the aid of viscosity of the water) forward progress with less energy than many patients experience on land. Backstroke and breaststroke generally prove to be favorite strokes, as the patients experience more security and more success than in sidestroke and some prone strokes. Diving, life saving, and skin and scuba diving are not indicated, but those who can swim can also enjoy boating, canoeing, and sailing.

Body Mechanics. Such activity is especially beneficial in helping these cases procure the greatest amount of work with the least amount of energy output.

Movement Exploration. These activities encourage the solving of problems related to movement, whether on the basis of space and time, or with definite sport skills in mind.

A Final Word

Any trouble taken to program the orthopaedically handicapped in isolated groups or, preferably, with other people is well worth the effort. To see a wheelchair patient become the best server on her Newcomb team, to watch a boy with Perthes' hip score more free-throws than any of his classmates, and to shake the hand of a boy on crutches who has just won the push-ups contest in his school are exciting moments. The cited instances are true, but they did not "just happen." Outcomes such as these result from thought, dedication, and careful cooperative planning so that the child develops as well as he can the abilities which are just waiting to be discovered.

14. The Tuberculous

Although modern chemotherapy has lessened the treatment time for tuberculosis, it is still a dreaded disease. Feelings of fear and depression, guilt, and secrecy have long shadowed it. Possibly these are due to the correlation between a high incidence of the disease and the substandard environmental conditions in which it thrives; perhaps they are related to the knowledge that the disease, apparently defeated, may recur without warning.

The dictionary defines it as follows:

. . . a specific disease caused by the presence of *Bacillus tuberculosis;* it may affect almost any tissue or organ of the body, the most common seats of the disease being the lungs and the joints . . . (178, p. 1438).

Late in the nineteenth century a German physician named Robert Koch was able to isolate and study the bacillus of the disease. At the time tuberculosis was present among all ages and conditions of mankind; in our century it centers mainly on the "young adult" or fifteen to forty year old group. It is interesting to realize that at the time that Koch took the steps which led to the discovery of the bacillus, he was in this special age range. At thirty-two years of age, the young district doctor presented his findings to a group of scientists who had gathered to hear him at the invitation of Professor Ferdinand Cohn, Director of the Botanical Institute in Breslau, Germany (61, p. 15).

The Tuberculous Student

Here is a disease which is often unrecognized in the incipient as well as in the convalescent stages. Unlike other handicapping conditions there are few dramatic signs; a person may cough or complain of undue fatigue, but these are the symptoms of at least a dozen other conditions, many of them far less serious than tuberculosis. Nevertheless, given such signs and a suspicion that the student is not as healthy as he ought to be, a teacher should make sure that a doctor is consulted and that whenever possible a test, either Mantoux or Vollmer Patch Test, is administered. The highly contagious nature of this disease forces extreme caution in follow-up of suspected cases.

The teacher is concerned, too, in the programming of post-tuberculosis cases. Such a student has generally proceeded through prolonged treatment with rest, diet, medication, and in some cases surgery. His physical weakness and social defenses as he re-enters a world in which he does not usually feel really welcome present problems which a wise teacher can help to solve.

As always, the physician will establish the limits of the program which the student will follow. The younger the student, the more he must be restrained, especially from such all-out efforts as running and chasing, which constitute an important part of elementary school physical education activities. The physician will tend to recommend activities which do not call for endurance, strength, or any real expenditure of energy.

Activity followed by rest becomes the pattern; thus shuffleboard, clock golf, and bait casting, which include periods of rest within the activity, are particularly valuable. As the patient improves, the physician will tend to increase the demands made upon him; more time spent in physical education activities, and stepped-up activities become the order of the day.

At this point it is important for the physical educator to remember that the student needs education, and in some cases re-education, in the type of activities which will be of lasting value. The former top-flight athlete who contracted the disease can no longer perform in the all-out way that he once did; the sports neophyte needs help too in learning some activities which might be described as hobby-type, semi-active, and all-age in character. All post-tuberculosis patients learn early in their illness that they have been infected by a bacillus which may be quiescent for years, then attack when the patient is fatigued or strained or in any other way has allowed his resistance to become low.

Selecting Activities

Physical education can provide him with many avenues for the building of resistance as well as for the enjoyment of life. Walking, swimming, dance of all kinds, and most sports which are individual or dual in character, such as table tennis and golf, are lifetime allies to the person with a history of tuberculosis infection. Such activities take him out of doors in moderate and dry weather and encourage him to spend his energy in reasonable amounts and at a reasonable pace. They help to communicate to him that the world will accept anyone who participates wholeheartedly and with social awareness of others.

The physical education teacher is in a position to supplement the work of the physician by helping the student to carry out any rehabilitative program recommended by the medical team. This is particularly true in cases which have required surgery with consequent involvement of muscle tissue. Often specific exercises are recommended; sometimes with the help of the physical educator the physician will prescribe participation by his patient in certain physical activities which promise help in rebuilding muscle strength, flexibility, or other components.

The recommendations of the physician will usually follow four general principles:

1. Patients with a history of tuberculosis must always avoid activities which are to be performed quickly, competitively, and with the physical strain and emotional excitement which are associated with some group activities. An example is basketball.

2. At first, such patients may be allowed to perform only activities which are more stationary than active, which require little or no use of the arms in such movements as lifting, which are mild in their demands for energy output, and which never force breathlessness upon the performer. Examples are putting in golf, lawn bowling with small, light balls, and moderate amounts of walking.

3. Regardless of improvement, such patients must have rest planned into the daily schedule.

4. With improvement, the recommendations will tend to permit increased activity as the time since the arrest of the disease increases. Gradually the patient may be taking part in a variety of activities chosen from the five categories of physical education areas: dance, sports, aquatics, body mechanics, and movement exploration.

15. Those With Weight Problems

The body has been compared to a machine, a work-producer. Good fuel is a basic requirement, and so is the balanced ratio between fuel-input and work-output. Most machines become less efficient as the ratio diminishes; man is no exception. When the body is provided with insufficient or poor fuel (food) or too much of it, it becomes less efficient and, in time, may suffer the consequences of various diseases and conditions which thrive on this imbalance.

Weight is one of the simplest signs of imbalance. When a person carries more or less weight than he should for his heredity, height, body build, age, sex, and occupation, he is said to be either overweight or underweight (29, p. 298). Both of these conditions are caused by one or more factors; each is modified best when the cause or causes have been determined and removed.

Actually one's weight is merely a mathematical expression of the pull between the body and the center of the earth, or the gravitational pull per person. The normal body is so constructed that bones, muscles, ligaments, and tendons operate most efficiently when a person maintains correct weight. For each extra 21 pounds which the overweight person carries, he may be thought of as carrying a 21-inch suitcase, fully packed! He is working harder than need be, every hour of the day. Meanwhile the seriously underweight person is asking more work of his body than can be provided by the food he gives it. Thus, correct weight represents the normal pull of gravity against which man exerts a normal expenditure of energy during a normal life expectancy.

The Overweight Person

The causes of this condition can be summarized under three headings:

1. Habitual overeating, sometimes linked to emotional factors such as security and satisfaction, and sometimes related to family eating traditions. Parents who allow continuous snacking, who are offended if children do not take second helpings, who serve food automatically during television commercials, are the parents who build the "hearty eating" tradition in a family.

2. Lack of exercise. Dozens of electrical appliances and continuous car-riding have crowded exercise out of day-to-day living. The results are seen in tired, slower, less agile people of all ages.

3. Glandular disturbances, usually involving the pituitary or thyroid glands. Only 3 per cent of the overweight suffer from this cause, but they fall victim to (1) hernias, (2) foot troubles, and (3) a decline in life expectancy because of potential development of such conditions as arthritis, cardiovascular conditions, diabetes, gallstones, and gout.

Many overweight children are handicapped. Often they cannot keep pace with classmates and because of inability to support their own weight, must be protected from injuring themselves in such activities as the headstand. Many obese persons are endomorphic in build with fragile bones hidden under layers of fat. And many are emotionally upset by their condition. The teacher should keep these possibilities in mind when selecting activities for such children. The starting point of planning is, of course, the physician who conducts the medical examination, gives advice to the student and his teacher, and provides follow-up care over a period of time.

Generally, activity selection centers about:

1. The factors of safety and consideration, both for the mental and physical protection of the student.

2. The need for development; activities which build strength and muscle tone are indicated.

3. The need to choose activities in which lack of endurance will not mean failure in performance.

Following these guidelines, the physical educator specifically seeks out:

1. Activities which permit:
   a. The subject to initiate whatever action is called for. Swimming and riflery are good examples.
   b. The subject to take part in nearly stationary activities. Horseshoes and table tennis are examples.

2. Activities which do not require:
   a. The subject to lift heavy objects which might cause strain, particularly in the abdominal area. Thus standing broad jump might be indicated and the wheelbarrow relay contraindicated.
   b. The subject to support his own weight or that of others. For this reason, head stands, rope climbing and stunts in which the overweight child acts as support man would be poor choices.
   c. That the subject come into rough contact with others. Thus soccer, tackle football, and similar games are not indicated.

With guidance, the overweight student is generally permitted to take part in most activities within the five areas of physical education. The proper balance between rest and activity is important, and in each area the student should be taught to rest before exhaustion forces him to do so. Most games of low organization include rest periods, and are permitted with the exception of rough activities such as Bull in the Ring. Among the activities classified as individual, dual, and team games, a few which are contraindicated for the overweight include:

1. Boxing.
2. Football.
3. Lacrosse.
4. Rebound tumbling.
5. Skiing.
6. Soccer.
7. Tumbling.
8. Pyramid building.
9. Wrestling.

Many of the scoring-systems of activities which are permitted to the overweight child may need modification. An example is basketball, which may be too strenuous for his limited endurance; played as Twenty-One, One Goal Basketball, or Basketball Relay, it may be completely acceptable. The child may be able to play certain games with position limitations; an example is field hockey, which is indicated if good sense places the overweight girl in either fullback or goalkeeper positions. To allow her to play on the speedy front line would be foolish and, because of her predictive failure in any of those positions, would call forth player resentment.

Authorities stress the need of caloric reduction if weight is to be lost. We agree, adding only that exercise has an equally important part to play. Byrd has said it very well:

Physical activity plays a role in weight reduction . . . If good judgment is used in the intensity of exercise, so that undesirable stress is not placed upon a heart already overburdened with fat, and if the major emphasis is still upon the decrease of food intake, physical activity may make a worthwhile contribution to weight loss.°

The Underweight Person

Generally life expectancy is considered greater for this group than for the overweight. However, a person who is 15 per cent or more underweight (in comparison with those of his build, age, and sex), may tire easily and become unable to resist disease. In the latter case, life expectancy may be shortened. The condition of being underweight results from one or more of the following causes:

1. Heredity.

2. Malnutrition.

3. Digestive problems, as, for example, intestinal ulcers.

4. Organic defects.

5. Illnesses, such as tuberculosis.

6. Overwork, with resulting tension and loss of sleep.

7. Glandular imbalance.

The underweight person tires quickly. His posture and muscle tone tend to be poor. This condition is especially unfortunate during the growing period because height, posture, stamina, and eventually self-image suffer.

Programming the underweight student requires thought and observation. If he seems low in energy and indifferent while taking part, he may be malnourished. Certainly examination by a physician is indicated. However, some underweight students have done so poorly in the past that they avoid participation whenever possible. Such students may need exercise for the development of circulatory and respiratory efficiency, and for the values which will accrue to them through socializing with others. Those who fall short in social adjustment should be scheduled primarily into activities in which they will probably succeed. This will encourage them, and, hopefully, motivate them to further participation. On the other hand, many underweight persons are active, want to participate, and should be allowed to do so provided they learn to rest as needed. Sometimes enforced rest periods must be scheduled for them.

It is important that the underweight student who engages in body

---

° Byrd, Oliver E., *Health*, 4th Ed. Philadelphia, W. B. Saunders Co., 1966, p. 130.

contact sports or tests of strength and endurance only does so against those who are equated with him. Two boys of the same age may be far apart in weight, height, strength, and endurance; the boy who measures lower in these categories may be injured when pitted against the bigger boy. Such uneven contests have sometimes resulted in the filing of charges of negligence against the teacher. Thus, the program for the underweight student should:

1. Protect him against ridicule due to his size or performance level.
2. Protect him against injury and exhaustion.
3. Build strength and endurance.
4. Guide him to food choices which will help him to gain weight.
5. Take place outdoors whenever possible as this tends to increase appetite.

Many underweight persons are of ectomorphic body build. Because of this they tend to prefer, and to excel in, individual and dual activities. Every effort should be made to provide them with opportunities for instruction in such activities as dance, racquet sports, and aquatics. Years later the teacher may have the privilege of seeing them as those enviably slim middle-aged people who still enjoy activity.

Summary

The intention of this chapter is to assist teachers and others to plan adapted physical education and recreation programs for the exceptional child. Adaptations may be made in regular activities by changing such factors as the amount of time, space, or object-weight which is usually involved.

From the five areas of the physical education program, choices have been made for each of the fifteen handicapping conditions which are usually found in a school population. Background material and program recommendations have been included for each condition. It is hoped that this information will encourage teachers to permit the exceptional pupil to take part. While it is true that the teacher is only one member of the education team, it is also true that he or she is the only one who can implement the agreements of the team and make it possible for the child to participate effectively in physical education.

Camping for the
Handicapped

Anyone who visits happy children in a well-run camp can only wish this experience for all children. Outdoor living, purposeful hobbies, daily swimming, and a host of other beneficial and joy-producing factors bring good complexions, big smiles, and improved circulation and stamina to all who camp.

Yet, despite these obvious advantages, relatively few atypical children go to camp. Camps for handicapped children are fewer and less often filled than those for typical youngsters. (On the other hand, atypical adults are more willing than typical adults to go to camp, especially in structured settings.)

Although the advantages of camping seem obvious to those who encourage, participate, administer, or sponsor camps for the handicapped, they are forced to join with many others who ask the question: WHY are these camps often undersubscribed? Surely there are many handicapped who would benefit. And surely there are many organizations which would pay (and have done so) the camp-costs for these children.

The problem seems to lie with the parents, or guardians, of the handicapped children. Many of these adults do not know of the camp opportunities for special children. Others are fearsome of the spiders, snakes and raccoons with whom they believe their children might come in contact. (When pressed on this point, they usually exclaim: "But what would they do? How would they cope?") Many of those who make decisions for the children have never attended camp and have at best only a hazy idea of organized camping. While they cannot give a reason for their objections to camp, they harbor a vague set of beliefs that camping is life in an unprotected setting, operated by a very young and inexperienced staff, and nurtured by poorly-chosen, ill-cooked meals offset by daily canteen "treats." (Such a description could very well be true for a few camps whose days, it is hoped, are numbered!)

Some few who lack funds to allow their children to attend camp also lack knowledge of the many camperships (tuition-free camping) which exist. Some low-income families know of the groups which sponsor camperships, but are too proud to ask for help. (They often forget that by the time they HAVE the funds to underwrite camp costs, their children may be too old to enjoy camp, and may even be seeing their own children off to camp!).

A small number of adults who oppose camping went to camp, and had a miserable experience there. They may have been too young for camp, too unready to leave the family circle, or they may have attended a camp where the staff, nutrition, program, facilities, or other factors deserved a poor rating. They may have felt "rejected" when their parents sent them to camp. Possibly they suffered some social trauma (bullying, or social isolation by their peers, for example), an accident which resulted in some disfiguration, or a near-drowning. The potential camper tends to "see" camp through the eyes of those who describe it to him, and so reject it, thereby robbing himself of an opportunity to enjoy the outdoors with others, whom he can teach and from whom he can learn.

The last category of objectors among adults includes those who feel that camping places participants in situations such as diving and fishing which are (to the objectors) inherently dangerous, or in situations which are dangerous because they call for facile mobility. They will point out, with regard to the latter, that a camper who goes from cabin to lake to dining hall may be called upon to travel over wooded trails, uneven terrain, and rough meadow-land; such travel, the objectors feel, may call for more judgment and endurance than the handicapped person can muster. They may express doubts as well about toilet areas which are fairly isolated, walkway-bridges over creek-beds, and vertical ladders out of swimming pools. However, a visit to the camp will usually confirm the fact that "ways" have been found to solve such problems. In most camps for the handicapped, campers help each other, the ambulatory pushing the wheelchairs over distances and up inclines, and the counselors lifting children out of the pool, or swinging out a lift in which they are elevated to pool-side. Many other situations and their problem-solutions could be cited; the important thing is for the adult to realize that the problems are known and understood and that solutions have been provided. The best thing he can do then is to permit the camper to experience the situations; they may be the best ones the child will ever encounter in his preparation for the future adult world. Moreover, the child's learning will take place among empathetic, helpful, and supportive peers and adults. Generally the threatening appearance of many situations "falls away" as the camper succeeds; and in the process he has learned a very valuable lesson: most problems are solvable if we will proceed "one step at a time."

There is just one other group of persons who may be responsible for a vote of "no" when camp opportunities are available; that group is made up of potential campers who would rather stay home! Some of their reasons are that they are afraid of the unknown or that they have heard "tales" from others who attended sub-standard camps. They rely on their own vivid imaginations and feel that they will be unable or are unwilling to cope with life in a near normal situation, instead of that in an over-protective home. There is no quick answer for such children, for few of their experiences have been supportive of independence, and many adults have expected little from them. There is no point in enrolling them as campers unless they can first be challenged, trained in skills with which they can live daily among others who treat them as independent persons, and educated toward better attitudes and expectancies about themselves. Otherwise, most would fail; few would enjoy camp. And they would make camp a difficult place for others, including the adults whom they left behind.

There is no question that in the past, many of these fears and problems reflected situations which needed attention. Many camps for the handicapped were opened and operated by persons with little or no experience; many were administered by people with good intentions but little knowledge of business, including recruiting, training and supervising staff, or choosing among various insurance plans. Some camps paid counselors so little (some still do), that they could obtain neither seasoned nor serious staff. Many tried to manage with too few counselors, and failed to meet the three-counselors-to-one-camper ratio which is considered necessary.

Such conditions continued for years because camps were considered peripheral and seasonal businesses, and most adults, never having been campers, hardly knew what to expect or to require of the camp operators. Fortunately, conditions have changed. During the past couple of decades, *standards* have been developed by several groups, notably the American Camping Association (160). Visitations are made by trained personnel, after which a camp may be certified. Camps have invested in health insurance and workmen's compensation plans. Also, lawsuits have become common enough to cause careless camp administrators to "mend their ways" with regard to such potentially suable conditions as food handling, water sources, personnel selection, and vehicle maintenance. These and other measures have lessened the fear of children or adults who are considering camp. For the handicapped child or adult who attends a properly operated camp, there are few experiences in life, from the point of view of fun, skill and fitness improvement, and maintenance, which can compete with this experience in creative living.

By now it is evident that camping can be of benefit to most people, and especially to the handicapped. Perhaps it would be well to consider what camping is, and what its purposes are, as well as to describe the types of camps among which the potential camper may choose.

What is a Camp

A camp is a place where outdoor and group living is emphasized. Everyone takes part with others in meals, common chores, and some mass activities. Depending on the type of camp, many other descriptive statements could be made. This is true even among camps which are considered to be of the same "type." Ultimately, a camp becomes an entity for the goals and purposes to which it is committed; from these flow the program it implements, the kinds of behaviors it rewards, and the kinds of satisfactions it offers its clientele.

General Purposes of Camps Which Enroll Handicapped Persons

Such camps attempt to do the following:
1. provide a "fun" experience for enrollees.
2. provide diverse and creative opportunities for campers, especially in the out of doors.
3. assist campers to "move ahead" in a positive way toward greater mobility and independence, toward greater knowledge, and toward increased ability to handle social relationships.
4. aid campers in their efforts to improve, or if that is not possible, to maintain whatever physical, social, emotional, and mental health they possess.

Types of Camps

Camps can be typed from the point of view of:
1. Length of Stay
   a. day camps, in which children come for the day, return to their living places each afternoon.
   b. resident camps, in which children spend 24 hours at the camp, or in camp-sponsored activities. Resident camps generally run from a few days to eight weeks in length.

2. Sponsorship
   a. private camps, owned and operated by a person or persons who earn a profit from tuitions paid by or for campers.
   b. agency camps, operated by and/or for social, labor, religious, or other agencies; they derive revenue from tuitions, donations, gifts, and other sources.
   c. school camps which are owned, leased, or rented by school districts for resident camping by school children, their teachers, and a permanent camp staff, for the purpose of studying at camp what is better studied there than on the school site; an example of program content is the environmental sciences.
3. Populations
   a. one sex only.
   b. peer group, of any age.
   c. a given type or types of handicap such as retardation, blindness, or orthopaedic difficulty.
   d. integrated, representing:
      1. all ages, as in family camps.
      2. all races, creeds, nationalities, neighborhoods, or social classes.
      3. coeducational camps.
4. Location
   a. existing primarily on one site, for example a resident camp.
   b. existing on many sites, as for example a touring camp.
5. Primary purpose
   a. enjoyment
   b. training in value-related special areas, such as religion or social skills.
   c. training in action-oriented area such as tennis, basketball, or weight-reduction.

It is obvious that many camps would fit well into more than one "type." For example, the parents of an integrated school group might pay three experienced counselors to take the youngsters on a two-week camping trip to Grand Canyon and back. Such a venture would be described as a private, integrated resident many-site camp whose purposes are to help the counselors to earn a living, and to help the campers to have fun and gain skills of many kinds while traveling and seeing the West.

Realistically, one must wonder whether his choices regarding camping are as numerous and as interesting for the handicapped as they are for the typical person. Do such factors as diseases, mobility-limitations, facility-needs, and fatigue-tolerances force the handicapped to choose more narrowly? The answer is both "yes" and "no." The ultimate answer for the handicapped is dependent on the individual: his willingness to try the untried, his ability to cope, as the unknown becomes known, his confidence in himself and those who are with him, and his ability to pay whatever charges are levied.

It is encouraging to know that time has improved the possibilities of locating worthy experiences for anyone who wants to camp. (This is as true for the handicapped as for the typical.) And most camps have improved over the years. Some of the reasons that one can make these statements are:

1. campers have become more mature, more outspoken, and more cooperative in evaluating and improving camping experiences which do not measure up to standards. Generally, camp directors have listened and acted.

2. those who pay for or otherwise are responsible for selecting camps for others include many who have been to camp, and so tend to have a realistic measure to use in evaluating what a camp is, or is not, and what it ought to be.

3. most camps conduct orientation sessions for staff, from one to seven days in length, just before the season opens. In most cases, this is supplemented by pre-season meetings, manuals, and other methods of educating personnel, and by evaluations of personnel during and at the end of the camp season.

4. such groups as the Association of Private Camps conduct self-studies, annual conferences and workshops, and other projects to upgrade the camps of their members.

5. most camps have earned or look forward to receiving the "Acorn" of the American Camping Association; this means that they have met the Camp Standards as established and approved by that group over a couple of decades (160).

6. professional associations and agencies, educational institutions and others have published lists of those camps which have been approved, certificated, or otherwise recognized; generally such listings include descriptions of the camps and whether or not they enroll handicapped children.

7. such groups as insurance companies, food distributors, and manufacturers of swimming pools take a keen look at camps in which their products are used. In case of liability claims or other law-based threats, they as well as the camps become "targets" for those who may go to court to prove that they have been wronged.

8. legislation at all levels of government has improved and will continue to improve camp conditions; examples of areas in which

such legislation exists are architectural barriers, equal opportunity, and workmen's compensation.

9. governmental requirements and public calls for more accountability have brought about the regular publication of annual reports by many groups which sponsor camps. Most contain pictures, program notes, and other material of interest and help to potential campers and their families.

Factors to Consider in Locating the Best Camp for a Handicapped Person

In considering various camps for a handicapped person, it is well to remember the old adage: "an ounce of prevention is worth a pound of cure." Time spent in investigating and checking on many camps is worth all the trouble involved, and is certainly worth far more than an evaluation at the end of a disastrous summer. The hope is that in the process, there will be revealed the best "match" between camp and camper; therein lies the probable success of the venture.

Factors which are important in the investigative process of any camp are as follows:

1. topography of the camp site: level or hilly, for example, are there some black-top or other permanent flat areas which drain and dry easily so that activities can be carried on safely, even after rain?
2. soil types found at the camp site: sand or clay, for example? both? soil types almost dictate whether there are trees for shade, grass, garden plot possibilities, and wild flowers in or near camp.
3. medical "climate" at the camp: are the personnel aware, careful, and able to handle medical problems which may develop, or are they unaware, casual, and unable to handle such problems?
4. the camp personnel: honest, interested, trained, experienced, healthy, and desirous of learning more, or selfish, disinterested, untrained, inexperienced, unable to keep up physically with the demands of their jobs, and unwilling to learn more in order to be of greater service?
5. program at the camp: is it creative, innovative, challenging, interesting, supervised, and balanced between active and passive activities and events, or traditional, over-protective, and unrelated to the needs and possible interests of the participants?
6. food provided at the camp: clean, plentiful, nutritious, varied, and appealing, or inadequate in variety and quantity, and substandard in quality and handling?

7. water at the camp: clean, plentiful, pleasant, or sub-standard in cleanliness, inadequate in quantity, noxious in odor or taste?
8. equipment, facilities, and vehicles at the camp: adequate, pleasant, accessible, safe, supportive, and efficient to use, or inadequate, unsafe, depressing, difficult of access and hard to keep clean and to enjoy? (26, 30, 45, 77, 154)

The merit of such a list is better seen when we use it to consider those factors which are most important for persons with specific handicaps. Let us use it, therefore, in thinking through the needs of six persons who would like to go to camp.

Case 1. a diabetic boy (diabetes mellitus) of ten years of age who has never been away from home but who is eager to attend a camp. He has learned to handle his own medication and does so, and enjoys activity with his peers. While the camp chosen for such a child should meet standards with regard to all of the factors listed, certain of them are less important than others, primarily #1 and 2. All of the others matter for him. Particular attention would be focused on #3, 4, 5, 6, 8; under #8 transportation would be of concern because of the possible necessity to take the child to the hospital for observation and/or treatment in connection with diabetes.

Case 2. an advanced case of muscular dystrophy in a fourteen-year-old girl who has attended camp for years, is now in a wheelchair, and is desirous of spending one of her last summers among peers at a camp. All factors listed would be of importance in camp selection for her because her limited mobility and endurance would require that she be on a site which is comparatively level, and accessible for activity in a wheelchair. A sandy beach with shade, reached by a ramped boardwalk, would be most helpful so that she could enjoy being with others, could "wade" while in her chair, or while support-seated on the shore, and could sculpture sand, or work with clay brought to the beach.

Cabins (or tents with floors) would have to be large enough to accommodate wheelchairs easily, and be reached by ramps. Toilet facilities would be located in or near cabins, be size- and level-planned for wheelchair users. Distances between facilities would have to be short (the usual standard of no longer than one-quarter mile in camps for the handicapped seems too long), and travel surfaces would have to be flat and smooth. Personnel would have to include at least one physician and a nurse as well as persons strong enough in body and "heart" to handle wheelchairs constantly and safely. Feeding might be necessary; if so, this would have to be planned so that the counselor would be given time to handle two meals: his own and that of the camper.

Case 3. an adult with an upper arm missing (amputation following an accident during childhood). This person attended school, including college, with his age-group, and holds a job as an accountant. He handles all *activities of daily living* on his own. He should attend any adult or family type of camp in which he will be accepted by staff as an independent person. He must realize that some of the other campers may stare, and may need some orientation, explanation, or other "help" in thinking of him as a person, not merely a "person without an arm."

Case 4. a totally blind camper who has attended camps for the blind for several summers. If and when he is ready to try to adjust to life in a typical camp, he should be allowed to do so, providing that the camp accepts him, is willing to help him become oriented and really accepted by everyone, and providing that there are no hazards which are dangerous to only the blind. The usual fenced pools and isolated archery ranges are safety measures which protect all campers, and so would protect the blind child. However, unguarded barbecue pits and unfenced fish ponds are typical of the unexpected hazards for a blind child which are not always considered hazardous for those who can see. The measure of safety which is sought is best stated in this way: the blind child must be able to go anywhere in the camp safely and confidently. Any other situation indicates a poor choice of camp for him.

Case 5. a moderately retarded woman (TMR) of 35 years of age who holds a routine position in a Sheltered Workshop, lives with her family, and has camped with members of her family for some summers. Such a person will probably enjoy the crafts, swimming, hiking, and other activities which are geared to her potential ability, but needs to be in a camp where she is safe and secure, and cannot become lost or confused, and where there is sufficient space for her group to work alone, without visits from those who "wander over" from nearby groups.

Many retarded persons have other handicaps in the physical, emotional, or perceptual areas. These must be taken into consideration too. The camp staff must be sufficiently educated to the problems facing them, and sufficiently strong to help with such daily activities as dressing, bathing, accompanying, and encouraging campers. *All* camps must have counselors with stamina and understanding; however, in camps for retarded persons these factors are especially important, and must exist in almost unlimited quantities within each staff person. Camper and counselor energy and productivity seem to "mesh" best in a campsite which includes a central area, surrounded by living quarters, and which keeps most activity areas in view of those who are responsible for the retarded campers.

Case 6.   an emotionally disturbed child of eight years of age. She attends a special school now, but attended kindergarten and first grade in a typical school. Inability to relate to her classmates and temper tantrums at school resulted in her parents' withdrawing her from school for counseling. She has shown considerable social progress during the past several months, and seems eager to go to a one-week camp for emotionally troubled persons where several of her classmates are also enrolled.

The camp has the staff and special medical personnel to handle such cases. Provision is made for academic remediation, psychotherapies, speech therapy, and whatever other work is appropriate to the needs of the campers. Site, facilities, and equipment are planned and administered with the special needs of the campers in mind; for example, there are no weapons or devices which can cause destruction or harm to persons or property. Another example is the labeling of trails, paths, and roads which campers use, to assure orientation and security of mind. Equipment and areas are planned so that "they might safely learn about themselves and their physical environment" (143, 145, 163, 165, 166, 194).

The program is centered around group activities, but plenty of time is scheduled for individual hobbies, conferences and supervised free time. The ratio of staff to children is high, so that staff members always have the time and energy to observe, record, and handle individual and situational behaviors and make recommendations on that basis. Above all, the camp is operated with one thought uppermost in mind: to assist the campers toward an ability to meet and solve their problems, and to relate well to others with whom they live.

The Program at Camp

Campers tend to remember two facets of camp more than any others: food and program. Visitors seem more aware of program activities than anything else. A camp which has a good program (appealing, joyful, progressive), but is poor otherwise may be rated higher by many than the camp which is more particular in other aspects of camping.

For example, some camps for handicapped youngsters devote much energy to developing medical histories of the campers, work hard to help them to improve personal habits and social relationships, and follow up on these items with parents after the season is over. Unless the child remembers a good program at the camp, however, he will probably not return next season. Indeed the program may have been poor enough to lessen the possible good results of the other efforts of the staff.

Since program is such a "show-case," it cannot be planned casually. And since it is the vehicle through which the aims and objectives of the camp are implemented, it should be thought through carefully. It affects campers; it provides opportunities for observation of behavior; it allows for some pragmatic proof of the effectiveness of the counseling services at camp.

It is generally agreed that the camp program consists of everything which happens at camp, whether scheduled or not. Under this definition, "program" includes such events as meals, free-play time after supper, and cabin cleanup. In addition, there is the scheduled program of activities which includes general all-camp activities such as flag-raising and camp barbecues as well as the instructional and recreational periods in which skills and appreciations are emphasized.

There follows a list of the usual program areas for which provision is made at many camps:

1. academic skills such as reading and writing, generally offered to individuals and groups when needed or otherwise appropriate. For example, "catch-up" skill sessions may be necessary for children who have been ill and missed school, or for campers whose conditions require constant academic work at their learning levels, if they are to continue to make progress.

2. active hobbies, and/or sports, including:
   a. aquatics: boating, canoeing, diving, water bikes, swimming and so on
   b. archery
   c. badminton
   d. bowling on the green, or on lanes
   e. dance in all forms, including modern, folk, square dancing
   f. fishing
   g. gymnastics
   h. horseback riding
   i. riflery
   j. team games such as kickball, basketball, softball
   k. table tennis
   l. tennis, including such modifications as paddle tennis, platform tennis
   m. tetherball

    n. therapeutic exercise

    o. track and field events

    p. trampoline

    q. wrestling

    r. use of some playground equipment, especially that which improves self-mobility, rather than mere transportation of the campers; thus, preference should be given to obstacle course items, sandboxes, and jungle gyms over merry-go-rounds and swings.

3. crafts and fine arts, including handcrafts, painting, sculpture and other media.

4. drama, from cabin skits to three-act plays.

5. musical activities including rhythm bands, opportunity to begin or continue to play a musical instrument, singing, musical presentations and concerts.

6. library activities from reading books to hearing records; from showing films to producing the camp newspaper.

7. campcrafts such as fire-making, outdoor cooking, whittling and carving, and shelter-building.

8. nature—interpretation through programs and activities such as hiking, "back-packing," canoe trips, bird-study, specimen-collecting, and astronomy.

9. service programs devoted to the needs of others.

10. social activities such as mixers, cookouts, and parties with persons from one's own and from other camps.

11. special programs, from bingo, campfires, and storytelling to scavenger hunts and olympic contests.

Many chapters of this textbook define, explain, and recommend ways of working with the handicapped, and of helping them and their companions to achieve success in activity. Chapters 4 and 9 are devoted to specific directions and suggestions by which feasible physical activities can be selected for those with various kinds of handicapping conditions. It is recommended that the material be reviewed in detail by those who are responsible for setting up programs of activity for any and all kinds of handicapped campers.

The program decisions which are reached should reflect knowledge, experience and judgment; they can be tested by asking the questions which follow. Unless a positive answer is returned for each, the activity in question should be omitted, at least for the time being:

1. does the camper know what the activity *is?*

2. does he show at least a mild *interest* in it?

3. can he *do* it? (that is, is it possible for him to become a performer?)

4. can he do it *safely?*
5. are orientation and any needed instruction available?
6. can the participant experience at least a small measure of success now, or eventually, if he participates?

Putting the Program to Work in Group Living (Camp)

To understand a camp, one must understand something of group living. Possibly the best place to start is to recognize that enrolling in a camp means joining the group which makes up that camp. If the camp group operates "in toto," intermingling in such facets of camp life as mealtimes, scheduled activities and evening programs, the camp is considered to be a centralized one. If, on the other hand, the original (all-camp) mass of persons breaks up into groups which plan and operate as separate living groups, the camp is considered to be a decentralized one. Most camps operate on primarily one or the other of these two group plans, with a few using both plans.

In addition to these two plans, camps operate through other groups, whose personnel are named:

1. owners, and/or directors, and/or camp committees.
2. counselors (instructional and group leaders), sometimes called staff members.
3. staff (for example, chefs, kitchen workers, maintenance personnel).
4. medical personnel (generally a physician, nurse, first-aid-nurse's aide).
5. campers.

There is a plethora of information on ways in which the first four groups are established. The criteria seem to reduce themselves to age, education, experience, talent, ability, opportunity, and sometimes, level of aspiration!

"Grouping" under #5 (campers) is a more fluid process and still somewhat in the experimental stage. Formation of groups seems to result from a consideration of the philosophy, goals, traditions, and population of a particular camp, modified by the realities (such as efficiency of operation) within the camp.

There is no one "best way" to group campers. The old expression: "if it is successful, don't change it" might be modified to read: "if it is successful, change it only to something which will be more successful." Possibly the decision can be made on the basis of priorities among goals of the camp: skill-learning and value-implementation, for instance. Possibly it can be made on the basis of camp strengths: leadership among counselors, volunteer leadership to supplement regular leadership, and availability of game-equipment donated by non-camp persons. (More leadership and equipment might make possible many small groups, instead of a few large ones, with resultant greater participation, fun, and learning by campers).

In many camps group living means cabin groups, assembled by such criteria as age, sex, camp experience, interests, or even social class lines. In other camps, group living means ever-changing groups from cabin, to meals, to activities, to campouts. There are many other plans between these two extremes.

Whether groups remain constant or change is often dependent on such a simple item as the length of time in which they will be at camp. Changes in the make-up of groups in an eight-week camp might be dictated, for example, by the necessity of providing variety among personalities (to prevent boredom), and opportunities to establish and develop new interests among those who seem to be attracted to the same activities. Whatever groupings are established, maintained, changed or discontinued, there should be evident a moving toward all, and attainment of at least some, of the goals of the camp.

As was indicated, populations which make up camps are important in deciding the number, size, kinds, and length-of-life of camp groups. Many camps for the retarded, for example, divide their campers into groups which demonstrate homogeneity in mental and social development, chronological age, and physical ability (10). Yet in other camps for the retarded, it is thought more important to form groups of persons whose chronological ages are relatively similar, with the hope that mental age will seem less important in the socializing process.

In camps for physically handicapped children, campers are often grouped by one of four means:

1. division by chronological age.
2. division by similarity of handicap, regardless of cause. Thus, those who have mobility problems would form one group, while the deaf and hard-of-hearing would form another. (An attempt would be made to keep age ranges narrow within each group.)
3. division by similarity of performance ability and interest level with regard to certain areas of activities, such as sports, fine arts.
4. a "match-up" of ambulatory and non-ambulatory (wheelchair) persons, so that the former can help the latter where transportation is necessary, and all can accomplish together.

Physically handicapped children are often placed in groups of typical children in integrated camps on what might be considered a "ratio" basis, for example, one or two handicapped children per group of cabin-mates. It is important that attitudes which represent empathy, patience, and willingness to live with such children are present. Support for these ideas must often be reinforced as the season moves along.

Sometimes such items as the size of cabins or the amount of space between tables in the dining hall make decisions about which handicapped campers operate in which groups. This is unfortunate, but must often be accepted as a reality to be "lived with." A camp which has ramped entrances to only a few cabins is forced to reserve those cabins for children who cannot handle steps. Even under such circumstances it is hoped that groups can be formed on the bases of compatibility and congeniality; usually this means proximity of age (chronological and mental), and leadership by counselors who possess sufficient maturity and understanding to remain counselors. (Immature counselors often become "campers" as the season progresses, thereby losing the respect of the campers, and, as a concomitant, the ability to lead.)

Group living is usually more successful and productive if it is understood that members may change from one group to another for sufficient reason, and if it is recognized that groups, as well as the individuals within them, may change during a season. Some flexibility in re-structuring groups should be acceptable, even encouraged at times.

There is a "Right" Camp for Your Camper

The following list is offered to those who are searching for a step-by-step method of locating the ideal camp for a potential camper:

1. long before the camp experience is to begin, locate lists of camps from magazine and newspaper advertisements, from professional associations, from parents and friends.
2. try to decide whether the potential campers can best handle a day camp experience or one in a residential camp.
3. at least a year prior to the proposed camp experience, choose some camps, and investigate concerning each:
   a. the camp record: number of years in existence, number of owners (past and present), credit rating, and respect accorded it by those who handle its business affairs.
   b. certification, by professional agencies or associations.
   c. reputation of the camp:
      1. among adults responsible for camp enrollees.
      2. among past and present campers.
      3. among counselors of the camp, past and present.
4. at least a year prior to the proposed camp experience, orient the person to the idea of becoming a camper:
   a. by talking about various camps, the benefits of camping, the possibility of going to camp.

    b. by listening to the aspirations and hopes of the potential camper, and trying to locate camps which seem worthy of consideration, in light of the information gained.

5. at least a year prior to the proposed camp experience, and while the camp season is running, visit various camps, with or without the potential camper, seeing, talking, listening on site, then evaluating your impressions.

6. following the current season:

    a. re-check your impressions by talking again with those who have been at the camp as campers or counselors or have been responsible for those who have attended camp.

    b. narrow your choices of camps to a half dozen or less, and have a serious, clarifying talk with the directors of those camps, to see whether they are aware of the needs of the potential camper, and whether they feel that their camps can satisfy those needs.

    c. re-check impressions with the potential camper, and "sell" the better of the camps to him or her.

    d. choose the camp which seems most suitable to you and the potential camper.

    e. enroll the person.

7. during the season in which the person is a camper, listen and exchange impressions. If there are conditions which need to be improved or changed, work toward that end, with an "eye" to the present and the future camp experiences of the camper.

Trends in Camping for the Handicapped

Trends in camping for the handicapped are many, and in general show positive progress. They can be summarized as follows:

1. programs include activities which tend to parallel those for typical campers, in contrast to the more passive and unimaginative programs selected for handicapped campers years ago.

2. camp counselors, kitchen and maintenance personnel, and medical staff are being procured whenever possible from nearby communities. This often results in more visitations by community members, with consequent development of greater empathy with the handicapped. It thus becomes one way of orienting and educating the public to the needs, the potential, and the successes of handicapped persons.

3. many persons from nearby communities and campuses are providing supplemental and volunteer leadership as:

FIG. 10-1. Fieldwork in a course can include: A. craft class outdoors, or B. supervision of a group whose slogan is: Let's Go Faster!! (Camp Courageous, Whitehouse, Ohio) C. Tetherball can be a game for all (just "bend" the rules a little). (Camp Pittinger, Ohio) D. Results of a college class project: games and toys for handicapped campers. (Bowling Green State University students, Ohio)

 a. leaders, or leader-aides for group activities at camp. Sometimes such efforts are used as practicums by students whose campus courses are concerned with communication, the humanities, religion, adapted physical education, camping, and other special areas.

 b. first-aid-nurse's aides as preparation for careers in nursing, medicine, and other health-related areas.

    c. observer-evaluators. This role is often taken by community leaders who provide in-put to the camp directors or committee as well as to community "service" groups who seek information about camp needs in the form of equipment or facilities to be built or funded.

    d. fund-raisers. Rummage sales and talent shows are examples which include all ages. Newer activities are exemplified by the "yard carnival" or day of games in someone's backyard, planned and staffed by children. Generally parents and a local business or two provide some leadership, and "help" in the form of monetary donations, or the donation of some saleable food and soft drink.

4. many camps which provide camping experiences for the handicapped are being winterized. This permits use by the handicapped, as well as an opportunity to raise funds by renting or leasing the camp or some of its facilities to non-handicapped groups whenever it is not in use by the handicapped.

5. some camps are renting a given area of the camp to outside groups during the season as a way of raising money. One example of this is a camp for the retarded whose swimming pool is made available to boys from a family center for an hour daily, while the retarded campers enjoy rest hour.

Summary

The material in this chapter is devoted to camping in all of its forms, particularly as it can be used for and by handicapped persons. Information is given about present practices, and those trends which help to describe the future, with regard to rationale for camping (or, why go to camp?), types of camps, camp learning/living groups, camp personnel and programs, and ways to evaluate, select and upgrade a camp for and with a camper.

Many examples are given, some as part of six case studies of specifically handicapped campers. And finally, a step-by-step method is given for finding the "right" camp for a potential camper, then making sure that it measures up to the standards which the search seemed to promise.

Bibliography

1. Abernathy, Ruth, and Waltz, Mary Ann: Toward a discipline: first steps first. Tucson, Arizona, Quest, Monograph II, Spring, 1964.
2. Adler, Alfred: *The Neurotic Constitution.* New York, Moffat, Yard and Co., 1917.
2A. Alm, I.: The long-term prognosis for prematurely born children: A follow-up study of 999 premature boys born in wedlock and of 1002 controls. Acta Paediatrica Supplement 94, 1953.
3. American Board of Certification of Corrective Therapists: Dr. John E. Davis, Executive Director; Association for Physical and Mental Rehabilitation: 105 St. Lawrence Street, Rehoboth Beach, Delaware.
4. Arnheim, Daniel D. Auxter, David, and Crowe, Walter C.: *Principles and Methods of Adapted Physical Education.* 2nd Ed., St. Louis, Missouri, C. V. Mosby Co., 1974.
4A. Barsch, R.: *Achieving Perceptual-Motor Efficiency.* Seattle, Special Child Publications, 1967.
5. Bartenieff, Ermgard, and Davis, Martha Ann: *Effort—Shape analysis of movement.* Unpublished paper, Bronx, New York, Albert Einstein College of Medicine, 1965.
6. Bartley, S. Howard: *Principles of Perception.* New York, Harper & Row, 1958.
6A. Bateman, B.: Learning disabilities—yesterday, today, and tomorrow. Exceptional Children 31:167–177, 1964.
7. Behanan, Kovoor T.: *Yoga.* New York, Dover Publications, Inc., 1937.
8. Biery, James: T'ai Chi for your muscles. *Popular Mechanics,* Oct., 1960.
9. Billig, Harvey, Jr.: *The Relief of Dysmenorrhea by Physical Mobilization Procedures.* Symposium on Dysmenorrhea, Phi Delta Pi, National Professional Physical Education Fraternity for Women, 1950.
10. Bogardus, LaDonna (Ed.): *Camping with Retarded Persons.* Nashville, Tennessee, Board of Education, The United Methodist Church, 1970.
11. Bortz, Edward L.: *Exercise and Fitness.* Chicago, Athletic Institute, 1960.

12. Bowsher, David: *Introduction to Neuroanatomy*. Oxford, Blackwell Scientific Publications, 1962.

13. Boyd, Jan A., Eyzaguire, Carlos, Matthews, Peter, and Rushworth, Geoffry: *Role of the Gamma System in Movement and Posture*. New York, Association for Aid to Crippled Children, 1964.

14. Bradley, R. C.: *The Education of Exceptional Children*. Denton, Texas, North Texas State University, 1970.

15. Broer, Marion R.: *Efficiency of Human Movement*. Philadelphia, W. B. Saunders Co., 1966.

16. Brunnstrom, Signe: *Clinical Kinesiology*. Philadelphia, F. A. Davis Co., 1962.

17. Buell, Charles E.: *Physical Education and Recreation for the Visually Handicapped*. Washington D.C., American Alliance for Health, Physical Education and Recreation, 1973.

18. Burke, Jack: Giving strength to the physically handicapped. Wisconsin Alumnus, 66: No. 1, August–September, 1965.

19. Cava, G. Lal: Some modern trends in sports medicine. Tucson, Arizona, Quest, Monograph III, Winter Issue, 1964.

20. Chapman, Frederick M.: *Recreation Activities for the Handicapped*. New York, The Ronald Press Co., 1960.

21. Chusid, Joseph G.: *Correlative Neuroanatomy and Functional Neurology*. Los Altos, California, Lange Medical Publications, 1970.

22. Cicero: De Senectute.

23. Clarke, H. Harrison, and Clarke, David H.: *Developmental and Adapted Physical Education*. Englewood Cliffs, N.J., Prentice-Hall, Inc., 1963.

24. Consolazio, C. Frank, Johnson, Robert E., and Pecora, Louis J.: *Physiological Measurements of Metabolic Function in Man*. New York, McGraw-Hill Book Co., 1963.

25. Coulter, J. S., and Morrison, Charlotte M.: Importance of a rehabilitation program in medical education. Physiotherapy Rev., 11, No. 2, March–April, 1931.

26. Crane, Helen (Ed.): *Easter Seal Guide to Special Camping Programs*. Chicago, Illinois, National Easter Seal Society for Crippled Children and Adults, 1968.

26A. Cruickshank, W.: *Psychology of Exceptional Children*. Englewood, N.J., Prentice-Hall, 1971.

27. Cratty, Bryant J.: *Movement Behavior and Motor Learning*. 3rd Ed., Philadelphia, Lea & Febiger, 1973.

28. Danford, Howard G.: *Creative Leadership in Recreation*. Rockleigh, N.J., Allyn, 1964.

29. Daniels, Arthur S., and Davies, Evelyn A.: *Adapted Physical Education*. 2nd Ed., New York, Harper & Row, 1975.

30. Dattner, Richard: *Design for Play*. New York, Van Nostrand Reinhold Co., 1969.

30A. Delacato, C.: *The Diagnosis and Treatment of Speech and Reading Problems*. Charles C Thomas, 1965.

31. Delza, Sophia: *Body and Mind in Harmony.* New York, David McKay Company, Inc., 1961.
32. Denver Public Schools: Annual Report. Health Service Department, Denver, Colorado, 1965.
33. Dorland, W. A. Newman (Ed.): *American Pocket Medical Dictionary.* Philadelphia, W. B. Saunders Co., 1942.
34. *Dorland's Medical Dictionary.* 25th Ed., Philadelphia, W. B. Saunders Co., 1974.
35. Drew, Lillian Curtiss, and Kinzly, Hazel L.: *Individual Gymnastics.* Philadelphia, Lea & Febiger, 1949.
36. Drowatzky, John N.: *Physical Education for the Mentally Retarded.* Philadelphia, Lea & Febiger, 1971.
37. Drury, Blanche J.: *Posture and Figure Control Through Physical Education.* Palo Alto, The National Press, 1965.
38. Eason, Byrdie, *et al:* Body image—implication and application to physical education. Unpublished paper, Michigan State University, Janet Wessel Workshop, 1964.
39. Extension Bulletin, H.D. 169—Revised—25 m-6:1932: U.S. Department of Agriculture and University of California, Berkeley.
40. Fait, Hollis F.: *Special Physical Education.* 3rd Ed., Philadelphia, W. B. Saunders Co., 1972.
41. Fearing, Franklin: *Reflex Action.* New York, Hafner Publishing Company, 1930.
41A. Ferguson-Smith, M.A., Johnston, A. W., and Handmaker, S. D.: Primary amentia and micro-orchidism associated with an XXXY sex chromosome constitution. Lancet, 2, 184–187, 1960.
41B. Fernald, G.: *Remedial Techniques in Basic School Subjects.* New York, McGraw-Hill Book Co., 1943.
42. Fischer, Ernst: Neurophysiology a physical therapist should know. Physical Ther. Rev., 38, Nov., 1958.
43. Fisher, Seymour, and Cleveland, Sidney E.: *Body Image and Personality.* Princeton, D. Van Nostrand Company, Inc., 1958.
44. Fitness for Youth: AAHPER Fitness Conference, December, 1956.
44A. Fölling, A.: Über Ausscheidung von Phenylbrenz-traubensäure in den Harn, als Stoffweckselanomalie in Verbendung mit Imbezillitat. Z. Physiology Chem., 227:169–176, 1934.
45. Ford, Phyllis M.: *Your Camp, and the Handicapped Child.* Bradford Woods, Martinsville, Indiana, American Camping Association, 1966.
45A. Fraser, F. C.: Genetic background of congenital malformations. 23rd Ross Pediatr. Res. Conf., pp. 59–63, Columbus, Ohio, 1956.
46. Freeburg, William H., Project Director: *Recreation for the Handicapped, A Bibliography.* Carbondale, Illinois, Southern Illinois University, 1965.
46A. Frostig, Marianne, and Horne, David: The Frostig Program for the Development of Visual Perception. Chicago, Follett Pub. Co., 1964.
47. Frost, Lorraine: Posture and body mechanics (Revised 1962). State University of Iowa Extension Bulletin, Iowa City, Iowa.

48. Gage, N. L.: *Toward a Cognitive Theory of Teaching*. Teachers College Board, Vol. 65, February, 1964; Columbus, Ohio. Reprint by Charles E. Merrill Books, Inc.

49. Gardiner, Ernest: *Neurology*. Philadelphia, W. B. Saunders Co., 1964.

50. Garrison, Fielding H.: *History of Medicine*. Philadelphia, W. B. Saunders Co., 1929.

51. Garvey, Joseph M.: Touch and see. Parks and Recreation, November, 1969, pp. 20–22 (Vol. IV, No. 11).

52. Gearheart, B. R.: *Learning Disabilities Educational Strategies*. St. Louis, Missouri, C. V. Mosby Co., 1973.

53. Geddes, Dolores: *Physical Activities for Individuals with Handicapping Conditions*. St. Louis, Missouri, C. V. Mosby Co., 1974.

53A. Getman, G. N.: The Visuomotor Complex in the Acquisition of Learning Skills. Learning Disorders. Vol. 1, Special Child Publication of the Seattle Sequin School, Inc., 1965.

54. Goldthwait, J. E., Brown, L. T., Swaim, L. T., Kuhns, J. G., and Kerr, W. S.: *Essentials of Body Mechanics*. Philadelphia, J. B. Lippincott Co., 1937.

55. Golub, Leib J., and Christaldi, Josephine: Reducing dysmenorrhea in young adolescents. J. Health, Physical Education and Recreation, 28, No. 5, May–June, 1957.

56. Golub, Leib J.: A new exercise for dysmenorrhea. Amer. J. Obstet. Gynec. 78, No. 1, pp. 152–155, July, 1959.

57. Gordon, Ira J.: *Human Development: From Birth through Adolescence*. New York, Harper & Bros., 1962.

57A. Greenbaum, J. V., and Lurie, L.: Encephalitis as a causative factor in behavior disorders of children: an analysis of seventy-eight cases. JAMA 136:923–930, 1948.

57B. Gregg, N. M.: Congenital cataract following German measles in the mother. Trans-opthal Soc. Australia, 3, 35, 1941.

58. Guthrie, D.: *History of Medicine*. Philadelphia, J. B. Lippincott, 1946.

59. Hackensmith, C. W.: *History of Physical Education*. New York, Harper & Row, 1966.

60. Hackett, Layne C.: *Movement Exploration and Games for the Mentally Retarded*. Palo Alto, California, Peek Publications, 1970.

61. Halleck, Grace T., and Turner, C. E.: *Robert Koch*. New York, Metropolitan Life Insurance Co., 1948.

62. Halsey, Elizabeth, and Porter, Lorena: *Physical Education for Children*. 2nd Ed., New York, Holt, Rinehart & Winston, 1963.

63. Harvard University: *The Occasional Speeches of Oliver Wendell Holmes*. Cambridge, Mass., Belknap Press, Harvard University, 1962.

64. Harvat, Robert W.: *Physical Education for Children with Perceptual-Motor Learning Disabilities*. Columbus, Ohio, Charles E. Merrill Books, Inc., 1971.

65. Havel, Richard C., and Seymour, Emery W.: *Administration of Health, Physical Education and Recreation for Schools*. New York, The Ronald Press Co., 1961.

66. Havighurst, Robert J.: *Developmental Tasks and Education.* New York, Longmans, Green & Co., 1952.

67. Hayden, Frank J.: Physical fitness for the mentally retarded. Toronto, Canada, Rotary Clubs, 1964.

67A. Hebb, D.: *The Organization of Behavior.* New York, Wiley, 1949.

68. Hendrickson, Andrew, and Barnes, Robert F.: *The Role of Colleges and Universities in the Education of the Aged.* Cooperative Research Project No. 1530, Columbus, Ohio: Center for Adult Education, College of Education, The Ohio State University, December, 1964.

69. Henry, Bill: *History of the Olympic Games.* New York, G. P. Putnam & Sons, 1948.

70. Hettinger, Theodor: *Physiology of Strength.* Springfield, Charles C Thomas, 1966.

70A. Hittleman, Richard L.: *The Yoga Way (to Figure and Facial Beauty).* New York, Hawthorne Books, 1968.

71. Hooley, Agnes M.: *A Survey of Practices in the Fifty States of the United States, concerning State Requirement or Recommendation, with regard to Training in Adapted Physical Education, for Those Who Would Teach Physical Education in the Given State.* Bowling Green State University, 1974.

72. Hooley, Agnes M.: Automation and the Recreationist. The Ohio High School Athlete, 24, No. 1, September, 1964.

73. Hooley, Agnes M.: Level of Aspiration of Good and Poor Performing Elementary and High School Girls in Selected Physical Education Activities. (Ph.D. dissertation, published by National Research Council, 1954).

74. Horowitz, H.: The cripple's place in society throughout the ages. Nation's Health, 5, No. 8, August, 1923.

75. Hubbard, K. T.: Who shall be in the adapted physical education program? AAHPER National Convention, Chicago, March, 1966. Paper presented at the Adapted Section.

76. Hunt, Valerie: Movement behavior: a model for action. Quest, Monograph II, Spring, 1964.

77. Indiana University, Reynold E. Carlson, Committee Chairman: *Camping for Emotionally Disturbed Boys.* Bloomington, Indiana, School of Health, Physical Education, and Recreation, Indiana University, 1962.

78. Johnson, Perry B., Updyke, Wynn F., Stolberg, Donald C., and Schaefer, Maryellen: *Physical Education.* New York, Holt, Rinehart & Winston, 1966.

78A. Johnson, D., and Myklebust, H.: *Learning Disabilities: Educational Principles and Practices.* New York, Grune & Stratton, Inc., 1967.

79. Johnson, Warren R.: Some psychological aspects of physical rehabilitation. J. Ass. Phys. Ment. Rehab., 16:165–168, Nov.–Dec., 1962.

80. Jokl, Ernst: *Medical Sociology and Cultural Anthropology of Sport and Physical Education.* Springfield, Charles C Thomas, 1964.

80A. Kanner, L.: *A Miniature Textbook of Feeblemindedness,* New York: Child Care Publications, 1949.

81. Karpovich, P.: *Physiology of Muscular Activity*. Philadelphia, W. B. Saunders Co., 1965.
82. Kaye, Richard A.: The use of a waist-type flotation device as an adjunct in teaching beginning swimming skills. Res. Quarterly, 36, No. 3, October, 1965.
83. Keller, Helen: *The Story of My Life*. Garden City, N.Y., Doubleday Doran and Co., Inc., 1933.
84. Kelly, Ellen Davis: *Adapted and Corrective Physical Education*. New York, The Ronald Press, 1965.
85. Kendall, Henry O., Kendall, Florence P., and Boynton, Dorothy A.: *Posture and Pain*. Baltimore, The Williams & Wilkins Co., 1952.
86. Kephart, Newell C.: *The Slow Learner in the Classroom*. Columbus, Ohio, Charles E. Merrill Books, Inc., 1971.
87. Kiernan, John, and Daley, Arthur: *The Story of the Olympic Games*. Philadelphia, J. B. Lippincott Co., 1952.
88. Kirk, Samuel A.: *Education of Exceptional Children*. 2nd Ed., Boston, Houghton Mifflin, 1973.
89. Kleinman, Seymour: Phenomenology—The Body Physical Education. Paper read at History and Philosophy Section of AAHPER, Chicago, March, 1966.
90. Knott, Margaret, and Voss, Dorothy E.: *Proprioceptive Neuromuscular Facilitation*. New York, Hoeber-Harper, 1956.
91. Kratz, Laura: *Movement Without Sight*. Palo Alto, California, Peek Publications, 1973.
92. Kraus, Hans, and Raab, Wilhelm: *Hypokinetic Disease*. Springfield, Charles C Thomas, 1961.
93. Kraus, Hans: Prevention of low back pain. J. Ass. Phys. Ment. Rehab. 6, No. 1, Sept.–October, 1952.
94. Kraus, Richard: Recreation and parks under fire. Parks and Recreation, January, 1973, pp. 25–26 (Vol. VIII, No. 1).
95. Kreps, J. M. (Ed.): *Employment, Income, and Retirement Problems of the Aged*. Durham, Duke University Press, 1963.
96. Krusen, Frank H., Kottke, F. C., and Ellword, P. M. Jr.: *Handbook of Physical Medicine and Rehabilitation*. Philadelphia, W. B. Saunders Co., 1965.
97. Krusen, Frank H.: History of physical therapeutics. The Physiotherapy Review, 11, No. 2, March–April, 1931.
98. Krusen Frank H.: *Physical Medicine*. Philadelphia, W. B. Saunders Co., 1941.
99. Kupfer, Donald M.: Recreation classes lead to improved physical abilities. Challenge, 1, No. 2, March, 1966.
100. Laban, Rudolf, and Lawrence, F. C.: *Effort*. London, MacDonald E. Evans, 1949.
101. Lee, Mabel, and Wagner, Miriam A.: *Fundamentals of Body Mechanics and Conditioning*. Philadelphia, W. B. Saunders Co., 1949.
102. Leland, Henry and Smith, Daniel E.: *Mental Retardation, Present and Future Perspectives*. Worthington, Ohio, Chas. A. Jones Pub. Co., 1974.

103. Lerch, Harold: Does physical excellence enhance social acceptance? The Ohio High School Athlete, 25, No. 2, November, 1965.

104. Lewin, Phillip: *The Foot and Ankle.* 4th Ed., Philadelphia, Lea & Febiger, 1959.

105. Licht, Sidney: *Therapeutic Exercise.* New Haven, Elizabeth Licht, 1961.

106. Life Magazine (Editors): The human body. October 26, 1962.

107. Littre, E.: *Oeuvres Complètes d'Hippocraté.* Paris, 1861.

108. Logan, Gene A., and Dunkelberg, James G.: *Adaptations of Muscular Activity.* Belmont, California, Wadsworth Publishing Co., Inc., 1964.

109. Lowman, C. L., and Young, C. H.: *Postural Fitness.* Philadelphia, Lea & Febiger, 1963.

110. Lucas, Carol: *Recreation Activity Development for the Aging in Home, Hospitals, and Nursing Homes,* Springfield, Charles C Thomas, 1962.

111. Madow, Pauline (Ed): *Recreation in America.* Vol. 37, No. 2 of *The Reference Shelf,* New York, H. W. Wilson Co., 1965.

112. Magnus, Rudolph: *"Haltung" Body Posture.* Abstracted by Signe Brunn-strom. Physical Ther. Rev., 33, Nos. 6 and 8, 1953.

113. Magoun, H. W., and Rhines, Ruth: *Spasticity—The Strength Reflex and Extrapyramidal Systems.* Springfield, Charles C Thomas, 1947.

114. Manter, John T., and Gatz, Arthur J.: *Clinical Neuroanatomy and Neuro-physiology.* Philadelphia, F. A. Davis Co., 1964.

115. Maresch, Marion M.: Variations in patterns of linear growth and skeletal maturity. Physical Therapy J., 44, No. 10, October, 1964.

116. Mathews, Donald K., Kruse, Robert, and Shaw, Virginia: *The Science of Physical Education for Handicapped Children.* New York, Harper & Bros., 1962.

117. Mayo Clinic, Rochester, Minnesota, School of Physical Medicine. Home Treatment Sheets.

118. McCarthy, James J., and McCarthy, Joan: *Learning Disabilities.* Boston, Allyn and Bacon, Inc. 1970.

118A. McClelland, D. C., Atkinson, J. W., Clark, R. A., and Lowell, E. L.: *The Achievement Motive.* New York, Appleton-Century-Crofts, 1953.

119. Menninger, William C.: Emotional adjustments for the handicapped. The Crippled Child, 27, No. 12, December, 1949.

120. Metheny, Eleanor: *Connotation of Movement in Sports and Dance.* Dubuque, Wm. C. Brown Co., 1965.

120A. Michaels, R. H., and Mellin, G. W.: Prospective experience with maternal rubella and associated congenital malformations. Pediatrics, 26, 200–209, 1960.

120B. Mikkelsen, M., and Stene, J.: Genetic counseling in Down's syndrome. Human Hered, 20: 457, 1970.

121. Mitchell, A. Viola, Crawford, Ida B., and Robberson, Julia D.: *Camp Counseling.* 4th Ed., Philadelphia, W. B. Saunders Co., 1970.

122. Moran, Joan May, and Kalakian, Leonard Harris: *Movement Experiences for the Mentally Retarded or Emotionally Disturbed Children.* Minne-apolis, Minn., Burgess Pub. Co., 1974.

123. Morehouse, Lawrence E., and Rasch, Phillip J.: *Scientific Basis of Athletic Training*. Philadelphia, W. B. Saunders Co., 1958.

124. Mosher, C. D.: *Personal Hygiene for Women*. Stanford, California, University Press, 1927.

124A. Mosston, Muska: *Teaching from Command to Discovery*. Wadsworth Publishing Co., Belmont, Calif., 1972.

124B. Mosston Muska: *Teaching Physical Education (from Command to Discovery)*. Charles E. Merrill Books, Inc., Columbus, Ohio, 1966.

125. Mueller, G. W., and Christaldi, J.: *Remedial Physical Education*. Philadelphia, Lea & Febiger, 1966.

126. Mulac, M. E.: *Leisure: Time for Living and Retirement*. New York, Harper & Bros., 1961.

127. Mullen, Frances A.: The physically handicapped child—how to keep him safe. School Safety, 1, No. 2, November–December, 1965.

128. Mussen, Paul H., and Newman, David K.: Acceptance of handicap, motivation, and adjustment in physically disabled children. Exceptional Children, 24, No. 6, February, 1958.

129. National Association for Retarded Children: *Facts on Mental Retardation*. New York, National Association for Retarded Children, Inc., 1964.

130. National Association for Retarded Children.: *The Retarded Can Be Helped*. Booklet C 632-9-63-60M, New York, National Association for Retarded Children, Inc., 1963.

131. National Society for Crippled Children and Adults: *"Hi There! Are You with It?"*, a Teen-Age Safety Checklist. Chicago, National Society for Crippled Children and Adults, undated.

132. National Wheelchair Athletic Committee: *Official Rules Book and Guide*, Woodside, N.Y., Joseph Bulova School of Watchmaking, 1965.

133. News Editor, in J. Rehabilitation, 32, No. 1, January–February, 1966.

134. Paterson, Ann, and Hallberg, Edmond C.: *Background Reading for Physical Education*. New York, Holt, Rinehart & Winston, 1965.

135. Peck, Robert F., and Mitchell, James V., Jr.: *Mental Health*. Washington, National Education Association, 1962.

135A. Piaget, J.: *The Origin of Intelligence in Children*. New York, International Universities Press, 1952.

136. Pilch, Judith: Physical education classes for mentally retarded. The Ohio High School Athlete, 25, No. 7, April, 1966.

137. Pintner, Rudolph, Eisenson, John, and Stanton, Mildred: *The Psychology of the Physically Handicapped*. New York, Appleton-Century-Crofts, 1941.

138. Pomeroy, Janet: *Recreation for the Physically Handicapped*. New York, The Macmillan Co., 1964.

139. Project, No. OEG-0-72-5454-233563, U.S. Department of Health, Education, and Welfare, Office of Education, Bureau of Education for the Handicapped. *Competitive Athletic Programs for Impaired, Disabled, and Handicapped Persons, Annotated Listing of Films, Guide for Financial Assistance and Program Support, Homemade Innovative Play Equipment*. Washington, D.C., American Alliance for Health, Physical Education and Recreation, 1973.

140. Rathbone, Josephine: *Corrective Physical Education*. Philadelphia, W. B. Saunders Co., 1959.

141. Rathbone, Josephine L., and Hunt, Valerie V.: *Corrective Physical Education*. 7th Ed., Philadelphia, W. B. Saunders Co., 1965.

142. Report of 1969 Conference on Problems of Education of Children in the Inner City: *The Six-Hour Retarded Child*. Obtainable from Supt. of Documents, U.S. Government Print. Office, Wash. D.C. 20402.

142A. Roach, E. G., and Kephart, N. C.: *The Purdue Perceptual-Motor Survey*. Charles E. Merrill Books, Inc., Columbus, Ohio, 1966.

143. Robinson, Frank M.: New dimensions in camping for the physically handicapped. Parks and Recreation, February, 1967, p. 21 (Vol. 11, No. 2).

144. Robinson, Halbert B., and Robinson, Nancy M.: *The Mentally Retarded Child*. New York, McGraw-Hill Book Co., 1965.

145. Rusk, Howard A.: Appearing on a program of The Prudential Life Insurance Co., Sunday, August 22, 1965, Columbia Broadcasting System Television Network.

146. Rusk, Howard A.: *The Handicapped and Their Rehabilitation*. St. Louis, The C. V. Mosby Company, 1964.

147. Schiller, Ronald: The Lonely World of Silence. Reprinted from The Christian Herald in The Reader's Digest, August, 1974, pp. 141–145 (Vol. 105, No. 628).

148. Schreiber, Meyer: Some basic concepts in social group work and recreation with the mentally retarded. Rehabilitation Literature, 26, No. 7, July, 1965.

149. Scientific Monthly: *Jonathan Wright Papers*. Philadelphia, Lea & Febiger, circa 1914.

150. Shivers, Jay S.: *Camping, Administration, Counseling, Programming*. New York, Meredith Corporation, 1971.

151. Simons, A.: Head posture and muscle tone. Abstracted by Signe Brunnstrom: Physical Ther. Rev., 33, June–August, 1953.

151A. Skeels, H. M., and Dye, H. B., A study of the effects of differential stimulation on the mental retardation child. Proceedings and Address of the Sixty-Third Annual Session of AAMD. Am. J. Ment. Defic., 44 (No. 1):114–130, 1939.

151B. Skinner, B. F.: *The Behavior of Organisms*. New York, Appleton-Century-Crofts, 1938.

151C. Skinner, B. F.: *An Operant Analysis of Problem Solving*. New York, Wiley, 1966.

152. Slavson, S. R.: *Recreation and the Total Personality*. New York, Association Press, 1946.

153. Smith, David W., and Wilson, Ann Asper: *The Child with Down's Syndrome*. Philadelphia, W. B. Saunders Co., 1973.

154. Sosne, Michael: *Handbook of Adapted Physical Education Equipment*. Springfield, Charles C Thomas, 1973.

155. Sports Illustrated: December, 1960, President's Council on Youth Fitness.

156. Staff: *A Fact Sheet*. New York, National Health Education Committee, Inc., 1964.

157. Staff, American Association Mental Deficiency: *AAMD Adaptive Behavior Scale for Children and Adults*, Washington, D.C., AAMD, Revised, 1974.

158. Staff, American Association Mental Deficiency: Herbert M. Grossman, M.D., Editor: *Manual on Terminology and Classification in Mental Retardation.* Washington, D.C., AAMD, Revised, 1974.

159. Staff, Bureau of Curriculum Development: *Education of the Physically Handicapped.* New York, Board of Education, City of New York, 1971.

160. Staff: *Camp Standards with Interpretations.* Bradford Woods, Martinsville, Indiana, American Camping Association, 1973.

161. Staff: *Condensed Listing of Standards for Organized Camps.* Bradford Woods, Martinsville, Indiana, American Camping Association, 1973.

162. Staff: *So You Want to Start A Day Camp.* Bradford Woods, Martinsville, Indiana, American Camping Association, 1964.

163. Staff: *Suggested Policies and Standing Orders for Camp Nursing Services.* Bradford Woods, Martinsville, Indiana, American Camping Association, 1971.

164. Staff: *Ninth National Wheelchair Games Program.* Woodside, New York, Joseph Bulova School for Watchmaking, 1965.

165. Staff: *The Easter Seal Directory of Resident Camps for Persons with Special Health Needs.* 8th Ed., Chicago, Illinois, The National Easter Seal Society for Crippled Children and Adults, 1973.

166. Staff: *USA Standards/Specifications for Making Buildings and Facilities Accessible to, and Usable by, the Physically Handicapped.* New York, United States of America Standards Institute, 1961.

167. Staff: *Working with the Handicapped, A Leader's Guide.* New York, Girl Scouts of the United States of America, 1964.

168. Stafford, George T.: *Preventive and Corrective Physical Education.* New York, A. S. Barnes & Company, 1934.

169. Stafford, George T.: *Sports for the Handicapped.* 2nd Ed., Englewood Cliffs, N.J., Prentice-Hall, Inc., 1947.

170. Stein, Julian U., Director Project: *Guidelines for Professional Preparation Programs for Personnel Involved in Physical Education and Recreation for the Handicapped.* Washington, D.C., American Alliance for Health, Physical Education and Recreation, 1973.

171. Steindler, Arthur: *Mechanics of Normal and Pathological Locomotion in Man.* Springfield, Charles C Thomas, 1935.

172. Steindler, Arthur: *Kinesiology of the Human Body.* Springfield, Charles C Thomas, 1973.

173. Steinhaus, Arthur H.: *Health and Physical Education.* Dubuque, Wm. C. Brown Co., 1963.

174. *How to Keep Fit and Like It.* Chicago, Dartnell Corporation, 1963.

175. Stern, Edith M., and Ross, Mabel: *You and Your Aging Parents.* New York, Harper & Row, 1962.

176. Stone, Edward H.: There's a wheelchair in the woods. Parks and Recreation, December, 1971, p. 19 (Vol. VI, No. 12).

177. Stone, Eleanor B., and Deyton, W.: *Corrective Therapy for the Handicapped Child.* Englewood Cliffs, N.J., Prentice-Hall, Inc., 1951.

177A. Strauss, A. A., and Lehtinen, L. E.: *Psychopathology and Education of the Brain-injured Child.*, New York, Grune & Stratton, 1947.

178. Taylor, Norman Burke (Ed.): *Stedman's Medical Dictionary.* 20th Ed., Baltimore, The Williams & Wilkins Co., 1961.

178A. Terman, L. A., and Merrill, M. A.: Stanford-Binet Intelligence Scale, Manual for the Third Revision Form L-M. Boston, Houghton Mifflin, 1960, p. 18.

179. Thompson, Morton: *Recreation for the Homebound Person with Cerebral Palsy.* New York, United Cerebral Palsy Association, undated.

179A. Ullman, L., and Krasner, L.: *Case Studies in Behavior Modification.* New York, Holt, Rinehart, and Winston, Inc., 1965.

180. Van Dalen, Deobold B., Mitchell, Elmer D., and Bennett, Bruce L.: *World History of Physical Education.* Englewood Cliffs, N.J., Prentice-Hall, Inc., 1971.

181. Viscardi, Henry, Jr.: *A Man's Stature.* New York, John Day Co., 1952.

182. Vodola, Thomas M.: *Individualized Physical Education Program for the Handicapped Child.* Englewood Cliffs, N.J., Prentice-Hall, Inc., 1973.

183. Wallin, J. E. W.: *Personality Maladjustments and Mental Hygiene.* New York, McGraw-Hill Book Co., 1949.

184. Wayne State University Women's Physical Education: *Workbook for Physical Education.* Detroit.

185. Wessel, Janet: *Fitness for the Modern Teenager.* New York, The Ronald Press Co., 1963.

186. Wessel, Janet: *Movement Fundamentals.* Englewood Cliffs, N.J., Prentice-Hall, Inc., 1961.

187. White House Conference on Child Health and Protection: *Body Mechanics: Education and Practice.* New York, The Century Co., 1932.

188. White, Paul Dudley: A plea for the health of our college men and women. Tucson, Arizona, Quest, December, 1964.

189. Whitman, Howard: Brightening old age in Houston. Today's Health. 41, No. 9, September, 1963.

190. Williams, F. Neil: Physical education adapts to the visually handicapped. J. Health, Physical Education and Recreation, 35, No. 3, March, 1964.

191. Williams, Marian, and Lissner, Herbert R.: *Biomechanics of Human Motion.* Philadelphia, W. B. Saunders Co., 1962.

191A. Wiseman, D.: A classroom procedure for identifying and remediating language problems. Mental Retardation 3:20, 1965.

192. Woods, Thomas: *Life and Education of Early Societies.* New York, Macmillan Company, 1949.

192A. Wortis, J.: International communication and cooperation in the field of mental retardation Am. J. Ment. Defic., 65, 426–433, 1961.

193. *Youth Fitness: A Medical View.* Pediatricians and Orthopedists, Image (Roche Medical) Vol. 7., No. 1., Feb. 1965, New York, International Medical Press, Inc., 10022.

194. Zweig, Franklin M., Research Monograph No. 1, *Therapeutic Camping.* Bradford Woods, Martinsville, Indiana, American Camping Association, 1962.

Index